STUDY GUIDE

Modern Business Statistics

with Microsoft® Excel

David R. Anderson
University of Cincinnati

Dennis J. Sweeney
University of Cincinnati

Thomas A. Williams
Rochester Institute of Technology

Prepared by

John S. Loucks
St. Edward's University

SOUTH-WESTERN
™
THOMSON LEARNING

Australia · Canada · Mexico · Singapore · Spain · United Kingdom · United States

Study Guide for Modern Business Statistics with Microsoft® Excel
by Anderson, Sweeney, and Williams; prepared by John Loucks

Publisher: Melissa Acuna
Sr. Acquisitions Editor: Charles E. McCormick, Jr.
Sr. Developmental Editor: Alice C. Denny
Sr. Marketing Manager: Joseph A. Sabatino
Sr. Production Editor: Deanna R. Quinn
Media Technology Editor: Diane Van Bakel
Media Developmental Editor: Chris Wittmer
Media Production Editor: Robin Browning
Manufacturing Coordinator: Diane Lohman
Printer: Globus Printing

Printed in the United States of America
1 2 3 4 5   04 03 02 01

For more information contact South-Western, 5191 Natorp Blvd., Mason, Ohio, 05040 or find us on the Internet at http://www.swcollege.com

For permission to use material from this text or product, contact us by
• telephone: **1-800-730-2214**
• fax: **1-800-730-2215**
• web: **http://www.thomsonrights.com**

ISBN 0-324-12177-6

Contents

Preface

The <u>Study Guide to Accompany Modern Business Statistics with Microsoft Excel</u> has been written with several objectives in mind. The objectives are:

1. To <u>provide an outline of the material</u> in the parent text via an opening key concepts section from which the student may design a course of study of the individual techniques and concepts of each chapter.

2. To <u>organize and summarize the material</u> in the parent text in a structured review section.

3. To <u>illustrate the basic concepts</u> of the parent text in detail through the presentation of 120 illustrated examples.

4. To <u>reinforce the basic concepts</u> by providing 130 additional exercises and 285 objective and fill-in-the-blank questions whose answers are at the ends of the chapters.

5. To <u>challenge the student</u> by including several exercises requiring more than simple, straightforward application of the techniques of the chapter.

6. To <u>expand the coverage</u> of certain areas beyond the parent text by offering additional insights and procedures to assist in the solution strategy.

7. To <u>illustrate business applications</u> areas in which statistical methodologies may be applied.

8. To <u>provide Excel worksheets</u> that students can use as templates for solving the exercises in the study guide and textbook.

To accomplish these goals, each chapter has been divided into seven basic parts:

1. Learning Objectives:
   Each chapter starts with a check-list of the learning objectives that should be achieved by the student upon completion of the chapter. This allows the student to assess his/her proficiency and identify areas needing additional attention.

2. Review:
   This section summarizes point by point the theoretical foundations, terminology, formulas, and methodologies for every topic area of the chapter. This provides an excellent outline for understanding the essential points of the chapters.

3. Key Concepts:
   This section notes the main topic areas of each chapter and denotes which examples illustrate the concept, and which answered exercises require the use of the concept in its solution. Examples that illustrate the use of an Excel spreadsheet are clearly marked. Every major concept of the text is illustrated in at least one example worked out in detail and in at least one exercise with its answer provided at the end of the chapter.

4. Examples:
   These are problems worked out in full, giving the step-by-step details as the problem is worked through to completion. For the vast majority of these examples, an Excel spreadsheet approach to solving the problem is demonstrated. The Excel worksheets presented in these examples can be used as templates for completing the exercises in the study guide and the textbook.

5. Exercises:
   These problems are for the student to do on his/her own with the answers provided at the end of the chapter. This enables the student to test him/herself on the individual concepts with brief answers to validate his results.

6. Self Test:
   Each chapter contains fifteen questions – 5 true/false, 5 fill-in-the-blank, and 5 multiple choice – designed to reinforce the theoretical concepts of the chapter. The answers are provided at the end of the chapter.

7. Answers:
   This section contains the answers to all of the self-test questions (true/false, fill-in-the-blank, and multiple choice), as well as the exercises, in the chapter.

We hope you find this study guide instructive and a useful supplement in your study of business statistics.

John S. Loucks
St. Edward's University
Austin, Texas 78704
johnsl@admin.stedwards.edu

CHAPTER 1

Data and Statistics

Applications in Business and Economics

Data

Data Sources

Descriptive Statistics

Statistical Inference

Statistical Analysis Using Microsoft Excel

LEARNING OBJECTIVES

1. Obtain an appreciation for the breadth of statistical applications in business and economics.

2. Understand the meaning of the terms elements, variables, and observations as they are used in statistics.

3. Understand that data are obtained using one of the following scales of measurement: nominal, ordinal, interval, and ratio.

4. Obtain an understanding of the difference between qualitative, quantitative, crossectional and time series data.

5. Learn about the sources of data for statistical analysis both internal and external to the firm.

6. Be aware of how errors can arise in data.

7. Know the meaning of descriptive statistics and statistical inference.

8. Be able to distinguish between a population and a sample.

9. Understand the role a sample plays in making statistical inferences about the population.

REVIEW

Applications in Business and Economics

- Public accounting firms use statistical sampling procedures when conducting audits for their clients.
- Financial advisors use a variety of statistical information, including price-earnings ratios and dividend yields, to guide their investment recommendations.
- Electronic point-of-sale scanners at retail checkout counters are being used to collect data for a variety of marketing research applications.
- A variety of statistical quality control charts are used to monitor the output of a production process.
- Economists use statistical information in making forecasts about the future of the economy or some aspect of it.

Data, Data Sets, Elements, Variables, and Observations

- Data are the facts and figures that are collected, summarized, analyzed, and interpreted.
- The data collected in a particular study are referred to as the data set.
- The elements are the entities on which data are collected.
- A variable is a characteristic of interest for the elements.
- The set of measurements collected for a particular element is called an observation.
- The number of observations is always the same as the number of elements.
- The total number of data values in a data set is the number of elements multiplied by the number of variables.

Qualitative and Quantitative Data

- The statistical analysis that is appropriate depends on whether the data for the variable are qualitative or quantitative.
- Qualitative data are labels or names used to identify an attribute of each element.
- Quantitative data indicate either how much or how many.
- Quantitative data are always numeric.
- Qualitative data can be either numeric or nonnumeric.
- Ordinary arithmetic operations are meaningful only with quantitative data.

Cross-Sectional and Time Series Data

- Cross-sectional data are collected at the same or approximately the same point in time.
- Example of cross-sectional data: data detailing the number of building permits issued in December 2000 in each of the counties of Texas.
- Time series data are collected over several time periods.
- Example of time series data: data detailing the number of building permits issued in Travis County, Texas in each of the last 36 months.

Data Sources: Internet

- The Internet has become an important source of data.
- Most government agencies, like the Bureau of the Census (www.census.gov), make their data available through a web site.
- More and more companies are creating web sites and providing public access to them.
- A number of companies now specialize in making information available over the Internet.

Data Sources: Statistical Studies

- Statistical studies can be classified as either experimental or observational.
- In experimental studies the variables of interest are first identified. Then one or more factors are controlled so that data can be obtained about how the factors influence the variables.
- In observational studies no attempt is made to control or influence the variables of interest.
- A survey is perhaps the most common type of observational study.

Data Acquisition Considerations

- Time Requirement: Searching for information can be time consuming. Information might no longer be useful by the time it is available.
- Cost of Acquisition: Organizations often charge for information even when it is not their primary business activity.
- Data Errors: Using any data that happens to be available or that were acquired with little care can lead to poor and misleading information.

Descriptive Statistics

- Summaries of data are referred to as descriptive statistics.
- Tabular Summary: An example is a table showing frequencies for a variable.
- Graphical Summary: An example, for qualitative data, is a bar graph. An example, for quantitative data, is a histogram.
- Numerical Summary: The most common numerical descriptive statistic is the average (or mean).

Statistical Inference
- Statistical inference is the process of using data obtained from a small group of elements (the <u>sample</u>) to make estimates and test hypotheses about the characteristics of a larger group of elements (the <u>population</u>).

Using Excel for Statistical Analysis
- Statistical analysis typically involves working with large amounts of data.
- <u>Computer software</u> is typically used to conduct the analysis.
- Frequently the data that is to be analyzed resides in a <u>spreadsheet</u>.
- Spreadsheet packages are capable of data management, analysis, and presentation.
- <u>MS Excel</u> is the most widely available spreadsheet software in business organizations.
- In using Excel for statistical analysis, three tasks might be necessary:
  - <u>Enter Data</u>: Select cell locations for the data and appropriate labels, and then enter the data and labels.
  - <u>Enter Functions and Formulas</u>: Select cell locations, enter Excel functions and formulas, and provide descriptive material to identify the results.
  - <u>Apply Tools</u>: Use Excel's tools for data management, data analysis, and presentation.

KEY CONCEPTS

<u>CONCEPT</u>	<u>EXAMPLES</u>	<u>EXERCISES</u>
Elements, Variables, and Observations	1	1
Qualitative and Quantitative Data	2	2
Cross-Sectional and Time Series Data	3	3,4
Experimental and Observational Studies	4	5
Data Sets and Excel Worksheets	⑤	6
Descriptive Statistics and Statistical Inference	6	7

◯ Excel Used

EXAMPLES

EXAMPLE 1

Elements, Variables, and Observations

Laura Naples, Manager of Heritage Inn, periodically collects and tabulates information about a sample of the hotel's overnight guests. This information aids her in planning and scheduling decisions she must make.

The table below lists data on ten randomly selected hotel registrants, collected as the registrants checked out. The data listed are:
- Number of people in the group
- Date of birth of person registering
- Shuttle service used: yes or no
- Total telephone charges incurred
- Reason for stay: business or personal

Name of Registrant	Number in Group	D.O.B (mm/dd/yy)	Shuttle Used	Telephone Charges ($)	Reason for Stay
Adam Sandler	1	05/07/59	yes	0.00	personal
Michelle Pepper	4	11/23/48	no	12.46	business
Claudia Shepler	2	04/30/73	no	1.20	business
Annette Rodriquez	2	12/16/71	no	2.90	business
Tony DiMarco	1	05/09/39	yes	0.00	personal
Amy Franklin	3	09/14/69	yes	4.65	business
Tammy Roberts	2	04/22/66	no	9.35	personal
Edward Blackstone	5	10/28/54	yes	2.10	personal
Mary Silverman	1	11/12/49	no	1.85	business
Todd Atherton	2	01/30/62	no	5.80	business

a) How many elements are there in the data set?

b) How many variables are there in the data set?

c) How many observations are there in the data set?

d) What are the observations for the second element listed?

e) What is the total number of measurements in the data set?

SOLUTION 1

a) There are 10 elements (registrants) in the data set.

b) There are 5 variables (number in party, DOB, shuttle used, telephone charges, and reason for stay).

c) There are 10 observations (one for each registrant) in the data set.

d) The observations for the second element are: 4, 11/23/48, no, 12.46, and business.

e) The total number of measurements in the data set is 50 (10 elements X 5 variables).

EXAMPLE 2

Qualitative and Quantitative Data

Refer to the Heritage Inn guest data presented in Example 1.

a) Which variables are quantitative?

b) Which variables are qualitative?

SOLUTION 2

a) There are two quantitative variables - number in party and telephone charges. Ordinary arithmetic operations such as computing an average value are meaningful for these variables.

b) There are three qualitative variables - DOB, shuttle used, and reason for stay. DOB contains numeric values, but it is considered a qualitative variable. We cannot <u>directly</u> perform any ordinary arithmetic operation on the DOB data. We can <u>derive</u> the age of each registrant from the DOB data and age would be considered a quantitative variable.

EXAMPLE 3

Cross-Sectional and Time Series Data

Refer again to the Heritage Inn guest data presented in Example 1. Does the data set represent cross-sectional or times series data? Explain the reason for your answer. What characteristic is lacking in the data set that, if it were present, would cause you to choose the other category as your answer? What is a potential shortcoming of this type of data?

SOLUTION 3

The data set represents cross-sectional data. The data might have been collected over several time periods (weeks or months), but the data is not sorted by time period. To use a photography analogy, the Heritage Inn data is a snapshot (still picture) and not a movie (motion picture).

The fact that it is a snapshot of conditions/circumstances at approximately one point in time might be a shortcoming, even if the sample was chosen in a purely random, unbiased manner. If the manager is interested in the ongoing status of the variables, this data set might not be representative.

EXAMPLE 4

Experimental and Observational Studies

Refer again to the Heritage Inn guest data presented in Example 1. Does the data set represent an experimental or an observational study? Explain the reason for your answer. How might the circumstances of the study be altered in order for you to categorize the study differently?

SOLUTION 4

The data set represents an observational (<u>non</u>experimental) study. There is no indication that an attempt was made to control or influence the variables of interest.

As an example of an experimental study, a controllable variable could be introduced and its effect on telephone charges could be examined. Such a controllable variable might be whether or not a guest party is given a discount on the telephone billing rate. Data on telephone charges could be collected for each group (guests given the discount and guests not given the discount). Statistical analysis of the experimental data could help determine the effect of lower telephone rates on charges guests incur.

EXAMPLE 5

Data Sets and Excel Worksheets

Refer again to the Heritage Inn guest data presented in Example 1. Enter the Heritage Inn data set, with appropriate labels, in an Excel worksheet. Compute the average number of guests in a group, the average telephone charge per group, and the average telephone charge per guest.

SOLUTION 5

Using Excel's *AVERAGE* Function

The two or three (depending on the problem) tasks involved with using Excel for statistical analysis are: 1) enter data, 2) enter functions and formulas, and/or 3) apply tools.

Enter Data: The appropriate labels for the columns of data are entered in cells A1:F1. The data are entered in cells A2:F11.

Enter Functions and Formulas: Excel's AVERAGE function can be used to compute the average number of guests in a group and the average telephone charge per group. For example, to compute the average number of guests in a group, the following formula is entered into cell B13:

=AVERAGE(B2:B11)

The average telephone charge per group is computed in a similar manner. To compute the average telephone charge per guest, it is not necessary or appropriate to use the AVERAGE function. The average telephone charge per guest is:

Average telephone charge per guest = <u>Average telephone charge per group</u>
Average number of guests in a group

B15 = B14/B13

To identify the results, appropriate labels are entered in cells A13:A15.

Formula Worksheet

	A	B	C	D	E	F
1	Name of Registrant	Number in Group	D.O.B (mm/dd/yy)	Shuttle Used	Telephone Charges ($)	Reason for Stay
2	Adam Sandler	1	05/07/59	yes	0.00	personal
3	Michelle Pepper	4	11/23/48	no	12.46	business
4	Claudia Shepler	2	04/30/73	no	1.20	business
5	Annette Rodriquez	2	12/16/71	no	2.90	business
6	Tony DiMarco	1	05/09/39	yes	0.00	personal
7	Amy Franklin	3	09/14/69	yes	4.65	business
8	Tammy Roberts	2	04/22/66	no	9.35	personal
9	Edward Blackstone	5	10/28/54	yes	2.10	personal
10	Mary Silverman	1	11/12/49	no	1.85	business
11	Todd Atherton	2	01/30/62	no	5.80	business
12						
13	Avg. Number in Group	=AVERAGE(B2:B11)				
14	Avg. Ph. Charge/Group	=AVERAGE(E2:E11)				
15	Avg. Ph. Charge/Guest	=B14/B13				

Value Worksheet

	A	B	C	D	E	F
1	Name of Registrant	Number in Group	D.O.B (mm/dd/yy)	Shuttle Used	Telephone Charges ($)	Reason for Stay
2	Adam Sandler	1	05/07/59	yes	0.00	personal
3	Michelle Pepper	4	11/23/48	no	12.46	business
4	Claudia Shepler	2	04/30/73	no	1.20	business
5	Annette Rodriquez	2	12/16/71	no	2.90	business
6	Tony DiMarco	1	05/09/39	yes	0.00	personal
7	Amy Franklin	3	09/14/69	yes	4.65	business
8	Tammy Roberts	2	04/22/66	no	9.35	personal
9	Edward Blackstone	5	10/28/54	yes	2.10	personal
10	Mary Silverman	1	11/12/49	no	1.85	business
11	Todd Atherton	2	01/30/62	no	5.80	business
12						
13	Avg. Number in Group	2.3				
14	Avg. Ph. Charge/Group	4.03				
15	Avg. Ph. Charge/Guest	1.75				

EXAMPLE 6

Descriptive Statistics and Statistical Inference

Refer again to the Heritage Inn guest data presented in Example 1.

a) Example 5 above involved computing several averages for the Heritage Inn guest data. Do these calculations fall under the heading of Descriptive Statistics or Statistical Inference methods?

b) Give two examples of descriptive statistics methods that could be applied to the Heritage Inn data.

c) Give two examples of statistical inference methods that could be applied to the Heritage Inn data.

SOLUTION 6

a) Calculating and reporting an average is an example of descriptive statistics. When an average pertaining to a sample is used to estimate a population average, statistical inference is being conducted.

b) Computing the proportion of the registrants in the sample who were staying at the hotel for business reasons is an example of descriptive statistics. Another example of a descriptive statistics method is constructing a histogram that shows the frequency of one guest in a group, two guests in a group, and so on.

c) An example of statistical inference is stating that the estimate of the proportion of all Heritage Inn registrants using the Inn's shuttle service is 0.4 with a margin of error of +/- .03. Another example is inferring that the overall average telephone expense per guest at the Heritage Inn is $1.75.

EXERCISES

EXERCISE 1

Elements, Variables, and Observations

Tony Zamora, a real estate investor, has just moved to Clarksville and wants to learn about the city's residential real estate market. Tony has randomly selected 25 house-for-sale listings from the Sunday newspaper and collected the data listed below.

Segment of City	Selling Price ($000)	House Size (00 sq. ft.)	Number of Bedrooms	Number of Bathrooms	Garage Size (cars)
Northwest	290	21	4	2	2
South	95	11	2	1	0
Northeast	170	19	3	2	2
Northwest	375	38	5	4	3
West	350	24	4	3	2
South	125	10	2	2	0
West	310	31	4	4	2
West	275	25	3	2	2
Northwest	340	27	5	3	3
Northeast	215	22	4	3	2
Northwest	295	20	4	3	2
South	190	24	4	3	2
Northwest	385	36	5	4	3
West	430	32	5	4	2
South	185	14	3	2	1
South	175	18	4	2	2
Northeast	190	19	4	2	2
Northwest	330	29	4	4	3
West	405	33	5	4	3
Northeast	170	23	4	2	2
West	365	34	5	4	3
Northwest	280	25	4	2	2
South	135	17	3	1	1
Northeast	205	21	4	3	2
West	260	26	4	3	2

a) How many elements are there in the data set and what are they?

b) How many variables are there in the data set and what are they?

c) How many observations are there in the data set?

d) What are the observations for the third element listed?

e) What is the total number of measurements in the data set?

EXERCISE 2

Qualitative and Quantitative Data

Refer again to the real estate data presented in Exercise 1.

a) Identify the variables that are quantitative?

b) What type of analysis can be done with the qualitative data?

EXERCISE 3

Cross-Sectional and Time Series Data

Refer again to the real estate data presented in Exercise 1. Is the data set cross-sectional or time series data? Explain.

EXERCISE 4

Cross-Sectional and Time Series Data

Molly Porter owns and operates two convenience stores, one on the East side of the city and the other on the South side. She has workforce-planning decisions to make and has collected some recent sales data that are relevant to her decisions. Listed below are the monthly sales ($000) at her two stores for the past six months.

Store	March	April	May	June	July	August
East	102	100	103	105	109	103
South	72	74	81	86	92	95

a) Is the data set cross-sectional or time series data? Explain.

b) Comment on any apparent patterns you see in the data.

EXERCISE 5

Experimental and Observational Studies

Refer again to the convenience store sales data presented in Exercise 4. Does the data set represent an experimental or an observational study? Explain the reason for your answer.

EXERCISE 6

Data Sets and Excel Worksheets

Refer again to the real estate data presented in Exercise 1. Enter the data set, with appropriate labels, in an Excel worksheet. Compute the average selling price of a house, average number of bedrooms per house, and average garage size.

EXERCISE 7

Descriptive Statistics and Statistical Inference

Refer again to the real estate data presented in Exercise 1.

a) What is the population being studied?

b) What are the population <u>characteristics</u> of interest to Tony Zamora?

c) What is the sample size?

d) Make an inference about the average garage size for a house in Clarksville.

e) Develop a descriptive statistic that can be used as an estimate of the percentage of houses in Clarksville that have four or more bedrooms.

SELF-TEST

TRUE/FALSE

____ 1. In an observational study, an attempt is made to control the variables of interest.

____ 2. The total number of data items in a complete data set is equal to the number of elements multiplied by the number of variables.

____ 3. The cost of data acquisition and the subsequent statistical analysis should not exceed the savings generated by using the information to make a better decision.

____ 4. A survey is a common form of observational study.

____ 5. Cross-sectional data are data collected over several time periods.

FILL-IN-THE-BLANK

1. When _____ data is recorded as numeric values, performing arithmetic operations on the values – such as computing the average value – provide meaningless results.

2. _____ are the entities on which data are collected.

3. The process of making estimates or testing hypotheses about the characteristics of a population is referred to as _____.

4. The data collected in a particular study are referred to as the _____ for the study.

5. _____ data indicates either how much or how many.

Multiple Choice

___ 1. How many observations are there in a complete data set having 10 elements and 5 variables?
   a) 2
   b) 5
   c) 10
   d) 50

___ 2. Which of the following is an example of qualitative data?
   a) a social security number
   b) a score on a multiple-choice exam
   c) the height, in meters, of a diving board
   d) the number of square feet of carpet laid

___ 3. Unusually large and small values in a data set are called
   a) errors
   b) cross-sectional data
   c) qualitative data
   d) outliers

___ 4. Which one of the following is not an example of descriptive statistics?
   a) a histogram depicting the age distribution for 30 randomly selected professors
   b) an estimate of the number of Alaska residents who have visited Canada
   c) a table summarizing the data collected in a sample of new-car buyers
   d) the proportion of mailed-out questionnaires that were completed and returned

___ 5. Which one of the following is an example of quantitative data?
   a) the number on a baseball uniform
   b) the serial number on a one-dollar bill
   c) the part number of an inventory item
   d) the number of dependents you claim on your income tax form

ANSWERS

EXERCISES

1) a) 25 elements (houses for sale)
   b) 6 variables (segment of city, selling price, house size, number of bedrooms, number of bathrooms, garage size)
   c) 25 observations (one for each element)
   d) Northeast, 170, 19, 3, 2, 2
   e) 150 (25 elements X 6 variables)

2) a) All are quantitative except Segment of City
   b) We can provide counts and compute the proportion or percentage of the houses being in each segment of the city.

3) Cross-sectional data. The data describe the six variables for the 25 houses at the same point in time.

4) a) Time series data for two variables: monthly sales for East store and monthly sales for South store.
   b) Both stores have been experiencing an overall rise in sales during the past six months. The South store's increase in sales (as a percentage of sales) has been greater than the East store's increase. The increases might be temporary, due to the seasonal nature of demand. It is also possible that the increases will continue.

5) The data set represents an observational (nonexperimental) study. There is no indication that an attempt was made to influence the sales from month to month for either store.

6) $261,800; 3.92 bedrooms; 2.00 cars

7) a) all of the houses in Clarksville
   b) the six variables on which Tony has collected data
   c) 25 houses
   d) the sample suggests that the average garage size for all houses in Clarksville is 2.00 cars
   e) the percentage of houses in the sample with 4 or more bedrooms (76%)

TRUE/FALSE

1) False
2) True
3) True
4) True
5) False

FILL-IN-THE-BLANK

1) qualitative
2) Elements
3) statistical inference
4) data set
5) Quantitative

MULTIPLE CHOICE

1) c
2) a
3) d
4) b
5) d

CHAPTER 2

Descriptive Statistics: Tabular and Graphical Methods

Summarizing Qualitative Data

Summarizing Quantitative Data

Exploratory Data Analysis:
The Stem-and-Leaf Display

Crosstabulations and Scatter Diagrams

LEARNING OBJECTIVES

1. Learn how to construct and interpret summarization procedures for qualitative data such as: frequency and relative frequency distributions, bar graphs and pie charts.

2. Be able to use Excel's COUNTIF function to construct a frequency distribution and the Chart Wizard to construct a bar graph and pie chart.

3. Learn how to construct and interpret tabular summarization procedures for quantitative data such as: frequency and relative frequency distributions, cumulative frequency and cumulative relative frequency distributions.

4. Be able to use Excel's FREQUENCY function to construct a frequency distribution and the Chart Wizard to construct a histogram.

5. Learn how to construct a histogram and an ogive as graphical summaries of quantitative data.

6. Be able to use and interpret the exploratory data analysis technique of a stem-and-leaf display.

7. Learn how to construct and interpret cross tabulations and scatter diagrams of bivariate data.

8. Be able to use Excel's Pivot Table report to construct a cross tabulation and the Chart Wizard to construct a scatter diagram.

REVIEW

Summarizing Qualitative Data

Frequency Distribution
*   A frequency distribution is a <u>tabular summary</u> of data showing the frequency (or number) of items in each of several nonoverlapping classes.
*   The objective is to <u>provide insights</u> about the data that cannot be quickly obtained by looking only at the original data.

Excel Function for Qualitative Frequency Distributions
*   Excel's <u>COUNTIF</u> function can be used to construct a frequency distribution for qualitative data.
*   The function has <u>two arguments</u>:
    *   First – the range of cell addresses containing the observations (qualitative data) to be counted by class.
    *   Second – the label, or cell address of the label, of the class to be counted.
*   Note that each time the function is employed, it counts the frequency of only one class – the class entered as the second argument in the function.
*   If, for example, you have four classes of data, you would employ the function four times.

Relative Frequency Distribution
- The <u>relative frequency</u> of a class is the fraction or proportion of the total number of data items belonging to the class.
- A <u>relative frequency distribution</u> is a tabular summary of a set of data showing the relative frequency for each class.

Percent Frequency Distribution
- The <u>percent frequency</u> of a class is the relative frequency multiplied by 100.
- A <u>percent frequency distribution</u> is a tabular summary of a set of data showing the percent frequency for each class.

Bar Graph
- A bar graph is a graphical device for depicting <u>qualitative data</u> that have been summarized in a frequency, relative frequency, or percent frequency distribution.
- On the horizontal axis we specify the labels that are used for each of the classes.
- A <u>frequency</u>, <u>relative frequency</u>, or <u>percent frequency</u> scale is used for the vertical axis.
- Using a <u>bar of fixed width</u> drawn above each class label, we extend the height appropriately.
- The <u>bars are separated</u> to emphasize the fact that each class is a separate category.

Pie Chart
- The pie chart is a commonly used graphical device for presenting <u>relative frequency distributions</u> for qualitative data.
- First draw a circle; then use the relative frequencies to subdivide the circle into sectors that correspond to the relative frequency for each class.
- Since there are 360 degrees in a circle, a class with a relative frequency of .25 would consume .25(360) = 90 degrees of the circle.

Excel's Tool for Bar Graphs and Pie Charts
- Excel's <u>Chart Wizard</u> can be used to construct bar graphs and pie charts.
- After frequencies, relative frequencies, or percent frequencies have been computed, these values can be graphically displayed using Chart Wizard.

Summarizing Quantitative Data

Frequency Distribution
- With quantitative data we have to be careful in defining the <u>nonoverlapping classes</u> to be used in the frequency distribution.
- The <u>three steps necessary to define the classes</u> are:
  - Determine the number of nonoverlapping classes.
  - Determine the width of each class.
  - Determine the class limits.
- The <u>guidelines for selecting number of classes</u> are:
  - Use between 5 and 20 classes.
  - Larger data sets usually require a larger number of classes.
  - Smaller data sets usually require fewer classes.

- The guidelines for selecting the width of classes are:
  - Use classes of equal width.
  - Approximate Class Width =

$$\frac{\text{Largest Data Value} - \text{Smallest Data Value}}{\text{Number of Classes}}$$

Excel Function for Quantitative Frequency Distributions

- Excel's FREQUENCY function can be used to construct a frequency distribution for quantitative data.
- Unlike simple Excel functions (COUNTIF for example), the FREQUENCY function can provide multiple values such as class frequencies.
- A formula containing a function that can return multiple values is called an array formula and must be entered in a special way.
- The function has two arguments:
  - First – the range of cell addresses containing the observations (quantitative data) to be counted by class.
  - Second – a list of the upper class limits (this tells Excel which frequency to put in each cell within the range of the array formula)
- After selecting the cells in which you want the frequencies to appear and typing in the array formula containing the FREQUENCY function, press CTRL+SHIFT+ENTER. The formula will be entered into each of the cells selected.
- Regardless of the number of classes, you enter the array formula only once and no copying/pasting is necessary.

Histogram

- A common graphical presentation of quantitative data is a histogram.
- The variable of interest is placed on the horizontal axis and the frequency, relative frequency, or percent frequency is placed on the vertical axis.
- A rectangle is drawn above each class interval with its height corresponding to the interval's frequency, relative frequency, or percent frequency.
- Unlike a bar graph, a histogram has no natural separation between rectangles of adjacent classes.

Excel's Tool for Histograms

- Excel's Chart Wizard can be used to construct histograms.
- After frequencies, relative frequencies, or percent frequencies have been computed, these values can be displayed graphically using Chart Wizard.

Cumulative Distributions

- The cumulative frequency distribution shows the number of items with values less than or equal to the upper limit of each class.
- The cumulative relative frequency distribution shows the proportion of items with values less than or equal to the upper limit of each class.
- The cumulative percent frequency distribution shows the percentage of items with values less than or equal to the upper limit of each class.

Ogive

- An ogive is a graph of a cumulative distribution.
- The data values are shown on the horizontal axis.
- Shown on the vertical axis is one of the following: cumulative frequency, cumulative relative frequency, or cumulative percent frequency.
- The frequency (one of the above) of each class is plotted as a point.
- Straight-line segments connect the plotted points.

Excel's Tool for Ogives

- Excel's Chart Wizard can be used to construct ogives.
- After cumulative frequencies have been computed, these values can be displayed graphically as a form of scatter diagram using Chart Wizard.

Exploratory Data Analysis

- The techniques of exploratory data analysis consist of simple arithmetic and easy-to-draw pictures that can be used to summarize data quickly.
- One such technique, for quantitative data, is the stem-and-leaf display.

Stem-and-Leaf Display

- A stem-and-leaf display shows both the rank order and shape of the distribution of the data.
- It is similar to a histogram on its side, but it has the advantage of showing the actual data values.
- The first digit(s) of each data item are arranged to the left of a vertical line.
- To the right of the vertical line we record the last digit for each item in rank order.
- Each line in the display is referred to as a stem.
- Each digit on a stem is a leaf.

Relationship Between Two Variables

- Often a manager is interested in tabular and graphical methods that will help understand the relationship between two variables.
- Crosstabulation and a scatter diagram are two methods for summarizing the data for two variables simultaneously.

Crosstabulation

- A crosstabulation is a tabular summary of data for two variables.
- The two variables might both be qualitative, both be quantitative, or be one of each.
- The classes for one variable are represented by the rows; the columns represent the classes for the other variable.
- Converting the entries in the table into row percentages or column percentages can provide additional insight about the relationship between the variables.

Excel's Tool for Crosstabulation

- Excel's PivotTable Report is a general tool for summarizing the data for two or more variables simultaneously.
- This tool can be used to construct a crosstabulation (an Excel PivotTable).

Scatter Diagram
- A scatter diagram is a <u>graphical presentation</u> of the relationship between <u>two quantitative variables</u>.
- One variable is shown on the horizontal axis and the other variable is shown on the vertical axis.
- A <u>positive relationship</u>, <u>negative relationship</u>, or <u>no relationship</u> might be apparent to a manager with the aid of a scatter diagram.

Excel's Tool for Scatter Diagrams
- Excel's <u>Chart Wizard</u> can be used to construct <u>scatter diagrams</u>.
- Once a scatter diagram has been developed, other Excel tools (covered in later chapters) can be used, for example to fit a trend line to the plotted data.

KEY CONCEPTS

<u>CONCEPT</u>	<u>EXAMPLES</u>	<u>EXERCISES</u>
Summarizing Qualitative Data		
Frequency Distribution	①	1
Relative Frequency Distribution	②	1
Percent Frequency Distribution	②	1
Bar Graph	③	2
Pie Chart	④	2
Summarizing Quantitative Data		
Frequency Distribution	⑤	3
Relative Frequency Distribution	⑤	3
Percent Frequency Distribution	⑤	3
Histogram	⑥	4
Cumulative Distributions	⑦	5
Ogive	⑧	5
Exploratory Data Analysis		
Stem-and-Leaf Display	9	6
Relationship Between Two Variables		
Crosstabulation	⑩	7
Scatter Diagram	⑪	8

◯ Excel Used

EXAMPLES

EXAMPLE 1

Frequency Distribution – Qualitative Data

Guests staying at Marada Inn were asked to rate the quality of their accommodations as being excellent, above average, average, below average, or poor. The ratings provided by a sample of 20 quests are shown below.

Below Average	Average	Above Average	Above Average
Above Average	Above Average	Above Average	Below Average
Below Average	Average	Poor	Poor
Above Average	Average	Above Average	Average
Excellent	Above Average	Average	Above Average

Provide a frequency distribution showing the number of occurrences of each rating level in the sample.

SOLUTION 1

Using Excel's COUNTIF Function for Frequency Distributions

Excel can be used to count the frequencies and construct a frequency distribution for the quality ratings data.

Enter Data: The label Rating Given and the data for the 20-guest sample are entered into cells A1:A21.

> (*Note:* Misspelled data will not be counted as it should. Misspelling includes typing any spaces before or after the phrases!)

Enter Functions and Formulas: Excel's COUNTIF function can be used to count the number of times each rating level appears in cells A2:A21. We first enter a label and the rating levels in cells C1:C6, the label Total in cell C7, and the label Frequency in cell D1. Then, we enter the following function into cell D2:

=COUNTIF($A$2:$A$21,C2)

To count the number of times the other rating levels appear in our data, we copy the **above** formula into cells D3:D6. Finally, we total the frequency counts using the SUM function in cell D7.

> (*Note:* It is a good idea to total your frequency count as a partial check of the accuracy of your data and function entries. We know from our sample size that the total frequency should be 20.)

Formula Worksheet:

	A	B	C	D
1	**Rating Given**		**Quality Rating**	**Frequency**
2	Above Average		Poor	=COUNTIF($A$2:$A$21,C2)
3	Below Average		Below Average	=COUNTIF($A$2:$A$21,C3)
4	Above Average		Average	=COUNTIF($A$2:$A$21,C4)
5	Average		Above Average	=COUNTIF($A$2:$A$21,C5)
6	Average		Excellent	=COUNTIF($A$2:$A$21,C6)
7	Above Average		**Total**	=SUM(D2:D6)
8	Above Average			
20	Excellent			
21	Poor			

Note: Rows 9-19 are hidden.

Value Worksheet:

	A	B	C	D
1	**Rating Given**		**Quality Rating**	**Frequency**
2	Above Average		Poor	2
3	Below Average		Below Average	3
4	Above Average		Average	5
5	Average		Above Average	9
6	Average		Excellent	1
7	Above Average		**Total**	20
8	Above Average			
20	Excellent			
21	Poor			

Note: Rows 9-19 are hidden.

EXAMPLE 2

Relative and Percent Frequency Distributions – Qualitative Data

Refer to the quality ratings data in Example 1. Construct a relative frequency distribution and percent frequency distribution for the data.

SOLUTION 2

Using Excel

For a data set with n observations, the relative frequency of each class is computed as follows:

Relative Frequency of a Class = (Frequency of the Class)/n

Continuing with the worksheet shown in the solution to Example 1, we can construct the relative frequency and percent frequency distributions for the quality ratings data.

Enter Data: The data set is already entered. We simply enter the label Relative Frequency in cell E1and "Percent Frequency" in cell F1.

Enter Functions and Formulas: Using the relative frequency formula above, we compute the relative frequency for the Poor rating by entering the formula =D2/$D$7 in cell E2. We then copy cell E2 to cells E3:E6.

To compute the percent frequency for the Poor rating we enter the formula =E2*100 into cell F2. We then copy cell F2 to cells F3:F6. Finally, we copy cell D7 to cells E7:F7 to compute the total of the relative frequencies (1.00) and the total of the percent frequencies (100).

Formula Worksheet

	C	D	E	F
			Relative Frequency	**Percent Frequency**
1	**Quality Rating**	**Frequency**		
2	Poor	=COUNTIF($A$2:$A$21,C2)	=D2/$D$7	=E2*100
3	Below Average	=COUNTIF($A$2:$A$21,C3)	=D3/$D$7	=E3*100
4	Average	=COUNTIF($A$2:$A$21,C4)	=D4/$D$7	=E4*100
5	Above Average	=COUNTIF($A$2:$A$21,C5)	=D5/$D$7	=E5*100
6	Excellent	=COUNTIF($A$2:$A$21,C6)	=D6/$D$7	=E6*100
7	Total	=SUM(D2:D6)	=SUM(E2:E6)	=SUM(F2:F6)
8				

Note: Columns A and B are not shown.

Value Worksheet

	C	D	E	F
			Relative Frequency	**Percent Frequency**
1	**Quality Rating**	**Frequency**		
2	Poor	2	0.10	10
3	Below Average	3	0.15	15
4	Average	5	0.25	25
5	Above Average	9	0.45	45
6	Excellent	1	0.05	5
7	Total	20	1.00	100
8				

Note: Columns A and B are not shown.

EXAMPLE 3

Bar Graph

Refer to the quality ratings data in Example 1. Display the frequencies (computed in Example 1) graphically with a bar graph.

SOLUTION 3

Using Excel's CHART WIZARD for Bar Graphs

Continuing with the worksheet shown in the solution to Example 1, we can construct the bar graph using Excel's Chart Wizard. A third task (in addition to Enter Data and Enter Functions and Formulas) is now necessary: Apply Tools.

Enter Data: The data set was entered in Example 1.

Enter Functions and Formulas: The functions and formulas for the relative frequencies we want to graph were entered in Example 1.

Apply Tools: The following steps describe how to use Excel's Chart Wizard to construct a bar graph using the frequency distribution appearing in cells C1:D6.

> Step 1 Select cells C1:D6
> Step 2 Select the **Chart Wizard** button
> Step 3 When the **Chart Wizard-Step 1 of 4-Chart Type** dialog box appears:
> > Choose **Column** in the **Chart type** list
> > Choose **Clustered Column** from the **Chart sub-type** display
> > Select **Next >**
> Step 4 When the **Chart Wizard-Step 2 of 4-Chart Source Data** dialog box appears
> > Select **Next >**
> Step 5 When the **Chart Wizard-Step 3 of 4-Chart Options** dialog box appears:
> > Select the **Titles** tab and then
> > > Type **Bar Graph of Quality Ratings** in the **Chart title** box
> > > Enter **Quality Rating** in the **Value (X)** axis box
> > > Enter **Frequency** in the **Value (Y)** axis box
> > Select the **Legend** tab and then
> > > Remove the check in the **Show Legend** box
> > > Select **Next >**
> Step 6 When the **Chart Wizard-Step 4 of 4-Chart Location** dialog box appears:
> > Specify the location for the new chart (we chose cell C9)
> > Select **Finish** to display the bar graph

You can alter the graph initially produced by Excel to look like the one below or to suit your personal preferences. A right-click on almost any item in the chart will bring up a menu of alteration options.

Bar Graph

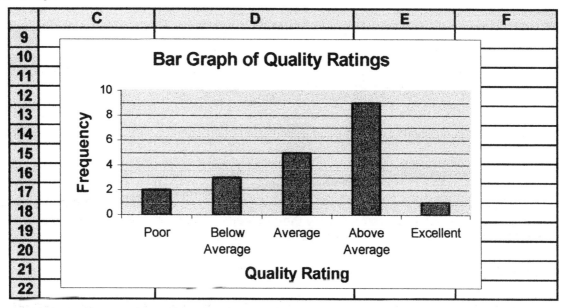

EXAMPLE 4

Pie Chart

Refer to the quality ratings data in Example 1. Display the percent frequencies (computed in Example 2) graphically with a pie chart.

SOLUTION 4

Using Excel's CHART WIZARD for Pie Charts

Excel's Chart Wizard provides a general tool for constructing graphical displays such as pie charts. Extending the worksheet shown in the solution to Example 2, we can construct the pie chart.

Enter Data: The data set was entered in Example 1.

Enter Functions and Formulas: The functions and formulas for the percent frequencies we want to graph were entered in Example 2.

Apply Tools: The following steps describe how to use Excel's Chart Wizard to construct a pie chart using the percent frequency distribution appearing in cells C1:C6 and F1:F6.

> Step 1 Select cells C1:C6 and F1:F6 (To select nonadjacent cells, select cells C1:C6 and then press the Control key while selecting cells F1:F6.)
> Step 2 Select the **Chart Wizard** button
> Step 3 When the **Chart Wizard-Step 1 of 4-Chart Type** dialog box appears:
> > Choose **Pie** in the **Chart type** list
> > Choose **Pie** from the **Chart sub-type** display
> > Select **Next >**

Step 4 When the **Chart Wizard-Step 2 of 4-Chart Source Data** dialog box appears
   Select **Next >**

Step 5 When the **Chart Wizard-Step 3 of 4-Chart Options** dialog box appears:
   Select the **Titles** tab and then
      Type **Customers' Quality Ratings at Marada Inn** in the **Chart title** box
   Select the **Legend** tab and then
      Remove the check in the **Show Legend** box
   Select the **Data Labels** tab and then
      Select **Show Label and percent**
      Select **Show leader lines**
      Select **Next >**

Step 6 When the **Chart Wizard-Step 4 of 4-Chart Location** dialog box appears:
   Specify the location for the new chart (we chose cell C9)
   Select **Finish** to display the pie chart

You can alter the chart initially produced by Excel to look like the one below or to suit your personal preferences. A right-click on almost any item in the chart will bring up a menu of alteration options.

Pie Chart

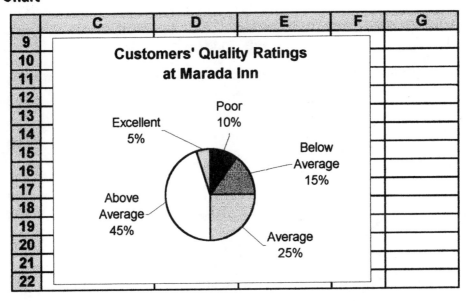

EXAMPLE 5

Frequency Distribution – Quantitative Data

The manager of Hudson Auto Repair would like to get a better picture of the distribution of costs for new parts used in the engine tune-up jobs done in the garage. A sample of 50 customer invoices for tune-ups has been taken and the costs of parts, rounded to the nearest dollar, are listed below.

91	78	93	57	75	52	99	80	73	62
71	69	72	89	66	75	79	95	72	76
104	74	62	68	97	105	77	65	80	109
85	97	88	68	83	68	71	69	67	74
62	82	98	101	79	105	79	69	62	73

Develop a frequency distribution for these cost data. Use your own judgment to determine the number of classes and class width that provide a distribution that will be meaningful and helpful to the manager.

SOLUTION 5

Using Excel's FREQUENCY Function

First, we must define the nonoverlapping classes to be used in the frequency distribution. The data is in dollars and most people will think in increments of $5, $10, $20, and so on. We should consider using one of these increments as the class width.

If we round <u>up</u> the largest data value (109) to 110 and we round <u>down</u> the smallest data value (52) to 50, we have a range of 110 – 50 = 60 for the frequency distribution to span. If we choose 10 as the class width, the result will be 60/10 = 6 classes, which is a reasonable number of classes.

The data is in integer dollar amounts. If we set the lower limit of the first class at 50, the upper limit of the first class will be 59 (not 60). There are 10 dollar amounts between 50 and 59, inclusively. The second class will have limits of 60 and 69, and so on.

Now we are ready to use Excel. Using Excel's COUNTIF function to construct a frequency distribution for quantitative data is cumbersome. Excel's FREQUENCY function is more appropriate here.

Enter Data: The label Parts Cost and the cost data from the 50 customer invoices are entered into cells A1:A51.

Enter Functions and Formulas: Descriptive labels are entered into cells C1 and D1, and the class limits 50-59, 60-69, and so on, are entered in a text format into cells C2:C7.

Data Worksheet: (Note: Rows 9-49 are hidden)

	A	B	C	D
	Parts Cost		Parts Cost	Frequency
1				
2	91		50-59	
3	71		60-69	
4	104		70-79	
5	85		80-89	
6	62		90-99	
7	78		100-109	
8	69			
50	74			
51	73			

The FREQUENCY function is not a "simple" Excel function. FREQUENCY is capable of providing multiple values and for this reason it is called an <u>array formula</u>. An array formula must be entered in a special way.

<u>Entering the Necessary Array Formula</u>

Step 1 Select cells D2:D7 (where the frequencies will appear)

Step 2 Type the following formula:
=FREQUENCY(A2:A51,{59,69,79,89,99,109})

Step 3 Hold down the CTRL and SHIFT keys while pressing the ENTER key
(Array formula will be entered into cells D2:D7)

Value Worksheet:

	A	B	C	D
1	Parts Cost		Parts Cost	Frequency
2	91		50-59	2
3	71		60-69	13
4	104		70-79	16
5	85		80-89	7
6	62		90-99	7
7	78		100-109	5
8	69			
50	74			
51	73			

Note: Rows 9-49 are hidden.

EXAMPLE 6

<u>Histogram</u>

Refer to the auto parts cost data in Example 5. Display the frequency distribution (constructed in Example 5) graphically with a histogram.

SOLUTION 6

<u>Using Excel's CHART WIZARD for Histograms</u>

Enter Data: The data set was entered in Example 5.

Enter Functions and Formulas: The functions and formulas for the frequencies we want to graph were entered in Example 5.

Apply Tools: The following steps describe how to use Excel's Chart Wizard to construct a histogram.

Step 1 Select cells C1:D7
Step 2 Select the **Chart Wizard** button
Step 3 When the **Chart Wizard-Step 1 of 4-Chart Type** dialog box appears:
      Choose **Column** in the **Chart type** list
      Choose **Clustered Column** from the **Chart sub-type** display
      Select **Next >**
Step 4 When the **Chart Wizard-Step 2 of 4-Chart Source Data** dialog box appears
      Select **Next >**
Step 5 When the **Chart Wizard-Step 3 of 4-Chart Options** dialog box appears:
      Select the **Titles** tab and then
          Type **Histogram for Parts Cost Data** in the **Chart title** box
          Enter **Parts Cost ($)** in the **Value (X)** axis box
          Enter **Frequency** in the **Value (Y)** axis box
      Select the **Legend** tab and then
          Remove the check in the **Show Legend** box
      Select **Next >**
Step 6 When the **Chart Wizard-Step 4 of 4-Chart Location** dialog box appears:
      Specify the location for the new chart (we chose cell C10)
      Select **Finish** to display the histogram

Initial Histogram:

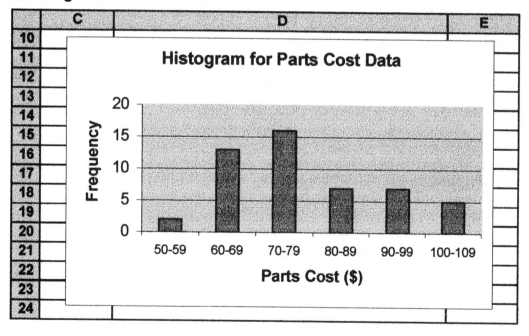

<u>Eliminating Gaps Between Rectangles</u>

Step 1 Right click on any rectangle in the column chart
Step 2 Select the **Format Data Series** option
Step 3 When the Format Data Series Option dialog box appears:
      Select the **Options** tab and then
          Enter **0** in the **Gap width** box
          Select **OK**

You can alter the chart initially produced by Excel to look like the one below or to suit your personal preferences. A right-click on almost any item in the chart will bring up a menu of alteration options.

Finished Histogram:

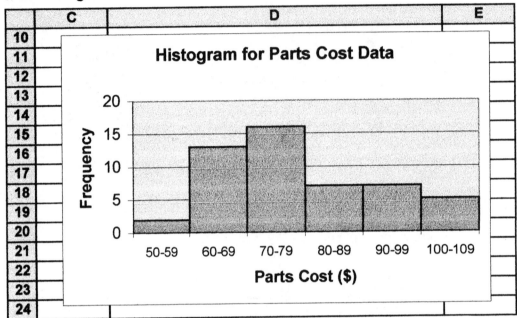

EXAMPLE 7

Cumulative Distributions

Refer to the auto parts cost data in Example 5. Develop a cumulative frequency distribution and a cumulative percent frequency distribution for this data.

SOLUTION 7

Using Excel's for Cumulative Distributions

Extending the worksheet shown in the solution to Example 5, we can construct the cumulative frequency and cumulative percent frequency distributions for the cost data.

Enter Data: The data set was entered in Example 5.

Enter Functions and Formulas: The functions and formulas for the frequencies we need were entered in Example 5. The first cumulative frequency (2) is simply the frequency for the first class, so we enter the formula =D2 in cell E2. The second cumulative frequency (15) is equal to the frequency of the second class (13) plus the prior cumulative frequency (2), so we enter the formula =D3+E2 in cell E3. Now, we copy cell E3 to cells E4:E7 to complete the cumulative distribution.

To compute the cumulative percent frequency distribution, we must convert each cumulative frequency value to a cumulative relative frequency value and then multiply it by 100. We enter the formula =E2/$D$8*100 into cell F2 to compute the first cumulative percent frequency. We then copy cell F2 to cells F3:F7 to complete our distribution.

Formula Worksheet:

	A	B	C	D	E	F	G
1	Parts Cost		Parts Cost	Frequency	Cumulative Frequency	Cumulative % Frequency	
2	91		$50-59	2	=D2	=E2/$D$8*100	
3	71		$60-69	13	=D3+E2	=E3/$D$8*100	
4	104		$70-79	16	=D4+E3	=E4/$D$8*100	
5	85		$80-89	7	=D5+E4	=E5/$D$8*100	
6	62		$90-99	7	=D6+E5	=E6/$D$8*100	
7	78		$100-109	5	=D7+E6	=E7/$D$8*100	
8	69		Sum	=SUM(D2:D7)			

Note: Rows 9-51 are not shown.

Value Worksheet:

	A	B	C	D	F	G	G
1	Parts Cost		Parts Cost	Frequency	Cumulative Frequency	Cumulative % Frequency	
2	91		$50-59	2	2	4	
3	71		$60-69	13	15	30	
4	104		$70-79	16	31	62	
5	85		$80-89	7	38	76	
6	62		$90-99	7	45	90	
7	78		$100-109	5	50	100	
8	69		Sum	50			

Note: Rows 9-51 are not shown.

EXAMPLE 8

Ogive

Refer to the auto parts cost data in Example 5. Construct an ogive showing the cumulative percent frequency distribution for the data.

SOLUTION 8

Using Excel's CHART WIZARD for Ogives

We will continue with the worksheet shown in the solution to Example 7 to develop the ogive. We need to modify the worksheet in two ways before we can apply the Chart Wizard tool. We will "insert" (figuratively) a new row between existing rows 1 and 2, and we will insert (literally) a new column between existing columns C and D.

The reason for a "new" row is that we need a starting point for the ogive showing that no data values fall below the 50-59 class. In other words, we need to create a 40-49 class with a cumulative percent frequency equal to 0. The reason for a new column is this: Because the class limits are 50-59, 60-69, and so on, there appear to be one-unit gaps from 59 to 60, 69 to 70, and so on. These gaps are eliminated by plotting points, on our ogive, at the midpoints of the gaps. Thus, 59.5 is used as the upper limit for the 50-59 class, 69.5 is used for the 60-69 class, and so on. We will enter these new upper limits in the new column.

Enter Data: The data set was entered in Example 5.

Enter Functions and Formulas: The formulas for the cumulative percent frequencies we need were entered in Example 7. Now, in order to enter the new 40-49 class in the worksheet we must free up a row. To do this, we drag cells C2:G8 down one row to cells C3:G9. This frees up cells C2:G2 for the new 40-49 class information. Next, we will insert a new column between existing columns C and D. To do this, select any cell in column D and then go to the main menu, select Insert, and select Columns in the drop-down menu.

The worksheet will now look like this:

	A	B	C	D	E	F	G
1	Parts Cost		Parts Cost		Frequency	Cumulative Frequency	Cumulative % Frequency
2	91						
3	71		50-59		2	2	4
4	104		60-69		13	15	30
5	85		70-79		16	31	62
6	62		80-89		7	38	76
7	78		90-99		7	45	90
8	69		100-109		5	50	100
9	74		Sum		50		

In the new column D, enter the label Parts Cost Upper Limit into cell D1 and enter the new upper limits 49.5, 59.5, and so on, into cells D2:D8. In cell C2 enter, in text format, 40-49. In cells E2:G2 enter zeros. Finally, drag the Sum label in cell C9 to cell D9.

The worksheet will now look like this:

	A	B	C	D	E	F	G
1	Parts Cost		Parts Cost	Parts Cost Upper Limit	Frequency	Cumulative Frequency	Cumulative % Frequency
2	91		40-49	49.5	0	0	0
3	71		50-59	59.5	2	2	4
4	104		60-69	69.5	13	15	30
5	85		70-79	79.5	16	31	62
6	62		80-89	89.5	7	38	76
7	78		90-99	99.5	7	45	90
8	69		100-109	109.5	5	50	100
9	74			Sum	50		

Apply Tools: The following steps describe how to use Excel's Chart Wizard to construct an ogive.

Step 1 Select cells D2:D8 and G2:G8 (To select nonadjacent cells, select cells D2:D8 and then press the Control key while selecting cells G2:G8.)

Step 2 Select the **Chart Wizard** button

Step 3 When the **Chart Wizard-Step 1 of 4-Chart Type** dialog box appears:
   Choose **XY (Scatter)** in the **Chart type** list
   Choose **Scatter with data points connected by lines** from the
      Chart sub-type display
   Select **Next >**

Step 4 When the **Chart Wizard-Step 2 of 4-Chart Source Data** dialog box appears
   Select **Next >**

Step 5 When the **Chart Wizard-Step 3 of 4-Chart Options** dialog box appears:
   Select the **Titles** tab and then
      Type **Ogive for the Parts-Cost Data** in the **Chart title** box
      Enter **Parts Cost ($)** in the **Value (X)** axis box
      Enter **Cumulative Percent Frequency** in the **Value (Y)** axis box
   Select the **Legend** tab and then
      Remove the check in the **Show Legend** box
      Select **Next >**

Step 6 When the **Chart Wizard-Step 4 of 4-Chart Location** dialog box appears:
   Specify the location for the new chart (we chose C12)
   Select **Finish** to display the ogive

Ogive:

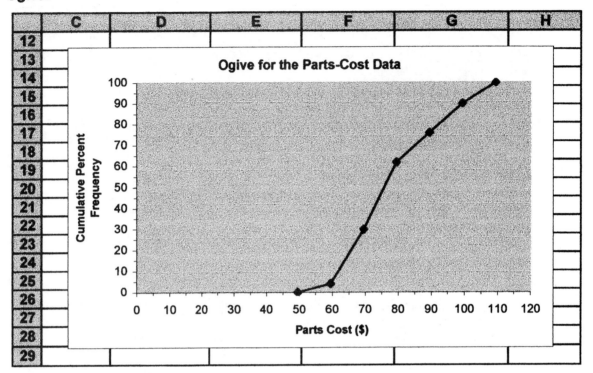

EXAMPLE 9

Stem-and-Leaf Display

Refer to the auto parts cost data in Example 5.

a) Develop a stem-and-leaf display showing both the rank order and shape of the data set simultaneously.

b) Also, develop a stretched stem-and-leaf display using two stems for each leading digit(s).

c) Which of the two displays is better in terms of revealing the natural grouping and variation in the data?

SOLUTION 9

a) To develop a stem-and-leaf display, we first arrange the leading digits (all but the last digit) of each data value to the left of a vertical line. To the right of the vertical line, we record the last digit for each data value as we pass through the observations in the order they are recorded. The last digit for each data value is placed on the line corresponding to its first digit.

At this point, the display will look like this:

```
 5 | 7 2
 6 | 2 9 6 2 8 5 8 8 9 7 2 9 2
 7 | 8 5 3 1 2 5 9 5 2 6 4 7 1 4 9 9 3
 8 | 0 9 0 5 8 3 2
 9 | 1 3 9 7 7 8
10 | 4 5 9 1 5
```

Next, we sort (in ascending order) the digits on each line. The result is the finished stem-and-leaf display.

```
 5 | 2 7
 6 | 2 2 2 2 5 6 7 8 8 8 9 9 9
 7 | 1 1 2 2 3 3 4 4 5 5 5 6 7 8 9 9 9
 8 | 0 0 2 3 5 8 9
 9 | 1 3 7 7 8 9
10 | 1 4 5 5 9
```

b) If we believe that our stem-and-leaf display has condensed the data too much, we can stretch the display by using two stems for each leading digit(s). All data values ending in 0, 1, 2, 3, and 4 are placed on one line, and all values ending in 5, 6, 7, 8, and 9 are placed on a second line.

The resulting <u>stretched stem-and-leaf display</u> will look like this:

```
 5 | 2
 5 | 7
 6 | 2 2 2 2
 6 | 5 6 7 8 8 8 9 9 9
 7 | 1 1 2 2 3 3 4 4
 7 | 5 5 5 6 7 8 9 9 9
 8 | 0 0 2 3
 8 | 5 8 9
 9 | 1 3
 9 | 7 7 8 9
10 | 1 4
10 | 5 5 9
```

c) The stretched stem-and-leaf display in (b) does a better job of revealing the dispersion of the data.

EXAMPLE 10

Crosstabulation

Ithaca Log Homes manufactures four styles of log houses that are sold in kits. The log homes the company has sold, by price (in $000) and style, for the past year is shown below.

≤99	Colonial	≥100	A-Frame	≥100	Colonial
≤99	Ranch	≥100	Split-Level	≤99	Colonial
≥100	Split-Level	≤99	Colonial	≤99	A-Frame
≥100	Split-Level	≥100	Ranch	≥100	Split-Level
≤99	Colonial	≥100	Colonial	≥100	Ranch
≤99	A-Frame	≤99	A-Frame	≤99	Split-Level
≤99	Split-Level	≤99	Split-Level	≥100	Split-Level
≤99	A-Frame	≤99	Split-Level	≥100	Colonial
≥100	Ranch	≤99	Colonial	≥100	Ranch
≥100	Split-Level	≤99	Ranch	≥100	Split-Level
≤99	A-Frame	≥100	Split-Level	≤99	Colonial
≤99	Colonial	≥100	Colonial	≥100	Colonial
≥100	Ranch	≤99	Split-Level	≤99	Split-Level
≤99	Colonial				

Prepare a crosstabulation for the variables price and style.

SOLUTION 10

Using Excel's PIVOTTABLE REPORT for Crosstabulation

On a new worksheet, enter the data in columns A, B, and C.

	A	B	C	D	E
1	Home	Price ($)	**Style**		
2	1	≥100K	Colonial		
3	2	≤99K	Ranch		
4	3	≥100K	Ranch		
5	4	≤99K	A-Frame		
6	5	≤99K	Colonial		
7	6	≤99K	Split-Level		
8	7	≥100K	A-Frame		
9	8	≥100K	Colonial		

Note: Rows 10-41 are not shown.

Changing the Default Order for the PivotTable Report

Step 1 Select the **Tools** pull-down menu
Step 2 Choose **Options**
Step 3 When the Options dialog box appears:
Select the **Custom lists** tab
In the **List entries:** box, type **≤99K** and press Enter, and type **≥100K**
Select **Add**
Select **OK**

We are now ready to use the PivotTable Report to construct a crosstabulation.

<u>Using the PivotTable Report</u>

Step 1 Select the **Data** pull-down menu

Step 2 Choose the **PivotTable and PivotChart Report**

Step 3 When the **PivotTable and PivotChart Wizard-Step 1 of 3** dialog box appears:
  Choose **Microsoft Excel list or database**
  Choose **PivotTable**
  Select **Next >**

Step 4 When the **PivotTable and PivotChart Wizard Step 2 of 3** dialog box appears:
  Enter A1:C41 in the **Range** box
  Select **Next >**

Step 5 When the **PivotTable and PivotChart Wizard Step 3 of 3** dialog box appears:
  Select **New Worksheet**
  Click on the **Layout** button
  When the **PivotTable and PivotChart Wizard – Layout** diagram appears:
    Drag the **Price ($)** field button to the **ROW** section of the diagram
    Drag the **Style** field button to the **COLUMN** section of the diagram
    Drag the **Home** field button to the **DATA** section of the diagram
    Double click the **Sum of Home** field button in the data section
    When the **PivotTable Field** dialog box appears:
      Choose **Count** under **Summarized by**:
      Select **OK**
    Select **OK**
  When the **PivotTable and PivotChart Wizard-Step 3 of 3** dialog box reappears:
    Select **Finish >**

Crosstabulation:

	E	F	G	H	I	J
1	Count of Home	Style				
2	Price ($)	Colonial	Ranch	Split-Level	A-Frame	Grand Total
3	≤99K	8	2	8	5	23
4	>100K	5	5	6	1	17
5	Grand Total	13	7	14	6	40
6						

EXAMPLE 11

Scatter Diagram

The Panthers football team is interested in investigating the relationship, if any, between interceptions made and points scored. The following data was collected for five recent games.

x = Number of Interceptions	y = Number of Points Scored
1	14
3	24
2	18
1	17
3	27

Develop a scatter diagram to show the relationship between the two variables, number of interceptions and number of points scored.

SOLUTION 11

Using Excel's CHART WIZARD for Scatter Diagrams

Enter Data: The appropriate labels and the data for the five football games are entered into cells A1:B6.

Data Worksheet:

	A	B	C
	Number of Interceptions	**Number of Points Scored**	
1			
2	1	14	
3	3	24	
4	2	18	
5	1	17	
6	3	27	
7			

Enter Functions and Formulas: No functions or formulas are needed.

Apply Tools: The following steps describe how to use Excel's Chart Wizard to produce a scatter diagram from the data in the worksheet.

Step 1 Select cells A1:B6
Step 2 Select the **Chart Wizard**
Step 3 When the **Chart Wizard-Step 1 of 4-Chart Type** dialog box appears:
Choose **XY (Scatter)** in the Chart type list
Choose **Scatter** from the Chart sub-type display
Select **Next >**
Step 4 When the **Chart Wizard-Step 2 of 4-Chart Source Data** dialog box appears
Select **Next >**
Step 5 When the **Chart Wizard-Step 3 of 4-Chart Options** dialog box appears:
Select the **Titles** tab and then

Delete **Number of Points Scored** in the Chart title box
Enter **Number of Interceptions** in the **Value (X)** axis box
Enter **Number of Points Scored** in the **Value (Y)** axis box
Select the **Legend** tab and then
Remove the check in the **Show Legend** box
Select **Next >**
Step 6 When the **Chart Wizard-Step 4 of 4-Chart Location** dialog box appears:
Specify the location for the new chart (we chose cell A8)
Select **Finish** to display the scatter diagram

Scatter Diagram:

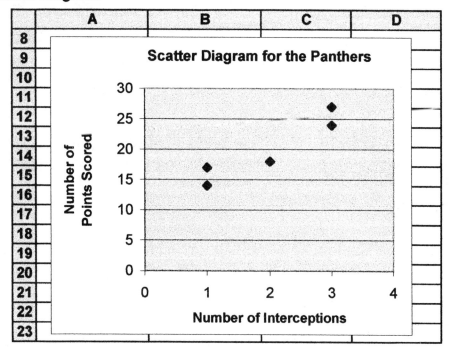

EXERCISES

EXERCISE 1

Frequency Distributions – Qualitative Data

It is time for Roger Hall, manager of new car sales at the Maxwell Ford dealership, to submit his order for new Mustang coupes. These cars will be parked in the lot, available for immediate sale to buyers who are not special-ordering a car. One of the decisions he must make is how many Mustangs of each color he should order. The new color options are very similar to the past year's options.

Roger believes that the colors chosen by customers who special-order their cars best reflect most customers' true color preferences. For that reason, he has taken a random sample of 40 special orders for Mustang coupes placed in the past year. The color preferences found in the sample are listed below.

Blue	Black	Green	White	Black	Red	Red	White
Black	Red	White	Blue	Blue	Green	Red	Black
Red	White	Blue	White	Red	Red	Black	Black
Green	Black	Red	Black	Blue	Black	White	Green
Blue	Red	Black	White	Black	Red	Black	Blue

Prepare a frequency distribution, relative frequency distribution, and percent frequency distribution for the data set.

EXERCISE 2

Bar Graph and Pie Chart

Refer to the Maxwell Ford data set in Exercise 1. Construct a bar graph showing the frequency distribution of the car colors. Also construct a pie chart showing the <u>percent</u> frequency distribution of the car colors.

EXERCISE 3

Frequency Distributions – Quantitative Data

Missy Walters owns a mail-order business specializing in clothing, linens, and furniture for children. She is considering offering her customers a discount on shipping charges for furniture based on the dollar-amount of the furniture order. Before Missy decides the discount policy, she needs a better understanding of the dollar-amount distribution of the furniture orders she receives.

Missy had an assistant randomly select 50 recent orders that included furniture. The assistant recorded the value, to the nearest dollar, of the furniture portion of each order. The data collected is listed below.

136	281	226	123	178	445	231	389	196	175
211	162	212	241	182	290	434	167	246	338
194	242	368	258	323	196	183	209	198	212
277	348	173	409	264	237	490	222	472	248
231	154	166	214	311	141	159	362	189	260

Prepare a frequency distribution, relative frequency distribution, and percent frequency distribution for the data set. Use your own judgment to determine the number of classes and class width that provide a distribution that will be meaningful and helpful to Missy in deciding the shipping discount policy.

EXERCISE 4

Histogram

Refer to the mail-order data in Exercise 3. Construct a histogram showing the <u>percent</u> frequency distribution of the furniture-order values in the sample.

EXERCISE 5

Cumulative Distributions and Ogive

Refer to the mail-order data in Exercise 3. Develop a cumulative frequency distribution and a cumulative percent frequency distribution for this data. Then construct an ogive showing the cumulative <u>percent</u> frequency distribution.

EXERCISE 6

Stem-and-Leaf Display

Refer to the mail-order data in Exercise 3. Develop a stem-and-leaf display for the data set. Employ the following tips to avoid having 38 stems and other shortcomings in your display.

1) Set the leaf unit equal to 10. In other words, convert the data to 10's of dollars. For example, the data value 226 would be treated as 22. The last digit, 6, is ignored.
2) Try using a <u>stretched</u> stem-and-leaf display. That is, have two stems labeled 1, two stems labeled 2, and so on. Values 10-14 are entered on the first stem labeled 1, values 15-19 are entered on the second stem labeled 1, and so on.

EXERCISE 7

Crosstabulation

Tony Zamora, a real estate investor, has just moved to Clarksville and wants to learn about the local real estate market. He wants to understand, for example, the relationship between geographical segment of the city and selling price of a house, the relationship between selling price and number of bedrooms, and so on.

Tony has randomly selected 25 house-for-sale listings from the Sunday newspaper and collected the data listed below.

a) Construct a crosstabulation for the variables *city segment* and *number of bedrooms*.

b) Compute the row percentages for your crosstabulation in part (a).

c) Comment on any apparent relationship between the variables.

Segment of City	Selling Price ($000)	House Size (00 sq. ft.)	Number of Bedrooms	Number of Bathrooms	Garage Size (cars)
Northwest	290	21	4	2	2
South	95	11	2	1	0
Northeast	170	19	3	2	2
Northwest	375	38	5	4	3
West	350	24	4	3	2
South	125	10	2	2	0
West	310	31	4	4	2
West	275	25	3	2	2
Northwest	340	27	5	3	3
Northeast	215	22	4	3	2
Northwest	295	20	4	3	2
South	190	24	4	3	2
Northwest	385	36	5	4	3
West	430	32	5	4	2
South	185	14	3	2	1
South	175	18	4	2	2
Northeast	190	19	4	2	2
Northwest	330	29	4	4	3
West	405	33	5	4	3
Northeast	170	23	4	2	2
West	365	34	5	4	3
Northwest	280	25	4	2	2
South	135	17	3	1	1
Northeast	205	21	4	3	2
West	260	26	4	3	2

EXERCISE 8

Scatter Diagram

Refer to the real estate data in Exercise 7. Develop a scatter diagram to show the relationship between the two variables *size of house* and *number of bathrooms*. Place the variable *number of bathrooms* on the horizontal axis.

SELF-TEST

TRUE/FALSE

___ 1. The lines that connect the points plotted in an ogive cannot have a negative slope.

___ 2. In a stem-and-leaf display, a single digit is used to define each leaf, while more than one digit can be used to define each stem.

___ 3. At least one of the variables in a crosstabulation must be a quantitative variable.

___ 4. There should be no gaps between adjacent bars in a histogram.

___ 5. For a bar graph to be worthwhile, the data being displayed must involve at least two variables.

FILL-IN-THE-BLANK

1. The techniques of _____ consist of simple arithmetic and easy-to-draw graphs that can be used to summarize data quickly.

2. A _____ is a tabular summary of data showing the number of items in each of several nonoverlapping classes.

3. The last entry in a _____ distribution is always 1.00.

4. In general practice, cumulative frequency distributions are appropriate for summarizing _____ data and not _____ data.

5. Adjacent bars are touching in a bar graph and are not touching in a _____.

MULTIPLE CHOICE

___ 1. Which one of the following graphical methods is most appropriate for qualitative data?
     a) ogive
     b) scatter diagram
     c) histogram
     d) pie chart

___ 2. A graphical method that will assist in the understanding of the relationship between two variables is a
     a) crosstabulation
     b) scatter diagram
     c) stem-and-leaf display
     d) bar graph

___ 3. A graphical method that can be used to show both the rank order and shape of a data set simultaneously is a
   a) relative frequency distribution
   b) pie chart
   c) stem-and-leaf display
   d) pivot table

___ 4. The proper way to construct a stem-and-leaf display for the data set {62,67,68,73,73,79,91,94,95,97} is to
   a) exclude a stem labeled '8'
   b) include a stem labeled '8' and enter no leaves on the stem
   c) include a stem labeled '(8)' and enter no leaves on the stem
   d) include a stem labeled '8' and enter one leaf value of '0' on the stem

___ 5. The graphical method presented in the chapter for displaying cumulative frequencies is
   a) an ogive
   b) a stem-and-leaf display
   c) a histogram
   d) a bar graph

ANSWERS

EXERCISES

1)

	C	D	E	F
1	**Color of Car**	**Frequency**	**Relative Frequency**	**Percent Frequency**
2	Black	12	0.300	30.0
3	Blue	7	0.175	17.5
4	Green	4	0.100	10.0
5	Red	10	0.250	25.0
6	White	7	0.175	17.5
7	**Total**	40	1.000	100.0

2) Bar Graph - Frequencies

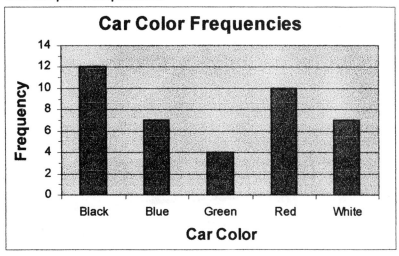

Pie Chart – Percent Frequencies

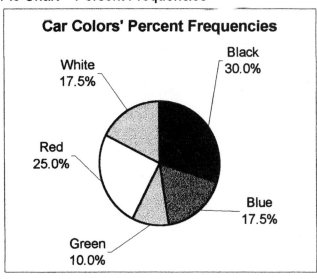

3)

	Furniture Order	Frequency	Relative Frequency	Cum. Rel. Frequency
	D	**E**	**F**	**G**
1	Furniture Order	Frequency	Relative Frequency	Cum. Rel. Frequency
2	100-149	3	0.06	0.06
3	150-199	15	0.30	0.36
4	200-249	14	0.28	0.64
5	250-299	6	0.12	0.76
6	300-349	4	0.08	0.84
7	350-399	3	0.06	0.90
8	400-449	3	0.06	0.96
9	450-499	2	0.04	1.00

4)

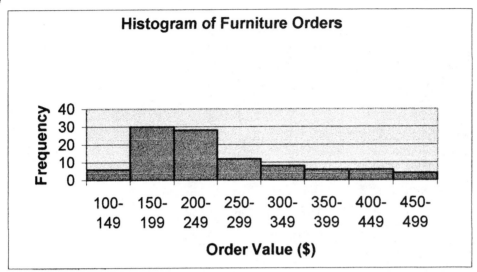

5)

	D	E	F	G
1	**Furniture Order**	**Frequency**	**Cumulative Frequency**	**Cumulative % Frequency**
2	100-149	3	3	6
3	150-199	15	18	36
4	200-249	14	32	64
5	250-299	6	38	76
6	300-349	4	42	84
7	350-399	3	45	90
8	400-449	3	48	96
9	450-499	2	50	100

6)

```
1 | 2 3 4
1 | 5 5 6 6 6 7 7 7 8 8 8 9 9 9 9
2 | 0 1 1 1 1 2 2 3 3 3 4 4 4 4
2 | 5 6 6 7 8 9
3 | 1 2 3 4
3 | 6 6 8
4 | 0 3 4
4 | 7 9
```

7) a) Crosstabulation:

	D	E	F	G	H	I
1	Count of Home	Number of Bedrooms				
2	Segment of City	2	3	4	5	Grand Total
3	Northeast	0	1	4	0	5
4	Northwest	0	0	4	3	7
5	South	2	2	2	0	6
6	West	0	1	3	3	7
7	Grand Total	2	4	13	6	25

b) Row Percentages:

	D	E	F	G	H	I
1	Percent of Home	Number of Bedrooms				
2	Segment of City	2	3	4	5	Grand Total
3	Northeast	0.0	20.0	80.0	0.0	100.0
4	Northwest	0.0	0.0	57.1	42.9	100.0
5	South	33.3	33.3	33.3	0.0	100.0
6	West	0.0	14.3	42.9	42.9	100.1

c) We see that fewest bedrooms are associated with the South, and the most bedrooms are associated with the West and particularly the Northwest.

8)

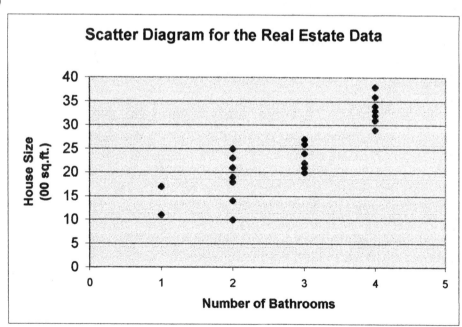

TRUE/FALSE

1) True
2) True
3) False
4) True
5) False

FILL-IN-THE-BLANK

1) exploratory data analysis
2) frequency distribution
3) cumulative relative frequency
4) quantitative, qualitative
5) histogram

MULTIPLE CHOICE

1) d
2) b
3) c
4) b
5) a

CHAPTER 3

Descriptive Statistics: Numerical Methods

Measures of Location

Measures of Variability

Measures of Relative Location
and Detecting Outliers

Exploratory Data Analysis

Measures of Association
Between Two Variables

The Weighted Mean and
Working with Grouped Data

LEARNING OBJECTIVES

1. Understand the purpose of measures of location.

2. Be able to compute the mean, median, mode, quartiles, and various percentiles.

3. Understand the purpose of measures of variability.

4. Be able to compute the range, interquartile range, variance, standard deviation, and coefficient of variation.

5. Understand how *z* scores are computed and how they are used as a measure of relative location of a data value.

6. Know how Chebyshev's theorem and the empirical rule can be used to determine the percentage of the data within a specified number of standard deviations from the mean.

7. Learn how to construct a 5-number summary and a box plot.

8. Be able to compute and interpret covariance and correlation as measures of association between two variables.

9. Be able to compute a weighted mean.

REVIEW

Measures of Location

Mean
- The <u>mean</u> of a data set is the average of all the data values.
- If the data are from a sample, the mean is denoted by $\bar{x}$.

$$\bar{x} = \frac{\sum x_i}{n}$$

- If the data are from a population, the mean is denoted by μ (mu).

$$\mu = \frac{\sum x_i}{N}$$

Median
- The <u>median</u> of a data set is the value in the middle when the data items are arranged in ascending order.
- If there are an odd number of items, the median is the value of the middle item.
- If there is an even number of items, the median is the average of the values for the middle two items.
- The median is most often reported for annual income and property value data because a few extremely large values can inflate the mean, making it misleading.

Mode
- The <u>mode</u> of a data set is the value that occurs with greatest frequency.
- The greatest frequency can occur at two or more different values.
- If the data have exactly two modes, the data are <u>bimodal</u>.
- If the data have more than two modes, the data are <u>multimodal</u>.

Excel's Functions for Mean, Median, and Mode
- The <u>AVERAGE</u> function can be used to compute the mean.
- The <u>MEDIAN</u> function will determine the median.
- The <u>MODE</u> function will determine the mode.
- These three functions have one and the same argument – the address range for the cells containing the data set.
- Caution – If the data are bimodal or multimodal, Excel's MODE function will <u>incorrectly</u> identify a single mode.

Percentiles
- The <u>pth percentile</u> of a data set is a value such that at least p percent of the items take on this value or less and at least $(100 - p)$ percent of the items take on this value or more.
  - Arrange the data in ascending order.
  - Compute index i, the position of the pth percentile.

$$i = (p/100)n$$

- If i is not an integer, round up. The pth percentile is the value in the ith position.
- If i is an integer, the pth percentile is the average of the values in positions i and $i + 1$.

Quartiles
- Quartiles are specific percentiles.
- First quartile = 25th percentile.
- Second quartile = 50th percentile = median.
- Third quartile = 75th percentile.

Using Excel to Compute Percentiles and Quartiles
- Excel provides functions for computing percentiles and quartiles.
- For small data sets, these functions do not always provide results that satisfy the definition of a percentile or quartile.
- We can use Excel to compute a percentile or quartile (converted to the equivalent percentile) another way.
- First, we sort the data in ascending order.
- Second, we compute an index that can be used to identify the position of the pth percentile.
- Then, we select the appropriate percentile or quartile from its indexed position in the ordered data set.

Measures of Variability

Range
- The range of a data set is the difference between the largest and smallest data values.
- It is the simplest measure of variability.
- It is very sensitive to the smallest and largest data values.

Interquartile Range
- The interquartile range of a data set is the difference between the third quartile and the first quartile.
- It is the range for the middle 50% of the data.
- It overcomes the sensitivity to extreme data values.

Variance
- The variance is the average of the squared differences between each data value and the mean.
- If the data set is a sample, the variance is denoted by s^2.

$$s^2 = \frac{\sum (x_i - \bar{x})^2}{n-1}$$

- If the data set is a population, the variance is denoted by σ^2.

$$\sigma^2 = \frac{\sum (x_i - \mu)^2}{N}$$

Standard Deviation
- The standard deviation of a data set is the positive square root of the variance.
- It is measured in the same units as the data, making it more easily comparable, than the variance, to the mean.
- If the data set is a sample, the standard deviation is denoted s.

$$s = \sqrt{s^2}$$

- If the data set is a population, the standard deviation is denoted σ (sigma).

$$\sigma = \sqrt{\sigma^2}$$

Excel's Functions for Sample Variance and Standard Deviation
- The VAR function can be used to compute the sample variance.
- The STDEV function can be used to compute the sample standard deviation.
- These two functions have one and the same argument – the address range for the cells containing the data set.

Coefficient of Variation
- The coefficient of variation indicates how large the standard deviation is in relation to the mean.
- If the data set is a sample, the sample coefficient of variation is computed as follows:

$$\frac{s}{\bar{x}}(100)$$

- If the data set is a population, the <u>population coefficient of variation</u> is computed as follows:

$$\frac{\sigma}{\mu}(100)$$

Excel's Descriptive Statistics Tool
- Excel provides statistical functions that can be used to compute <u>one statistic at a time</u>.
- Excel also provides a <u>Data Analysis Tool called Descriptive Statistics</u> that allows the user to compute <u>a variety of statistics at once</u>.
- After the user answers a few questions in the Descriptive Statistics dialog box, <u>more than a dozen summary statistics</u> are produced at once.
- The summary statistics include many of the measures discussed above, such as the mean, median, mode, standard deviation, variance, and range.

Measures of Relative Location and Detecting Outliers

z-Score
- The <u>z-score</u> is often called the standardized value.
- z denotes the number of standard deviations a data value x_i is from the mean.

$$z_i = \frac{x_i - \overline{x}}{s}$$

- A data value less than the sample mean will have a z-score less than zero.
- A data value greater than the sample mean will have a z-score greater than zero.
- A data value equal to the sample mean will have a z-score of zero.

Chebyshev's Theorem
- At least $(1 - 1/k^2)$ of the items in <u>any data set</u> will be within k standard deviations of the mean, where k is any value greater than 1.
- At least <u>75%</u> of the items must be <u>within $k = 2$ standard deviations</u> of the mean.
- At least <u>89%</u> of the items must be <u>within $k = 3$ standard deviations</u> of the mean.
- At least <u>94%</u> of the items must be <u>within $k = 4$ standard deviations</u> of the mean.

Empirical Rule
- The empirical rule is based on the normal (bell-shaped) probability distribution.

- Approximately <u>68%</u> of the data values will be <u>within one standard deviation</u> of the mean.
- Approximately <u>95%</u> of the data values will be <u>within two standard deviations</u> of the mean.
- <u>Almost all</u> of the items (<u>99.7%</u>) will be <u>within three standard deviations</u> of the mean.

Detecting Outliers
- An <u>outlier</u> is an unusually small or unusually large value in a data set.
- A data value with a z-score less than -3 or greater than +3 might be considered an outlier.
- It might be an <u>incorrectly recorded</u> data value.
- It might be a data value that was <u>incorrectly included</u> in the data set.
- It might be a correctly recorded data value that belongs in the data set !

Exploratory Data Analysis
- Exploratory data analysis enables us to use simple arithmetic and easy-to-draw pictures to summarize data.

Five-Number Summary
- The five numbers used to summarize the data are: <u>smallest value</u>, <u>first quartile</u>, <u>median</u>, <u>third quartile</u>, and <u>largest value</u>.

Box Plot
- A box is drawn with its ends located at the first and third quartiles.
- A vertical line is drawn in the box at the location of the median.
- Limits are located (not drawn) using the interquartile range (IQR).
    - The <u>lower limit</u> is located 1.5(IQR) below Q1.
    - The <u>upper limit</u> is located 1.5(IQR) above Q3.
    - Data outside these limits are considered <u>outliers</u>.
- <u>Dashed lines</u> are drawn from the ends of the box to the smallest and largest data values inside the limits.
- The location of each outlier is shown with the symbol * .

Measures of Association Between Two Variables

Covariance
- The <u>covariance</u> is a measure of the linear association between two variables.
- Positive values indicate a positive relationship.
- Negative values indicate a negative relationship.
- If the data set is a sample, the covariance is denoted by s_{xy}.

$$s_{xy} = \frac{\sum(x_i - \bar{x})(y_i - \bar{y})}{n-1}$$

$$\sigma_{xy} = \frac{\sum(x_i - \mu_x)(y_i - \mu_y)}{N}$$

- If the data set is a population, the covariance is denoted by σ_{xy}.

<u>Correlation Coefficient</u>
- The coefficient can take on values between -1 and +1.
- Values near -1 indicate a <u>strong negative linear relationship</u>.
- Values near +1 indicate a <u>strong positive linear relationship</u>.

- If the data sets are samples, the coefficient is r_{xy}.

$$r_{xy} = \frac{s_{xy}}{s_x s_y}$$

- If the data sets are populations, the coefficient is p_{xy}.

$$\rho_{xy} = \frac{\sigma_{xy}}{\sigma_x \sigma_y}$$

Excel's Functions for Covariance and Correlation Coefficient
- The <u>COVAR</u> function can be used to compute the <u>population covariance</u>.
- The <u>STDEV</u> function can be used to compute the <u>sample correlation coefficient</u>.
- The <u>user must be careful</u> when using these two functions because one treats the data as if it were a population while the other treats the data as a sample!
- These two functions have the same two arguments:
  - First – the address range for the cells containing the data for variable x.
  - Second – the address range for the cells containing the data for variable y.
- The <u>user must be careful</u> when using these two functions because one treats the data as if it were a population while the other treats the data as a sample!
- The results obtained using <u>COVAR must be adjusted</u> to provide the <u>sample covariance</u>.
- Simply <u>multiply the population covariance by $n/(n-1)$</u> to get the sample covariance.

Weighted Mean
- When the mean is computed by giving each data value a weight that reflects its importance, it is referred to as a <u>weighted mean</u>, $\bar{x}$.

$$x_{wt} = (\Sigma w_i x_i)/\Sigma w_i$$

where: x_i = value of observation i
w_i = weight for observation i

- In the computation of a <u>grade point average</u> (GPA), the weights are the number of credit hours earned for each grade.
- When <u>data values vary in importance</u>, the analyst must choose the weight that best reflects the importance of each value.
- The weighted mean computation can be used to obtain approximations of the mean, variance, and standard deviation for grouped data.

Working with Grouped Data

Mean for Grouped Data
- To compute the weighted mean, we treat the <u>midpoint of each class</u> as though it were the mean of all items in the class.
- We compute a weighted mean of the class midpoints using the <u>class frequencies</u> as weights.
- If the data set is a sample, the approximated mean is:

$$\bar{x} = \frac{\sum f_i M_i}{n}$$

- If the data set is a population, the approximated mean is:

$$\mu = \frac{\sum f_i M_i}{N}$$

- In both formulas above, f_i = frequency of class i and M_i = midpoint of class i

Variance for Grouped Data
- If the data set is a sample, the approximated variance is:

$$s^2 = \frac{\sum f_i (M_i - \bar{x})^2}{n-1}$$

- If the data set is a population, the approximated variance is:

$$\sigma^2 = \frac{\sum f_i (M_i - \mu)^2}{N}$$

Standard Deviation for Grouped Data
- If the data set is a sample, the approximated standard deviation is:

$$s = \sqrt{s^2}$$

- If the data set is a population, the approximated standard deviation is:

$$\sigma = \sqrt{\sigma^2}$$

KEY CONCEPTS

CONCEPT	EXAMPLES	EXERCISES
Measures of Location		
Mean	① ⑤	1,5
Median	① ⑤	1,5
Mode	① ⑤	1,5
Percentiles	②	2
Quartiles	②	2
Measures of Variability		
Range	③ ⑤	3,5
Interquartile Range	③	3
Variance	④ ⑤	4,5
Standard Deviation	④ ⑤	4,5
Coefficient of Variation	④	4

CONCEPT	EXAMPLES	EXERCISES
Measures of Relative Location		
z-Scores	⑥	6
Chebyshev's Theorem	⑥	6
Empirical Rule	⑥	6
Detecting Outliers	⑥	6
Exploratory Data Analysis		
Five-Number Summary	7	7
Box Plot	7	7
Measures of Assoc. Between Two Variables		
Covariance	⑧	8
Correlation Coefficient	⑧	8
Weighted Mean	9	9
Grouped Data		
Mean	⑩	10
Variance	⑩	10
Standard Deviation	⑩	10

◯ Excel Used

EXAMPLES

EXAMPLE 1

Mean, Median, and Mode

A sample of monthly rent values ($) for one-bedroom apartments in a particular city was taken. The data collected from the 70-apartment sample is listed below in ascending order. Determine the mean, median, and mode for this data set.

```
425 430 430 435 435 435 435 435 440 440
440 440 440 445 445 445 445 445 450 450
450 450 450 450 450 460 460 460 465 465
465 470 470 472 475 475 475 480 480 480
480 485 490 490 490 500 500 500 500 510
510 515 525 525 525 535 549 550 570 570
575 575 580 590 600 600 600 600 615 615
```

SOLUTION 1

Using Excel's AVERAGE, MEDIAN, and MODE Functions

Excel provides functions for computing the mean, median, and mode.

Enter Data: Labels and the rent amounts are entered in cells A1:B71 of the worksheet.

Enter Functions and Formulas: Excel's AVERAGE function can be used to compute the mean by entering the following formula is entered into cell E2:

$$=AVERAGE(B2:B71)$$

Similarly, the formulas =MEDIAN(B2:B71) and =MODE(B2:B71) are entered into cells E3 and E4, respectively, to compute the median and the mode. The labels Mean, Median, and Mode are entered into cells D2:D4 to identify the output.

Formula Worksheet:

	A	B	C	D	E
1	Apart-ment	Monthly Rent ($)			
2	1	525		Mean	=AVERAGE(B2:B71)
3	2	440		Median	=MEDIAN(B2:B71)
4	3	450		Mode	=MODE(B2:B71)
5	4	615			

Note: Rows 6-71 are not shown.

Value Worksheet:

	A	B	C	D	E
1	Apart-ment	Monthly Rent ($)			
2	1	525		Mean	490.8
3	2	440		Median	475.0
4	3	450		Mode	450.0
5	4	615			

Note: Rows 6-71 are not shown.

EXAMPLE 2

Percentiles and Quartiles

Refer again to the apartment rent data presented in Example 1. What is the 90th percentile? What is the third quartile?

SOLUTION 2

Using Excel

Excel provides functions for computing percentiles and quartiles. However, for small data sets these functions do not always provide results that satisfy the true definition of the terms. Shown below is another way to compute these values. We will first sort the data and then compute the appropriate index i that can be used to identify the position of the p th percentile. This procedure also provides quartiles because they are also percentiles.

Sorting Data:

Step 1 Select any cell containing data in column B
Step 2 Select the **Data** pull-down menu
Step 3 Choose the **Sort** option
Step 4 When the Sort dialog box appears:
>   In the **Sort by** box, make sure that **Monthly Rent ($)** appears and that **Ascending** is selected
>   In the **My list has** box, make sure that **Header row** is selected
>   Click **OK**

Enter Data: The rent data are already entered (see solution to Example 1).

Enter Functions and Formulas: The labels Number of Observations, Percentile, and Index i in cells D1:F1, respectively. The number of observations, 70, is entered into cell D2 and the desired percentile, 90, is entered into cell E2. Recall that the formula for computing the index is $i = (p/100)n$. The corresponding formula =(E2/100)*D2 is entered into cell F2.

Formula Worksheet:

	A	B	C	D	E	F
1	Apart-ment	Monthly Rent ($)		Number of Observations	Percentile	Index i
2	1	425		70	90	=(E2/100)*D2
3	2	430				
4	3	430				
5	4	435				
6	5	435				

Note: Rows 7-71 are not shown.

We see in the worksheet below that the index value is the integer 63.

Value Worksheet:

	A	B	C	D	E	F
1	Apart-ment	Monthly Rent ($)		Number of Observations	Percentile	Index i
2	1	425		70	90	63.00
3	2	430				
4	3	430				
5	4	435				
6	5	435				

Note: Rows 7-71 are not shown.

When i is an integer, the p th percentile is the average of the data values in positions i and $i + 1$. Therefore, we should compute the average of the data values in the 63rd and 64th positions of the ordered data set.

Value Worksheet:

	A	B	C	D	E	F
1	Apart-ment	Monthly Rent ($)		Number of Observations	Percentile	Index i
62	61	575				
63	62	575				
64	63	580				
65	64	590				
66	65	600				
67	66	600				

Note: Rows 2-61 are hidden.

We see in the worksheet above that the value of the 90th percentile is the average of the data values 580 and 590. The answer is 585.

The third quartile is found in a similar way. The 3rd quartile equals the 75th percentile, so we enter the value 75 into cell E2.

Value Worksheet:

	A	B	C	D	E	F
1	Apart-ment	Monthly Rent ($)		Number of Observations	Percentile	Index i
2	1	425		70	75	52.50
3	2	430				
4	3	430				
5	4	435				
6	5	435				

Note: Rows 7-71 are not shown.

The index value 52.5 is not an integer, so we round it up to 53. The <u>position</u> of the data value being the 3rd quartile (75th percentile) is 53. The 3rd quartile is 525.

	A	B	C	D	E	F
1	**Apart-ment**	**Monthly Rent ($)**		**Number of Observations**	**Percentile**	**Index *i***
52	51	510				
53	52	515				
54	53	525				
55	54	525				
56	55	525				

Note: Rows 2-51 are hidden.

EXAMPLE 3

Range and Interquartile Range

Refer again to the apartment rent data presented in Example 1. Compute the range and interquartile range for the data set.

SOLUTION 3

Using Excel's MAX and MIN Functions

The range equals the largest data value minus the smallest data value. The interquartile range equals the 3rd quartile minus the 1st quartile (or 75th percentile minus the 25th percentile).

Enter Data: The rent data and labels are already entered (see solution to Example 1).

Enter Functions and Formulas: The following formula for computing the range is entered into cell E2:

$$=MAX(B2:B71)-MIN(B2:B71)$$

Formula Worksheet:

	A	B	C	D	E
1	**Apart-ment**	**Monthly Rent ($)**			
2	1	425		**Range**	=MAX(B2:B71)-MIN(B2:B71)
3	2	430			
4	3	430			
5	4	435			
6	5	435			

Note: Rows 7-71 are not shown.

We see in the worksheet below that the range is 190.

Value Worksheet:

	A	B	C	D	E
1	Apart-ment	Monthly Rent ($)			
2	1	425		**Range**	190
3	2	430			
4	3	430			
5	4	435			
6	5	435			

Note: Rows 7-71 are not shown.

To compute the interquartile range, we must determine the 75th percentile and 25th percentile. Refer to the solution to Example 2 for explanation of the steps involved in finding percentiles. Executing those steps, we find that the 75th percentile is 525, and the 25th percentile is 445. Hence, the interquartile range is 525 – 445 = 80.

EXAMPLE 4

Variance, Standard Deviation, and Coefficient of Variation

Refer again to the apartment rent data presented in Example 1. Compute the sample variance, sample standard deviation, and the coefficient of variation.

SOLUTION 4

Using Excel's VAR and STDEV Functions

We will use Excel functions to compute the sample variance and standard deviation. There is no function in Excel for solely computing the coefficient of variation, so we will use a formula.

Enter Data: The rent data and labels are already entered (see solution to Example 1).

Enter Functions and Formulas: In order to compute the coefficient of variation, we need the value of the mean that was found in the solution to Example 1. The sample variance is computed by entering the following formula into cell E5:

=VAR(B2:B71)

The sample standard deviation is computed by entering the following formula into cell E6:

=STDEV(B2:B71)

The formula for the coefficient of variation (CV) is:

$$\frac{\text{Standard Deviation}}{\text{Mean}} \times 100$$

To compute the CV we enter the formula =E6/E2*100 into cell E7. Last, we enter labels to identify the output.

Formula Worksheet:

	A	B	C	D	E
1	Apart-ment	Monthly Rent ($)			
2	1	525		Mean	=AVERAGE(B2:B71)
3	2	440		Median	=MEDIAN(B2:B71)
4	3	450		Mode	=MODE(B2:B71)
5	4	615		Variance	=VAR(B2:B71)
6	5	480		Std. Dev.	=STDEV(B2:B71)
7	6	510		C.V.	=E6/E2*100

Note: Rows 8-71 are not shown.

Value Worksheet:

	A	B	C	D	E
1	Apart-ment	Monthly Rent ($)			
2	1	525		Mean	490.80
3	2	440		Median	475.00
4	3	450		Mode	450.00
5	4	615		Variance	2996.16
6	5	480		Std. Dev.	54.74
7	6	510		C.V.	11.15

Note: Rows 8-71 are not shown.

EXAMPLE 5

Descriptive Statistics

Refer again to the apartment rent data presented in Example 1. Use Excel's Descriptive Statistics tool to compute a variety of descriptive statistics at once rather than one by one using individual functions such as AVERAGE, MEDIAN, and STDEV.

SOLUTION 5

Using Excel's DESCRIPTIVE STATISTICS Tool

Enter Data: The rent data and labels are already entered (see solution to Example 1).

Enter Functions and Formulas: No functions or formulas are needed.

Apply Tools: The following steps describe how to use Excel's Descriptive Statistics tool.

Step 1 Select the **Tools** pull-down menu
Step 2 Choose the **Data Analysis** option
Step 3 Choose **Descriptive Statistics** from the list of Analysis Tools
Step 4 When the **Descriptive Statistics** dialog box appears:

               Enter B1:B71 in the **Input Range** box
               Select **Grouped By Columns**
               Select **Labels in First Row**
               Select **Output Range**
               Enter D1 in the **Output Range** box
               Select **Summary Statistics**
               Select **OK**

Value Worksheet:

	A	B	C	D	E
1	Apart-ment	Monthly Rent ($)		Monthly Rent ($)	
2	1	525		Mean	490.8
3	2	440		Standard Error	6.542348114
4	3	450		Median	475
5	4	615		Mode	450
6	5	480		Standard Deviation	54.73721146
7	6	510		Sample Variance	2996.162319
8	7	575		Kurtosis	-0.334093298
9	8	430		Skewness	0.924330473
10	9	440		Range	190
11	10	450		Minimum	425
12	11	470		Maximum	615
13	12	485		Sum	34356
14	13	515		Count	70

EXAMPLE 6

z-Scores, Chebyshev's Theorem, Empirical Rule, and Outliers

Refer again to the apartment rent data presented in Example 1. Compute the z-score for every value in the data set and then answer the following questions.

a) What is the z-score for the minimum value in the data set? What is the z-score for the maximum value in the data set?

b) Based on Chebyshev's Theorem, what percentage of the data values must be within 1.5 standard deviations of the mean. What percentage of the data values <u>actually</u> falls within +/- 1.5 standard deviations?

c) Apply the empirical rule to the data set. How close are the actually percentages to the percentages dictated by the empirical rule?

d) Using +/- 3 standard deviations as the criterion, identify any outliers in the data set.

SOLUTION 6

Using Excel

Enter Data: The rent data and labels are already entered (see solution to Example 1).

Enter Functions and Formulas: We need the mean and standard deviation in order to compute z-scores, so we will use the worksheet we developed in Example 4. First, sort the data in cells B2:B71 in ascending order. Next, expand column C and enter the label **z-Score** into cell C1. The formula for computing a z-score is:

$$z_i = \frac{x_i - \overline{x}}{s}$$

Hence, we enter the formula =(B2-$E$2)/$E$6 into cell C2. Then, cell C2 is copied to cells C3:C71.

Formula Worksheet:

	A	B	C	D	E
1	Apart-ment	Monthly Rent ($)	z-Score		
2	1	425	=(B2-$E$2)/$E$6	Mean	=AVERAGE(B2:B71)
3	2	430	=(B3-$E$2)/$E$6	Median	=MEDIAN(B2:B71)
4	3	430	=(B4-$E$2)/$E$6	Mode	=MODE(B2:B71)
5	4	435	=(B5-$E$2)/$E$6	Variance	=VAR(B2:B71)
6	5	435	=(B6-$E$2)/$E$6	Std. Dev.	=STDEV(B2:B71)
7	6	435	=(B7-$E$2)/$E$6	C.V.	=E6/E2*100

Note: Rows 8-71 are not shown.

Value Worksheet:

	A	B	C	D	E
1	Apart-ment	Monthly Rent ($)	z-Score		
2	1	425	-1.20	Mean	490.80
3	2	430	-1.11	Median	475.00
4	3	430	-1.11	Mode	450.00
5	4	435	-1.02	Variance	2996.16
6	5	435	-1.02	Std. Dev.	54.74
7	6	435	-1.02	C.V.	11.15

Note: Rows 8-71 are not shown.

a) From the resulting worksheet we see that the z-scores for the minimum and maximum data values are −1.20 and 2.27, respectively. (Scroll down to the last data value in your worksheet to see the last z-score of 2.27.)

b) Let $k = 1.5$ with $\bar{x} = 490.80$ and $s = 54.74$. At least $(1 - 1/(1.5)^2) = 1 - 0.44 = 0.56$ or 56% of the rent values must be between:

$$\bar{x} - k(s) = 490.80 - 1.5(54.74) = \underline{409}$$
and
$$\bar{x} + k(s) = 490.80 + 1.5(54.74) = \underline{573}$$

Actually, 86% of the data values are between 409 and 573.

c)

	Interval	Actual % in Interval	Emp.Rule % in Interval
Within +/- 1s	436.06 to 545.54	48/70 = 69%	approx. 68%
Within +/- 2s	381.32 to 600.28	68/70 = 97%	approx. 95%
Within +/- 3s	326.58 to 655.02	70/70 = 100%	almost 100%

d) The most extreme z-scores are -1.20 and 2.27. Using $|z| \geq 3$ as the criterion for an outlier, there are no outliers in this data set.

EXAMPLE 7

Five-Number Summary and Box Plot

Refer again to the apartment rent data presented in Example 1. Provide a five-number summary of the data set and graph your results using a box plot.

SOLUTION 7

The five-number summary includes the minimum data value, first quartile, median, third quartile, and maximum data value. We solved for all of these values in previous examples.

Five-Number Summary:

Minimum   = 425 (computed in Example 5)
First Quartile = 445 (computed in Example 3)
Median   = 475 (computed in Example 5)
Third Quartile = 525 (computed in Example 3)
Maximum   = 615 (computed in Example 5)

Box Plot:

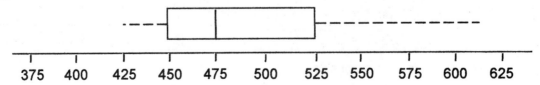

375   400   425   450   475   500   525   550   575   600   625

EXAMPLE 8

Covariance and Correlation Coefficient

Angela Lopez, a golf instructor, is interested in investigating the relationship between a golfer's average driving distance and 18-hole score. She recently observed the performance of six golfers during one round of a tournament and measured, as accurately as possible, the distances of their drives and noted their final scores. She then computed each golfer's average drive distance for 18 holes. The results of her sample are shown below.

Golfer	Avg. Drive Distance	18-Hole Score
1	277.6	69
2	259.5	71
3	269.1	70
4	267.0	70
5	255.6	71
6	272.9	69

Compute and interpret both the sample covariance and the sample correlation coefficient.

SOLUTION 8

Using Excel's COVAR and CORREL Functions

Excel provides functions for computing the covariance and correlation coefficient. However, the covariance function treats the data as if it were a population, while the correlation coefficient function treats the data as if it were a sample.

Enter Data: Labels and data on the six golfers are entered into cells A1:C7 of a new worksheet. The rent data and labels are already entered (see solution to Example 1).

Data Worksheet:

	A	B	C	D	E
1	Golfer	Avg. Drive Distance	18-Hole Score		
2	1	277.6	69		
3	2	259.5	71		
4	3	269.1	70		
5	4	267.0	70		
6	5	255.6	71		
7	6	272.9	69		
8					

Enter Functions and Formulas: Excel's covariance function, COVAR, can be used to compute the <u>population</u> covariance by entering the following formula into cell E2:

$$=COVAR(B2:B7,C2:C7)$$

To convert the population covariance to the sample covariance we multiply the former by $n/(n-1)$. In this example, the sample size is 6, so the conversion factor is $6/(6-1) = 6/5$. For this reason we enter the formula $= 6/5*E2$ into cell E3.

Excel's correlation function, CORREL, can be used to compute the sample correlation coefficient by entering the following formula into cell E5:

$$=CORREL(B2:B7,C2:C7)$$

Formula Worksheet:

	A	B	C	D	E
		Avg. Drive	**18-Hole**		
1	**Golfer**	**Distance**	**Score**		
2	1	277.6	69	**Popul. Covariance**	=COVAR(B2:B7,C2:C7)
3	2	259.5	71	**Sample Covariance**	=6/5*E2
4	3	269.1	70		
5	4	267.0	70	**Samp. Correlation**	=CORREL(B2:B7,C2:C7)
6	5	255.6	71		
7	6	272.9	69		
8					

The value worksheet below shows a sample covariance value of −7.08 that indicates a negative relationship between driving distance and final score. This is not surprising. Unless a golfer's putting performance is relatively poor, we would expect longer driving distances to lead to lower final scores. To judge the strength of the relationship between the two variables we turn to interpreting the correlation coefficient. Its value is -.96 that indicates (because it is so close to −1.00) an exceptionally strong negative correlation between driving distance and final score.

Value Worksheet:

	A	B	C	D	E
		Avg. Drive	**18-Hole**		
1	**Golfer**	**Distance**	**Score**		
2	1	277.6	69	**Popul. Covariance**	-5.90
3	2	259.5	71	**Sample Covariance**	-7.08
4	3	269.1	70		
5	4	267.0	70	**Samp. Correlation**	-0.96
6	5	255.6	71		
7	6	272.9	69		
8					

EXAMPLE 9

Weighted Mean

Del Michaels had a successful morning, or so he thinks, selling 1300 surplus notebook computers over the telephone to three commercial customers. The three customers were not equally skillful at negotiating a low unit price. Customer A bought 600 computers for $1252 each, B bought 300 units at $1310 each, and C bought 400 at $1375 each.

Del's manager told him he expected Del to sell, by the end of the day, the 2500 surplus computers being held in the warehouse at an average price of $1312 each. How is Del doing so far? What should be Del's strategy in the afternoon, considering his morning results?

SOLUTION 9

To determine the average price he got for the 1300 computers Del sold we must compute a weighted average of the three prices he charged, not a simple average (because he did not sell the same number of computers at each price).

The formula for computing a weighted mean is:

$$x_{wt} = (\Sigma w_i x_i)/\Sigma w_i$$

where: x_i = value of observation i
w_i = weight for observation i

The weight we place on each price, in computing the average price, is the number of computers sold at that price. Essentially, the steps to computing a weighted mean in this example are: 1) multiply each price by its respective weight, 2) sum the products from step 1, and 3) divide the sum from step 2 by the sum of the weights.

$$(600(1252) + 300(1310) + 400(1375))/1300 = 1303.23$$

Del is not meeting his manager's expectation of an average selling price of $1312. He under priced the computers he sold by an average of $8.77. He needs to sell the remaining 1200 computers at an average price of $1321.50 in order to meet expectations.

EXAMPLE 10

Grouped Data

Given below is a sample of 70 monthly rents for one-bedroom apartments presented as grouped data in the form of a frequency distribution. Compute the sample mean, variance, and standard deviation.

Rent ($)	Frequency	Rent ($)	Frequency
420-439	8	520-539	4
440-459	17	540-559	2
460-479	12	560-579	4
480-499	8	580-599	2
500-519	7	600-619	6

SOLUTION 10

Using Excel for Grouped Data

Computing the Sample Mean:

Enter Data: Labels and the rent classes and their corresponding frequencies are entered into cells A1:B11 of a new worksheet.

Enter Functions and Formulas: The first step is to compute the midpoint of each rent class as follows:

$$\text{Midpoint of a Class} = (\text{Lower Limit} + \text{Upper Limit})/2$$

For example, the midpoint of the first class is $(420 + 439)/2 = 429.5$. Now we are ready to multiply the midpoint of each class by the class' frequency. To do this we enter the formula = B2*C2 into cell D2 and then copy cell D2 to cells D3:D11.

Next, we sum the frequencies in cells B2:B11 by entering the formula =SUM(B2:B11) into cell B12. Then, we sum the products in cells D2:D11 by entering the formula =SUM(D2:D11) into cell D12.

Finally, we compute the sample mean by entering the formula =D12/B12 into cell B13 and enter appropriate labels to identify the output.

Formula Worksheet:

	A	B	C	D
1	Rent ($)	Frequency f_i	Class Midpt. M_i	$f_i M_i$
2	420-439	8	429.5	=B2*C2
3	440-459	17	449.5	=B3*C3
4	460-479	12	469.5	=B4*C4
5	480-499	8	489.5	=B5*C5
6	500-519	7	509.5	=B6*C6
7	520-539	4	529.5	=B7*C7
8	540-559	2	549.5	=B8*C8
9	560-579	4	569.5	=B9*C9
10	580-599	2	589.5	=B10*C10
11	600-619	6	609.5	=B11*C11
12	Totals	=SUM(B2:B11)		=SUM(D2:D11)
13	Sample Mean	=D12/B12		

Value Worksheet:

	A	B	C	D
	Rent ($)	**Frequency** f_i	**Class Midpt.** M_i	f_iM_i
1				
2	420-439	8	429.5	3436.0
3	440-459	17	449.5	7641.5
4	460-479	12	469.5	5634.0
5	480-499	8	489.5	3916.0
6	500-519	7	509.5	3566.5
7	520-539	4	529.5	2118.0
8	540-559	2	549.5	1099.0
9	560-579	4	569.5	2278.0
10	580-599	2	589.5	1179.0
11	600-619	6	609.5	3657.0
12	**Totals**	70		34525.0
13	**Sample Mean**	493.21		

Computing the Sample Variance and Standard Deviation:

Enter Data: We will continue with the worksheet (above) that we developed to compute the sample mean. We chose to erase the contents of column D and use the column for new calculations. (You can choose to start your new work in column E if you like.) We replaced the formula for the sample mean in cell B13 with the value 493.21.

Enter Functions and Formulas: We begin by subtracting the sample mean from the midpoint of each of the rent classes. To do this we enter the formula = C2-$B$13 into cell D2 and then copy cell D2 to cells D3:D11. Next, we square the deviations in cells D2:D11 by entering the formula = D2^2 into cell E2 and then copying cell E2 to cells E3:E11. Next, we multiply the squared deviations in cells E2:E11 by their respective class frequencies in cells B2:B11. We do this by entering the formula =B2*E2 into cell F2 and then copying cell F2 to cells F3:F11. And then we sum the values in cells F2:F11 by entering the formula =SUM(F2:F11) into cell F12.

Now we are ready to compute the sample variance by entering the formula =F12/(B12-1) into cell B14. The sample standard deviation is the square root of the sample variance, so we enter the formula =SQRT(B14) into cell B15. We finish by entering labels to identify the output.

Formula Worksheet:

	A	B	C	D	E	F
1	Rent ($)	Frequency f_i	Class Midpt. M_i	Deviation M_i - Mean	Sq. Dev.	f_i(Sq.Dev.)
2	420-439	8	429.5	=C2-$B$13	=D2^2	=B2*E2
3	440-459	17	449.5	=C3-$B$13	=D3^2	=B3*E3
4	460-479	12	469.5	=C4-$B$13	=D4^2	=B4*E4
5	480-499	8	489.5	=C5-$B$13	=D5^2	=B5*E5
6	500-519	7	509.5	=C6-$B$13	=D6^2	=B6*E6
7	520-539	4	529.5	=C7-$B$13	=D7^2	=B7*E7
8	540-559	2	549.5	=C8-$B$13	=D8^2	=B8*E8
9	560-579	4	569.5	=C9-$B$13	=D9^2	=B9*E9
10	580-599	2	589.5	=C10-$B$13	=D10^2	=B10*E10
11	600-619	6	609.5	=C11-$B$13	=D11^2	=B11*E11
12	Totals	=SUM(B2:B11)				=SUM(F2:F11)
13	Sample Mean	493.21				
14	Sample Var.	=F12/(B12-1)				
15	Sample S.D.	=SQRT(B14)				

Value Worksheet:

	A	B	C	D	E	F
1	Rent ($)	Frequency f_i	Class Midpt. M_i	Deviation M_i - Mean	Sq. Dev.	f_i(Sq.Dev.)
2	420-439	8	429.5	-63.7	4058.96	32471.71
3	440-459	17	449.5	-43.7	1910.56	32479.59
4	460-479	12	469.5	-23.7	562.16	6745.97
5	480-499	8	489.5	-3.7	13.76	110.11
6	500-519	7	509.5	16.3	265.36	1857.55
7	520-539	4	529.5	36.3	1316.96	5267.86
8	540-559	2	549.5	56.3	3168.56	6337.13
9	560-579	4	569.5	76.3	5820.16	23280.66
10	580-599	2	589.5	96.3	9271.76	18543.53
11	600-619	6	609.5	116.3	13523.36	81140.18
12	Totals	70				208234.29
13	Sample Mean	493.21				
14	Sample Var.	3017.89				
15	Sample S.D.	54.94				

EXERCISES

EXERCISE 1

Mean, Median, and Mode

Missy Walters owns a mail-order business specializing in clothing, linens, and furniture for children. She is considering offering her customers a discount on shipping charges for furniture based on the dollar-amount of the furniture order. Before Missy decides the discount policy, she needs a better understanding of the dollar-amount distribution of the furniture orders she receives.

Missy had an assistant randomly select 50 recent orders that included furniture. The assistant recorded the value, to the nearest dollar, of the furniture portion of each order. The data collected is listed below.

136	281	226	123	178	445	231	389	196	175
211	162	212	241	182	290	434	167	246	340
194	242	368	258	323	196	183	209	198	210
277	348	173	409	264	237	490	222	472	248
231	154	166	214	311	141	159	362	189	260

Determine the mean, median, and mode for this data set.

EXERCISE 2

Percentiles and Quartiles

Refer again to the furniture data presented in Exercise 1. What is the 80th percentile? What is the first quartile?

EXERCISE 3

Range and Interquartile Range

Refer again to the furniture data presented in Exercise 1. Compute the range and interquartile range for the data set.

EXERCISE 4

Variance, Standard Deviation, and Coefficient of Variation

Refer again to the furniture data presented in Exercise 1. Compute the sample variance, sample standard deviation, and the coefficient of variation.

EXERCISE 5

Descriptive Statistics

Refer again to the furniture data presented in Exercise 1. Use Excel's Descriptive Statistics tool to compute a variety of descriptive statistics at once rather than one by one using individual functions such as AVERAGE, MEDIAN, and STDEV.

EXERCISE 6

z-Scores, Chebyshev's Theorem, Empirical Rule, and Outliers

Refer again to the furniture data presented in Exercise 1. Compute the z-score for every value in the data set and then answer the following questions.

a) What is the z-score for the minimum value in the data set? What is the z-score for the maximum value in the data set?

b) Based on Chebyshev's Theorem, what percentage of the data values must be within 1.5 standard deviations of the mean. What percentage of the data values <u>actually</u> falls within +/- 1.5 standard deviations?

c) Apply the empirical rule to the data set. How close are the actually percentages to the percentages dictated by the empirical rule?

d) Using +/- 3 standard deviations as the criterion, identify any outliers in the data set.

EXERCISE 7
Five-Number Summary and Box Plot

Refer again to the furniture data presented in Exercise 1. Provide a five-number summary of the data set and graph your results using a box plot.

EXERCISE 8

Covariance and Correlation Coefficient

Reed Auto periodically has a special week-long sale. As part of the advertising campaign Reed runs one or more television commercials during the weekend preceding the sale. Data from a sample of 5 previous sales are shown below.

Week	TV Ads	Cars Sold
1	1	14
2	3	24
3	2	18
4	1	17
5	3	27

Compute and interpret both the sample covariance and the sample correlation coefficient.

EXERCISE 9

Weighted Mean

Ron Butler, a custom home builder, is looking over the expenses he incurred for a house he just completed constructing. For the purpose of pricing future construction projects, he would like to know the average wage ($/hour) he paid the workers he employed. (The cost of materials is estimated in advance by the architect.) Listed below are the categories of worker he employed, along with their respective wage and total hours worked.

Worker	Wage ($/hr)	Total Hours
Carpenter	21.60	520
Electrician	28.72	230
Laborer	11.80	410
Painter	19.75	270
Plumber	24.16	160

What is the average wage ($/hour) he paid the workers?

EXERCISE 10

Grouped Data

The manager of Hudson Auto Repair has recorded the following frequency distribution for the cost of new parts used in doing an engine tune-up in a sample of 50 tune-ups.

Parts Cost ($)	Frequency
50-59	2
60-69	13
70-79	17
80-89	7
90-99	6
100-109	5

Compute the sample mean, variance, and standard deviation.

SELF-TEST

TRUE/FALSE

___ 1. The interquartile range is the difference between the third and second quartiles.

___ 2. The absolute value of the correlation coefficient is equal to the value of the coefficient of determination.

___ 3. The descriptive statistics for grouped data are only approximations of the descriptive statistics that would result from using the original data directly.

___ 4. The steps for computing percentiles can be directly applied in the computation of quartiles.

___ 5. When a data set contains an even number of data values, there can be two median values for the data set.

FILL-IN-THE-BLANK

1. When observations vary in importance, the analyst must choose the _____ that best reflects the importance of each observation in the determination of the mean.

2. In computing descriptive statistics for grouped data, the _____ are used to approximate the data values in each class.

3. It is better to use the median than the mean as a measure of central location when the data set contains _____.

4. The _____ is an important measure of location for qualitative data.

5. Although the _____ is the easiest of the measures of variability to compute, it is seldom used as the only measure.

MULTIPLE CHOICE

___ 1. Which one of the following is not a measure of variability of a single variable?
   a) range
   b) covariance
   c) standard deviation
   d) coefficient of variation

___ 2. The empirical rule states that, for data having a bell-shaped distribution, the percentage of data values being within one standard deviation of the mean is approximately
   a) 34
   b) 50
   c) 68
   d) 95

___ 3. A box plot is a graphical representation of data that is based on
   a) the empirical rule
   b) z-scores
   c) a histogram
   d) a five-number summary

___ 4. The coefficient of variation indicates how large the standard deviation is relative to the
   a) mean
   b) median
   c) range
   d) variance

___ 5. Which one of the following descriptive statistics is not measured in the same units as the data?
   a) 35th percentile
   b) standard deviation
   c) variance
   d) interquartile range

ANSWERS

EXERCISES

1) mean = 251.46; median = 228.5; modes are 196 and 231 (data set is bimodal)

2) 80th percentile = 331.5; first quartile = 183

3) range = 367 ; interquartile range = 107

4) variance = 8398.50; standard deviation = 91.64; coefficient of variation = 36.44

5) (compare your output with several of the answers above)

6) a) min. z = -1.40; max. z = 2.60
   b) 55.5%; 44/50 = 88%
   c) 72% are +/- 1σ; 94% are +/- 2σ; 100% are +/- 3σ; all are relatively close
   d) no outliers

7) 123, 183, 228.5, 290, 490

8) sample covariance = 5.0 ; sample correlation coefficient = 0.937

9) $20.05

10) sample mean = 77.9; sample variance = 186.16; sample standard deviation = 13.64

TRUE/FALSE

1) False
2) False
3) True
4) True
5) False

FILL-IN-THE-BLANK

1) weight
2) class midpoints
3) extreme values
4) mode
5) range

MULTIPLE CHOICE

1) b
2) c
3) d
4) a
5) c

CHAPTER 4

Introduction to Probability

Experiments, Counting Rules,
and Assigning Probabilities

Events and Their Probabilities

Some Basic Relationships of Probability

Conditional Probability

Bayes' Theorem

1. Obtain an appreciation of the role probability information plays in the decision making process.

2. Understand probability as a numerical measure of the likelihood of occurrence.

3. Know the three methods commonly used for assigning probabilities and understand when they should be used.

4. Know how to use the laws that are available for computing the probabilities of events.

5. Understand how new information can be used to revise initial (prior) probability estimates using Bayes' theorem.

REVIEW

Probability
- <u>Probability</u> is a numerical measure of the likelihood that an event will occur.
- Probability values are always assigned on a scale from 0 to 1.
- A probability near 0 indicates an event is very unlikely to occur.
- A probability near 1 indicates an event is almost certain to occur.
- A probability of 0.5 indicates the occurrence of the event is just as likely as it is unlikely.

An Experiment and Its Sample Space
- An <u>experiment</u> is any process that generates well-defined outcomes.
- The <u>sample space</u> for an experiment is the set of all experimental outcomes.
- A <u>sample point</u> is an element of the sample space, any one particular experimental outcome.
- The sum of the probabilities of all the sample points in the sample space must equal 1.

Counting Rules

Counting Rule for Multiple-Step Experiments
- If an experiment consists of a sequence of k steps in which there are n_1 possible results for the first step, n_2 possible results for the second step, and so on, then the total number of experimental outcomes is given by $(n_1)(n_2) \ldots (n_k)$.
- A helpful graphical representation of a multiple-step experiment is a <u>tree diagram</u>.

Counting Rule for Combinations
- Another useful counting rule enables us to count the number of experimental outcomes when n objects are to be selected from a set of N objects.
- The number of <u>combinations</u> of N objects taken n at a time is

$$C_n^N = \binom{N}{n} = \frac{N!}{n!(N-n)!}$$

$$\text{where} \quad N! = N(N-1)(N-2)\ldots(2)(1)$$
$$n! = n(n-1)(n-2)\ldots(2)(1)$$
$$0! = 1$$

Counting Rule for Permutations
- A third useful counting rule enables us to count the number of experimental outcomes when n objects are to be selected from a set of N objects where the <u>order of selection is important</u>.
- An experiment will have <u>more permutations than combinations</u> for the same number of objects because every selection of n objects has $n!$ different ways to order them.
- The number of <u>permutations</u> of N objects taken n at a time is

$$P_n^N = n!\binom{N}{n} = \frac{N!}{(N-n)!}$$

Excel's Functions for Combinations and Permutations
- The <u>COMBIN</u> function can be used to compute the number of combinations.
- The <u>PERMUT</u> function can be used to compute the number of combinations.
- These two functions have the same two arguments:
    - First – the total number of objects, N.
    - Second – the number of objects selected, n.

Assigning Probabilities

Classical Method
- Assigning probabilities based on the assumption of <u>equally likely outcomes</u>.
- If an experiment has n possible outcomes, this method would assign a probability of $1/n$ to each outcome.

Relative Frequency Method
- Assigning probabilities based on <u>experimentation or historical data</u>.
- The probability assigned to an outcome is found by dividing the frequency of the outcome by the total frequency for all of the outcomes.

Subjective Method
- Assigning probabilities based on the <u>assignor's judgment</u>.
- When economic conditions and a company's circumstances change rapidly it might be inappropriate to assign probabilities based solely on historical data.
- We can use any data available as well as our experience and intuition, but ultimately a probability value should express our <u>degree of belief</u> that the experimental outcome will occur.
- The best probability estimates often are obtained by combining the estimates from the classical or relative frequency approach with the subjective estimates.

Events and Their Probability
- An event is a collection of sample points.
- The probability of any event is equal to the sum of the probabilities of the sample points in the event.
- If we can identify all the sample points of an experiment and assign a probability to each, we can compute the probability of an event.

Some Basic Relationships of Probability
- There are some basic probability relationships that can be used to compute the probability of an event without knowledge of all the sample point probabilities.
- One method frequently used for visualizing relationships between event sets is the Venn diagram. This is a picture with a rectangle representing the entire sample space, S, and event sets represented by circles within the rectangle.

Complement of an Event
- The complement of event A is defined to be the event consisting of all sample points that are not in A.
- The complement of A is denoted by A^c.
- The probability of the complement of the event A is $P(A^c) = 1 - P(A)$.
- The Venn diagram below illustrates the concept of a complement.

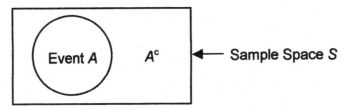

Union of Two Events
- The union of events A and B is the event containing all sample points that are in A or B or both.
- The union is denoted by $A \cup B$.
- The union of A and B is illustrated below.

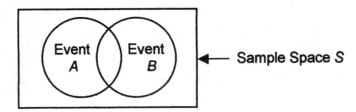

Intersection of Two Events
- The intersection of events A and B is the set of all sample points that are in both A and B.
- The intersection is denoted by $A \cap B$.
- The intersection of A and B is the area of overlap in the illustration below.

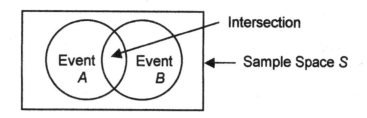

Addition Law
- The <u>addition law</u> provides a way to compute the probability of event *A*, or *B*, or both *A* and *B* occurring.
- The addition law is written as:

$$P(A \cup B) = P(A) + P(B) - P(A \cap B)$$

Mutually Exclusive Events
- Two events are said to be <u>mutually exclusive</u> if the events have no sample points in common. (*A* and A^c are mutually exclusive.)

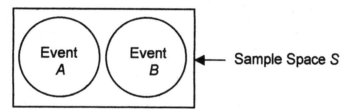

- Two events are mutually exclusive if, when one event occurs, the other cannot occur.
- For mutually exclusive events $P(A|B) = P(B|A) = 0$, (e.g. the probability a coin comes up heads given it comes up tails is 0.)

Addition Law for Mutually Exclusive Events
- Addition Law for Mutually Exclusive Events is written as:

$$P(A \cup B) = P(A) + P(B)$$

Conditional Probability
- The probability of an event given that another event has occurred is called a <u>conditional probability</u>.
- The conditional probability of <u>*A* given *B*</u> is denoted by $P(A|B)$.
- A conditional probability is computed as follows:

$$P(A \mid B) = \frac{P(A \cap B)}{P(B)}$$

Multiplication Law
- The <u>multiplication law</u> provides a way to compute the probability of an intersection of two events.
- The law is written as:

$$P(A \cap B) = P(B)P(A|B)$$

- $P(A \cap B)$ is the <u>joint probability</u> of events *A* and *B*.

Independent Events
- Events A and B are <u>independent</u> if $P(A|B) = P(A)$ or $P(B|A) = P(B)$.

Multiplication Law for Independent Events
- Multiplication Law for Independent Events:
$$P(A \cap B) = P(A)P(B)$$
- The multiplication law also can be used as a test to see if two events are independent.

Bayes' Theorem
- Often we begin probability analysis with initial or <u>prior probabilities</u>.
- Then, from a sample, special report, or a product test we obtain some additional information.
- Given this information, we calculate revised or <u>posterior probabilities</u>.
- <u>Bayes' theorem</u> provides the means for revising the prior probabilities.

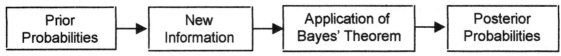

- To find the posterior probability that event A_i will occur given that event B has occurred we apply <u>Bayes' theorem</u>.
$$P(A_i \mid B) = \frac{P(A_i)P(B \mid A_i)}{P(A_1)P(B \mid A_1) + P(A_2)P(B \mid A_2) + \ldots + P(A_n)P(B \mid A_n)}$$
- Bayes' theorem is applicable when the events for which we want to compute posterior probabilities are mutually exclusive and their union is the entire sample space.

Tabular Approach to Bayes' Theorem Calculations
- Step 1   Prepare the following three columns:
  <u>Column 1</u> - The mutually exclusive events for which posterior probabilities are desired.
  <u>Column 2</u> - The prior probabilities for the events.
  <u>Column 3</u> - The conditional probabilities of the new information *given* each event.
- Step 2   In <u>Column 4</u>, compute the joint probabilities for each event and the new information B by using the multiplication law. Multiply the prior probabilities in column 2 by the corresponding conditional probabilities in column 3. That is, $P(A_i \cap B) = P(A_i) P(B|A_i)$.
- Step 3   Sum the joint probabilities in column 4. The sum is the probability of the new information $P(B)$.
- Step 4   In <u>Column 5</u>, compute the posterior probabilities using the basic relationship of conditional probability.
$$P(A_i \mid B) = \frac{P(A_i \cap B)}{P(B)}$$

CONCEPT	EXAMPLES	EXERCISES
Experiments, Sample Spaces, and Counting Rule	1	1
Assignment of Probabilities	2,4	5
Probability Relationships: Complement Union Intersection Mutually Exclusive Addition Law Conditional Probability Independence Multiplication Law	2,3,4,5	1,2,3,6,7,8
Tree Diagram	6	10
Bayes' Theorem	⑥,7	4,9,10

◯ Excel Used

EXAMPLES

EXAMPLE 1

Experiments, Sample Spaces, and Counting Rule

Mini Car Motors offers its luxury car in three colors: gold, silver and blue. The vice president of advertising is interested in the order of popularity of the color choices by customers during the first month of sales.

a) How many sample points are there in this experiment?

b) If the event A = gold is the most popular color, list the outcome(s) in event A.

c) If the event B = blue is the least popular color, list the outcome(s) in $A \cap B$.

d) List the outcome(s) in $A \cap B^C$.

SOLUTION 1

a) Sample space = {(GSB),(GBS),(SGB),(SBG),(BGS),BSG)} = 6 sample points

b) Event *A* = {(GSB),(GBS)} = 2 sample points

c) *A*∩*B* = sample points common to both Event *A* and Event *B* = {(GSB)}

d) *A*∩*B*^{C} = sample points in Event *A* that are not in Event *B* = {(GBS)}

EXAMPLE 2

Assignment of Probabilities and Probability Relationships

A market study taken at a local sporting goods store showed that of 20 people questioned, 6 owned tents, 10 owned sleeping bags, 8 owned camping stoves, 4 owned both tents and camping stoves, and 4 owned both sleeping bags and camping stoves.

Let: Event *A* = owns a tent
       Event *B* = owns a sleeping bag
       Event *C* = owns a camping stove

and let the sample space be the 20 people questioned.

a) Find P(*A*), P(*B*), P(*C*), P(*A*∩*C*), P(*B*∩*C*).

b) Are the events *A* and *C* mutually exclusive? Explain briefly.

c) Are the events *B* and *C* independent events? Explain briefly.

d) If a person questioned owns a tent, what is the probability he also owns a camping stove?

e) If two people questioned own a tent, a sleeping bag, and a camping stove, how many own only a camping stove? In this case is it possible for 3 people to own both a tent and a sleeping bag, but not a camping stove?

SOLUTION 2

a) Using the relative frequency method, the probability equals the number of sample points in the event divided by the number of sample points in the sample space. Thus,

P(*A*) = 6/20 = .3
P(*B*) = 10/20 = .5
P(*C*) = 8/20 = .4

P(*A*∩*B*) = P(owns a tent and owns a camping stove) = 4/20 = .2
P(*B*∩*C*) = P(owns a sleeping bag and owns a camping stove) = 4/20 = .2

b) Events B and C are not mutually exclusive because there are people (4 people) who both own a tent and a camping stove.

c) To see whether events B and C are independent, check to see if $P(B \cap C) = P(B)P(C)$. Since $P(B \cap C) = .2$ and $P(B)P(C) = (.5)(.4) = .2$, then <u>these events are independent</u>.

d) Here the probability that a person owns a camping stove <u>given</u> he owns a tent or $P(C|A)$ must be determined. Using conditional probability,

$$P(C|A) = P(A \cap C)/P(A) = .2/.3 = .667$$

e) Using a Venn diagram gives the following:

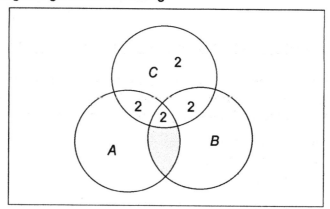

Note that <u>two</u> people own only a camping stove. To determine whether it is possible for three people to own both a tent and a sleeping bag, but not a camping stove, note that the total size of event A is 6. Thus, the shaded area above could not have a value of 3.

EXAMPLE 3

Probability Relationships

The Bidwell Valve Company requires all prospective employees to be interviewed by a three-person committee. Each member of the committee votes individually for or against a recommendation of employment. Upon examining the company's records over the past year, the personnel director has noted the following probabilities for eight possible outcomes:

	Vote Of Member			
Outcome	1	2	3	Probability
E_1	for	for	for	.20
E_2	for	for	against	.14
E_3	for	against	for	.12
E_4	for	against	against	.07
E_5	against	for	for	.08
E_6	against	for	against	.11
E_7	against	against	for	.06
E_8	against	against	against	.22

Denote the following events: A = Member 1 votes for employment
B = Member 2 votes for employment
C = Member 3 votes for employment

a) Find $P(A)$, $P(B)$, and $P(C)$.

b) Which sample outcomes correspond to the event $D = A \cup B$ (Member 1 <u>or</u> Member 2 votes for employment)? Find $P(D)$.

c) Which sample outcomes correspond to the event $G = A \cap B$ (Member 1 <u>and</u> Member 2 vote for employment)? Use the addition law of probability to find $P(G)$.

d) Let the event $F = B^c \cap C$ (Member 2 votes against employment and Member 3 votes for employment). Draw a Venn diagram to represent the event $G \cup F$.

e) If a new employee is hired only if a majority of the committee members vote for employment, what is the probability that a prospective employee is hired? Does a job applicant stand a better or worse chance of being employed going before the committee than one of the individuals?

SOLUTION 3

a) Find the outcomes corresponding to events A, B, and C.

$A = \{E_1, E_2, E_3, E_4\}$. Thus $P(A) = P(E_1) + P(E_2) + P(E_3) + P(E_4)$
$= .20 + .14 + .12 + .07 = .53$

$B = \{E_1, E_2, E_5, E_6\}$. Thus $P(B) = P(E_1) + P(E_2) + P(E_5) + P(E_6)$
$= .20 + .14 + .08 + .11 = .53$

$C = \{E_1, E_3, E_5, E_7\}$. Thus $P(C) = P(E_1) + P(E_3) + P(E_5) + P(E_7)$
$= .20 + .12 + .08 + .06 = .46$

b) The event D corresponds to all sample points that are either in event A or event B or both. Thus $D = \{E_1, E_2, E_3, E_4, E_5, E_6\}$.

$P(D) = P(E_1) + P(E_2) + P(E_3) + P(E_4) + P(E_5) + P(E_6)$
$= .20 + .14 + .12 + .07 + .08 + .11 = .72$

c) The event G corresponds to sample points in both event A and event B. Thus $G = \{E_1, E_2\}$.

The addition law states: $P(A \cup B) = P(A) + P(B) - P(A \cap B)$
or in this case: $P(G) = P(A) + P(B) - P(D) = .53 + .53 - .72 = .34$
Note that this checks with $P(G) = P(E_1) + P(E_2) = .20 + .14 = .34$

d) Event $B^c = \{E_3, E_4, E_7, E_8\}$. $F = B^c \cap C$ = the events common to both B^c and $C = \{E_3, E_7\}$. The Venn diagram for $G \cup F$ is:

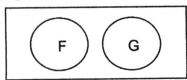

e) Let event L = the event that the majority of the committee members vote for employment, i.e. two or three vote for employment. Thus, $L = \{E_1, E_2, E_3, E_5\}$. $P(L) = P(E_1) + P(E_2) + P(E_3) + P(E_5)$. Thus $P(L) = .20 + .14 + .12 + .08 = .54$. Since this is higher than $P(A)$, $P(B)$, and $P(C)$, the job applicant has a better chance of being employed by going before the committee.

EXAMPLE 4

Assignment of Probabilities and Probability Relationships

Harry owns shares of stock in both Bidwell Valve Company and Mini Car Motors, Inc. Harry has recorded the performance of these shares on each day for a 200-day period as to whether the price has risen, fallen or remained unchanged. Harry's data is as follows:

Event	Bidwell	Mini Car	# of Days
E_1	Rise	Rise	40
E_2	Rise	Unchanged	14
E_3	Rise	Fall	20
E_4	Unchanged	Rise	18
E_5	Unchanged	Unchanged	12
E_6	Unchanged	Fall	14
E_7	Fall	Rise	28
E_8	Fall	Unchanged	16
E_9	Fall	Fall	38

a) Using this data and the relative frequency approach, find the following probabilities:
  (1) a rise in the price of Bidwell stock
  (2) a fall in the price of Mini Car stock
  (3) a rise in Bidwell and a fall in Mini Car stock
  (4) a rise in Bidwell or a fall in Mini Car stock (Use the addition law.)

b) Suppose Harry is told that Bidwell stock has risen. What is the probability that Mini Car stock has fallen?

c) Suppose Harry is told that Mini Car stock has fallen. What is the probability that Bidwell stock has risen?

d) Are the events "a rise in Bidwell stock" and "a fall in Mini Car stock" independent?

SOLUTION 4

a) Let: event A = "rise in Bidwell stock" = $\{E_1, E_2, E_3\}$
    event B = "fall in Mini Car stock" = $\{E_3, E_6, E_9\}$

Using the relative frequency approach,

$$P(E_1) = 40/200 = .20 \qquad P(E_6) = 14/200 = .07$$
$$P(E_2) = 14/200 = .07 \qquad P(E_7) = 28/200 = .14$$
$$P(E_3) = 20/200 = .10 \qquad P(E_8) = 16/200 = .08$$
$$P(E_4) = 18/200 = .09 \qquad P(E_9) = 38/200 = .19$$
$$P(E_5) = 12/200 = .06$$

(1) $P(A) = P(E_1) + P(E_2) + P(E_3) = .20 + .07 + .10 = .37$
(2) $P(B) = P(E_3) + P(E_6) + P(E_9) = .10 + .07 + .19 = .36$
(3) $P(A \cap B) = P(E_3) = .10$
(4) $P(A \cup B) = P(A) + P(B) - P(A \cap B) = .37 + .36 - .10 = .63$

b) $P(B|A) = P(A \cup B)/P(A) = .10/.37 = .27$

c) $P(A|B) = P(A \cup B)/P(B) = .10/.36 = .28$

d) There are several ways to check if events A and B are independent. One method is to see if $P(A|B) = P(A)$. Since $P(A|B) = .28$ and $P(A) = .37$, these events are <u>dependent</u>.

EXAMPLE 5

Probability Relationships

The Board of Directors of Bidwell Valve Company has made the following estimates for the upcoming year's annual earnings:

$$P(\text{earnings lower than this year}) \qquad = .30$$
$$P(\text{earnings about the same as this year}) = .50$$
$$P(\text{earnings higher than this year}) \qquad = .20$$

After talking with union leaders, the human resource department has drawn the following conclusions:

$$P(\text{Union will request wage increase|lower earnings next year}) = .25$$
$$P(\text{Union will request wage increase|same earnings next year}) = .40$$
$$P(\text{Union will request wage increase|higher earnings next year}) = .90$$

a) Are the probabilities developed by the directors and personnel manager based on the classical, relative frequency, or subjective method?

b) Calculate the following probabilities:
   (1) The company earns the same as this year and the union requests a wage increase
   (2) The company has higher earnings next year and the union does not request a wage increase
   (3) The union requests a wage increase

SOLUTION 5

a) Since the predicted outcomes of earnings and wage increase requests have unequal probabilities, they are not based on the classical method. Similarly, since the outcomes arise from a unique situation, the relative frequency method is not applicable. Instead, the probabilities stated reflect the judgment of the individuals involved, and hence are developed by the <u>subjective method</u>.

b) Define the following events: L = lower earnings next year; S = about the same earnings next year; H = higher earnings next year. Further define R = union requests a pay increase next year, so R^c = union does not request a pay increase next year.

    (1) This is $P(S \cap R)$. Now, $P(S) = .50$ and $P(R|S) = .40$.
        Thus, $P(S \cap R) = P(S)P(R|S) = (.50)(.40) = .20$

    (2) This is $P(H \cap R^c)$. Now, $P(H) = .20$ and $P(R^c|H) = 1 - P(R|H) = .10$
        Thus, $P(H \cap R^c) = P(H)P(R^c|H) = (.20)(.10) = .02$

    (3) This is $P(R)$. $P(R) = P(R|H)P(H) + P(R|S)P(S) + P(R|L)P(L)$
                  $= (.25)(.30) + (.40)(.50) + (.90)(..20) = .455$

EXAMPLE 6

Tree Diagram and Bayes' Theorem

    A proposed shopping center will provide strong competition for downtown businesses like L. S. Clothiers. If the shopping center is built, the owner of L. S. Clothiers feels it would be best to relocate. The shopping center cannot be built unless the town council approves a zoning change. The planning board must first make a recommendation, for or against the zoning change, to the council.

    Let: A_1 = town council approves the zoning change
          A_2 = town council disapproves the change

    Prior to the planning board making a recommendation, the probabilities of A_1 and A_2 were subjective judged to be: $P(A_1) = .7$ and $P(A_2) = .3$
    New information is now available! The planning board has recommended <u>against</u> the zoning change. Let B denote the event of a negative recommendation by the board.
    Given that B has occurred, L. S. Clothiers can revise the probabilities that the town council will approve or disapprove the zoning change. Past history with the planning board and the town council indicates the following: $P(B|A_1) = .2$ and $P(B|A_2) = .9$

a) Draw a tree diagram to represent, and better understand, this multiple-step experiment.

b) Using Excel, compute the posterior (revised) probability of the town council approving the zoning change.

SOLUTION 6

a) Tree diagram:

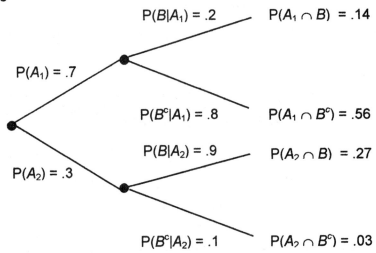

$P(B|A_1) = .2$ $P(A_1 \cap B) = .14$

$P(A_1) = .7$

$P(B^c|A_1) = .8$ $P(A_1 \cap B^c) = .56$

$P(B|A_2) = .9$ $P(A_2 \cap B) = .27$

$P(A_2) = .3$

$P(B^c|A_2) = .1$ $P(A_2 \cap B^c) = .03$

b) To find the posterior probability that event A_1 will occur given that event B has occurred we apply Bayes' theorem. The steps for using Excel in this problem are as follows:

<u>Excel Steps</u>

1. Open a new worksheet and enter the following labels and data.

	A	B	C	D	E
1	CHAPTER 4 - EXAMPLE 5 - BAYES' THEOREM				
2					
3		Prior	Conditional	Joint	Posterior
4	Events	Probabilities	Probabilities	Probabilities	Probabilities
5	A_1	0.7	0.2		
6	A_2	0.3	0.9		
7			$P(B) =$		
8					

Col. A - The mutually exclusive events for which posterior probabilities are desired.
Col. B - The prior probabilities for the events.
Col. C - The conditional probabilities of the new information *given* each event.

2. In column D, enter the formulas for computing the joint probabilities for each event and the new information B using the multiplication law. Multiply the prior probabilities in column B by the corresponding conditional probabilities in column C. That is, $P(A_i | B) = P(A_i) \, P(B|A_i)$.

3. Enter the formula for summing the joint probabilities in column D. The sum is the probability of the new information $P(B)$.

4. In column E, enter the formulas for computing the posterior probabilities using the basic relationship of conditional probability.

$$P(A_i \mid B) = \frac{P(A_i \cap B)}{P(B)}$$

Note that the joint probabilities $P(A_i \mid B)$ are in column D and the probability $P(B)$ is the sum of column D.

Formula Worksheet:

	A	B	C	D	E
1	CHAPTER 4 - EXAMPLE 5 - BAYES' THEOREM				
2					
3		Prior	Conditional	Joint	Posterior
4	Events	Probabilities	Probabilities	Probabilities	Probabilities
5	A_1	0.7	0.2	=B5*C5	=D5/$D$7
6	A_2	0.3	0.9	=B6*C6	=D6/$D$7
7				P(B)=SUM(D5:D6)	=SUM(E5:E6)
8					

We see in the resulting worksheet below, in column D, that there is a .14 probability of the town council approving the zoning change and a negative recommendation by the planning board. There is a .27 probability of the town council disapproving the zoning change and a negative recommendation by the planning board. The sum .14 + .27 shows an overall probability of .41 of a negative recommendation by the planning board.

Value Worksheet:

	A	B	C	D	E
1	CHAPTER 4 - EXAMPLE 5 - BAYES' THEOREM				
2					
3		Prior	Conditional	Joint	Posterior
4	Events	Probabilities	Probabilities	Probabilities	Probabilities
5	A_1	0.7	0.2	0.14	0.34
6	A_2	0.3	0.9	0.27	0.66
7				P(B)	0.41	1.00
8					

<u>Conclusion</u> - The planning board's recommendation is good news for L. S. Clothiers. The posterior probability of the town council approving the zoning change is <u>.34</u> (compared to a prior probability of .70).

EXAMPLE 7

Bayes' Theorem

An accounting firm has noticed that of the companies it audits, 85% show no inventory shortages, 10% show small inventory shortages and 5% show large inventory shortages. The firm has devised a new accounting test for which it believes the following probabilities hold:

$$P(\text{company will pass test}|\text{no shortage}) = .90$$
$$P(\text{company will pass test}|\text{small shortage}) = .50$$
$$P(\text{company will pass test}|\text{large shortage}) = .20$$

a) If a company being audited fails this test, what is the probability of a large or small inventory shortage?

b) If a company being audited passes this test, what is the probability of no inventory shortage?

SOLUTION 7

a) Let: A_1 = no inventory shortage P = company passes test
          A_2 = small inventory shortage F = company fails test
          A_3 = large inventory shortage

Event	Prior Probabilities $P(A_i)$	Conditional Probabilities $P(F|A_i)$	Joint Probabilities $P(A_i \cap F)$	Posterior Probabilities $P(A_i|F)$
A_1	.85	.10	.085	.486
A_2	.10	.50	.050	.286
A_3	.05	.80	.040	.229
			$P(F) = .175$	

Here, $P(F|A_i) = 1 - P(P|A_i)$; the joint probabilities are the multiples of the prior and conditional probabilities and the posterior probabilities are the joint probabilities divided by $P(F)$. The probability of a large or small shortage = .286 + .229 = <u>.515</u>

b)

Event	Prior Probabilities $P(A_i)$	Conditional Probabilities $P(P|A_i)$	Joint Probabilities $P(A_i \cap P)$	Posterior Probabilities $P(A_i|P)$
A_1	.85	.90	.765	.927
A_2	.10	.50	.050	.061
A_3	.05	.20	.010	.012
			$P(P) = .825$	

The solution is $P(A_1|P) = $ <u>.927</u>

EXERCISES

EXERCISE 1

Experiments, Sample Spaces, and Counting Rule

Providence Land Development Company has just hired four new salespersons. After six months on the job each salesperson will be rated as either poor, average or excellent and will be compensated accordingly. Assume that Providence is concerned with the number of salespersons in each category.

a) List the outcomes of this experiment.

b) Let event A = at least two salespersons are rated average and let event B = exactly one salesperson is rated poor. List the outcomes in $A \cap B$.

c) Let event C = exactly two salespersons are rated excellent. List the outcomes in $D = B \cap C$.

d) Are events D and A mutually exclusive?

e) Are events D and A collectively exhaustive?

f) Let the event E = at most one salesperson is rated average. Are events A and E mutually exclusive and collectively exhaustive?

EXERCISE 2

Probability Relationships

Global Airlines operates two types of jet planes: jumbo and ordinary. On jumbo jets, 25% of the passengers are on business while on ordinary jets 30% of the passengers are on business. Of Global's air fleet, 40% of its capacity is provided on jumbo jets.

a) What is the probability a randomly chosen business customer flying with Global is on a jumbo jet?

b) What is the probability a randomly chosen non-business customer flying with Global is on an ordinary jet?

EXERCISE 3

Probability Relationships

The following probability model describes the number of snowstorms for Washington, D. C. for a given year:

# of Snowstorms	0	1	2	3	4	5	6
Probability	.25	.33	.24	.11	.04	.02	.01

The probability of 7 or more snowstorms in a year is 0.

a) What is the probability of more than 2 but less than 5 snowstorms?

b) Given this a particularly cold year (in which 2 snowstorms have already been observed), what is the conditional probability that 4 or more snowstorms will be observed?

c) If at the beginning of winter there is a snowfall, what is the probability of at least one more snowstorm before winter is over?

EXERCISE 4

Bayes' Theorem

Safety Insurance Company has compiled the following statistics. For any one year period:

$$P(accident|male\ driver\ under\ 25)\ \ = .22$$
$$P(accident|male\ driver\ over\ 25)\ \ \ = .15$$
$$P(accident|female\ driver\ under\ 25) = .16$$
$$P(accident|female\ driver\ over\ 25)\ \ = .14$$

The percentage of Safety's policyholders in each category is:

Male Under 25	20%
Male Over 25	40%
Female Under 25	10%
Female Over 25	30%

a) What is the probability that a randomly selected policyholder will have an accident within the next year?

b) Given that a driver has an accident, what is the probability the driver is a male over 25?

c) Given that a driver has no accident, what is the probability the driver is a female?

d) Does knowing the fact that a driver has had no accidents give us a great deal of information regarding the driver's sex?

EXERCISE 5

Assignment of Probabilities

Sales of the first 500 luxury Mini Cars were as follows: 250 gold, 150 silver, and 100 blue. Assume the relative frequency method is used to assign probabilities for color choice and the color of each car sold is independent of that of any other car sold.

a) What is the probability that the next two cars sold will both be gold?

b) What is the probability that neither of the next two cars sold will be silver?

c) What is the probability that of the next two cars sold, one will be silver and the other will be blue?

EXERCISE 6

Probability Relationships

The sales manager for Widco Distributing Company has estimated demand for a new combination microwave oven and color television will be between 0 and 2 units per day. He believes the probability of selling no units is .65, of one unit is .25, and two units is .10. The company is interested in sales over a two-day period.

a) What is the probability of selling no units during the two days?

b) What is the probability of selling one unit during the two days?

c) What is the probability of selling three or more units during the two days?

d) What is the probability of selling two units during the two days?

EXERCISE 7

Probability Relationships

Super Cola sales breakdown as 80% regular soda and 20% diet soda. Men purchase 60% of the regular soda, but only 30% of the diet soda. If a woman purchases Super Cola, what is the probability that it is a diet soda?

EXERCISE 8

Probability Relationships

Stanton Marketing conducted a taste preference test among married and single persons for the Super Cola Company. Among single people, 11% of the population questioned preferred Super Cola to all other brands. For married people the data was:

	Wife Prefers	Wife Does Not Prefer
Husband Prefers	.08	.06
Does Not Prefer	.07	.79

a) Using this study as a basis for a probability measure, find the probability that if two single people are questioned: (1) they both prefer Super Cola; (2) they both do not prefer Super Cola; and (3) one prefers Super Cola and the other does not.

b) What is the probability that a married female prefers Super Cola?

c) Given that a husband prefers Super Cola, what is the probability his wife also prefers it?

d) Is the event "husband prefers Super Cola" independent of the event "wife prefers Super Cola"?

e) Do married people prefer Super Cola more than single people?

EXERCISE 9

Bayes' Theorem

Higbee Manufacturing Corp. has recently received 5 cases of a certain part from one of its suppliers. The defect rate for the parts is normally 5%, but the supplier has just notified Higbee that one of the cases shipped to them has been made on a misaligned machine that has a defect rate of 97%. So the plant manager selects a case at random and tests a part.

a) What is the probability that the part is defective?

b) Suppose the part is defective, what is the probability that this is from the case made on the misaligned machine?

c) After finding that the first part was defective, suppose a second part from the case is tested. However, this part is found to be good. Using the revised probabilities from part (b) compute the new probability of these parts being from the defective case.

d) Do you think you would obtain the same posterior probabilities as in part (c) if the first part was not found to be defective but the second part was?

e) Suppose, because of other evidence, the plant manager was 80% certain this case was the one made on the misaligned machine. How would your answer to part (b) change?

EXERCISE 10

Tree Diagram and Bayes' Theorem

An investment advisor recommends the purchase of shares in Probaballistics, Inc. He has made the following predictions:

$$P(\text{Stock goes up 20\%}|\text{Rise in GDP}) = .6$$
$$P(\text{Stock goes up 20\%}|\text{Level GDP}) = .5$$
$$P(\text{Stock goes up 20\%}|\text{Fall in GDP}) = .4$$

An economist has predicted that the probability of a rise in the GDP is 30%, whereas the probability of a fall in the GDP is 40%.

a) Draw a tree diagram to represent, and better understand, this multiple-step experiment.

b) What is the probability that the stock will go up 20%?

b) We have been informed that the stock has gone up 20%. What is the probability of a rise or fall in the GDP?

SELF-TEST

TRUE/FALSE

____ 1. $P(A|B) = 1 - P(B|A)$ for all events A and B.

____ 2. If A and B are mutually exclusive, $P(A \cap B) = 0$.

____ 3. $P(A|B) + P(A|B^C) = 1$ for all A and B.

____ 4. A joint probability can have a value greater than 1.

____ 5. Posterior probabilities are conditional probabilities.

FILL-IN-THE-BLANK

1. A method of assigning probabilities that assumes the experimental outcomes are equally likely is the _____ method.

2. Events that have no sample points in common are _____.

3. An element of the sample space is a _____.

4. _____ is a numerical measure of the likelihood that an event will occur.

5. The _____ law is used to compute the probability of an intersection of two events.

MULTIPLE CHOICE

___ 1. A graphical representation helpful in defining sample points of an experiment involving multiple steps is a
   a) Venn diagram
   b) Bayes' table
   c) Scatter diagram
   d) Tree diagram

___ 2. The probability of at least one head in two flips of a coin is
   a) 0.33
   b) 0.50
   c) 0.75
   d) 1.00

___ 3. Revised probabilities of events based on additional information are
   a) joint probabilities
   b) posterior probabilities
   c) marginal probabilities
   d) complementary probabilities

___ 4. Posterior probabilities are computed using
   a) the classical method
   b) the subjective method
   c) the relative frequency method
   d) Bayes' theorem

___ 5. The complement of $P(A|B)$ is
   a) $P(A^C|B)$
   b) $P(A|B^C)$
   c) $P(B|A)$
   d) $P(A \cap B)$

ANSWERS

EXERCISES

1) a) Let E_j = (# poor, # average, # excellent).
   E_1 = (4,0,0), E_2 = (3,1,0), E_3 = (3,0,1), E_4 = (2,2,0), E_5 = (2,1,1),
   E_6 = (2,0,2), E_7 = (1,3,0), E_8 = (1,2,1), E_9 = (1,1,2), E_{10} = (1,0,3),
   E_{11} = (0,4,0), E_{12} = (0,3,1), E_{13} = (0,2,2), E_{14} = (0,1,3), E_{15} = (0,0,4).
   b) {E_7,E_8}
   c) {E_9}
   d) yes
   e) no
   f) yes

2) a) .357
   b) .583

3) a) .15
   b) .167
   c) .56

4) a) .162
   b) .370
   c) .408
   d) no

5) a) .25
   b) .49
   c) .12

6) a) .4225
   b) .325
   c) .06
   d) .1925

7) .304

8) a) (1) .0121; (2) .7921 (3) .1958
   b) .15
   c) .571
   d) No
   e) .145; more

9) a) .234
   b) .829
   c) .133
   d) yes
   e) .987

10) a) see below
    b) .490
    c) .694

10) a)

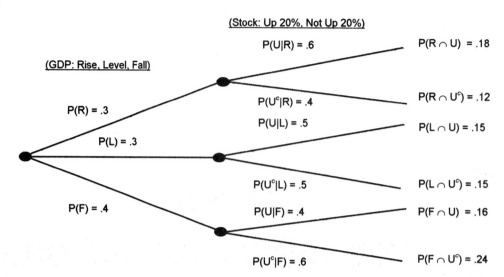

TRUE/FALSE	FILL-IN-THE-BLANK	MULTIPLE CHOICE
1) False	1) classical method	1) d
2) True	2) mutually exclusive	2) c
3) False	3) sample point	3) b
4) False	4) Probability	4) d
5) True	5) multiplication	5) a

CHAPTER 5

Discrete
Probability Distributions

Random Variables

Discrete Probability Distributions

Expected Value and Variance

Binomial Probability Distribution

Poisson Probability Distribution

Hypergeometric Probability Distribution

LEARNING OBJECTIVES

1. Understand the concepts of a random variable and a probability distribution.

2. Be able to distinguish between discrete and continuous random variables.

3. Be able to compute and interpret the expected value, variance, and standard deviation for a discrete random variable and understand how an Excel worksheet can be used to ease the burden of the calculations.

4. Be able to compute probabilities using a binomial probability distribution and be able to compute these probabilities using Excel's BINOMDIST function.

5. Be able to compute probabilities using a Poisson probability distribution and be able to compute these probabilities using Excel's POISSON function.

6. Know when and how to use the hypergeometric probability distribution and be able to compute these probabilities using Excel's HYPGEOMDIST function.

REVIEW

Random Variables
*   A <u>random variable</u> is a numerical description of the outcome of an experiment.
*   A random variable can be classified as being either discrete or continuous depending on the numerical values it assumes.
*   A <u>discrete random variable</u> may assume either a finite number of values or an infinite sequence of values.
*   A <u>continuous random variable</u> may assume any numerical value in an interval or collection of intervals.

Discrete Probability Distributions
*   The <u>probability distribution</u> for a random variable describes how probabilities are distributed over the values of the random variable.
*   The probability distribution is defined by a <u>probability function</u>, denoted by $f(x)$, which provides the probability for each value of the random variable.
*   The required conditions for a discrete probability function are:
$$f(x) \geq 0$$
$$\Sigma f(x) = 1$$
*   We can describe a discrete probability distribution with a table, graph, or equation.

Discrete Uniform Probability Distribution
*   The <u>discrete uniform probability distribution</u> is the simplest example of a discrete probability distribution given by a formula.
*   The <u>discrete uniform probability function</u> is

$$f(x) = 1/n \quad \text{where: } n = \text{the number of values the random variable may assume}$$
*   Note that the values of the random variable are equally likely.

Expected Value and Variance

- The <u>expected value</u>, or mean, of a random variable is a measure of its central location.
- Expected value of a discrete random variable:
$$E(x) = \mu = \Sigma x f(x)$$
- The <u>variance</u> summarizes the variability in the values of a random variable.
- Variance of a discrete random variable:
$$Var(x) = \sigma^2 = \Sigma(x - \mu)^2 f(x)$$
- The <u>standard deviation</u>, σ, is defined as the positive square root of the variance.
- The standard deviation is measured in the same units as the random variable and therefore is often preferred in describing variability.

Binomial Probability Distribution

- The binomial probability distribution is associated with a multiple-step experiment that we call the <u>binomial experiment</u>
- A binomial experiment has the following four properties:
  - The experiment consists of a sequence of n identical trials.
  - Two outcomes, <u>success</u> and <u>failure</u>, are possible on each trial.
  - The probability of a success, denoted by p, does not change from trial to trial (this property is called the stationarity assumption).
  - The trials are independent.
- A special mathematical formula, called the <u>binomial probability function</u>, can be used to compute the probability of x successes in n trials.

Binomial Probability Function

- The function can be viewed as consisting of two parts.
- Part 1: Number of experiments; outcomes providing exactly x successes in n trials is:
$$\frac{n!}{x!(n-x)!}$$
- Part 2: Probability of a particular sequence of trial outcomes with x successes in n trials is:
$$p^x(1-p)^{(n-x)}$$
- Putting the two parts together, we get the binomial probability function:
$$f(x) = \frac{n!}{x!(n-x)!} p^x(1-p)^{(n-x)}$$
where: $f(x)$ = probability of x successes in n trials
n = number of trials
p = probability of a success on any one trial
$(1 - p)$ = probability of a failure on any one trial

Expected Value and Variance for the Binomial Distribution

- The expected value is:
$$E(x) = \mu = np$$
- The variance is:
$$Var(x) = \sigma^2 = np(1 - p)$$

Excel Function for Binomial Distribution

- Excel's <u>BINOMDIST</u> function can be used to compute probabilities and cumulative probabilities for the binomial distribution.
- The function has <u>four arguments</u>:
    - First – the value of the random variable x, the number of successes
    - Second – the value of n, the number of trials
    - Third – the value of p, the probability of a success on any one trial
    - Fourth – "TRUE" or "FALSE" ("TRUE" if a cumulative probability is desired; "FALSE" if a probability is desired)

Poisson Probability Distribution

- The Poisson probability distribution is often useful in estimating the number of occurrences over a specified interval of time or space.
- A Poisson experiment has the following <u>two properties</u>:
    - The probability of an occurrence is the same for any two intervals of equal length.
    - The occurrence or nonoccurrence in any interval is independent of the occurrence or nonoccurrence in any other interval.
- The Poisson probability function is:

$$f(x) = \frac{\mu^{x} e^{-\mu}}{x!}$$

where: $f(x)$ = probability of x occurrences in an interval
μ = mean number of occurrences in an interval
e = 2.71828

Excel Function for Poisson Distribution

- Excel's <u>POISSON</u> function can be used to compute probabilities and cumulative probabilities for the Poisson distribution.
- The function has <u>three arguments</u>:
    - First – the value of μ, the expected number of occurrences in an interval
    - Second – the value of the random variable x, the number of occurrences
    - Third – "FALSE" or "TRUE" ("FALSE" if a probability is desired; "TRUE" if a cumulative probability is desired)

Hypergeometric Probability Distribution

- The <u>hypergeometric distribution</u> is closely related to the binomial distribution.
- With the hypergeometric distribution, the trials are not independent, and the probability of success changes from trial to trial.
- The <u>hypergeometric probability function</u> is used to compute the probability that in a random sample of n elements, selected without replacement, we will obtain x elements labeled success and $n - x$ elements labeled failure.
- The hypergeometric probability function is:

$$f(x) = \frac{\binom{r}{x}\binom{N-r}{n-x}}{\binom{N}{n}} \quad \text{for } 0 \leq x \leq r$$

where: $f(x)$ = probability of x successes in n trials

n = number of trials

N = number of elements in the population

r = number of elements in the population labeled success

- The function can be viewed as consisting of three parts.
- Part 1: Number of ways a sample of size n can be selected from a population of size N:

$$\binom{N}{n}$$

- Part 2: Number of ways that x successes can be selected from a total of r successes in the population:

$$\binom{r}{x}$$

- Part 3: Number of ways that $n - x$ failures can be selected from a total of $N - r$ failures in the population:

$$\binom{N-r}{n-x}$$

Excel Function for Hypergeometric Distribution

- Excel's <u>HYPGEOMDIST</u> function can be used to compute probabilities for the hypergeometric distribution.
- It only computes probabilities, not cumulative probabilities.
- The function has <u>four arguments</u>:
  - First – the value of the random variable x, the number of successes
  - Second – the value of n, the number of trials
  - Third – the value of r, the number of elements in the population labeled success
  - Fourth – the value of N, the number of elements in the population

KEY CONCEPTS

CONCEPT	EXAMPLES	EXERCISES
Random Variables	1	1
Discrete Probability Distribution	2,③	2,3
Expected Value and Variance	④	4,5
Binomial Probability Distribution	⑤	6,7,8
Poisson Probability Distribution	⑥	9,10,11
Hypergeometric Probability Distribution	⑦	12

○ Excel Used

EXAMPLES

EXAMPLE 1

Random Variables

Dollar Department Stores is planning to open a new store on the corner of Main and Vine Streets. It has asked the Stanton Marketing Company to do a market study of randomly selected families within a five-mile radius of the store. Among the questions it wishes Stanton to ask each homeowner are: (a) family income; (b) family size; (c) distance from home to the store site; and, (d) whether or not the family owns a dog or a cat.

For each of the four questions, develop a random variable of interest to Dollar Department Stores. Denote which of these are discrete and which are continuous random variables.

SOLUTION 1

Question	Random Variable	Discrete or Continuous
(a) Family income	x = Annual dollar gross income the family reported on their tax return	Discrete
(b) Family size	x = Number of dependents in the family reported on their tax return	Discrete
(c) Distance from home to store	x = Distance in miles from home to the store site	Continuous
(d) Dog/Cat	x = 1 if own no pet; = 2 if own dog(s) only; = 3 if own cat(s) only; = 4 if own dog(s) and cat(s)	Discrete

EXAMPLE 2

Discrete Probability Distribution

Stanton Marketing reported back to Dollar Department Stores the following information. Out of 400 families surveyed, 260 owned no pet, 120 owned dogs and 50 owned cats.

a) On the basis of this information, find the probability distribution for the random variable x, defined in (d) in Example 1.

b) Dollar Department Stores is considering opening a pet department if the expected number of families owning pets shopping at its store exceeds 4,000. If Dollar expects to serve 12,000 families, should it open a pet department?

SOLUTION 2

Since 260 owned no pets, 140 owned pets. Since 120 owned dogs and 50 owned cats (total = 170), then 30 must own both dogs and cats.

a) Since 120 owned dogs and 30 owned dogs and cats, 120 - 30 = 90 own dogs only. Similarly, 50 - 30 = 20 own cats only. Using the relative frequency method to calculate $f(x)$:

$$f(1) = 260/400 = .65 \qquad f(3) = 20/400 = .05$$
$$f(2) = \ 90/400 \ = .225 \qquad f(4) = \ 30/400 = .075$$

b) The probability of owning a pet = 1 - the probability of not owning a pet = $1 - f(1)$ = 1 - .65 = .35. Multiply this probability by the total number of families Dollar expects to serve to obtain the expected number of families owning pets = (.35)(12,000) = 4,200. Since this is greater than 4,000, Dollar should open a pet department.

EXAMPLE 3

Discrete Probability Distribution

Abbey Grant is a part-time salesperson at McNair's Appliances. For the last 200 days she has kept a record of the number of televisions she sold each day.

Units Sold	Number of Days
0	80
1	50
2	40
3	10
4	20
	200

a) Develop a probability distribution for the number of televisions sold in a day.

b) What is the most probable number of televisions Abbey will sell in a day?

c) What is the probability that Abbey will sell more than one television in a day?

d) Draw a graph of the probability distribution.

SOLUTION 3

Using Excel

Enter Data: The data needed are the values for the random variable and their corresponding frequencies. These data and the appropriate labels are entered into cells A1:B6.

Enter Functions and Formulas: To develop the probability distribution we compute the probability of each value of the random variable using the relative frequency approach. That is, the probability is equal to the frequency of the value relative to the total frequency for all values of the random variable. So, we compute the sum of the frequencies by entering the formula =SUM(B2:B6) into cell B7. Next, we enter the formula =B2/$B$7 into cell C2 and then copy cell C2 to cells C3:C6.

Formula Worksheet:

	A	B	C
1	Sales	Frequency	Probability
2	0	80	=B2/$B$7
3	1	50	=B3/$B$7
4	2	40	=B4/$B$7
5	3	10	=B5/$B$7
6	4	20	=B6/$B$7
7		Total	=SUM(B2:B6)	

Value Worksheet:

	A	B	C
1	Sales	Frequency	Probability
2	0	80	0.40
3	1	50	0.25
4	2	40	0.20
5	3	10	0.05
6	4	20	0.10
7	Total	200	

b) Abbey is most likely to sell 0 televisions in a day.

c) $P(x \geq 2) = P(x = 2) + P(x = 3) + P(x = 4) = .20 + .05 + .10 = \underline{.35}$

d)

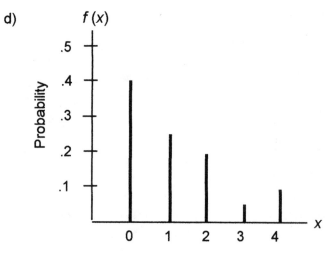

Number of Televisions Sold During a Day

EXAMPLE 4

Expected Value and Variance

Refer to the probability distribution for daily television sales developed in Example 3. Compute the expected value, variance, and standard deviation for the distribution.

SOLUTION 4

Using Excel's SUMPRODUCT Function

Excel's SUMPRODUCT function can be used to the expected value and variance for daily television sales. We will continue with the worksheet we developed in Solution 3.

Enter Data: The data is already entered (see Solution 3).
Enter Functions and Formulas: To compute the mean or expected value for the distribution, we do the following. The SUMPRODUCT function multiplies each value in one range by the corresponding value in another range, and sums the products. We enter the following formula into cell C8:

$$=SUMPRODUCT(A2:A6,C2:C6)$$

To compute the variance for the distribution, we first compute the squared deviation from the mean value for each value of the random variable. To do this, we enter the formula =(A2-$C$8)^2 into cell D2 and then copy cell D2 to cells D3:D6. The variance is the sum of the products of the squared deviations and the corresponding probabilities. So, we enter the following formula into cell C9:

$$=SUMPRODUCT(D2:D6,C2:C6)$$

To compute the standard deviation for the distribution, we enter the formula =SQRT(C9) into cell C10.

Formula Worksheet:

	A	B	C	D
1	**Sales**	**Frequency**	**Probability**	**Sq. Dev. from Mean**
2	0	80	=B2/$B$7	=(A2-$C$8)^2
3	1	50	=B3/$B$7	=(A3-$C$8)^2
4	2	40	=B4/$B$7	=(A4-$C$8)^2
5	3	10	=B5/$B$7	=(A5-$C$8)^2
6	4	20	=B6/$B$7	=(A6-$C$8)^2
7	**Total**	=SUM(B2:B6)		
8		**Mean**	=SUMPRODUCT(A2:A6,C2:C6)	
9		**Variance**	=SUMPRODUCT(D2:D6,C2:C6)	
10		**Std. Dev.**	=SQRT(C9)	

Value Worksheet:

	A	B	C	D
1	**Sales**	**Frequency**	**Probability**	**Sq. Dev. from Mean**
2	0	80	0.40	1.44
3	1	50	0.25	0.04
4	2	40	0.20	0.64
5	3	10	0.05	3.24
6	4	20	0.10	7.84
7	**Total**	200		
8		**Mean**	1.20	
9		**Variance**	1.66	
10		**Std. Dev.**	1.29	

EXAMPLE 5

Binomial Distribution

Evans Electric is concerned about a low retention rate for employees. On the basis of past experience, management has seen an annual turnover of 10% of the hourly employees. Thus, for any hourly employee chosen at random, management estimates a probability of 0.1 that the person will not be with the company next year.

Choosing 3 hourly employees at random, what is the probability that 1 of them will leave the company this year? (Draw a tree diagram to represent this multiple-trial experiment.) What is the probability that <u>at least</u> one of the three chosen workers stays?

SOLUTION 5

Using Excel's BINOMDIST Function

Tree Diagram:

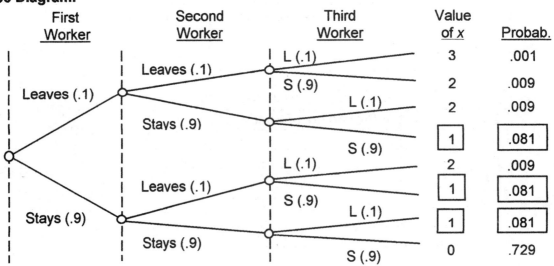

We see in the tree diagram that the probability of one employee leaving, out of the sample of three, is .081 + .081 + .081 = .243.

In order to compute a binomial probability we must know the number of trials (n), the probability of success (p), and the value of the random variable (x). For Evans Electric, the number of trials is 3, the probability of success (leaving) is .1, and the value of x is 1.

Enter Data: We enter the value 3 for n into cell A1, the value .1 for p into cell A2, and the appropriate labels into cell B1:B2. We are specifically interested in the probability of $x = 1$, however we can find the probabilities for all possible values of x quite easily using Excel. With this in mind, we enter the x values 0, 1, 2, and 3 into cells A5:A8.

Enter Functions and Formulas: The BINOMDIST function has four arguments: the first is the value of x, the second is the value of n, the third is the value of p, and the fourth is FALSE or TRUE. We choose FALSE because we want a probability, not a cumulative probability. The formula =BINOMDIST(A5,$A$1,$A$2,FALSE) is entered into cell B5 to compute the probability of 0 successes (persons leaving) in 3 trials. Then, the formula in B5 is copied to cells B6:B8 to compute the probabilities for $x = 1$, 2, and 3 successes, respectively.

Formula Worksheet:

	A	B
1	3	**= Number of Trials (n)**
2	0.1	**= Probability of Success (p)**
3		
4	*x*	*f(x)*
5	0	=BINOMDIST(A5,$A$1,$A$2,FALSE)
6	1	=BINOMDIST(A6,$A$1,$A$2,FALSE)
7	2	=BINOMDIST(A7,$A$1,$A$2,FALSE)
8	3	=BINOMDIST(A8,$A$1,$A$2,FALSE)

We see below in the resulting worksheet that the probability of one of the three chosen workers leaving is .243, which agrees with our result using the tree diagram.

Value Worksheet:

	A	B
1	3	**= Number of Trials (n)**
2	0.1	**= Probability of Success (p)**
3		
4	*x*	*f(x)*
5	0	0.729
6	1	0.243
7	2	0.027
8	3	0.001

The second part of the problem we are solving asks "what is the probability that at least one of the three chosen workers stays?" This is equivalent to asking "what is the probability that the number of workers leaving is two or less?" The answer can be computed by again using the BINOMDIST function, but this time we will enter TRUE for the fourth argument in the function. Also, we must add the word Cumulative to the label in cell B4.

Formula Worksheet:

	A	B
1	3	= Number of Trials (*n*)
2	0.1	= Probability of Success (*p*)
3		
4	*x*	Cumulative Probability
5	0	=BINOMDIST(A5,$A$1,$A$2,TRUE)
6	1	=BINOMDIST(A6,$A$1,$A$2,TRUE)
7	2	=BINOMDIST(A7,$A$1,$A$2,TRUE)
8	3	=BINOMDIST(A8,$A$1,$A$2,TRUE)
9		

We see in the resulting worksheet below that the probability of two or less of the three chosen workers leaving is .999.

Value Worksheet:

	A	B
1	3	= Number of Trials (*n*)
2	0.1	= Probability of Success (*p*)
3		
4	*x*	Cumulative Probability
5	0	0.729
6	1	0.972
7	2	0.999
8	3	1.000
9		

EXAMPLE 6

Poisson Probability Distribution

Patients arrive at the emergency room of Mercy Hospital at the average rate of 6 per hour on weekend evenings. What is the probability of 4 arrivals in 30 minutes on a weekend evening? What is the probability of 6 or fewer arrivals in one hour?

SOLUTION 6

Using Excel's POISSON Function

In order to compute a Poisson probability we must know the mean number of occurrences (μ) per time period and the number of occurrences (x) for which we want to compute the probability. For this problem, x equals 4.

For our purposes, μ does not equal 6. The average number of arrivals in <u>one hour</u> is 6, but we are interested in a 30-minute time period. For this reason we convert the hourly average to a half-hour average by dividing 6 by 2. Thus $\mu = 3$.

Enter Data: We enter the value 3, for the mean number of arrivals, into cell A1 and an appropriate label into B1. We are specifically interested in the probability of $x = 4$, but we can find the probabilities for a wide range of all possible values of x quite easily using Excel. With this in mind, we enter the x values 0, 1, 2, ..., 8 into cells A4:A12. And we enter appropriate labels in cells A3 and B3.

Enter Functions and Formulas: The POISSON function has three arguments: the first is the value of μ, the second is the value of x, and the third is TRUE or FALSE. We choose FALSE because we want a probability, not a cumulative probability. The formula =POISSON(A4,$A$1,FALSE) is entered into cell B4 to compute the probability of 0 arrivals in 30 minutes. Then, the formula in B4 is copied to cells B5:B12 to compute the probabilities for $x = 1, 2, ..., 8$, respectively.

Formula Worksheet:

	A	B
1	3	= Mean No. of Occurrences (μ)
2		
3	**Number of Arrivals (x)**	**Probability $f(x)$**
4	0	=POISSON(A4,$A$1,FALSE)
5	1	=POISSON(A5,$A$1,FALSE)
6	2	=POISSON(A6,$A$1,FALSE)
7	3	=POISSON(A7,$A$1,FALSE)
8	4	=POISSON(A8,$A$1,FALSE)
9	5	=POISSON(A9,$A$1,FALSE)
10	6	=POISSON(A10,$A$1,FALSE)
11	7	=POISSON(A11,$A$1,FALSE)
12	8	=POISSON(A12,$A$1,FALSE)

We see in the resulting worksheet below that the probability of four arrivals in 30 minutes is <u>.168</u>.

Value Worksheet:

	A	B
1	3	= Mean No. of Occurrences (μ)
2		
3	Number of Arrivals (x)	Probability $f(x)$
4	0	0.0498
5	1	0.1494
6	2	0.2240
7	3	0.2240
8	4	0.1680
9	5	0.1008
10	6	0.0504
11	7	0.0216
12	8	0.0081

The second part of the problem we are solving asks "What is the probability of 6 or fewer arrivals in one hour? Now we use $\mu = 6$ because we are examining a one-hour time period. Also, this time we enter TRUE as the third argument in the POISSON function because we want a cumulative probability. Lastly, we add the word Cumulative to the label in cell B3.

Formula Worksheet:

	A	B
1	6	= Mean No. of Occurrences (μ)
2		
3	Number of Arrivals (x)	Cumulative Probability
4	0	=POISSON(A4,$A$1,TRUE)
5	1	=POISSON(A5,$A$1,TRUE)
6	2	=POISSON(A6,$A$1,TRUE)
7	3	=POISSON(A7,$A$1,TRUE)
8	4	=POISSON(A8,$A$1,TRUE)
9	5	=POISSON(A9,$A$1,TRUE)
10	6	=POISSON(A10,$A$1,TRUE)
11	7	=POISSON(A11,$A$1,TRUE)
12	8	=POISSON(A12,$A$1,TRUE)

We see in the resulting worksheet below that the probability of six or fewer arrivals in one hour is .6063.

Value Worksheet:

	A	B
1	6	= Mean No. of Occurrences (μ)
2		
3	Number of Arrivals (x)	Cumulative Probability
4	0	0.0025
5	1	0.0174
6	2	0.0620
7	3	0.1512
8	4	0.2851
9	5	0.4457
10	6	0.6063
11	7	0.7440
12	8	0.8472

EXAMPLE 7

Hypergeometric Distribution

Bob Neveready has removed two dead batteries from a flashlight and inadvertently mingled them with the two good batteries he intended as replacements. The four batteries look identical.

Bob now randomly selects two of the four batteries. What is the probability he selects the two good batteries?

SOLUTION 7

Using Excel's HYPGEOMDIST Function

We can use the hypergeometric probability function to compute the probability we are solving for. The computation is as follows:

$$f(x) = \frac{\binom{r}{x}\binom{N-r}{n-x}}{\binom{N}{n}} = \frac{\binom{2}{2}\binom{2}{0}}{\binom{4}{2}} = \frac{\left(\frac{2!}{2!0!}\right)\left(\frac{2!}{0!2!}\right)}{\left(\frac{4!}{2!2!}\right)} = \frac{1}{6} = .167$$

where: $x = 2$ = number of <u>good</u> batteries selected
$n = 2$ = number of batteries selected
$N = 4$ = number of batteries in total
$r = 2$ = number of <u>good</u> batteries in total

The Excel function for computing hypergeometric probabilities, HYPERGEOMDIST, only computes probabilities, not cumulative probabilities. The function has four arguments: x for the number of successes, n for the number of trials, r for the number of elements in the population labeled success, and N for the total number of elements in the population. In this problem, $x = 2$, $n = 2$, $r = 2$, and $N = 4$.

Enter Data: We enter the value 2, for the number of successes, into cell A1. We enter the value 2, for the number of trials, into cell A2. We enter the value 2, for the number of elements in the population labeled success (good batteries), into cell A3. We enter the value 4, for the total number of elements (batteries), into cell A4.

Enter Functions and Formulas: We enter the formula =HYPERGEOMDIST (A1,A2,A3,A4) into cell B6 and an appropriate label into cell A6.

Formula Worksheet:

	A	B
1	2	= **Number of Successes (x)**
2	2	= **Number of Trials (n)**
3	2	= **Number of Elements in the Population Labeled Success (r)**
4	4	= **Number of Elements in the Population (N)**
5		
6	$f(x)$ =	=HYPGEOMDIST(A1,A2,A3,A4)
7		

We see in the resulting worksheet below that the probability of selecting two good batteries from a group of four batteries containing only two good batteries is .167.

Value Worksheet:

	A	B
1	2	= **Number of Successes (x)**
2	2	= **Number of Trials (n)**
3	2	= **Number of Elements in the Population Labeled Success (r)**
4	4	= **Number of Elements in the Population (N)**
5		
6	$f(x)$ =	0.167
7		

EXERCISES

EXERCISE 1

Random Variables

Waters' Edge is a clothing retailer that promotes its products via catalog and accepts customer orders by all of the conventional ways including the Internet. Waters' Edge has an excellent reputation as a result of the superior service, speed of delivery, and product value it provides its customers. The company has gained these competitive advantages in part by collecting data about its operations and the customer each time an order is processed.

Among the data collected with each order are: (a) order quantity, (b) shipping weight of order, (c) inventory status of items ordered, (d) customer's prior orders, (e) method of payment, and (f) gender of orderer. For each of the six categories of data, develop a random variable of interest to the managers of Waters' Edge. Denote which of the variables are discrete and which are continuous.

EXERCISE 2

Discrete Probability Distribution

June's Specialty Shop sells designer original dresses. On 10% of her dresses, June makes a profit of $10, on 20% of her dresses she makes a profit of $20, on 30% of her dresses she makes a profit of $30, and on 40% of her dresses she makes a profit of $40.

a) What is the expected profit June earns on the sale of a dress?

b) On a given day, the probability of June having no customers is .05, of one customer is .10, of two customers is .20, of three customers is .35, of four customers is .20, and of five customers is .10. June's daily operating cost is $0 per day. Using your answer to (a), find the expected net profit June earns per day. (Hint: To find the expected daily gross profit, multiply the expected profit per dress by the expected number of customers per day.)

c) June is considering moving to a larger store. She estimates that doing so will double the expected number of customers. If the larger store will increase her operating costs to $100 per day, should she make the move?

EXERCISE 3

Discrete Probability Distribution

Ace Mopeds sells mopeds with a one-month warranty. Over a one-year period the following data were compiled.

Month	Number Sold in Month	Number Returned for Warranty Service	Month	Number Sold in Month	Number Returned for Warranty Service
Jan	4	1	Jul	20	4
Feb	6	2	Aug	20	4
Mar	3	0	Sep	20	4
Apr	20	1	Oct	16	3
May	10	2	Nov	16	3
Jun	16	4	Dec	10	3

a) Based on this data, determine the probability distribution for: (1) the number of mopeds sold in a month; (2) the number of mopeds returned for warranty in a given month; (3) the percentage of mopeds returned for warranty in a given month.

b) Which of these distributions are for discrete and which are for continuous random variables.

c) Which distribution would be of concern to (1) the quality control engineer at the moped factory; (2) the sales department at Ace; and, (3) the service department at Ace.

d) What is the probability that the percentage of Mopeds returned for service in a randomly selected month is between 10% and 21%?

e) What is the probability that the number of mopeds returned for service in a randomly selected month is greater than 1 and less than 4?

f) What is the expected number of mopeds Ace sells in a month?

g) What is the expected number of mopeds returned for service in a month?

h) What is the expected percentage of mopeds returned for service in a month?

i) Is the answer to part (h) equal to the answer in part (g) divided by the answer to part (f)?

EXERCISE 4

Expected Value and Variance

Two headache remedies, Relief and Comfort are waging an advertising campaign. Each claims it eliminates a headache faster. The data compiled by an independent testing agency is as follows:

Time (in minutes) after taking remedy	Percentage of headaches cured at that time using	
	Relief	Comfort
5	.60	0
10	0	.10
15	0	.75
20	0	.15
25	0	0
30	.40	0

a) What are the means and variances of the time until headache cure (1) using Relief; (2) using Comfort?

b) Which remedy has the maximum probability of relieving a headache within 10 minutes?

c) Which remedy has the maximum probability of relieving a headache within 20 minutes?

EXERCISE 5

Expected Value and Variance

The salespeople at Gold Key Realty sell up to 9 houses per month. The probability distribution of a salesperson selling x houses in a month is as follows:

Sales (x)	0	1	2	3	4	5	6	7	8	9
Probability $f(x)$	.05	.10	.15	.20	.15	.10	.10	.05	.05	.05

a) What are the mean and standard deviation for the number of houses sold by a salesperson per month?

b) Any salesperson selling more houses than the amount equal to the mean plus two standard deviations receives a bonus. How many houses per month must a salesperson sell to receive a bonus?

EXERCISE 6

Binomial Probability Distribution

Sandy's Pet Center grooms large and small dogs. It takes Sandy 40 minutes to groom a small dog and 70 minutes to groom a large dog. Large dogs account for 20% of Sandy's business. Sandy has 5 appointments on August 15.

a) What is the probability that all 5 dogs are small?

b) What is the probability that two of the dogs are large?

c) What is the expected amount of time to finish all five dogs?

EXERCISE 7

Binomial Probability Distribution

Ralph's Gas Station is running a giveaway promotion. With every fill-up of gasoline, Ralph gives out a lottery ticket that has a 25% chance of being a winning ticket. Customers who collect four winning lottery tickets are eligible for the "BIG SPIN" for large payoffs.

What is the probability of qualifying for the big spin if a customer fills up: (a) 3 times; (b) 4 times; (c) 7 times?

EXERCISE 8

Binomial Probability Distribution

Chez Paul is an exclusive French restaurant that seats only 10 couples for dinner. Paul is famous for his "truffle salad for two" which must be prepared one day in advance. The probability of any couple ordering the salad is .4 and each couple orders independently of other couples.

a) What is the expected number of "truffle salads for two" that Paul serves per dinner? What is the variance?

b) What is the probability that on a given evening, at most three couples want a "truffle salad for two"?

c) How many salads should Paul prepare if he wants the probability of not having enough salads for all customers who desire one to be no greater than .10?

d) There is a 70% chance a couple will order coffee after dinner. What is the probability that on a given evening, exactly eight of the ten couples will order coffee? (Again assume that couples order independently of each other.)

EXERCISE 9

Poisson Probability Distribution

The number of customers at Winkies Donuts between 8:00a.m. and 9:00a.m. is believed to follow a Poisson distribution with a mean of 2 customers per minute.

a) During a randomly selected one-minute interval during this time period, what is the probability of 6 customers arriving to Winkies?

b) What is the probability that at least 2 minutes elapse between customer arrivals?

EXERCISE 10

Poisson Probability Distribution

During lunchtime, customers arrive at Bob's Drugs according to a Poisson distribution with $\lambda = 4$ per minute.

a) During a one minute interval, determine the following probabilities: (1) no arrivals; (2) one arrival; (3) two arrivals; and, (4) three or more arrivals.

b) What is the probability of two arrivals in a two-minute period?

EXERCISE 11

Poisson Probability Distribution

Telephone calls arrive at the Global Airline reservation office in Lemonville according to a Poisson distribution with a mean of 1.2 calls per minute.

a) What is the probability of receiving exactly one call during a one-minute interval?

b) What is the probability of receiving at most 2 calls during a one-minute interval?

c) What is the probability of receiving at least two calls during a one-minute interval?

d) What is the probability of receiving exactly 4 calls during a five-minute interval?

e) What is the probability that at most 2 minutes elapse between one call and the next?

EXERCISE 12

Hypergeometric Probability Distribution

Before dawn Josh hurriedly packed some clothes for a job-interview trip while his roommate was still sleeping. He reached in his disorganized sock drawer where there were five black socks and five navy blue socks, although they appeared to be the same color in the dimly lighted room. Josh grabbed six socks, hoping that at least two, and preferably four, of them were black to match the gray suit he had packed. With no time to spare, he then raced to the airport to catch his plane.

a) What is the probability that Josh packed at least two black socks so that he will be dressed appropriately the day of his interview?

b) What is the probability that Josh packed at least four black socks so that he will be dressed appropriately the latter day of his trip as well?

SELF-TEST

TRUE/FALSE

___ 1. The binomial probability distribution is most symmetric when *p* equals 0.5.

___ 2. A discrete random variable may assume an infinite sequence of values.

___ 3. If one wanted to find the probability of ten customer arrivals in an hour at a service station, one would generally use the Poisson distribution.

___ 4. The binomial probability function cannot be applied to all binomial experiments.

___ 5. There is an upper limit on the value of *x*, the number of occurrences in an interval, when *x* is a random variable described by the Poisson probability function.

FILL-IN-THE-BLANK

1. A _____ is a numerical description of the outcome of an experiment.

2. To compute the probability that in a random sample of *n* elements, selected without replacement, we will obtain *x* successes, we would use the _____ probability function.

3. The _____ probability function is based in part on the counting rule for combinations.

4. A _____ probability distribution shows the probability of *x* occurrences of an event over a specified interval of time or space.

5. Experimental outcomes that are based on measurement scales such as time, weight, and distance can be described by _____ random variables.

MULTIPLE CHOICE

___ 1. Which one of the following properties of a binomial experiment is called the stationarity assumption?
   a) The experiment consists of *n* identical trials.
   b) Two outcomes are possible on each trial.
   c) The probability of success is the same for each trial.
   d) The trials are independent.

___ 2. The function used to compute the probability of x successes in n trials, when the trials are dependent, is the
   a) binomial probability function
   b) hypergeometric probability function
   c) Poisson probability function
   d) discrete uniform probability function

___ 3. The expected value of a random variable is the
   a) most probable value
   b) simple average of all the possible values
   c) median value
   d) mean value

___ 4. In a binomial experiment consisting of five trials, the number of different values that x (the number of successes) can assume is
   a) 2
   b) 5
   c) 6
   d) 10

___ 5. A binomial probability distribution with $p = .3$ is
   a) negatively skewed
   b) symmetrical
   c) positively skewed
   d) bimodal

ANSWERS

EXERCISES

1) (a)	Order quantity	x = Number of items ordered	Discrete
(b)	Shipping weight	x = Weight (in pounds) of package(s) shipped	Continuous
(c)	Inventory status	x = 0 if any items unavailable 1 if all items available	Discrete
(d)	Order fill time	x = Time (in hours) from order receipt until shipped	Continuous
(d)	Prior orders	x = Number of orders in last 12 months	Discrete
(e)	Payment method	x = 0 if gift certificate 1 if personal check 2 if credit card 3 if debit card	Discrete

2) a) $30
   b) $45.50
   c) Yes, new daily profit = $71

3) a) (1) P(3) = 1/12, P(4) = 1/12, P(6) = 1/12, P(10) = 1/6, P(16) = 1/4, P(20) = 1/3,
         all other P(x) = 0.
      (2) P(0) = 1/12, P(1) =1/6, P(2) = 1/6, P(3) = 1/6, P(4) = 1/3, all other P(y) = 0
      (3) P(0) = 1/12, P(.05) = 1/12, P(.1875) = 1/6, P(.20) = 1/3, P(.25) = 1/6,
          P(.3) = 1/12, P(.333) = 1/12, all other P(z) = 0
   b) all distributions are for discrete random variables
   c) (1) the third; (2) the first; (3) the second.
   d) 1/2   e) 5/12   f) 13.417   g) 2.583   h) 17.15%   i) No

4) a) Relief μ = 15, σ^2 = 150; Comfort μ = 15.25, σ^2 = 6.19
   b) Relief
   c) Comfort

5) a) mean = 3.9, standard deviation = 2.34
   b) 8.58 or 9 houses

6) a) .3277
   b) .2048
   c) 300 minutes

7) a) 0
   b) .0039
   c) .0705

8) a) μ = 4, σ^2 = 2.4
   b) .3822
   c) 6
   d) .2335

9) a) .0120
   b) .0183

10) a) .0183, .0733, .1465, .7619
    b) .0107
    c) .8647

11) a) .36
    b) .88
    c) .34
    d) .135
    e) .9093

12) a) .976
    b) .262

TRUE/FALSE

1) True
2) True
3) True
4) False
5) False

FILL-IN-THE-BLANK

1) random variable
2) hypergeometric
3) binomial
4) Poisson
5) continuous

MULTIPLE CHOICE

1) c
2) b
3) d
4) c
5) c

CHAPTER 6

Continuous
Probability Distributions

Uniform Probability Distribution

Normal Probability Distribution

Exponential Probability Distribution

LEARNING OBJECTIVES
LEARNING OBJECTIVES

1. Understand the difference between how probabilities are computed for discrete and continuous random variables.

2. Know how to compute probability values for a continuous uniform probability distribution and be able to compute the expected value and variance for such a distribution.

3. Be able to compute probabilities using a normal probability distribution. Understand the role of the standard normal distribution in this process.

4. Be able to use tables for the standard normal probability distribution to compute both standard normal probabilities and probabilities for any normal distribution.

5. Given a cumulative probability be able to compute the z-value and x-value that cuts off the corresponding area in the left tail of a normal distribution.

6. Be able to use Excel's NORMSDIST and NORMDIST functions to compute probabilities for the standard normal distribution and any normal distribution.

7. Be able to use Excel's NORMSINV and NORMINV function to find z and x values corresponding to given cumulative probabilities.

8. Be able to compute probabilities using an exponential probability distribution and using Excel's EXPONDIST function.

9. Understand the relationship between the Poisson and exponential probability distributions.

REVIEW

Continuous Probability Distributions
- A <u>continuous random variable</u> can assume any value in an interval on the real line or in a collection of intervals.
- It is not possible to talk about the probability of the random variable assuming a particular value.
- Instead, we talk about the probability of the random variable assuming a value within a given interval.
- The probability of the random variable assuming a value within some given interval from x_1 to x_2 is defined to be the <u>area under the graph</u> of the <u>probability density function</u> between x_1 and x_2.
- The total area under the graph $f(x)$ is equal to 1.

Area as a Measure of Probability
- The area under the graph of $f(x)$ and probability are the same.
- The probability that x takes a value between some lower value x_1 and some higher value x_2 can be found by computing the area under the graph of $f(x)$ over the interval x_1 and x_2.

Uniform Probability Distribution
- If a random variable is restricted to be within some interval and the probability density function is constant over the interval, (a,b), the continuous random variable is said to have a uniform distribution between a and b.
- Its density function is given by:
  $$f(x) = 1/(b\text{-}a) \text{ for } a \le x \le b, \text{ and } = 0 \text{ outside this interval.}$$
- The formula for the expected value of x is:
  $$E(x) = (a + b)/2$$
- The formula for the variance of x is:
  $$Var(x) = (b - a)^2/12$$

Normal Probability Distribution
- The normal distribution is perhaps the most widely used distribution for describing a continuous random variable.
- The normal probability density function is:
  $$f(x) = \frac{1}{\sigma\sqrt{2\pi}} e^{-(x-\mu)^2/2\sigma^2}$$
  where: μ = mean
  σ = standard deviation
  π = 3.14159
  e = 2.71828

Characteristics of the Normal Probability Distribution
- The shape of the normal curve is often illustrated as a bell-shaped curve.
- Two parameters, μ (mean) and σ (standard deviation), determine the location and shape of the distribution.
- The highest point on the normal curve is at the mean, which is also the median and mode.
- The mean can be any numerical value: negative, zero, or positive.
- The normal curve is symmetric (left and right halves are mirror images).
- The standard deviation determines the width of the curve: larger values result in wider, flatter curves.
- The total area under the curve is 1 (0.5 to the left of the mean and 0.5 to the right).
- Areas under the curve give probabilities for the normal random variable.
- Unlike the uniform distribution, the height of the normal distribution's curve varies and calculus is required to compute the areas that represent probability.
- Areas under the normal curve have been computed and are available in tables that can be used in computing probabilities.
- The percentage of values in some commonly used intervals are:
  - 68.26% of values of a normal random variable are within +/- 1 standard deviation of its mean.
  - 95.44% of values of a normal random variable are within +/- 2 standard deviations of its mean.
  - 99.72% of values of a normal random variable are within +/- 3 standard deviations of its mean.

Standard Normal Probability Distribution
- A random variable that has a normal distribution with a mean of zero and a standard deviation of one is said to have a standard normal probability distribution.
- The letter z is commonly used to designate this normal random variable.
- We can think of z as a measure of the number of standard deviations x is from μ..
- The formula used to convert any normal random variable x, with mean μ and standard deviation σ, to the standard normal distribution is:
$$z = (x - \mu)/\sigma$$

Excel Functions for Normal Distribution
- For a standard normal probability distribution:
  - NORMSDIST is used to compute the cumulative probability, given a z value.
  - NORMSINV is used to compute the z value, given a cumulative probability.
- For any normal probability distribution:
  - NORMDIST is used to compute the cumulative probability, given an x value.
  - NORMINV is used to compute the x value, given a cumulative probability.

Exponential Probability Distribution
- A continuous probability distribution frequently used for computing the probability of the time to complete a task is the exponential distribution.
- If the average time to complete a task is denote by μ, then the probability density function for the amount of time, x, to complete the task is given by:
$$f(x) = (1/\mu)e^{-(x/\mu)} \text{ for } x \geq 0 \text{ and } \mu > 0.$$
- From this distribution, the probability a task is completed within a specified time, x_0, is:
$$P(x < x_0) = 1 - e^{-(x_0/\mu)}.$$

Excel Function for Exponential Distribution
- Excel's EXPONDIST function can be used to compute cumulative probabilities for the exponential distribution.
- The function has three arguments:
  - First – the value of the random variable x
  - Second – $1/\mu$ (the inverse of the mean number of occurrences in an interval)
  - Third – "TRUE" or "FALSE" (we will always enter "TRUE" because we are seeking a cumulative probability)

Relationship Between the Poisson and Exponential Distributions
- If the Poisson distribution provides an appropriate description of the number of occurrences per interval, the exponential distribution provides a description of the length of the interval between occurrences.
- As an example: If customers arrive according to a Poisson distribution with a mean of λ customers, then the interarrival times of customers follows an exponential distribution with $\mu = 1/\lambda$.

KEY CONCEPTS

CONCEPT	EXAMPLES	EXERCISES
Uniform Probability Distribution	1,2	1,2
Normal Probability Distribution	③	3,4,5,6,7
Exponential Probability Distribution	④	8

◯ Excel Used

EXAMPLES

EXAMPLE 1

Uniform Probability Distribution

Customers of Slater's Buffet are charged for the amount of salad they take. Sampling suggests that the amount of salad taken is uniformly distributed between 5 ounces and 15 ounces.

a) Compute the expected value and variance for the distribution.

b) What is the probability that a customer will take between 12 and 15 ounces of salad?

c) Graph the probability density function.

SOLUTION 1

a) Expected Value of x = E(x) = ($a + b$)/2 = (5 + 15)/2 = 10

Variance of x = Var(x) = ($b - a$)^2/12 = (15 - 5)^2/12 = 8.33

b) P(12 $\leq x \leq$ 15) = 1/10(3) = .3

c)

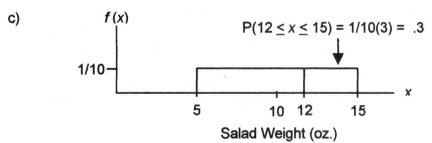

EXAMPLE 2

Uniform Probability Distribution

     Suppose a random variable x has a continuous uniform distribution with values ranging from 5 to 15.

a) What is the probability that x has a value between 8 and 10?

b) What is the probability that the value for x is less than 7 or greater than 12?

c) What is the probability that x has a value less than 20?

d) What is the probability that x equals 11?

SOLUTION 2

Since x has a uniform distribution between 5 and 15, $f(x)$ = 1/10 for $5 \leq x \leq 15$
$$= 0 \text{ elsewhere.}$$

a) To find the probability x has a value between 8 and 10, multiply the interval width (2) by $f(x)$. This equals (2)(.1) = .2.

b) The event "7 or less" is the interval between 5 and 7 = 2, and "greater than 12" is between 12 and 15 = 3. The total interval width of the event is 3+2 = 5. Hence its probability is 5(.1) = .50

c) Since x can only be 15 or less, the probability $x \leq 20$ is 1.

d) The probability that x exactly equals 11 is 0 by definition.

EXAMPLE 3

Normal Probability Distribution

     Pep Zone sells auto parts and supplies including a popular multi-grade motor oil. When the stock of this oil drops to 20 gallons, a replenishment order is placed.
     The store manager is concerned that sales are being lost due to stockouts while waiting for a replenishment order. It has been determined that lead-time demand is normally distributed with a mean of 15 gallons and a standard deviation of 6 gallons.

a) The manager would like to know the probability of a stockout, $P(x > 20)$.

b) If the manager of Pep Zone wants the probability of a stockout to be no more than .05, what should the reorder point be?

SOLUTION 3

Using Excel's NORMDIST, NORMSDIST, NORMINV, NORMSINV Functions

a) We are solving for the (tail) area to the right of the 20-gallon line in the graph below of the normal probability density function for the random variable x. The <u>Areas for the Standard Normal Distribution</u> (normal probabilities) table in the textbook does not directly provide areas for the tail regions of the distribution. So, we will first determine the area of the region between the center (mean) line and the reorder point line.

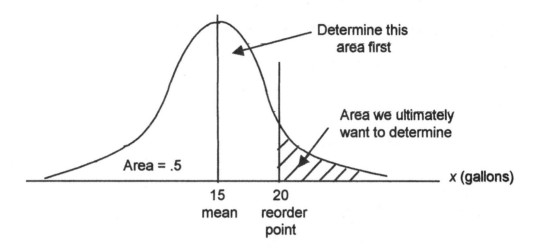

We begin by converting our normal distribution (measured in gallons here) to the standard normal distribution so that we can use the Standard Normal table of areas. Essentially, we must compute how many standard deviations lie between the mean demand value μ (15) and the reorder point value x (20).

$$z = (x - \mu)/\sigma = (20 - 15)/6 = .83$$

The Standard Normal table shows an area of .2967 for the region between the mean (where $z = 0$) and the reorder point (where $z = .83$).

z	.00	.01	.02	.03	.04	.05	.06	.07	.08	.09
.5	.1915	.1950	.1985	.2019	.2054	.2088	.2123	.2157	.2190	.2224
.6	.2257	.2291	.2324	.2357	.2389	.2422	.2454	.2486	.2518	.2549
.7	.2580	.2612	.2642	.2673	.2704	.2734	.2764	.2794	.2823	.2852
.8	.2881	.2910	.2939	.2967	.2995	.3023	.3051	.3078	.3106	.3133
.9	.3159	.3186	.3212	.3238	.3264	.3289	.3315	.3340	.3365	.3389

The upper (right) tail area is .5 - .2967 = .2033. The probability of a stock-out is <u>.2033</u>.

NORMSDIST Function

Excel's NORMSDIST function can be used to solve this portion of the problem. The NORMSDIST function is used to compute the cumulative probability for the standard normal distribution. Essentially, we are converting a normal distribution to the standard normal distribution by computing and using a z value rather than an x value.

Enter Data: We enter the mean value, 15, into cell B2, the standard deviation value, 6, into cell B3, and the x value (for which we want a cumulative probability) into cell B4.

Enter Functions and Formulas: The NORMSDIST function requires one argument (input), a z value, so we compute the z value by entering the formula =(B4-B2)/B3 into cell B5. To compute the probability of the random variable assuming a value <u>less</u> than the x value entered into cell B4, we enter the formula =NORMSDIST(B5) into cell B6. To compute the probability of the random variable assuming a value <u>greater</u> than the x value entered into cell B4, we enter the formula =1-NORMSDIST(B5) into cell B7. (We could also simply enter the formula =1-B6 into cell B7.)

Formula Worksheet:

	A	B
1	FINDING A PROBABILITY, USING A z VALUE	
2	Mean	15
3	Standard Deviation	6
4	x Value	20
5	z Value	=(B4-B2)/B3
6	Probability of a Lesser x Value	=NORMSDIST(B5)
7	Probability of a Greater x Value	=1-NORMSDIST(B5)

We see in the resulting worksheet below that the probability of demand during replenishment lead time exceeding 20 gallons is .2023. This probability differs slightly from the one we earlier computed manually (.2033) because in our manual calculation we rounded the z value to .83.

Value Worksheet:

	A	B
1	FINDING A PROBABILITY, USING A z VALUE	
2	Mean	15
3	Standard Deviation	6
4	x Value	20
5	z Value	0.8333
6	Probability of a Lesser x Value	0.7977
7	Probability of a Greater x Value	0.2023

<u>NORMDIST Function</u>

Excel's NORMDIST function can also be used to solve this portion of the problem. The NORMDIST function computes the cumulative probability for <u>any normal distribution</u>. We do not need to convert an x value to a z value.

Enter Data: We enter the mean value, 15, into cell B2, the standard deviation value, 6, into cell B3, and the x value (for which we want a cumulative probability) into cell B4.

Enter Functions and Formulas: The NORMSDIST function requires four arguments: (1) the x value for which we want to compute the cumulative probability, (2) the mean, (3) the standard deviation, and (4) a value of TRUE or FALSE. We want a cumulative probability, so we enter TRUE. To compute the probability of the random variable assuming a value <u>less</u> than the x value entered into cell B4, we enter the formula =NORMDIST(B4,B2,B3,TRUE) into cell B6. To compute the probability of the random variable assuming a value <u>greater</u> than the x value specified, we enter the formula =1-B6 into cell B7. (We could also enter the formula =1- NORMSDIST(B4,B2,B3,TRUE) into cell B7.)

Formula Worksheet:

	A	B
1	FINDING A PROBABILITY, USING AN x VALUE	
2	Mean	15
3	Standard Deviation	6
4	x Value	20
5		
6	Probability of a Lesser x Value	=NORMDIST(B4,B2,B3,TRUE)
7	Probability of a Greater x Value	=1-B6

The result of using the NORMDIST function is identical to that of the NORMSDIST function as evidenced below.

Value Worksheet:

	A	B
1	FINDING A PROBABILITY, USING AN x VALUE	
2	Mean	15
3	Standard Deviation	6
4	x Value	20
5		
6	Probability of a Lesser x Value	0.7977
7	Probability of a Greater x Value	0.2023

b) Rather than having an x value and solving for the cumulative probability, we now have a cumulative probability and we are solving for the x value. We are solving for the reorder point (x) value that corresponds to an upper (right) tail area of .05.

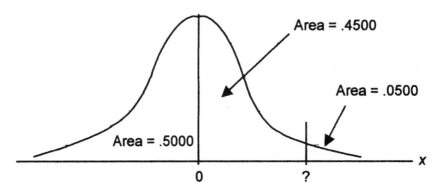

Let $z_{.05}$ represent the z value cutting the .05 tail area. We now look up the .4500 area in the Standard Normal Probability table to find the corresponding $z_{.05}$ value.

z	.00	.01	.02	.03	.04	.05	.06	.07	.08	.09
1.5	.4332	.4345	.4357	.4370	.4382	.4394	.4406	.4418	.4429	.4441
1.6	.4452	.4463	.4474	.4484	.4495	.4505	.4515	.4525	.4535	.4545
1.7	.4554	.4564	.4573	.4582	.4591	.4599	.4608	.4616	.4625	.4633
1.8	.4641	.4649	.4656	.4664	.4671	.4678	.4686	.4693	.4699	.4706
1.9	.4713	.4719	.4726	.4732	.4738	.4744	.4750	.4756	.4761	.4767

$z_{.05} = 1.645$ is a reasonable estimate. The corresponding value of x is given by

$$x = \mu + z_{.05}\sigma$$
$$= 15 + 1.645(6)$$
$$= 24.87$$

A reorder point of 24.87 gallons will place the probability of a stockout during lead time at .05. Perhaps Pep Zone should set the reorder point at 25 gallons to keep the probability under .05.

NORMINV Function

Excel's NORMINV function can be used to solve this portion of the problem. The NORMINV function is used to compute the x value for a given cumulative probability.

Enter Data: We enter the mean value, 15, into cell B2, the standard deviation value, 6, into cell B3, and the cumulative probability, .95, into cell B4. (Note: the tail area is .05, but the cumulative probability or area up to the tail is .95.)

Enter Functions and Formulas: The NORMINV function requires three arguments (inputs): the cumulative probability, the mean, and the standard deviation. To compute the x value we enter the formula =NORMINV(B4,B2,B3) into cell B6.

Formula Worksheet:

	A	B
1	FINDING AN x VALUE, GIVEN A PROBABILITY	
2	Mean	15
3	Standard Deviation	6
4	Cumulative Probability	0.95
5		
6	x Value	=NORMINV(B4,B2,B3)

The result, shown below, agrees with our manual calculation. The reorder point necessary for a .05 probability of a stockout during lead time is 24.87.

Value Worksheet:

	A	B
1	FINDING AN x VALUE, GIVEN A PROBABILITY	
2	Mean	15
3	Standard Deviation	6
4	Cumulative Probability	0.95
5		
6	x Value	24.87

EXAMPLE 4

Exponential Probability Distribution

The time between arrivals of cars at Al's Carwash follows an exponential probability distribution with a mean time between arrivals of 3 minutes. Al would like to know the probability that the time between two successive arrivals will be 2 minutes or less.

SOLUTION 4

Using Excel's EXPONDIST Function

To compute the exponential probability asked for here we use the formula:

$$P(x \leq x_0) = 1 - e^{-x_0/\mu}$$

It provides the cumulative probability of obtaining a value for the exponential random variable of less than or equal to some specific value of x, denoted by x_0.

In this problem, $\mu = 3$ and $x_0 = 2$. The result is:

$$P(x \leq 2) = 1 - 2.71828^{-2/3} = 1 - .5134 = \underline{.4866}$$

There is a .4866 probability that the time between two successive arrivals at the car wash will be two minutes or less.

The exponential probability distribution in this problem can be graphed as follows:

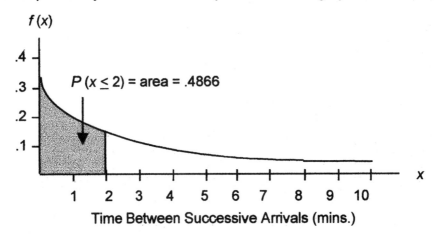

Excel's EXPONDIST function can be used to compute exponential probabilities.

Enter Data: No data are entered in the worksheet. We simply enter the appropriate values for the exponential random variable (time between successive arrivals) directly into the formula as needed.

Enter Functions and Formulas: The EXPONDIST function has three arguments: the first is the value of x_0, the second is $1/\mu$, and the third is TRUE or FALSE. We will always select TRUE because we are seeking a cumulative probability. Hence, we enter the formula =EXPONDIST(2,1/3,TRUE) into cell B3 and enter labels to identify the output.

Formula Worksheet:

	A	B
1	\multicolumn{2}{c}{**Probabilities: Exponential Distribution**}	
2		
3	$P(x \le 2) =$	=EXPONDIST(2,1/3,TRUE)
4		

Value Worksheet:

	A	B
1	\multicolumn{2}{c}{**Probabilities: Exponential Distribution**}	
2		
3	$P(x \le 2) =$	0.4866
4		

EXERCISES

EXERCISE 1

Uniform Probability Distribution

The Harbour Island Ferry leaves on the hour and at 15-minute intervals. The time, x, it takes John to drive from his house to the ferry has a uniform distribution with x between 10 and 20 minutes. One morning John leaves his house at precisely 8:00a.m.

a) What is the probability John will wait less than 5 minutes for the ferry?

b) What is the probability John will wait less than 10 minutes for the ferry?

c) What is the probability John will wait less than 15 minutes for the ferry?

d) What is the probability John will not have to wait for the ferry?

e) Suppose John leaves at 8:05a.m. What is the probability John will wait (1) less than 5 minutes for the ferry; (2) less than 10 minutes for the ferry?

f) Suppose John leaves at 8:10a.m. What is the probability John will wait (1) less than 5 minutes for the ferry; (2) less than 10 minutes for the ferry?

g) What appears to be the best time for John to leave home if he wishes to maximize the probability of waiting less than 10 minutes for the ferry?

EXERCISE 2

Uniform Probability Distribution

Delicious Candy markets a two-pound box of assorted chocolates. Because of imperfections in the candy making equipment, the actual weight of the chocolate has a continuous uniform distribution ranging from 31.8 and 32.6 ounces.

a) Define a probability density function for the weight of the box of chocolate.

b) What is the probability that a box weighs (1) exactly 32 ounces; (2) more than 32.3 ounces; (3) less than 31.8 ounces?

c) The government requires that at least 60% of all products sold weigh at least as much as the stated weight. Is Delicious violating government regulations?

EXERCISE 3

Normal Probability Distribution

The time at which the mailman delivers the mail to Ace Bike Shop follows a normal distribution with mean 2:00 PM and standard deviation of 15 minutes.

a) What is the probability the mail will arrive after 2:30 PM?

b) What is the probability the mail will arrive before 1:36 PM?

c) What is the probability the mail will arrive between 1:48 PM and 2:09 PM?

EXERCISE 4

Normal Probability Distribution

Dollar Department Stores has compiled the following data concerning its daily sales. The sales for each day of the week are normally distributed with the following parameters:

Day	Mean = μ	Standard Deviation = σ
Monday	$120,000	$20,000
Tuesday	$100,000	$25,000
Wednesday	$100,000	$10,000
Thursday	$120,000	$40,000
Friday	$140,000	$20,000
Saturday	$160,000	$50,000

For each day of the week, find the probability that the store sales are between $110,000 and $150,000.

EXERCISE 5

Normal Probability Distribution

The township of Middleton sets the speed limit on its roads by conducting a traffic study and determining the speed (to the nearest 5 miles per hour) at which 80% of the drivers travel at or below. A study was done on Brown's Dock Road that indicated driver's speeds follow a normal distribution with a mean of 36.25 miles per hour and a variance of 6.25.

a) What should the speed limit be?

b) What percent of the drivers travel below that speed?

EXERCISE 6

Normal Probability Distribution

Joe's Record World has two stores. The sales at each store follow a normal distribution. For store 1, μ = $2,000 and σ = $200 per day. For store 2, μ = $1,900 and σ = $400 per day.

a) Which store has the higher average daily sales?

b) What is the probability that daily sales are greater than $2,200 for store 1? for store 2?

c) Is there a contradiction between parts (a) and (b)? Explain.

PROBLEM 7

Exponential Probability Distribution

A light bulb manufacturer claims his light bulbs will last 500 hours on the average. The lifetime of a light bulb is assumed to follow an exponential distribution.

a) What is the probability that the light bulb will have to be replaced within 500 hours?

b) What is the probability that the light bulb will last more than 1000 hours?

c) What is the probability that the light bulb will last between 200 and 800 hours.

SELF-TEST

TRUE/FALSE

_____ 1. The height of a probability density function is a probability.

_____ 2. If x is a continuous random variable, then $P(a \leq x \leq b) = P(a < x < b)$.

_____ 3. For the normal probability distribution, larger values of the standard deviation result in taller probability density curves.

_____ 4. If arrivals follow a Poisson distribution, the time between arrivals must follow an exponential distribution.

_____ 5. For the uniform, normal, and exponential probability distributions, the area to the left of the mean is .5.

FILL-IN-THE-BLANK

1. A fundamental difference separates discrete and continuous random variables in terms of how _____ are computed.

2. Whenever the probability is proportional to the length of the interval, the random variable is _____ distributed.

3. A continuous probability distribution that is useful in computing probabilities for the time or space between occurrences of an event is the _____ distribution.

4. Given a z value, we use the _____ to find the appropriate probability (an area under the curve).

5. The probability of any particular value for a continuous random variable is _____.

MULTIPLE CHOICE

___ 1. There is a lower limit but no upper limit for a random variable that follows the
        a) uniform probability distribution
        b) normal probability distribution
        c) exponential probability distribution
        d) none of the above

___ 2. The form of the continuous uniform probability distribution is
        a) triangular
        b) rectangular
        c) bell-shaped
        d) a series of vertical lines

___ 3. The mean, median, and mode have the same value for which one of the following probability distributions?
        a) uniform
        b) normal
        c) exponential
        d) none of the above

___ 4. The probability distribution that can be described by just one parameter is the
        a) uniform
        b) normal
        c) exponential
        d) none of the above

___ 5. The values of the mean and standard deviation for the standard normal probability distribution are, respectively,
        a) 0, 1
        b) .5, .5
        c) 1, .5
        d) 1, 1

ANSWERS

EXERCISES

1) a) 1/2
   b) 1/2
   c) 1
   d) 0
   e) (1) 0   (2) 1/2
   f) (1) 1/2 (2) 1
   g) 8:10

2) a) f(x) = 1.25 for 31.8 < x < 32.6,
           = 0 otherwise
   b) 0, .375, 0

3) a) .0228
   b) .0548
   c) .5138

4) M- .6247
   T- .3218
   W- .1587
   R- .3721
   F- .6247
   S- .2620

5) a) 40 mph
   b) 93.32%

6) a) 0, .5, .5, .1587
   b) $2

7) a) Store 1
   b) Store 1 - .1587, Store 2 - .2266
   c) No - Store has larger std. deviation

8) a) .632
   b) .135
   c) .468

TRUE/FALSE

1) False
2) True
3) False
4) True
5) False

FILL-IN-THE-BLANK

1) probabilities
2) uniformly
3) exponential
4) standard normal table
5) zero

MULTIPLE CHOICE

1) c
2) b
3) b
4) c
5) a

CHAPTER 7

Sampling and Sampling Distributions

Simple Random Sampling

Point Estimation

Introduction to Sampling Distributions

Sampling Distribution of $\bar{x}$

Sampling Distribution of $\bar{p}$

Other Sampling Methods

LEARNING OBJECTIVES

1. Understand the importance of sampling and how results from samples can be used to provide estimates of population parameters such as the population mean, the population standard deviation and/or the population proportion.

2. Know what simple random sampling is and how simple random samples are selected.

3. Be able to select a simple random sample using Excel.

4. Understand the concept of a sampling distribution.

5. Know the central limit theorem and the important role it plays in sampling.

6. Know the characteristics of the sampling distribution of the sample mean ($\bar{x}$) and the sampling distribution of the sample proportion ($\bar{p}$).

7. Learn about a variety of sampling methods including stratified random sampling, cluster sampling, systematic sampling, convenience sampling and judgment sampling.

8. Know the definition of the following terms:

   simple random sampling   finite population correction factor
   sampling with replacement   standard error
   sampling without replacement
   sampling distribution
   point estimator

REVIEW

Purpose of Sampling
- A <u>population</u> is the set of all the elements of interest.
- A <u>parameter</u> is a numerical characteristic of a population.
- Often times we cannot examine the entire population (conduct a <u>census</u>) in order to learn the value of a parameter.
- Examining the entire population might be <u>time and/or cost prohibitive</u> or simply <u>not feasible</u>.
- Instead, we examine a sample taken from the population.
- A <u>sample</u> is a subset of the population.
- The sample results provide <u>estimates</u> of the values of the population characteristics.
- With <u>proper sampling methods</u>, the sample results will provide <u>"good" estimates</u> of the population characteristics.
- Several methods can be used to select a sample from a population.
- One of the most common methods is simple random sampling.

Simple Random Sampling

Finite Population
- A simple random sample from a finite population of size N is a sample selected such that each possible sample of size n has the same probability of being selected.
- Replacing each sampled element before selecting subsequent elements is called sampling with replacement.
- Sampling without replacement is the procedure used most often.
- One approach to sampling without replacement is to choose the element for the sample one at a time in such a way that each of the elements remaining in the population has the same probability of being selected.
- In large sampling projects, computer-generated random numbers are often used to automate the sample selection process.

Using Excel to Select a Simple Random Sample
- Excel can be used to select a simple random sample without replacement.
- The method used is based on random numbers generated by Excel's RAND function.
- The RAND function generates random numbers in the interval from 0 to 1.
- The random numbers are values of a uniformly distributed random variable.
- The steps involved are:
  - Generate a random number for each of the N items in the population.
  - Turn off the automatic recalculation of the random numbers.
  - Sort the N items in ascending order of their corresponding random numbers.
  - Choose as the sample the n items corresponding to the n smallest random numbers.

Infinite Population
- A simple random sample from an infinite population is a sample selected such that the following conditions are satisfied.
  - Each element selected comes from the same population.
  - Each element is selected independently.
- The population is usually considered infinite if it involves an ongoing process that makes listing or counting every element impossible.
- The random number selection procedure cannot be used for infinite populations because a listing of the population is impossible.

Point Estimation
- In point estimation we use the data from the sample to compute a value of a sample statistic that serves as an estimate of a population parameter.
- We refer to $\bar{x}$ as the point estimator of the population mean μ.
- s is the point estimator of the population standard deviation σ.
- $\bar{p}$ is the point estimator of the population proportion p.

Sampling Error

- The absolute difference between an unbiased point estimate and the corresponding population parameter is called the <u>sampling error</u>.
- Sampling error is the result of using a subset of the population (the sample), and not the entire population to develop estimates.
- The sampling errors are:
  - $|\bar{x} - \mu|$ for sample mean
  - $|s - \sigma|$ for sample standard deviation
  - $|\bar{p} - p|$ for sample proportion

Sampling Distribution of $\bar{x}$

- The sampling distribution of $\bar{x}$ is the probability distribution of all possible values of the sample mean $\bar{x}$.
- The expected value of $\bar{x}$ is

$$E(\bar{x}) = \mu$$
where μ is the population mean.

- The standard deviation of $\bar{x}$ for a finite population is

$$\sigma_{\bar{x}} = (\frac{\sigma}{\sqrt{n}})\sqrt{\frac{N-n}{N-1}}$$

where $\sqrt{(N-n)/(N-1)}$ is the finite correction factor.

- The standard deviation of $\bar{x}$ for a infinite population is

$$\sigma_{\bar{x}} = \frac{\sigma}{\sqrt{n}}$$

- A finite population is treated as being infinite if $n/N \le .05$.
- $\sigma_{\bar{x}}$ is referred to as the <u>standard error of the mean</u>.
- If we use a large ($n \ge 30$) simple random sample, the <u>central limit theorem</u> enables us to conclude that the sampling distribution of $\bar{x}$ can be approximated by a normal probability distribution.
- When the simple random sample is small ($n < 30$), the sampling distribution of $\bar{x}$ can be considered normal only if we assume the population has a normal probability distribution.

Sampling Distribution of $\bar{p}$

- The sampling distribution of $\bar{p}$ is the probability distribution of all possible values of the sample proportion $\bar{p}$.
- The expected value of $\bar{p}$ is

$$E(\bar{p}) = p$$
where p = the population proportion

- The standard deviation of $\bar{p}$ for a finite population is

$$\sigma_{\bar{p}} = \sqrt{\frac{p(1-p)}{n}}\sqrt{\frac{N-n}{N-1}}$$

- The standard deviation of $\bar{p}$ for a infinite population is

$$\sigma_{\bar{p}} = \sqrt{\frac{p(1-p)}{n}}$$

- $\bar{p}$ is referred to as the <u>standard error of the proportion</u>.

Other Sampling Methods

Stratified Random Sampling
- The population is first divided into groups of elements called <u>strata</u>.
- Each element in the population belongs to one and only one stratum.
- Best results are obtained when the elements within each stratum are as much alike as possible (i.e. <u>homogeneous group</u>).
- A simple random sample is taken from each stratum.
- Formulas are available for combining the stratum sample results into one population parameter estimate.
- <u>Advantage</u>: If strata are homogeneous, this method is as "precise" as simple random sampling but with a smaller total sample size.
- <u>Example</u>: The basis for forming the strata might be department, location, age, industry type, etc.

Cluster Sampling
- The population is first divided into separate groups of elements called <u>clusters</u>.
- Ideally, each cluster is a representative small-scale version of the population (i.e. <u>heterogeneous group</u>).
- A simple random sample of the clusters is then taken.
- All elements within each sampled (chosen) cluster form the sample.
- <u>Advantage</u>: The close proximity of elements can be cost effective (I.e. many sample observations can be obtained in a short time).
- <u>Disadvantage</u>: This method generally requires a larger total sample size than simple or stratified random sampling.
- <u>Example</u>: A primary application is area sampling, where clusters are city blocks or other well-defined areas.

Systematic Sampling
- If a sample size of n is desired from a population containing N elements, we might sample one element for every n/N elements in the population.
- We randomly select one of the first n/N elements from the population list.
- We then select every n/Nth element that follows in the population list.
- This method has the properties of a simple random sample, especially if the list of the population elements is a random ordering.
- <u>Advantage</u>: The sample usually will be easier to identify than it would be if simple random sampling were used.
- <u>Example</u>: Select every 100th listing in a telephone book after the first randomly selected listing.

Convenience Sampling
- It is a <u>nonprobability sampling technique</u>. Items are included in the sample without known probabilities of being selected.
- The sample is identified primarily by <u>convenience</u>.
- <u>Advantage</u>: Sample selection and data collection are relatively easy.
- <u>Disadvantage</u>: It is impossible to determine how representative of the population the sample is.
- <u>Example</u>: A professor conducting research uses student volunteers to constitute a sample.

Judgment Sampling
- The person most knowledgeable on the subject of the study selects elements of the population that he or she feels are most representative of the population.
- It is a <u>nonprobability sampling technique</u>.
- <u>Advantage</u>: It is a relatively easy way of selecting a sample.
- <u>Disadvantage</u>: The quality of the sample results depends on the judgment of the person selecting the sample.
- <u>Example</u>: A reporter might sample three or four senators, judging them as reflecting the general opinion of the senate.

KEY CONCEPTS

<u>CONCEPT</u>	<u>EXAMPLES</u>	<u>EXERCISES</u>
Simple Random Sampling		
Using a Random Number Table	1	1
Using a Random Number Generator	②	2
Point Estimation		
Population Mean and Standard Deviation	③	3
Population Proportion	③	7
Sampling Distribution of $\bar{x}$		
Expected Value and Standard Deviation of $\bar{x}$	④	4
Probability Information about the Size of the Sampling Error	⑤	5
Sample Size and Sampling Distribution of $\bar{x}$	⑥	6
Sampling Distribution of $\bar{p}$		
Expected Value and Standard Deviation of $\bar{p}$	⑦	8
Probability Information about the Size of the Sampling Error	⑧	9

◯ Excel Used

EXAMPLE 1

Simple Random Sampling from a Finite Population

St. Andrew's College receives 900 applications annually from prospective students. A completed application contains a variety of information including the individual's scholastic aptitude test (SAT) score and whether or not the individual desires on-campus housing.

The director of admissions would like to know the average SAT score for the applicants and the proportion of applicants that want to live on campus. The director decides, for the sake of expedience, to take a simple random sample of 30 applicants and tally their SAT scores and housing preferences.

Use the random number table below to select the applicants the director will include in her sample. Starting in the sixth row of the table, moving from left to right, and continuing down the rows, identify the numbers of the 30 applicants for the sample. Let's assume that the SAT scores and housing preferences of the 900 applicants are already entered into an Excel worksheet.

Random Numbers

63271	59986	71744	51102	15141	80714	58683	93108	13554	79945
88547	09896	95436	79115	08303	01041	20030	63754	08459	28364
55957	57243	83865	09911	19761	66535	40102	26646	60147	15702
46276	87453	44790	67122	45573	84358	21625	16999	13385	22782
55363	07449	34835	15290	76616	67191	12777	21861	68689	03263
69393	92785	49902	58447	42048	30378	87618	26933	40640	16281
13186	29431	88190	04588	38733	81290	89541	70290	40113	08243
17726	28652	56836	78351	47327	18518	92222	55201	27340	10493
36520	64465	05550	30157	82242	29520	69753	72602	23756	54935
81628	36100	39254	56835	37636	02421	98063	89641	64953	99337
84649	38968	75215	75498	49539	74240	03466	49292	36401	45525
63291	11618	12613	75055	43915	26499	41116	64531	56827	30825
70502	53225	03655	05915	37140	57051	48393	91322	25653	06543
06426	24771	59935	49801	11082	66762	94477	02494	88215	27191
20711	55609	29430	70165	45406	78484	31639	52009	18873	96927

SOLUTION 1

Using a Random Number Table

Since the finite population has 900 elements, we will need 3-digit random numbers to randomly select applicants numbered from 1 to 900. The numbers we draw will be the numbers of the applicants we will sample unless the random number is greater than 900 or the random number has already been used. We will continue to draw random numbers until we have selected 30 applicants for our sample.

The 3-digit numbers we encounter in the table, including unacceptable numbers, are listed below. The numbers in bold print are unacceptable because they are greater than 900. Note that we had to draw 34 numbers from the table in order to get 30 acceptable numbers.

693 **939** 278 549 **902** 584 474 204 803 788 761 826 **933** 406 401
628 113 186 294 318 819 004 588 387 338 129 089 541 702 **904**
011 308 243 177

EXAMPLE 2

Simple Random Sampling from a Finite Population

Refer to the St. Andrew's sampling problem in Example 1. Use an Excel worksheet and the RAND function to select a simple random sample of 30 applicants without replacement.

SOLUTION 2

Using Excel's RAND Function

We begin by generating 900 random numbers, one for each applicant in the population. Then we choose the 30 applicants corresponding to the 30 smallest random numbers as our sample. Each of the 900 applicants has the same probability of being included.

Enter Data: We will assume that the following data were already entered into columns A, B, and C. The applicant numbers 1-900 are shown in Column A. The SAT score and housing preference are shown in columns B and C, respectively.

Enter Functions and Formulas: The formula =RAND() is entered into cells D2:D901 to generate a random number between 0 and 1 for each of the 900 applicants.

Formula Worksheet:

	A	B	C	D
	Applicant Number	SAT Score	On-Campus Housing	Random Number
1				
2	1	1008	Yes	=RAND()
3	2	1025	No	=RAND()
4	3	952	Yes	=RAND()
5	4	1090	Yes	=RAND()
6	5	1127	Yes	=RAND()
7	6	1015	No	=RAND()
8	7	965	Yes	=RAND()

Note: Rows 9-901 are not shown.

We see that the random number generated for the first applicant is .34194, the random number generated for the second applicant is .07560, and so on.

Value Worksheet:

	A	B	C	D
1	Applicant Number	SAT Score	On-Campus Housing	Random Number
2	1	1008	Yes	0.34194
3	2	1025	No	0.07560
4	3	952	Yes	0.42331
5	4	1090	Yes	0.06674
6	5	1127	Yes	0.27756
7	6	1015	No	0.62837
8	7	965	Yes	0.21312

Note: Rows 9-901 are not shown.

Apply Tools: All that remains is to find the applicants associated with the 30 smallest random numbers. To do so, we sort the data in columns A through D into ascending order by random numbers in column D.

Putting Random Numbers in Ascending Order

Step 1   Select cells A2:A901
Step 2   Select the **Data** pull-down menu
Step 3   Choose the **Sort** option
Step 4   When the **Sort** dialog box appears:
  Choose **Random Numbers** in the **Sort by text** box
  Choose **Ascending**
  Click **OK**

After completing these steps we obtain the worksheet shown below. The applicants listed in rows 2-31 are the ones corresponding to the smallest 30 random numbers that were generated. Hence, this group of 30 applicants is our simple random sample.
Note: Prior to sorting we turned off the automatic recalculation option for the worksheet. With the option turned on, any change made to the worksheet will trigger a recalculation of the random numbers. To turn the recalculation option off, select **Tools**, choose **Options**, select the **Calculation** tab, and in the calculation section select **Manual**.

Sorted Worksheet:

	A	B	C	D
1	Applicant Number	SAT Score	On-Campus Housing	Random Number
2	12	1107	No	0.00027
3	773	1043	Yes	0.00192
4	408	991	Yes	0.00303
5	58	1008	No	0.00481
6	116	1127	Yes	0.00538
7	185	982	Yes	0.00683
8	510	1163	Yes	0.00749

Note: Rows 9-901 are not shown.

EXAMPLE 3

Point Estimation

Refer to the St. Andrew's sampling problem in Example 1. What is the point estimate of the mean SAT score for the 900 applicants? What is the point estimate of the standard deviation of the 900 SAT scores? What is the point estimate of the proportion of the 900 applicants who want on-campus housing?

SOLUTION 3

Using Excel

We will first compute the point estimates manually to demonstrate the mathematical operations. If you could (you cannot) see here all of the data for the sample of 30 applicants in the exhibits above, you would make the following computations.

$\bar{x}$ as Point Estimator of μ

$$\bar{x} = \frac{\sum x_i}{30} = \frac{29,910}{30} = 997$$

s as Point Estimator of σ

$$s = \sqrt{\frac{\sum (x_i - \bar{x})^2}{n-1}} = \sqrt{\frac{163,996}{29}} = 75.20$$

$\bar{p}$ as Point Estimator of p

$$\bar{p} = 20/30 = .667$$

Now we will demonstrate how Excel can be used to compute the point estimate. We will continue with the worksheet developed in Example 2.

Enter Data: The data for the simple random sample of 30 applicants are already entered into cells A2:C31 (See Solution 2).

Enter Functions and Formulas: We are using the mean SAT score in the sample as the point estimate of the population's average SAT score. To compute the sample mean we enter the formula =AVERAGE(B2:B31) into cell F3.

We are using the standard deviation of the SAT scores in the sample as the point estimate of the standard deviation of the population's SAT scores. To compute the sample standard deviation we enter the formula =STDEV(B2:B31) into cell F4.

We are using the proportion of the sample that wants on-campus housing as the point estimate of the proportion of the population that wants on-campus housing. To compute the sample proportion we count the number of Yes responses in the sample and divide the number by 30. So, we enter the formula =COUNTIF(C2:C31,"Yes")/30 into cell F5.

Formula Worksheet:

	A	B	C	D	E	F
1	Applicant Number	SAT Score	On-Campus Housing	Random Number		Point Estimates
2	12	1107	No	0.00027		
3	773	1043	Yes	0.00192	Estimate μ	=AVERAGE(B2:B31)
4	408	991	Yes	0.00303	Estimate σ	=STDEV(B2:B31)
5	58	1008	No	0.00481	Estimate p	=COUNTIF(C2:C31,"Yes")/30
6	116	1127	Yes	0.00538		

Note: Rows 7-31 are not shown.

The results are shown in the worksheet below. Keep in mind that different random numbers would have identified a different sample, which would have resulted in different point estimates.

Value Worksheet:

	A	B	C	D	E	F
1	Applicant Number	SAT Score	On-Campus Housing	Random Number		Point Estimates
2	12	1107	No	0.00027		
3	773	1043	Yes	0.00192	Estimate μ	997
4	408	991	Yes	0.00303	Estimate σ	75.20
5	58	1008	No	0.00481	Estimate p	0.667
6	116	1127	Yes	0.00538		

EXAMPLE 4

Sampling Distribution of $\bar{x}$

Refer to the St. Andrew's sampling problem in Example 1. Assume we know the mean and standard deviation are 990 and 80, respectively, for the 900 applicants' SAT scores. Show the sampling distribution of $\bar{x}$ where $\bar{x}$ is the mean SAT score for the 30 applicants.

SOLUTION 4

If we use a large ($n \geq 30$) simple random sample, the <u>central limit theorem</u> enables us to conclude that the sampling distribution of $\bar{x}$ can be approximated by a normal probability distribution.

Expected Value of $\bar{x}$

$$E(\bar{x}) = \mu = 990$$
where: μ = the population mean

Standard Deviation of $\bar{x}$

$$\sigma_{\bar{x}} = \frac{\sigma}{\sqrt{n}} = \frac{80}{\sqrt{30}} = 14.6$$
where: σ = the population standard deviation
n = the sample size

Sampling Distribution of $\bar{x}$

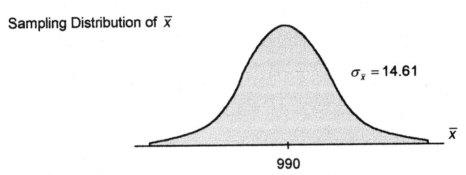

$$\sigma_{\bar{x}} = 14.61$$

$\bar{x}$

990

Now we will demonstrate how Excel can be used to compute the expected value and standard deviation of $\bar{x}$.

Enter Data: We enter the values of the population mean and standard deviation into cells B2 and B3, respectively. The sample size is entered into cell B6.

Enter Functions and Formulas: The expected value of $\bar{x}$ is simply the value of the population mean, so we enter the formula =B2 into cell B7. We compute the standard error of the mean by entering the formula =B3/SQRT(B6) into cell B8.

Formula Worksheet:

	A	B
1	POPULATION PARAMETERS	
2	Population Mean (μ) =	990
3	Population Standard Deviation (σ) =	80
4		
5	SAMPLING DISTRIBUTION OF xbar	
6	Sample Size (n) =	30
7	Expected x bar =	=B2
8	Standard Error of the Mean =	=B3/SQRT(B6)

Value Worksheet:

	A	B
1	POPULATION PARAMETERS	
2	Population Mean (μ) =	990
3	Population Standard Deviation (σ) =	80
4		
5	SAMPLING DISTRIBUTION OF xbar	
6	Sample Size (n) =	30
7	Expected x bar =	990
8	Standard Error of the Mean =	14.61

EXAMPLE 5

Probability Information about the Size of the Sampling Error

Refer to the St. Andrew's problem in Example 1. What is the probability that a simple random sample of 30 applicants will provide an estimate of the population mean SAT score that is within plus or minus 10 of the actual population mean μ, assuming $\mu = 990$?
In other words, what is the probability that $\bar{x}$ will be between 980 and 1000?

SOLUTION 5

Using Excel's NORMDIST Function

We will continue with the worksheet we developed in Example 4.

Enter Data: We enter the value of the sampling error into cell B11.

Enter Functions and Formulas: The upper limit for $\bar{x}$ is the expected value of $\bar{x}$ plus the sampling error, so we enter the formula =B2+B11 into cell B12. Similarly, we compute the lower limit for $\bar{x}$ by entering the formula =B2-B11 into cell B13.
The probability of $\bar{x}$ being between the specified lower and upper limits is computed in three steps. 1) We compute the probability of $\bar{x}$ being less than the upper limit by entering the formula =NORMSDIST(B12,B2,B8,TRUE) into cell B14. 2) We compute the probability of $\bar{x}$ being less than the lower limit by entering the formula =NORMSDIST(B13,B2,B8,TRUE) into cell B15. 3) Finally, we compute the probability of $\bar{x}$ being between the lower and upper limits by entering the formula =B14-B15 into cell B16.

Formula Worksheet:

	A	B
1	POPULATION PARAMETERS	
2	Population Mean (μ) =	990
3	Population Standard Deviation (σ) =	80
4		
5	SAMPLING DISTRIBUTION OF xbar	
6	Sample Size (*n*) =	30
7	Expected *x* bar =	=B2
8	Standard Error of the Mean =	=B3/SQRT(B6)
9		
10	PROBABILITY OF GIVEN SAMPLING ERROR	
11	Sampling Error (μ +/-) =	10
12	Upper Limit for *x* bar =	=B2+B11
13	Lower Limit for *x* bar =	=B2-B11
14	Probability of xbar <= Upper Limit =	=NORMDIST(B12,B2,B8,TRUE)
15	Probability of xbar < Lower Limit =	=NORMDIST(B13,B2,B8,TRUE)
16	Probability of xbar between Lower and Upper Limits =	=B14-B15

We see in the resulting worksheet below that the probability of the mean SAT score for the sampled applicants being within +/- 10 points of the mean SAT score for the population of applicants is .5064.

Value Worksheet:

	A	B
1	POPULATION PARAMETERS	
2	Population Mean (μ) =	990
3	Population Standard Deviation (σ) =	80
4		
5	SAMPLING DISTRIBUTION OF xbar	
6	Sample Size (*n*) =	30
7	Expected *x* bar =	990
8	Standard Error of the Mean =	14.61
9		
10	PROBABILITY OF GIVEN SAMPLING ERROR	
11	Sampling Error (μ +/-) =	10
12	Upper Limit for *x* bar =	1000
13	Lower Limit for *x* bar =	980
14	Probability of xbar <= Upper Limit =	0.7532
15	Probability of xbar < Lower Limit =	0.2468
16	Probability of xbar between Lower and Upper Limits =	0.5064

EXAMPLE 6

Sample Size and the Sampling Distribution of $\bar{x}$

Refer to Example 5. What happens to the sampling distribution of $\bar{x}$ when the sample size is increased from 30 to 100? With a sample size of 100, what is the probability that $\bar{x}$ will be between 980 and 1000?

SOLUTION 6

Using Excel's NORMDIST Function

Enter Data: We simply enter the new value, 100, for the sample size into cell B6.

Enter Functions and Formulas: There are no additions or changes necessary.

We can see in the worksheet below the impact of increasing the sample size from 30 to 100 on two values in particular. The standard error of the mean has decreased from 14.61 to 8.00. This means the bell curve representing the sampling distribution of $\bar{x}$ is narrower and more peaked. This results in more area under the curve lying between the lower and upper limits defined by the specified sampling error (μ +/- 10). In other words, the probability of $\bar{x}$ having a value between 980 and 1000 is now greater. Notice that the probability has increased from .5064 to .7887.

Value Worksheet:

	A	B
1	POPULATION PARAMETERS	
2	Population Mean (μ) =	990
3	Population Standard Deviation (σ) =	80
4		
5	SAMPLING DISTRIBUTION OF xbar	
6	Sample Size (n) =	100
7	Expected x bar =	990
8	Standard Error of the Mean =	8.00
9		
10	PROBABILITY OF GIVEN SAMPLING ERROR	
11	Sampling Error (μ +/-) =	10
12	Upper Limit for x bar =	1000
13	Lower Limit for x bar =	980
14	Probability of xbar <= Upper Limit =	0.8944
15	Probability of xbar < Lower Limit =	0.1056
16	Probability of xbar between Lower and Upper Limits =	0.7887

Sampling Distributions of $\bar{x}$

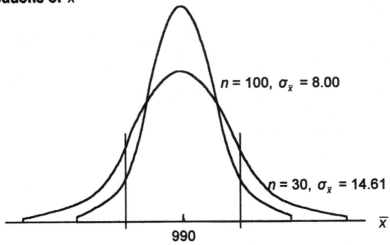

$n = 100, \sigma_{\bar{x}} = 8.00$

$n = 30, \sigma_{\bar{x}} = 14.61$

$\bar{x}$

990

EXAMPLE 7

Sampling Distribution of $\bar{p}$

Refer to the St. Andrew's sampling problem in Example 1. Describe the sampling distribution of $\bar{p}$ where $\bar{p}$ is the proportion of the 30 applicants who want on-campus housing.

SOLUTION 7

Using Excel

We will first manually compute the expected value and standard deviation of $\bar{p}$ to demonstrate the mathematical operations. The sampling distribution of $\bar{p}$ is the probability distribution of all possible values of the sample proportion $\bar{p}$. The normal probability distribution is an acceptable approximation since $np = 30(.72) = 21.6 \geq 5$ and $n(1 - p) = 30(.28) = 8.4 \geq 5$.

Expected Value of $\bar{p}$

$$E(\bar{p}) = p = .72$$

where: p = the population proportion

Standard Deviation of $\bar{p}$

$$\sigma_{\bar{p}} = \sqrt{\frac{p(1-p)}{n}}$$

where: n = the sample size

$$\sigma_{\bar{p}} = \sqrt{\frac{.72(.28)}{30}} = .082$$

Now we will demonstrate how Excel can be used to compute the expected value and standard deviation of $\bar{p}$.

Enter Data: We enter the value of the population proportion into cell B2. The sample size is entered into cell B5.

Enter Functions and Formulas: The expected value of $\bar{p}$ is simply the value of the population proportion, so we enter the formula =B2 into cell B6. We compute the standard error of the proportion by entering the formula =SQRT(B2(1-B2)/B5) into cell B7.

Formula Worksheet:

	A	B
1	POPULATION PARAMETERS	
2	Population Mean (p) =	0.72
3		
4	SAMPLING DISTRIBUTION OF pbar	
5	Sample Size (n) =	30
6	Expected $p$bar =	=B2
7	Standard Error of the Mean =	=SQRT(B2(1-B2)/B5)

Value Worksheet:

	A	B
1	POPULATION PARAMETERS	
2	Population Mean (p) =	0.72
3		
4	SAMPLING DISTRIBUTION OF pbar	
5	Sample Size (n) =	30
6	Expected $p$bar =	0.72
7	Standard Error of the Mean =	0.0820

EXAMPLE 8

Probability Information about the Size of the Sampling Error

Refer to the St. Andrew's problem in Example 1. What is the probability that a simple random sample of 30 applicants will provide an estimate of the population proportion of applicants desiring on-campus housing that is within plus or minus .05 of the actual population proportion, assuming p = .72? In other words, what is the probability that $\bar{p}$ will be between .67 and .77?

SOLUTION 8

Using Excel's NORMDIST Function

We will continue with the worksheet we developed in Example 7.

Enter Data: We enter the value of the sampling error into cell B10.

Enter Functions and Formulas: The upper limit for $\bar{p}$ is the expected value of $\bar{p}$ plus the sampling error, so we enter the formula =B2+B10 into cell B11. Similarly, we compute the lower limit for $\bar{p}$ by entering the formula =B2-B10 into cell B12.

The probability of $\bar{p}$ being between the specified lower and upper limits is computed in three steps. 1) We compute the probability of $\bar{p}$ being less than the upper limit by entering the formula =NORMSDIST(B11,B2,B7,TRUE) into cell B13. 2) We compute the probability of $\bar{p}$ being less than the lower limit by entering the formula =NORMSDIST(B12,B2,B7,TRUE) into cell B14. 3) Finally, we compute the probability of $\bar{p}$ being between the lower and upper limits by entering the formula =B13-B14 into cell B15.

Formula Worksheet:

	A	B
1	POPULATION PARAMETERS	
2	Population Mean (p) =	0.72
3		
4	SAMPLING DISTRIBUTION OF pbar	
5	Sample Size (n) =	30
6	Expected $p$bar =	=B2
7	Standard Error of the Mean =	=SQRT(B2(1-B2)/B5)
8		
9	PROBABILITY OF GIVEN SAMPLING ERROR	
10	Sampling Error (p +/-) =	0.05
11	Upper Limit for $p$bar =	=B2+B10
12	Lower Limit for $p$bar =	=B2-B10
13	Probability of $p$bar <= Upper Limit =	=NORMDIST(B11,B2,B7,TRUE)
14	Probability of $p$bar < Lower Limit =	=NORMDIST(B12,B2,B7,TRUE)
15	Probability of $p$bar Between Lower and Upper Limits =	=B13-B14

We see in the resulting worksheet below that the probability of the proportion of the 30 sampled applicants who desire on-campus housing being within +/- .05 of the population proportion is .4581.

Value Worksheet:

	A	B
1	POPULATION PARAMETERS	
2	Population Mean (p) =	0.72
3		
4	SAMPLING DISTRIBUTION OF pbar	
5	Sample Size (n) =	30
6	Expected $p$bar =	0.72
7	Standard Error of the Mean =	0.0820
8		
9	PROBABILITY OF GIVEN SAMPLING ERROR	
10	Sampling Error (p +/-) =	0.05
11	Upper Limit for $p$bar =	0.77
12	Lower Limit for $p$bar =	0.67
13	Probability of $p$bar <= Upper Limit =	0.7290
14	Probability of $p$bar < Lower Limit =	0.2710
15	Probability of $p$bar Between Lower and Upper Limits =	0.4581

EXERCISES

EXERCISE 1

Using a Random Number Table

Missy Walters owns a mail-order business specializing in clothing, linens, and furniture for children. She is considering offering her customers a discount on shipping charges for furniture based on the dollar-amount of the furniture order. Before Missy decides the discount policy, she needs a better understanding of the average dollar-amount of the furniture orders she receives.

Missy had an assistant identify all of the company's orders in the past two years that included furniture. The assistant found 750 furniture orders. Missy needs help in using the random number table shown in Example 1 to select 30 orders to include in her sample. Starting in the eleventh row of the table and moving from left to right, and then to the next row if necessary, identify the numbers of the 30 furniture orders for the sample.

EXERCISE 2

Simple Random Sampling from a Finite Population

Refer to the mail-order problem in Exercise 1. Missy's assistant found a total of 750 orders in the past two years that included furniture. To save you time, the dollar amounts of just 50 of the orders are listed below.

136	281	226	123	178	445	231	389	196	175
211	162	212	241	182	290	434	167	246	338
194	242	368	258	323	196	183	209	198	212
277	348	173	409	264	237	490	222	472	248
231	154	166	214	311	141	159	362	189	260

Use an Excel worksheet and the RAND function to select a simple random sample of 30 orders without replacement. (When you are finished, you should have 30 randomly selected order numbers in the 1 to 50 range.)

EXERCISE 3

Point Estimation of μ and σ

Refer to the mail-order problem in Exercise 1 and your sample orders in Exercise 2. What is the point estimate of the mean dollar-amount of all furniture orders? What is the point estimate for the standard deviation of the dollar-amount of all furniture orders? (Hint: Base your estimates on the sample statistics you compute using the sample orders you identified in Exercise 2.

EXERCISE 4

Sampling Distribution of $\bar{x}$

Refer to the mail-order problem in Exercise 1. Assume we know the mean and standard deviation are $249 and $46, respectively, for the 750 furniture orders. Show the sampling distribution of $\bar{x}$, where $\bar{x}$ is the mean dollar-amount of a furniture order for the 30 sampled orders.

EXERCISE 5

Probability Information about the Size of the Sampling Error

Refer to the mail-order problem in Exercise 1. What is the probability that a simple random sample of 30 furniture orders will provide an estimate of the population mean dollar-amount of a furniture order that is within plus or minus $10 of the actual population mean, assuming μ = $249 and σ = $46.?

EXERCISE 6

Sample Size and the Sampling Distribution of $\bar{x}$

Refer to the mail-order problem in Exercise 5. What happens to the sampling distribution of $\bar{x}$ when the sample size is increased from 30 to 90? With a sample size of 90, what is the probability that $\bar{x}$ will be between $229 and $269?

EXERCISE 7

Point Estimation of p

It is time for Roger Hall, manager of new car sales at the Maxwell Ford dealership in Los Angeles, to submit his order for new Mustang coupes. These cars will be parked in the lot, available for immediate sale to buyers who are not special-ordering a car. One of the decisions he must make is how many Mustangs of each color he should order. The new color options are very similar to the past year's options.

Roger believes that the colors chosen by customers who special-order their cars best reflect most customers' true color preferences. For that reason, he has tabulated the color preferences specified in a sample of 56 Mustang coupe special orders placed in the past year. The sample data are listed below.

Black	Red	White	Blue	Blue	Green	Red	Black
Red	White	Blue	White	Red	Red	Black	Black
Green	Black	Red	Black	Blue	Black	White	Green
Blue	Red	Black	White	Black	Red	Black	Blue
Blue	Black	Green	White	Black	Red	Red	White
Red	Red	Blue	Black	Red	Black	Green	Black
Green	Red	Black	White	Black	Red	Black	White

What is the point estimate of the proportion of all Mustang coupe special orders that specify a color preference of black?

EXERCISE 8

Sampling Distribution of $\bar{p}$

Refer to the Maxwell Ford problem in Exercise 7. Describe the sampling distribution of $\bar{p}$ where $\bar{p}$ is the proportion of Mustang coupe special orders that specify a color preference of black. Assume that the proportion of all (1200) Mustang coupe special orders having a color preference of black is .36.

EXERCISE 9

Probability Information about the Size of the Sampling Error

Refer to the Maxwell Ford problem in Exercise 7. What is the probability that a simple random sample of 30 special orders will provide an estimate of the population proportion of special orders specifying the color black that is within plus or minus .05 of the actual population proportion, assuming $p = .36$? In other words, what is the probability that $\bar{p}$ will be between .31 and .41?

SELF-TEST

TRUE/FALSE

____ 1. The expected value of $\bar{x}$ equals the mean of the population from which the sample is drawn, regardless of the sample size.

____ 2. An advantage of cluster sampling is that it generally requires a smaller total sample size than simple random sampling.

____ 3. The finite population correction should be used in the computation of the standard error of the mean whenever the population being sampled is finite.

____ 4. Whenever the population has a normal probability distribution, the sampling distribution of $\bar{x}$ has a normal probability distribution, regardless of the sample size.

____ 5. The process of selecting a simple random sample depends on whether the population is finite or infinite.

FILL-IN-THE-BLANK

1. The _____ provides the basis for using a normal probability distribution to approximate the sampling distribution of $\bar{x}$ and $\bar{p}$.

2. The value of the _____ is used to estimate the value of the population parameter.

3. The standard deviation of $\bar{p}$ is referred to as the _____.

4. The _____ can be used to provide probability information about how close the sample mean is to the population mean.

5. The population being studied is usually considered _____ if it involves an ongoing process that makes listing or counting every element in the population impossible.

MULTIPLE CHOICE

___ 1. A probability sampling method in which we randomly select one of the first *k* elements and then select every *k* th element thereafter is
a) stratified random sampling
b) cluster sampling
c) systematic sampling
d) convenience sampling

___ 2. The standard deviation of a point estimator is the
a) standard error
b) sample statistic
c) point estimate
d) sampling error

___ 3. Which one of the following sampling methods is classified as a nonprobability sampling method?
a) stratified random sampling
b) cluster sampling
c) systematic sampling
d) convenience sampling

___ 4. The finite population correction factor should be used in the computation of σ_x and $\sigma_{\bar{p}}$ when *n/N* is greater than
a) .01
b) .025
c) .05
d) .10

___ 5. The extent of the sampling error may be affected by all of the following factors except
a) the sampling method used
b) the sample size
c) the expected value of the sample statistic being used
d) the variability of the population

ANSWERS

EXERCISES

1) **846** 493 **896 875** 215 **754 984 953 974** 240 034 664 **929** 236 401 455 256
329 111 618 126 137 505 543 **915** 264 **994** 111 664 531 568 273 082 570
502 532 250 365 505 **915** 371   (exclude the bold-printed numbers, those > 750)

2) no <u>one</u> right answer (different random numbers result in different items selected)

3) no <u>one</u> right answer (different items sampled results in different sample statistics)

4) Normally distributed with E(x) = \$249 and $\sigma_{\bar{x}}$ = \$8.40

5) .7660

6) .9606

7) .32143

8) Normally distributed with $\bar{p}$ = .36 and $\sigma_{\bar{p}}$ = .064

9) .5646

TRUE/FALSE

1) True
2) False
3) False
4) True
5) True

FILL-IN-THE-BLANK

1) central limit theorem
2) sample statistic
3) standard error of the proportion
4) sampling distribution of $\bar{x}$
5) infinite

MULTIPLE CHOICE

1) c
2) a
3) d
4) c
5) c

CHAPTER 8

Interval Estimation

Interval Estimation of a Population Mean:
Large-Sample Case

Interval Estimation of a Population Mean:
Small-Sample Case

Determining the Sample Size to Estimate

Interval Estimation of a Population Proportion

LEARNING OBJECTIVES

1. Be able to construct and interpret an interval estimate of a population mean and/or a population proportion.

2. Understand the concept of a sampling error.

3. Be able to use knowledge of a sampling distribution to make probability statements about the sampling error.

4. Understand and be able to compute the margin of error.

5. Learn about the *t* distribution and when it should be used in constructing an interval estimate for a population mean.

6. Be able to use the worksheets presented in the chapter as templates for constructing interval estimates.

7. Be able to determine the size of a simple random sample necessary to estimate a population mean and a population proportion with a specified level of precision.

8. Know the definition of the following terms:

   confidence interval   precision
   confidence coefficient   sampling error
   confidence level   margin of error
                               degrees of freedom

REVIEW

Interval Estimation of a Population Mean: Large-Sample Case

Sampling Error
- The absolute value of the difference between an unbiased point estimate and the population parameter it estimates is called the <u>sampling error</u>.
- For the case of a sample mean estimating a population mean, the sampling error is:
$$|\bar{x} - \mu|$$
- Knowledge of the sampling distribution of $\bar{x}$ enables us to make <u>probability statements</u> about the sampling error even though the population mean μ is not known.
- A probability statement about the sampling error is a <u>precision statement</u>.
- Precision statement: "There is a $1 - \alpha$ probability that the value of a sample mean will provide a sampling error of $z_{\alpha/2}\sigma_{\bar{x}}$ or less."

Constructing an Interval Estimate

- When the population standard deviation σ is assumed known, the interval is:

$$\bar{x} \pm z_{\alpha/2} \frac{\sigma}{\sqrt{n}}$$

where: $\bar{x}$ is the sample mean

$1 - \alpha$ is the confidence coefficient

$z_{\alpha/2}$ is the z value providing an area of $\alpha/2$ in the upper

tail of the standard normal probability distribution

σ is the population standard deviation

n is the sample size

- In most applications the value of the population standard deviation is unknown.
- We use the value of the sample standard deviation, s, as the point estimate of the population standard deviation.
- When the population standard deviation σ is estimated by s, the interval is compute as:

$$\bar{x} \pm z_{\alpha/2} \frac{s}{\sqrt{n}}$$

Using Excel to Construct a Confidence Interval: σ Estimated by s

- The <u>AVERAGE</u> function is used to compute the sample mean, $\bar{x}$.
- The <u>STDEV</u> function is used to compute the sample standard deviation, s.
- The estimated standard error of the mean, $\sigma_{\bar{x}}$, is computed by formula using s and n.
- The level of significance, α, is computed by formula using the confidence coefficient.
- The <u>NORMSINV</u> function (with α as input) is used to compute the appropriate z value.
- The margin of error is computed by formula using z and $\sigma_{\bar{x}}$.
- The upper and lower limits of the confidence interval are computed by formula using $\bar{x}$ and the margin of error.

Determining the Sample Size

- Let E = the maximum sampling error mentioned in the precision statement.
- E is the amount added to and subtracted from the point estimate to obtain an interval estimate.
- E is often referred to as the <u>margin of error</u>.
- We have:

$$E = z_{\alpha/2} \frac{\sigma}{\sqrt{n}}$$

- Solving for n we have:

$$n = \frac{(z_{\alpha/2})^2 \sigma^2}{E^2}$$

Interval Estimation of a Population Mean: Small-Sample Case

- If the population is not normally distributed, the only option is to increase the sample size to $n \geq 30$ and use the large-sample interval-estimation procedures.
- If the population is normally distributed and σ is known, the large-sample interval-estimation procedure can be used.
- If the Population is normally distributed and σ is unknown, the appropriate interval estimate is based on a probability distribution known as the *t* distribution.

t Distribution

- The *t* distribution is a family of similar probability distributions.
- A specific *t* distribution depends on a parameter known as the degrees of freedom.
- As the number of degrees of freedom increases, the difference between the *t* distribution and the standard normal probability distribution becomes smaller.
- A *t* distribution with more degrees of freedom has less dispersion.
- The mean of the *t* distribution is zero.

Constructing an Interval Estimate

- When the population standard deviation σ is estimated by *s*, the interval is compute as follows:

$$\overline{x} \pm t_{\alpha/2} \frac{s}{\sqrt{n}}$$

where: $1 - \alpha$ is the confidence coefficient

$t_{\alpha/2}$ is the *t* value providing an area of

$\alpha/2$ in the upper tail of a *t* distribution
with $n - 1$ degrees of freedom

s   is the sample standard deviation

n   is the sample size

Using Excel to Construct a Confidence Interval: σ Estimated by *s*

- The AVERAGE function is used to compute the sample mean, $\overline{x}$.
- The STDEV function is used to compute the sample standard deviation, *s*.
- The estimated standard error of the mean, $\sigma_{\overline{x}}$, is computed by formula using *s* and *n*.
- The level of significance, α, is computed by formula using the confidence coefficient.
- The degrees of freedom value is computed by formula using *n*.
- The TINV function (with α and degrees of freedom as input) is used to compute the appropriate *t* value.
- The margin of error is computed by formula using *t* and $\sigma_{\overline{x}}$.
- The upper and lower limits of the confidence interval are computed by formula using $\overline{x}$ and the margin of error.

Interval Estimation of a Population Proportion

- The interval estimate of the population proportion is computed as follows:

$$\bar{p} \pm z_{\alpha/2} \sqrt{\frac{\bar{p}(1-\bar{p})}{n}}$$

where: $1 - \alpha$ is the confidence coefficient

       $z_{\alpha/2}$ is the z value providing an area of

            $\alpha/2$ in the upper tail of the standard
            normal probability distribution

       s is the sample proportion
       n is the sample size

Using Excel to Construct a Confidence Interval

- The <u>COUNTIF</u> function is used to compute the number of "successes" in the sample.
- The sample proportion, $\bar{p}$, is computed by formula using n and the number of "successes".
- The estimated standard error of the proportion, $\sigma_{\bar{p}}$, is computed by formula using n and $\bar{p}$.
- The level of significance, α, is computed by formula using the confidence coefficient.
- The <u>NORMSINV</u> function (with α as input) is used to compute the appropriate z value.
- The margin of error is computed by formula using z and $\sigma_{\bar{p}}$.
- The upper and lower limits of the confidence interval are computed by formula using $\bar{p}$ and the margin of error.

Determining the Sample Size

- Let E = the maximum sampling error mentioned in the precision statement.
- We have:

$$E = z_{\alpha/2} \sqrt{\frac{p(1-p)}{n}}$$

- Solving for n we have:

$$n = \frac{(z_{\alpha/2})^2 \, p(1-p)}{E^2}$$

KEY CONCEPTS

CONCEPT	EXAMPLES	EXERCISES
Interval Estimation of a Population Mean		
Large-Sample Case	①	1
Determining the Sample Size	2	2
Small-Sample Case	③	3
Interval Estimation of a Population Proportion	④	4
Determining the Sample Size	5	5

◯ Excel Used

EXAMPLES

EXAMPLE 1

Interval Estimate of a Population Mean:
Large-Sample Case ($n \geq 30$) and σ Estimated by s

National Discount has 260 retail outlets throughout the United States. National evaluates each potential location for a new retail outlet in part on the mean annual income of the households in the marketing area of the new location. National develops an interval estimate of the mean annual income in a potential marketing area after taking a random sample of households.

For a marketing area being studied, a sample of 36 households was taken and their incomes are listed below. Develop a 95% confidence interval for the mean annual income of households in this marketing area.

Household	Income	Household	Income	Household	Income
1	25,600	13	19,250	25	26,550
2	19,615	14	27,500	26	15,900
3	20,035	15	23,650	27	18,450
4	21,735	16	30,000	28	14,750
5	17,600	17	19,250	29	20,000
6	26,080	18	24,557	30	19,250
7	28,925	19	19,382	31	27,500
8	25,350	20	20,050	32	23,650
9	15,900	21	21,750	33	18,450
10	17,550	22	17,500	34	14,750
11	14,745	23	19,340	35	20,000
12	20,000	24	30,000	36	15,000

SOLUTION 1

Using Excel's NORMSINV Function

Excel's NORMSINV function is used to compute the appropriate z value. Because σ is unknown, s and the sample size n are used to estimate the standard error of the mean. The margin of error is computed as the product of the z value and the estimated standard error. Then by subtracting and adding the margin of error to the point estimate (the sample mean) we obtain the confidence interval.

Enter Data: A label and the income data for the 36 households are entered into cells A1:A37.

Enter Functions and Formulas: The descriptive statistics we need are provided in cells C1:C3. The sample size (n = 36) is entered into cell C1. The formula =AVERAGE(A2:A37) is entered into cell C2 to compute the sample mean, $\bar{x}$. The STDEV function is used in cell C3 to compute the standard deviation, s, for the sample data in cell A2:A37.

Cells C5:C7 are used to compute the appropriate z value. The confidence coefficient is entered into cell C5 and the level of significance, α, is computed in cell C6 by entering the formula =1-C5. Now recall from Chapter 6 that if we provide a cumulative probability as input to the NORMSINV function, it provides the corresponding z value. We want an area of $\alpha/2$ in the upper tail, so the appropriate cumulative probability is $1 - \alpha/2$. Thus, we enter the formula =NORMSINV(1-C6/2) into cell C7.

Cells C9:C10 provide the estimate of the standard error and the margin of error. In cell C9 we enter the formula =C3/SQRT(C1) to estimate the standard error. The formula =C7*C9 is entered into cell C10 to compute the margin of error.

Cells C12:C14 provide the point estimate and the lower and upper limits for the confidence interval. The point estimate of the population mean is simply the sample mean, so we enter the formula =C2 into cell C12. The lower limit of the confidence interval is the point estimate minus the margin of error, so we enter the formula =C12-C10 into cell C13. To find the upper limit of the confidence interval we add the margin of error to the point estimate, so we enter the formula =C12+C10 into cell C14.

We see the results of our computations in the value worksheet below. The sample mean and standard deviation equal $21,100.39 and $4,499.95, respectively. The appropriate z-value for a 95% confidence interval is 1.96. The estimated standard deviation for $\bar{x}$, referred to as the standard error, is $749.99. The product of the z-value and the standard error, referred to as the margin of error, is $1,469.95. Finally, the lower and upper limits of the interval estimate are computed to be $19,630.43 and $22,570.34, respectively.

Formula Worksheet:

	A	B	C
1	Income	Sample Size	36
2	25,600	Sample Mean	=AVERAGE(A2:A37)
3	19,615	Sample Std. Deviation	=STDEV(A2:A37)
4	20,035		
5	21,735	Confidence Coefficient	0.95
6	17,600	Level of Signif. (alpha)	=1-C5
7	26,080	z Value	=NORMSINV(1-C6/2)
8	28,925		
9	25,350	Standard Error	=C3/SQRT(C1)
10	15,900	Margin of Error	=C7*C9
11	17,550		
12	14,745	Point Estimate	=C2
13	20,000	Lower Limit	=C12-C10
14	19,250	Upper Limit	=C12+C10

Note: Rows 15-37 are not shown.

Value Worksheet:

	A	B	C
1	Income	Sample Size	36
2	25,600	Sample Mean	21,100.39
3	19,615	Sample Std. Deviation	4499.95
4	20,035		
5	21,735	Confidence Coefficient	0.95
6	17,600	Level of Signif. (alpha)	0.05
7	26,080	z Value	1.960
8	28,925		
9	25,350	Standard Error	749.99
10	15,900	Margin of Error	1469.95
11	17,550		
12	14,745	Point Estimate	21,100.39
13	20,000	Lower Limit	19,630.43
14	19,250	Upper Limit	22,570.34

Note: Rows 15-37 are not shown.

To recap, we are <u>95% confident</u> that the average annual income for all households in the market area being studied falls in the interval $19,630.43 to $22,570.34. As a precision statement regarding our sampling error, we can say that there is a .95 probability that the value of the sample mean for National Discount will provide a sampling error of $1,469.95 or less.

EXAMPLE 2

Sample Size for an Interval Estimate of a Population Mean

Refer again to the information in Example 1. Suppose that National's management team wants an estimate of the population mean such that there is a .95 probability that the sampling error is $500 or less. How large a sample size is needed to meet the required precision?

SOLUTION 2

Using Excel's NORMSINV Function

In the large-sample case with σ known, the margin of error E is computed as follows:

$$E = z_{\alpha/2} \frac{s}{\sqrt{n}}$$

Given values of $z_{\alpha/2}$ and σ, we can determine the sample size n needed to provide any desired margin of error. We arrange the formula above (solving for n) to get:

$$n = \frac{(z_{\alpha/2})^2 \sigma^2}{E^2}$$

We do not know the population standard deviation, σ, in this problem, so we will use the prior sample standard deviation, s, as a suitable substitute.

$$n = \frac{(1.96)^2 (4499.95)^2}{(500)^2} = 311.2$$

Thus, we will need to sample 312 households to reach a desired precision of +/- $500 at 95% confidence. In other words, in order to <u>reduce</u> the margin of error by a factor of approximately 3, we have to <u>increase</u> the sample size by a factor of nearly 9.

EXAMPLE 3

Interval Estimation of a Population Mean:
Small-Sample Case ($n < 30$) with σ Estimated by s

A reporter for a student newspaper is writing an article on the cost of off-campus housing. A sample was taken of 10 one-bedroom units within a half-mile of campus and the rents paid are listed below.

Unit	Rent	Unit	Rent
1	600	6	625
2	635	7	570
3	550	8	465
4	535	9	550
5	465	10	505

Provide a 95% confidence interval estimate of the mean rent per month for the population of one-bedroom units within a half-mile of campus. We'll assume this population to be normally distributed.

SOLUTION 3

Using Excel's TINV Function

With this being a small-sample case, σ unknown, and the population approximately normally distributed, we can use the t distribution to construct a confidence interval. At 95% confidence, $1 - \alpha = .95$, $\alpha = .05$, and $\alpha/2 = .025$. $t_{.025}$ is based on $n - 1 = 10 - 1 = 9$ degrees of freedom. In the partial t distribution table below we see that $t_{.025} = 2.262$.

Degrees	Area in Upper Tail				
of Freedom	.10	.05	.025	.01	.005
.	.	.	.	.	.
7	1.415	1.895	2.365	2.998	3.499
8	1.397	1.860	2.306	2.896	3.355
9	1.383	1.833	2.262	2.821	3.250
10	1.372	1.812	2.228	2.764	3.169
.	.	.	.	.	.

Excel's TINV function can be used to compute the appropriate t value. Because σ is unknown, s and the sample size n are used to estimate the standard error of the mean. The margin of error is computed as the product of the t value and the estimated standard error. Then by subtracting and adding the margin of error to the point estimate (the sample mean) we obtain the confidence interval. The confidence interval is of the form:

$$\bar{x} \pm t_{.025} \frac{s}{\sqrt{n}}$$

Enter Data: A label and the rent data for the 10 households are entered into cells A1:A11.

Enter Functions and Formulas: The descriptive statistics we need are provided in cells C1:C3. The sample size ($n = 10$) is entered into cell C1. The formula =AVERAGE(A2:A11) is entered into cell C2 to compute the sample mean, $\bar{x}$. The STDEV function is used in cell C3 to compute the standard deviation, s, for the sample data in cell A2:A11.

Cells C5:C8 are used to compute the appropriate t value. The confidence coefficient is entered into cell C5 and the level of significance, α, is computed in cell C6 by entering the formula =1-C5. We enter the formula =C1-1 into cell C7 to compute the degrees of freedom as the sample size minus one. Next, the t value corresponding to an upper tail area of $\alpha/2$ is computed by using the TINV function. The TINV function has two arguments, level of significance (in cell C6) and degrees of freedom (in cell C7). Now we enter the formula =TINV(C6,C7) into cell C8.

Cells C10:C11 provide the estimate of the standard error and the margin of error. In cell C10 we enter the formula =C3/SQRT(C1) to estimate the standard error. The formula =C8*C10 is entered into cell C11 to compute the margin of error.

Cells C13:C15 provide the point estimate and the lower and upper limits for the confidence interval. The point estimate of the population mean is simply the sample mean, so we enter the formula =C2 into cell C13. The lower limit of the confidence interval is the point estimate minus the margin of error, so we enter the formula =C13-C11 into cell C14. To find the upper limit of the confidence interval we add the margin of error to the point estimate, so we enter the formula =C13+C11 into cell C15.

Formula Worksheet:

	A	B	C
1	Rent	Sample Size	10
2	600	Sample Mean	=AVERAGE(A2:A11)
3	635	Sample Std. Deviation	=STDEV(A2:A11)
4	550		
5	535	Confidence Coefficient	0.95
6	465	Level of Signif. (alpha)	=1-C5
7	625	Degrees of Freedom	=C1-1
8	570	*t* Value	=TINV(C6,C7)
9	465		
10	550	Standard Error	=C3/SQRT(C1)
11	505	Margin of Error	=C8*C10
12			
13		Point Estimate	=C2
14		Lower Limit	=C13-C11
15		Upper Limit	=C13+C11

We see the results of our computations in the worksheet below. The sample mean and standard deviation equal $550.00 and $60.05, respectively. The appropriate *t*-value for a 95% confidence interval is 2.2622. The estimated standard deviation for $\bar{x}$, referred to as the standard error, is $18.988. The product of the z-value and the standard error, referred to as the margin of error, is $42.955. Finally, the lower and upper limits of the interval estimate are computed to be $507.05 and $592.95.

Value Worksheet:

	A	B	C
1	Rent	Sample Size	10
2	600	Sample Mean	550.00
3	635	Sample Std. Deviation	60.05
4	550		
5	535	Confidence Coefficient	0.95
6	465	Level of Signif. (alpha)	0.05
7	625	Degrees of Freedom	9
8	570	*t* Value	2.2622
9	465		
10	550	Standard Error	18.988
11	505	Margin of Error	42.955
12			
13		Point Estimate	550.00
14		Lower Limit	507.05
15		Upper Limit	592.95

To summarize, we are 95% confident that the mean rent per month for the population of one-bedroom units within a half-mile of campus is between $507.05 and $592.95. These limits found using Excel are virtually the same (only a 3-cent difference) as the limits we manually computed earlier. (The *t* value used in Excel is more accurate than the one we found in the *t* Distribution table.)

EXAMPLE 4

Interval Estimation of a Population Proportion

Political Science, Inc. (PSI) specializes in voter polls and surveys designed to keep political office seekers informed of their position in a race. Using telephone surveys, interviewers ask registered voters who they would vote for if the election were held that day.

In a recent election campaign, PSI found that 220 registered voters, out of 500 contacted, favored a particular candidate. PSI wants to develop a 95% confidence interval estimate for the proportion of the population of registered voters that favors the candidate.

SOLUTION 4

Using Excel's NORMSINV Function

Excel can be used to develop a 95% confidence interval estimate for the proportion of the population of registered voters that favors the candidate. Assume that the responses to PSI's voter poll had been recorded as a Yes or No for each registered voter polled. The form of the confidence interval is $\bar{p} \pm z_{\alpha/2}\sqrt{\bar{p}(1-\bar{p})/n}$.

Enter Data: A label and the Yes-No data for the 500 registered voters are entered into cells A1:A501.

Enter Functions and Formulas: The descriptive statistics we need are entered into cells C1:C3. The sample size ($n = 500$) is entered into cell C1. The COUNTIF function is used to count the number of Yes responses in the data. Thus, we enter the formula =COUNTIF(A2:A501,"Yes") into cell C2. The sample proportion is computed in cell C3 by dividing the number of Yes responses by the sample size (=C2/C1).

Cells C5:C7 are used to compute the appropriate z value. The confidence coefficient (0.95) is entered into cell C5 and the level of significance (α) is computed in cell C6 by entering the formula =1-C5. The z value corresponding to an upper tail area of $\alpha/2$ is computed by entering the formula =NORMSINV(1-C6/2) into cell C7.

Cells C9:C10 provide the estimate of the standard error of the proportion and the margin of error. In cell C9 we enter the formula =SQRT(C3*(1-C3)/C1) to compute the standard error using the sample proportion and the sample size as inputs. The formula =C7*C9 is entered into cell C10 to compute the margin of error.

Cells C12:C14 provide the point estimate and the lower and upper limits for a confidence interval. The point estimate in cell C12 is the sample proportion. The lower and upper limits in cells C13 and C14 are obtained by subtracting and adding the margin of error to the point estimate.

Formula Worksheet:

	A	B	C
1	Favored	Sample Size	500
2	Yes	Total Yes	=COUNTIF(A2:A501,"Yes")
3	Yes	Sample Proportion	=C2/C1
4	No		
5	Yes	Confid. Coefficient	0.95
6	No	Lev. of Signif. (alpha)	=1-C5
7	No	z Value	=NORMSINV(1-C6/2)
8	No		
9	No	Standard Error	=SQRT(C3*(1-C3)/C1)
10	Yes	Margin of Error	=C7*C9
11	No		
12	Yes	Point Estimate	=C3
13	No	Lower Limit	=C12-C10
14	No	Upper Limit	=C12+C10

Note: Rows 15-501 are not shown.

We see in the value worksheet below that we are 95% confident that the proportion of the population of registered voters that favors the candidate is between .3965 and .4835.

Value Worksheet:

	A	B	C
1	Favored	Sample Size	500
2	Yes	Total Yes	220
3	Yes	Sample Proportion	0.4400
4	No		
5	Yes	Confid. Coefficient	0.95
6	No	Lev. of Signif. (alpha)	0.05
7	No	z Value	1.9600
8	No		
9	No	Standard Error	0.02220
10	Yes	Margin of Error	0.04351
11	No		
12	Yes	Point Estimate	0.4400
13	No	Lower Limit	0.3965
14	No	Upper Limit	0.4835

Note: Rows 15-501 are not shown.

EXAMPLE 5

Sample Size for an Interval Estimate of a Population Proportion

Refer again to Example 4. Suppose that PSI would like a .99 probability that the sample proportion is within +/- .03 of the population proportion. How large a sample size is needed to meet the required precision?

SOLUTION 5

Using Excel's NORMSINV Function

The margin of error, *E*, associated with an estimate of a population proportion is:

$$E = z_{\alpha/2}\sqrt{p(1-p)/n}$$

We see that the margin of error is based on the values of $z_{\alpha/2}$, *p*, and *n*. We can determine the sample size *n* needed to provide any desired margin of error by rearranging the formula above (solving for *n*) to get:

$$n = \frac{(z_{\alpha/2})^2 p(1-p)}{E^2}$$

We do not know the population proportion, *p*, in this problem, so we will use the prior sample proportion, $\bar{p}$ = .44, as a suitable substitute. At 99% confidence, $z_{.005}$ = 2.575, approximately.

$$n = \frac{(z_{\alpha/2})^2 p(1-p)}{E^2} = \frac{(2.575)^2(.44)(.56)}{(.03)^2} = 1815.32$$

The required sample size is 1816. Note: If the prior sample of 500 voters had not been taken and no estimate of p was available, then $p = .5$ could be assumed because it provides the largest sample size recommendation. (If we had used $p = .5$, the recommended n would have been 1842.)

EXERCISES

EXERCISE 1

Interval Estimate of a Population Mean:
Large-Sample Case ($n > 30$) and σ Estimated by s

An apartment complex developer is considering building apartments in College Town, but first wants to do a market study. A sample of monthly rent values ($) for one-bedroom apartments in College Town was taken. The data collected from the 70-apartment sample is presented below. Develop a 98% confidence interval for the mean monthly rent for all one-bedroom apartments in this city.

```
440 575 580 435 600 435 435 600 615 425
440 515 525 445 525 445 445 550 570 450
450 485 490 450 490 460 460 500 500 465
480 480 480 475 475 475 472 470 470 465
510 500 500 490 480 465 460 450 450 450
510 440 440 525 445 535 549 445 450 615
575 440 435 590 435 600 600 430 430 570
```

EXERCISE 2

Sample Size for an Interval Estimate of a Population Mean

Refer to the apartment rent problem in Exercise 1. Suppose that the apartment developer wants an estimate of the population mean such that there is a .98 probability that the sampling error is $10 or less. How large a sample size is needed to meet the required precision?

EXERCISE 3

Interval Estimation of a Population Mean:
Small-Sample Case ($n < 30$) with σ Estimated by s

The manager of Hudson Auto Repair wants to advertise one price for an engine tune-up, with parts included. Before he decides the price to advertise, he needs a good estimate of the average cost of tune-up parts. A sample of 20 customer invoices for tune-ups has been taken and the costs of parts, rounded to the nearest dollar, are listed below.

Provide a 90% confidence interval estimate of the mean cost of parts per tune-up for all of the tune-ups performed at Hudson Auto Repair. We will assume this population to be normally distributed.

| 91 | 78 | 93 | 57 | 75 | 52 | 99 | 80 | 105 | 62 |
| 104 | 74 | 62 | 68 | 97 | 73 | 77 | 65 | 80 | 109 |

EXERCISE 4

Interval Estimation of a Population Proportion

The manager of University Credit Union (UCU) is concerned about checking account transaction discrepancies. Customers are bringing transaction errors to the attention of the bank's staff three months or more after they occur. The manager would like to know what proportion of his customers balance their checking accounts within 30 days of receiving a transaction statement from the bank.

Using systematic random sampling, 400 checking account customers are contacted by telephone and asked if they routinely balance their accounts within 30 days of receiving a statement. 271 of the 400 customers respond Yes.

Develop a 95% confidence interval estimate for the proportion of the population of checking account customers at UCU that routinely balance their accounts in a timely manner.

EXERCISE 5

Sample Size for an Interval Estimate of a Population Proportion

Refer again to the University Credit Union problem in Exercise 4. Suppose that UCU would like a .95 probability that the sample proportion is within +/- .025 of the population proportion. How large a sample size is needed to meet the required precision?

SELF-TEST

TRUE/FALSE

____ 1. As the degrees of freedom increase, the *t* distribution approaches the normal distribution.

____ 2. If the margin of error in an interval estimate of μ is 4.6, the interval estimate equals $\bar{x} \pm 2.3$.

____ 3. The level of significance is the probability of correctly concluding that a confidence interval estimate of μ will contain μ.

____ 4. The *t* distribution is based on the assumption that the population has a normal, or approximately normal, probability distribution.

____ 5. In actual practice, only one sample is selected to develop an interval estimate.

FILL-IN-THE-BLANK

1. The *t* distribution is a family of similar probability distributions, with each individual distribution depending on a parameter known as the _____.

2. "There is a .90 probability that the sample proportion will provide a sampling error of .035 or less" is an example of a _____.

3. The sample mean $\bar{x}$ can be used as a(n) _____ of the population mean μ.

4. To compute the minimum sample size for an interval estimate of μ or p, we must first decide the desired _____.

5. The use of the normal distribution as an approximation of the sampling distribution of $\bar{p}$ is based on the condition that both np and $n(1 - p)$ equal _____ or more.

MULTIPLE CHOICE

____ 1. The sample size that guarantees all estimates of proportions will meet the margin of error requirement is computed using a planning value of p equal to
   a) .01
   b) .50
   c) .51
   d) .99

___ 2. We can reduce the margin of error in an interval estimate by doing any one of the following <u>except</u>
   a) increasing the sample size
   b) increasing the level of significance
   c) using the *t* distribution rather than the standard normal distribution
   d) reducing the confidence coefficient

___ 3. In determining an interval estimate of a population mean based on a small sample, we use a *t* distribution with
   a) $\sqrt{n-1}$ degrees of freedom
   b) $\sqrt{n}$ degrees of freedom
   c) $n - 1$ degrees of freedom
   d) n degrees of freedom

___ 4. The expression used to compute an interval estimate of μ may depend on any of the following factors <u>except</u>
   a) the sample size
   b) whether the population standard deviation is known
   c) whether the population has an approximately normal probability distribution
   d) whether there is sampling error

___ 5. The mean of the *t* distribution is
   a) 0
   b) .5
   c) 1
   d) problem specific

ANSWERS

EXERCISES

1) 475.58 to 506.02   2) 162

3) 80.05 to 86.59   4) .632 to .723

5) 1343

TRUE/FALSE

1) True
2) False
3) False
4) True
5) True

FILL-IN-THE-BLANK

1) degrees of freedom
2) statement of precision
3) point estimator
4) margin of error
5) 5

MULTIPLE CHOICE

1) b
2) c
3) c
4) d
5) a

CHAPTER 9

Hypothesis Testing

Developing Null and Alternative Hypotheses

Type I and Type II Errors

One-Tailed Tests About a Population Mean:
Large-Sample Case

Two-Tailed Tests About a Population Mean:
Large-Sample Case

Tests About a Population Mean: Small-Sample Case

Tests About a Population Proportion

Hypothesis Testing and Decision Making

Calculating the Probability of Type II Errors

Determining the Sample Size for a
Hypothesis Test About a Population Mean

LEARNING OBJECTIVES

1. Learn how to formulate and test hypotheses about a population mean and a population proportion.

2. Be able to use an Excel worksheet to conduct hypothesis tests about population means and proportions.

3. Understand the types of errors possible when conducting a hypothesis test.

4. Be able to determine the probability of making various errors in hypothesis tests.

5. Know how to compute and interpret *p*-values.

6. Know the definition of the following terms:

    null hypothesis   level of significance
    alternative hypothesis   one-tailed test
    type I error   two-tailed test
    type II error   *p*-value
    critical value

REVIEW

Developing Null and Alternative Hypotheses
- <u>Hypothesis testing</u> can be used to determine whether a statement about the value of a population parameter should or should not be rejected.
- The <u>null hypothesis</u>, denoted by H_0, is a tentative assumption about a population parameter.
- The <u>alternative hypothesis</u>, denoted by H_a, is the opposite of what is stated in the null.
- Hypothesis testing is similar to a criminal trial. The hypotheses are:
    - H_0: The defendant is innocent
    - H_a: The defendant is guilty

Testing Research Hypotheses
- The research hypothesis should be expressed as the alternative hypothesis.
- The conclusion that the research hypothesis is true comes from sample data that contradict the null hypothesis.

Testing the Validity of a Claim
- Manufacturers' claims are usually given the benefit of the doubt and stated as the null hypothesis.
- The conclusion that the claim is false comes from sample data that contradict the null hypothesis.

Testing in Decision-Making Situations
- A decision maker might have to choose between two courses of action, one associated with the null hypothesis and another associated with the alternative hypothesis.
- Example: Accepting a shipment of goods from a supplier or returning the shipment of goods to the supplier.

Summary of Forms for Null and Alternative Hypotheses about a Population Mean
- The equality part of the hypotheses always appears in the null hypothesis.
- In general, a hypothesis test about the value of a population mean μ must take one of the following three forms (where μ_0 is the hypothesized value of the population mean).

$$H_0 : \mu \geq \mu_0 \qquad H_0 : \mu \leq \mu_0 \qquad H_0 : \mu = \mu_0$$
$$H_a : \mu < \mu_0 \qquad H_a : \mu > \mu_0 \qquad H_a : \mu \neq \mu_0$$

Type I and Type II Errors
- Since hypothesis tests are based on sample data, we must allow for the chance of errors.
- A <u>Type I error</u> is rejecting H_0 when it is true.
- A <u>Type II error</u> is accepting H_0 when it is false.
- The person conducting the hypothesis test specifies the maximum allowable probability of making a Type I error, denoted by α and called the <u>level of significance.</u>
- Generally, we cannot control for the probability of making a Type II error, denoted by β.
- Statisticians avoid the risk of making a Type II error by using "do not reject H_0" and not "accept H_0".

One-Tailed Tests About a Population Mean: Large-Sample Case

p -Values for One-Tailed Tests
- The <u>p -value</u> is the probability of obtaining a sample result that is at least as unlikely as what is observed.
- The p -value can be used to make the decision in a hypothesis test by noting that if the p -value is less than the level of significance α, the value of the test statistic is in the rejection region. If the p -value is greater than or equal to α, the value of the test statistic is not in the rejection region.
- Reject H_0 if the p-value < α.

Steps of Hypothesis Testing: One-Tailed Case
- Determine the <u>appropriate hypotheses</u>.
    - $H_0 : \mu \geq \mu_0$ and $H_a : \mu < \mu_0$ (left-tailed test)
    - $H_0 : \mu \leq \mu_0$ and $H_a : \mu > \mu_0$ (right-tailed test)
- Select the <u>test statistic</u> for deciding whether or not to reject the null hypothesis.
    - If σ is assumed known:

$$z = \frac{\overline{x} - \mu_0}{\sigma / \sqrt{n}}$$

    - If σ is estimated by s:

$$z = \frac{\overline{x} - \mu_0}{s / \sqrt{n}}$$

- Specify the <u>level of significance</u> α for the test.
- Use α to develop the <u>rule for rejecting</u> H_0.
  - Reject H_0 if $z < -z_\alpha$ (if left-tailed test)
  - Reject H_0 if $z > z_\alpha$ (if right-tailed test)
  - Reject H_0 if p-value $< \alpha$
- Collect the sample data and compute the value of the test statistic.
- Compare the test statistic to the critical value(s) in the rejection rule, or compute the p-value based on the test statistic and compare it to α, to determine whether or not to reject H_0.

Using Excel to Conduct a One-Tailed Hypothesis Test
- The <u>AVERAGE</u> function is used to compute the sample mean, $\bar{x}$.
- The <u>STDEV</u> function is used to compute the sample standard deviation, s.
- The estimated standard error of the mean, $\sigma_{\bar{x}}$, is computed by formula using s and n.
- The level of significance, α, is computed by formula using the confidence coefficient.
- The <u>NORMSINV</u> function (with $1 - \alpha$ as input) is used to compute the critical value, z_α.
- The test statistic, z, is computed by formula using $\bar{x}$, μ_0, and $\sigma_{\bar{x}}$.
- The <u>NORMSDIST</u> function (with z as input) is used to compute the p-value.
- The decision to reject or not reject H_0 is made based on a comparison of the p-value and α (or on a comparison of the test statistic and the critical value).

Two-Tailed Tests About a Population Mean: Large-Sample Case

p-Values for Two-Tailed Tests
- In a two-tailed test, the p-value is found by doubling the area in the tail.
- The doubling of the area in the tail is done so that the p-value can be compared directly to α and the same rejection rule can be maintained.
- Without the doubling of the area in the tail, a p-value rule based on the tail area of $\alpha/2$ would be needed.
- The advantage of this definition of the p-value is that the p-value can be compared directly to the level of significance α. In other words, reject H_0 if p-value $< \alpha$.

Steps of Hypothesis Testing: Two-Tailed Case
- The steps are the same as in the one-tailed case with the following exceptions:
  - <u>Hypotheses</u>
  $$H_0 : \mu = \mu_0 \text{ and } H_a : \mu \neq \mu_0$$
  - <u>Rejection Rule</u>
  Reject H_0 if $z < -z_{\alpha/2}$ or if $z > z_{\alpha/2}$ or if p-value $< \alpha$

Using Excel to Conduct a Two-Tailed Hypothesis Test
- The <u>AVERAGE</u> function is used to compute the sample mean, $\bar{x}$.
- The <u>STDEV</u> function is used to compute the sample standard deviation, s.
- The estimated standard error of the mean, $\sigma_{\bar{x}}$, is computed by formula using s and n.
- The level of significance, α, is computed by formula using the confidence coefficient.

- The <u>NORMSINV</u> function is used twice, to compute lower-tail and upper-tail critical values.
  - For the lower-tail critical value, the NORMSINV function argument is $\alpha/2$.
  - For the upper-tail critical value, the NORMSINV function argument is $1 - \alpha/2$.
- The test statistic, z, is computed by formula using $\bar{x}$, μ_0, and $\sigma_{\bar{x}}$.
- The <u>NORMSDIST</u> function (with $|z|$ as input) is used to compute the p-value.
- The decision to reject or not reject H_0 is made based on a comparison of the p-value and α (or on a comparison of the test statistic and the two critical values).

Confidence Interval Approach to a Two-Tailed Hypothesis Test
- The steps are the same as above with one exception, the rejection rule.
- Reject H_0 if the confidence interval does <u>not</u> contain the hypothesized value μ_0.

One-Tailed Tests About a Population Mean: Small-Sample Case
- If the distribution of the population <u>is not</u> approximately normal, the sample size must be increased to 30 or more in order to conduct the hypothesis test.
- If the distribution of the population <u>is</u> approximately normal, we can proceed below.

Steps of Hypothesis Testing
- The steps are the same as in the large-sample case with the following exceptions.
- <u>Test statistic</u>:
  - The test statistic has a t distribution with $n - 1$ degrees of freedom.
  - If σ is assumed known:

$$t = \frac{\bar{x} - \mu_0}{\sigma/\sqrt{n}}$$

  - If σ is estimated by s:

$$t = \frac{\bar{x} - \mu_0}{s/\sqrt{n}}$$

- <u>Rejection rule</u>:
  - Reject H_0 if $t < -t_\alpha$ (if left-tailed test)
  - Reject H_0 if $t > t_\alpha$ (if right-tailed test)
  - Reject H_0 if p-value $< \alpha$

Using Excel to Conduct a One-Tailed Hypothesis Test: Small-Sample Test
- The <u>AVERAGE</u> function is used to compute the sample mean, $\bar{x}$.
- The <u>STDEV</u> function is used to compute the sample standard deviation, s.
- The estimated standard error of the mean, $\sigma_{\bar{x}}$, is computed by formula using s and n.
- The level of significance, α, is computed by formula using the confidence coefficient.
- The degrees of freedom (df) value is computed by formula using n.
- The <u>TINV</u> function (with 2α and df as input) is used to compute the critical value, t_α.
- The test statistic, t, is computed by formula using $\bar{x}$, μ_0, and $\sigma_{\bar{x}}$.
- The <u>TDIST</u> function (with t, degrees of freedom, and 1 tail as input) is used to compute the p-value. (Note: if t is negative, enter a value of $-t$ in TDIST.)
- The decision to reject or not reject H_0 is made based on a comparison of the p-value and α (or a comparison of t and t_α).

Two-Tailed Tests About a Population Mean: Small-Sample Case

Steps of Hypothesis Testing
- The steps are the same as the two-tail case with the following exceptions.
- <u>Hypotheses</u>: $H_0 : \mu = \mu_0$ and $H_a : \mu \neq \mu_0$
- <u>Rejection rule</u>:   Reject H_0 if $t < -t_{\alpha/2}$ or $t > t_{\alpha/2}$ or p-value $< \alpha$

Using Excel to Conduct a Two-Tailed Hypothesis Test: Small-Sample Test
- The <u>AVERAGE</u> function is used to compute the sample mean, $\overline{x}$.
- The <u>STDEV</u> function is used to compute the sample standard deviation, s.
- The estimated standard error of the mean, $\sigma_{\overline{x}}$, is computed by formula using s and n.
- The level of significance, α, is computed by formula using the confidence coefficient.
- The degrees of freedom value is computed by formula using n.
- The lower-tail and upper-tail critical values are computed as follows:
  - For the lower tail, the <u>TINV</u> function is used with α and degrees of freedom as input.
  - For the upper tail, -<u>TINV</u> is used with α and degrees of freedom as input.
- The test statistic, t, is computed by formula using $\overline{x}$, μ_0, and $\sigma_{\overline{x}}$.
- The <u>TDIST</u> function (with t, degrees of freedom, and 2 tails as input) is used to compute the p-value. (Note: if t is negative, enter a value of $-t$ in TDIST.)
- The decision to reject or not reject H_0 is made based on a comparison of the p-value and α (or a comparison of t and the two critical values).

Tests About a Population Proportion

Summary of Forms for Hypotheses about a Population Proportion
- The equality part of the hypotheses always appears in the null hypothesis.
- In general, a hypothesis test about the value of a population proportion p must take one of the following three forms (where p_0 is the hypothesized value of the population mean):

$$H_0 : p \geq p_0 \qquad H_0 : p \leq p_0 \qquad H_0 : p = p_0$$
$$H_a : p < p_0 \qquad H_a : p > p_0 \qquad H_a : p \neq p_0$$

One-Tailed Tests About a Population Proportion: Large-Sample Case

Steps of Hypothesis Testing
- The steps are the same as in the one-tailed, large-sample test of a population mean with the following exception.
- <u>Test statistic</u>:

$$z = \frac{\overline{p} - p_0}{\sigma_{\overline{p}}}$$

$$\text{where: } \sigma_p = \sqrt{\frac{p_0(1 - p_0)}{n}}$$

Using Excel to Conduct One-Tailed Hypothesis Tests about a Population Proportion
- The <u>COUNTIF</u> function is used to compute the number of "successes" in the sample.
- Sample proportion, $\bar{p}$, is computed by formula using the number of successes and n.
- Estimated standard error of the proportion, $\sigma_{\bar{p}}$, is computed by formula using p_0 and n.
- The level of significance, α, is computed by formula using the confidence coefficient.
- The <u>NORMSINV</u> function (with α as input) is used to compute the critical value, z_α.
- The test statistic, z, is computed by formula using $\bar{p}$, p_0, and $\sigma_{\bar{p}}$.
- The <u>NORMSDIST</u> function (with z as input) is used to compute the p-value.
- The decision to reject or not reject H_0 is made based on a comparison of the p-value and α (or a comparison of the test statistic and the critical value).

KEY CONCEPTS

<u>CONCEPT</u>	<u>EXAMPLES</u>	<u>EXERCISES</u>
Tests About a Population Mean		
Developing Null and Alternative Hypotheses	1,2,4,5	1,2,3,4
One-Tailed Test: Large-Sample	①	1
Two-Tailed Test: Large-Sample	②	2
One-Tailed Test: Small-Sample	④	3
Two-Tailed Test: Small-Sample	5	4
p-Value Approach	①②④⑤	1,2,3,4
Confidence Interval Approach	③	2
Tests About a Population Proportion		
Developing Null and Alternative Hypotheses	6	5
Two-Tailed Test: Large-Sample	⑥	5
p-Value Approach	⑥	5

○ Excel Used

 **EXAMPLES**

EXAMPLE 1

One-Tailed Test about a Population Mean: Large *n*

A major west coast city provides one of the most comprehensive emergency medical services in the world. Operating in a multiple hospital system with approximately 20 mobile medical units, the service goal is to respond to medical emergencies with a mean time of 12 minutes or less.

The director of medical services wants to conduct a hypothesis test, using a sample of emergency response times, to determine whether or not the service goal of 12 minutes or less is being achieved. A random sample of 40 emergencies was taken. The average response time was 13.25 minutes with a standard deviation of 3.2 minutes.

Complete the hypothesis test with α = .05 and draw your conclusion using both the test statistic and *p*-value approaches.

SOLUTION 1

Using Excel's *NORMSINV* and *NORMSDIST* Functions

We illustrate below each step of this one-tailed hypothesis test. The necessary calculations are performed both manually, to illustrate the mathematical operations, and with the use of Excel.

Step 1: Determine the null and alternative hypotheses

H_0: $\mu \le 12$ The emergency service is meeting the response goal.
No follow-up action is necessary.

H_a: $\mu > 12$ The emergency service is not meeting the response goal.
Appropriate follow-up action is necessary.

where: μ = mean response time for the population of medical emergency requests.

Step 2: Select the test statistic to be used to decide whether to reject H_0

With $n \ge 30$ and σ unknown, the appropriate test statistic is:

$$z = \frac{\bar{x} - \mu_0}{s / \sqrt{n}}$$

Step 3: Specify the level of significance α

α = .05

Step 4: Develop the rejection rule based on the level of significance

Reject H_0 if $z > 1.645$

Step 5: Collect the data and compute the value of the test statistic

With $n = 40$, $\bar{x} = 13.25$ minutes, and $s = 3.2$ minutes, the value of z is:

$$z = \frac{\bar{x} - \mu_0}{s/\sqrt{n}} = \frac{13.25 - 12}{3.2/\sqrt{40}} = 2.47$$

Step 6: a) Compare the value of the test statistic to the critical value(s)

$z = 2.47 > 1.645$

or b) Compute the *p*-value and compare it to α

With $z = 2.47$, the upper tail area $= .5000 - .4932 = .0068$

$p = .0068 < .05$

Step 7: State your conclusion regarding H_0

Reject H_0. We are 95% confident that Metro EMS is not meeting the response goal of 12 minutes or less. Appropriate action should be taken to improve service.

Now we will use Excel to conduct a hypothesis test for the emergency medical services study.

Enter Data: The response times for the sample of 40 emergencies are entered into cells A2:A41 along with an appropriate label.

Enter Functions and Formulas: The descriptive statistics we need are entered into cells C1:C3. The sample size, 40, is entered into cell C1. The AVERAGE function is used in cell C2 to compute the sample mean, and the STDEV function is used in cell C3 to compute the sample standard deviation.

The level of significance, .05, is entered into cell C5. Because this is an upper-tail test, we must compute a critical value for the upper tail of the sampling distribution. We compute the critical value by entering the formula =NORMSINV(1-C5) into cell C6.

Next, the hypothesized value of the population mean, 12, is entered into cell C8. We obtain an estimate of the standard error of the mean in cell C9 by dividing the sample standard deviation in cell C3 by the square root of the sample size in cell C1. The value of the test statistic z is computed in cell C10 by dividing the difference between the sample mean and the hypothesized population mean by the standard error. The *p*-value is computed by entering the formula =1-NORMSDIST(C10) into cell C11.

Finally, if the *p*-value is less than α, we reject H_0; otherwise we do not reject H_0. Hence, we enter the formula =IF(C11<C5,"Reject","Do Not Reject") into cell C12. Similarly, if the test statistic, z, is greater than the critical value, we reject H_0. Hence, we could have entered the formula =IF(C10>C6,"Reject","Do Not Reject") into cell C12. Either approach will yield the same conclusion.

Formula Worksheet:

	A	B	C
1	Response Time	Sample Size	40
2	19.5	Sample Mean	=AVERAGE(A2:A41)
3	15.2	Sample Std. Dev.	=STDEV(A2:A41)
4	11.0		
5	12.8	Lev. of Signif.	0.05
6	12.4	Critical Value	=NORMSINV(1-C5)
7	20.3		
8	9.6	Hypoth. Value	12
9	10.9	Standard Error	=C3/SQRT(C1)
10	16.2	Test Statistic	=(C2-C8)/C9
11	13.4	*p*-Value	=1-NORMSDIST(C10)
12	19.7	Conclusion	=IF(C11<C5,"Reject","Do Not Reject")

Note: Rows 13-41 are not shown.

We see in the resulting worksheet below that the value of the test statistic, *p*-value, and conclusion agree with the results from our earlier, manual calculations.

Value Worksheet:

	A	B	C
1	Response Time	Sample Size	40
2	19.5	Sample Mean	13.25
3	15.2	Sample Std. Dev.	3.20
4	11.0		
5	12.8	Lev. of Signif.	0.05
6	12.4	Critical Value	1.645
7	20.3		
8	9.6	Hypoth. Value	12
9	10.9	Standard Error	0.5060
10	16.2	Test Statistic	2.471
11	13.4	*p*-Value	0.0067
12	19.7	Conclusion	Reject

Note: Rows 13-41 are not shown.

EXAMPLE 2

Two-Tailed Test about a Population Mean: Large *n*

The production line for Glow toothpaste is designed to fill tubes of toothpaste with a mean weight of 6 ounces.

Periodically, a sample of 30 tubes will be selected in order to check the filling process. Quality assurance procedures call for the continuation of the filling process if the sample results are consistent with the assumption that the mean filling weight for the population of toothpaste tubes is 6 ounces; otherwise the filling process will be stopped and adjusted.

The mean and standard deviation for the most recent sample were 6.1 ounces and .2 ounces, respectively. Using both the test statistic and *p*-value approaches, conduct a hypothesis test with $\alpha = .02$ to determine if the process requires adjustment.

SOLUTION 2

Using Excel's *NORMSINV* and *NORMSDIST* Functions

A two-tailed hypothesis test about the population mean can be used to help determine whether the filling process should be allowed to continue or be stopped and adjusted.

Step 1: Determine the null and alternative hypotheses

H_0: $\mu = 6$ The population mean equals the desired mean of 6 ounces.
No process adjustment is necessary.

H_a: $\mu \neq 6$ The population mean does not equal the desired mean of 6 oz.
Appropriate corrective action is necessary.

Step 2: Select the test statistic to be used to decide whether to reject H_0

With $n \geq 30$ and σ unknown, the appropriate test statistic is:

$$z = \frac{\bar{X} - \mu_0}{s/\sqrt{n}}$$

Step 3: Specify the level of significance α

$\alpha = .02$

Step 4: Develop the rejection rule based on the level of significance

Reject H_0 if $z < -2.33$ or if $z > 2.33$

Step 5: Collect the data and compute the value of the test statistic
With $n = 30$, $\bar{x} = 6.1$ ounces, and $s = .2$ ounces, the value of z is:

$$z = \frac{\bar{X} - \mu_0}{s/\sqrt{n}} = \frac{6.1 - 6.0}{.2/\sqrt{30}} = 2.74$$

Step 6: a) <u>Compare the value of the test statistic to the critical value(s)</u>

$z = 2.74 > 2.33$

or b) <u>Compute the *p*-value and compare it to α</u>

With $z = 2.74$, the upper tail area = .5000 - .4969 = .0031

$p = 2(.0031) = .0062 < .02$ (Note: *p*-value is doubled; this is a two-tailed test.)

Step 7: <u>State your conclusion regarding H_0</u>

Reject H_0. We are 98% confident that that the mean filling weight of the toothpaste tubes is not 6 ounces. The filling process should be stopped and the filling mechanism adjusted.

Now we will use Excel to conduct a two-tailed hypothesis test for the toothpaste tube-filling study. The steps involved are nearly identical to those outlined in the solution to Example 1. The primary difference is that here, because this is a two-tailed test, we must compute <u>two</u> critical values for the test statistic.

Enter Data: The fill weights for the sample of 30 toothpaste tubes are entered into cells A2:A31 along with an appropriate label.

Enter Functions and Formulas: The descriptive statistics we need are entered into cells C1:C3. The sample size, 30, is entered into cell C1. The AVERAGE function is used in cell C2 to compute the sample mean, and the STDEV function is used in cell C3 to compute the sample standard deviation.

The level of significance, .02, is entered into cell C5. Because this is a two-tailed test, we must compute a critical value for the lower tail and a critical value for the upper tail of the sampling distribution. We compute the lower-tail critical value by entering the formula =NORMSINV(C5/2) into cell C6. We compute the upper-tail critical value by entering the formula =NORMSINV(1-C5/2) into cell C7.

Next, the hypothesized value of the population mean, 6, is entered into cell C9. We obtain an estimate of the standard error of the mean in cell C10 by dividing the sample standard deviation in cell C3 by the square root of the sample size in cell C1. The value of the test statistic *z* is computed in cell C11 by dividing the difference between the sample mean and the hypothesized population mean by the standard error. The *p*-value is computed by entering the formula =2*(1-NORMSDIST(C11)) into cell C12.

Finally, if the *p*-value is less than α, we reject H_0; otherwise we do not reject H_0. Hence, we enter the formula =IF(C12<C5,"Reject","Do Not Reject") into cell C13. Similarly, if the test statistic, *z*, is less than the lower-tail critical value or is greater than the upper-tail critical value, we reject H_0. Hence, we could have entered the formula =IF(C11<C6,"Reject",IF(C11>C7,"Reject","Do Not Reject")) into cell C13. Either approach will yield the same conclusion.

Formula Worksheet:

	A	B	C
1	Weight	Sample Size	30
2	6.04	Sample Mean	=AVERAGE(A2:A31)
3	5.99	Sample Std. Dev.	=STDEV(A2:A31)
4	5.92		
5	6.03	Lev. of Signif.	0.02
6	6.01	Crit. Value (lower)	=NORMSINV(C5/2)
7	5.95	Crit. Value (upper)	=NORMSINV(1-C5/2)
8	6.09		
9	6.07	Hypoth. Value	6
10	6.07	Standard Error	=C3/SQRT(C1)
11	5.97	Test Statistic	=(C2-C9)/C10
12	5.96	*p*-Value	=2*(1-NORMSDIST(C11))
13	6.08	Conclusion	=IF(C12<C5,"Reject","Do Not Reject")

Note: Rows 14-31 are not shown.

Value Worksheet:

	A	B	C
1	Weight	Sample Size	30
2	6.04	Sample Mean	6.1
3	5.99	Sample Std. Dev.	0.2
4	5.92		
5	6.03	Lev. of Signif.	0.02
6	6.01	Crit. Value (lower)	-2.33
7	5.95	Crit. Value (upper)	2.33
8	6.09		
9	6.07	Hypoth. Value	6
10	6.07	Standard Error	0.0365
11	5.97	Test Statistic	2.74
12	5.96	*p*-Value	0.0062
13	6.08	Conclusion	Reject

EXAMPLE 3

Confidence Interval Approach to Hypothesis Testing

Refer to the Glow toothpaste study in Example 2. Conduct the same hypothesis test, but this time use a confidence interval approach rather than a *p*-value or test statistic approach.

SOLUTION 3

Using Excel's NORMSINV Function

First we will manually compute the interval estimate to illustrate the mathematical operations. The interval estimate is computed as:

Point Estimate of μ +/- Margin of Error

We use the sample mean, $\bar{x}$, as the point estimate of μ. The margin of error is the product of $z_{\alpha/2}$ times the standard error of the mean. The value of $z_{\alpha/2}$ is 2.33. The standard error of the mean equals the sample standard deviation divided by the square root of the sample size. Hence, we can compute a 98% confidence interval for μ as follows:

$$\bar{x} \pm z_{\alpha/2}\frac{s}{\sqrt{n}} = 6.1 \pm 2.33(.2/\sqrt{30}) = 6.1 \pm .08508$$

Hence, we are 98% confident that the value of μ is in the interval 6.01492 to 6.18508. Since the hypothesized value for the population mean, $\mu_0 = 6$, is not in this interval, the conclusion is that the null hypothesis, H_0: $\mu = 6$, should be rejected.

Excel can be used to compute an interval estimate and carry out a hypothesis test.

Enter Data: We already entered the sample data into column A. (See Solution 2 above.)

Enter Functions and Formulas: The descriptive statistics we need are provided in cells C1:C3. The sample size ($n = 30$) is entered into cell C1. The formula =AVERAGE(A2:A31) is entered into cell C2 to compute the sample mean, $\bar{x}$. The STDEV function is used in cell C3 to compute the standard deviation, s, for the sample data in cell A2:A31. The hypothesized value of the population mean is entered into cell C5.

Cells C7:C8 are used to compute the appropriate z value. The level of significance, α, is entered into cell C7. Now recall from Chapter 6 that if we provide a cumulative probability as input to the NORMSINV function, it provides the corresponding z value. We want an area of $\alpha/2$ in the upper tail, so the appropriate cumulative probability is $1 - \alpha/2$. Thus, we enter the formula =NORMSINV(1-C7/2) into cell C8.

Cells C10:C11 provide the estimate of the standard error and the margin of error. In cell C10 we enter the formula =C3/SQRT(C1) to estimate the standard error. The formula =C8*C10 is entered into cell C11 to compute the margin of error.

Cells C13 and C14 provide the lower and upper limits for the confidence interval. The lower limit of the confidence interval is the point estimate minus the margin of error, so we enter the formula =C2-C11 into cell C13. To find the upper limit of the interval we add the margin of error to the point estimate, so we enter the formula =C2+C11 into cell C14.

Finally, if the hypothesized value of μ does not lie between the lower and upper limits of the interval estimate, we reject H_0; otherwise we do not reject H_0. Hence, we enter the formula =IF(C5<C13,"Reject",IF(C5>C14,"Reject","Do Not Reject")) into cell C15.

Formula Worksheet:

	B	C
1	Sample Size	30
2	Sample Mean	=AVERAGE(A2:A31)
3	Sample Std. Dev.	=STDEV(A2:A31)
4		
5	Hypoth. Value	6
6		
7	Lev. of Signif.	0.02
8	z value	=NORMSINV(1-C7/2)
9		
10	Standard Error	=C3/SQRT(C1)
11	Margin of Error	=C8*C10
12		
13	Lower Limit	=C2-C11
14	Upper Limit	=C2+C11
15	Conclusion	=IF(C5<C13,"Reject",IF(C5>C14,"Reject","Do Not Reject"))

Note: Column A and rows 16-31 are not shown.

We see in the resulting worksheet below that the interval estimate and the test conclusion agree with the results from our earlier, manual calculations.

Value Worksheet:

	B	C
1	Sample Size	30
2	Sample Mean	6.1
3	Sample Std. Dev.	0.2
4		
5	Hypoth. Value	6
6		
7	Lev. of Signif.	0.02
8	z value	2.33
9		
10	Standard Error	0.0365
11	Margin of Error	0.085
12		
13	Lower Limit	6.0151
14	Upper Limit	6.185
15	Conclusion	Reject

EXAMPLE 4

One-Tailed Test about a Population Mean: Small *n*

A State Highway Patrol periodically samples vehicle speeds at various locations on a particular roadway. The sample of vehicle speeds is used to test the hypothesis H_0: $\mu \leq 65$ mph. The locations where H_0 is rejected are deemed the best locations for radar traps.

At Location F, a sample of 16 vehicles shows a mean speed of 68.2 mph with a standard deviation of 3.8 mph. Use the test statistic and *p*-value approaches to test the hypothesis with $\alpha = .05$.

SOLUTION 4

Using Excel's *TINV* and *TDIST* Functions

A one-tailed hypothesis test about the population mean can be used to help determine whether Location F is a good location for a radar trap.

Step 1: Determine the null and alternative hypotheses

H_0: $\mu \leq 65$ The population of vehicles have a mean speed of 65 or less. Location F is not a good location for a radar trap.

H_a: $\mu > 65$ The population mean speed is greater than 65. Location F is a good location for a radar trap.

Step 2: Select the test statistic to be used to decide whether to reject H_0

With $n < 30$ and σ unknown, the appropriate test statistic is:

$$t = \frac{\overline{x} - \mu_0}{s / \sqrt{n}}$$

Step 3: Specify the level of significance α

$\alpha = .05$

Step 4: Develop the rejection rule based on the level of significance

Reject H_0 if $t > 1.753$ (based on $\alpha = .05$ and d.f. = 16 - 1 = 15)

Step 5: Collect the data and compute the value of the test statistic

With $n = 16$, $\overline{x} = 68.2$ mph, and $s = 3.8$ mph, the value of t is:

$$t = \frac{\overline{x} - \mu_0}{s / \sqrt{n}} = \frac{68.2 - 65.0}{3.8 / \sqrt{16}} = 3.37$$

Step 6: a) Compare the value of the test statistic to the critical value(s)

$t = 3.37 > 1.753$

or b) <u>Compute the *p*-value and compare it to α</u>

Generally, it is not possible to be very precise with the *p*-value approach when doing the problem manually (without the aid of Excel).

<u>Step 7</u>: <u>State your conclusion regarding H_0</u>

Reject H_0. We are 95% confident that that the mean speed of all vehicles in Location F is greater than 65 mph. Location F is a good location for a radar trap.

Now we will use Excel to conduct a one-tailed hypothesis test for this small-sample study of vehicle speeds. The steps involved are nearly identical to those outlined in the solution to Example 1. The primary difference is that here, because this is a small-sample case, we must compute use *t*, rather than *z*, as the test statistic.

Enter Data: The vehicle speeds for the sample of 16 vehicles are entered into cells A2:A17 along with an appropriate label.

Enter Functions and Formulas: The steps involved here are the same as those in Example 1 with two exceptions. (The two exceptions are discussed here; refer to Solution 1 for details on the other entries.)

Exception 1: In cell C6 we use the TINV function rather than the NORMSINV function because our test statistic is *t* not *z*. The TINV function has two arguments: the upper-tail area and the degrees of freedom. We enter 2*C5 (see chapter 8 for an explanation) as the first argument. We enter C1-1 (sample size − 1) as the second argument.

Exception 2: In cell C11 we use the TDIST function rather than the NORMSDIST function. The function's first argument is the test statistic value in cell C10. The function's second argument is the degrees of freedom value. The third argument is the number of tails in the test, which in this case is 1.

Formula Worksheet:

	A	B	C
	Vehicle Speed		
1		**Sample Size**	16
2	69.6	**Sample Mean**	=AVERAGE(A2:A17)
3	73.5	**Sample Std. Dev.**	=STDEV(A2:A17)
4	74.1		
5	64.4	**Lev. of Signif.**	0.05
6	66.3	**Critical Value**	=TINV(2*C5,C1-1)
7	68.7		
8	69.0	**Hypoth. Value**	65
9	65.2	**Standard Error**	=C3/SQRT(C1)
10	71.1	**Test Statistic**	=(C2-C8)/C9
11	70.8	***p*-Value**	=TDIST(C10, C1-1,1)
12	64.6	**Conclusion**	=IF(C11<C5,"Reject","Do Not Reject")

Note: Rows 13-17 are not shown.

Value Worksheet:

	A	B	C
1	Vehicle Speed	Sample Size	16
2	68.2	Sample Mean	68.20
3	77.0	Sample Std. Dev.	3.80
4	71.0		
5	64.2	Lev. of Signif.	0.05
6	66.8	Critical Value	1.753
7	68.3		
8	65.9	Hypoth. Value	65
9	63.9	Standard Error	0.9490
10	71.1	Test Statistic	3.372
11	71.6	*p*-Value	0.0021
12	60.7	Conclusion	Reject

Note: Rows 13-17 are not shown.

EXAMPLE 5

Two-Tailed Test about a Population Mean: Small *n*

Refer to the Glow toothpaste study in Example 2. Recall that the sample mean was 6.1 ounces and the sample standard deviation was .2 ounces. Also recall that, with a sample size of 30, we rejected the null hypothesis. Conduct the same hypothesis test, but this time assume that the sample statistics come from a sample of size 12 rather than 30. Should we again reject the null hypothesis?

SOLUTION 5

A two-tailed hypothesis test about the population mean can be used to help determine whether the filling process should be allowed to continue or be stopped and adjusted.

Step 1: Determine the null and alternative hypotheses

H_0: $\mu = 6$ The population mean equals the desired mean of 6 ounces. No process adjustment is necessary.

H_a: $\mu \neq 6$ The population mean does not equal the desired mean of 6 oz. Appropriate corrective action is necessary.

Step 2: Select the test statistic to be used to decide whether to reject H_0

With $n < 30$ and σ unknown, the appropriate test statistic is:

$$t = \frac{\overline{x} - \mu_0}{s/\sqrt{n}}$$

Step 3: Specify the level of significance α

$\alpha = .02$

Step 4: Develop the rejection rule based on the level of significance

Reject H_0 if $t < -2.718$ or if $t > 2.718$

Step 5: Collect the data and compute the value of the test statistic

With $n = 12$, $\bar{x} = 6.1$ ounces, and $s = .2$ ounces, the value of t is:

$$t = \frac{\bar{x} - \mu_0}{s/\sqrt{n}} = \frac{6.1 - 6.0}{.2/\sqrt{12}} = 1.73$$

Step 6: a) Compare the value of the test statistic to the critical value(s)

$t = 1.73 < 2.718$

or b) Compute the *p*-value and compare it to α

Generally, it is not possible to be very precise with the *p*-value approach when doing the problem manually (without the aid of Excel).

Step 7: State your conclusion regarding H_0

Do not reject H_0. We are not 98% confident that that the mean filling weight of the toothpaste tubes is not 6 ounces. The filling process should be allowed to continue.

EXAMPLE 6

Test about a Population Proportion: Large *n*

For a Christmas and New Year's week, the National Safety Council estimated that 500 people would be killed and 25,000 injured on the nation's roads. The NSC claimed that drunk driving would cause 50% of the accidents.

A sample of 120 accidents showed that 67 were caused by drunk driving. Use these data to test the NSC's claim with $\alpha = 0.05$. Use the test statistic and *p*-value approaches to hypothesis testing.

SOLUTION 6

Using Excel's *NORMSINV* and *NORMSDIST* Functions

A two-tailed hypothesis test about the population proportion can be used to help determine whether 50% of all the accidents during the holiday week were caused by drunk driving.

Step 1: Determine the null and alternative hypotheses

    H_0: $p = .5$ The population proportion equals .5

    H_a: $p \neq .5$ The population proportion does not equal .5

Step 2: Select the test statistic to be used to decide whether to reject H_0

$$z = \frac{\bar{p} - p_0}{\sqrt{\dfrac{p_0(1 - p_0)}{n}}}$$

Step 3: Specify the level of significance α

    $\alpha = .05$

Step 4: Develop the rejection rule based on the level of significance

    Reject H_0 if $z < -1.96$ or if $z > 1.96$

Step 5: Collect the data and compute the value of the test statistic

    With $n = 120$, $\bar{p} = 67/120 = .5583$, the value of z is:

$$z = \frac{\bar{p} - p_0}{\sqrt{\dfrac{p_0(1 - p_0)}{n}}} = \frac{.5583 - .5}{\sqrt{\dfrac{.5(1 - .5)}{120}}} = 1.278$$

Step 6: a) Compare the value of the test statistic to the critical value(s)

    $z = 1.278 < 1.96$

    or b) Compute the *p*-value and compare it to α

    With $z = 1.28$, the upper tail area = .5000 - .3997 = .1003

    $p = 2(.1003) = .2006 > .05$ (Note: *p*-value is doubled; this is a two-tailed test.)

Step 7: State your conclusion regarding H_0

    Do not reject H_0. We are <u>not</u> 95% confident that the proportion of all accidents during the holiday week caused by drunk driving was .5.

Now we will use Excel to conduct a two-tailed hypothesis test for the holiday accident study. The steps involved are nearly identical to those outlined in the solution to Example 2. The primary difference is that this is a population proportion, not a population mean, problem.

Enter Data: The Yes or No responses for the sample of 120 accidents are entered into cells A2:A121 along with an appropriate label.

Enter Functions and Formulas: The descriptive statistics we need are entered into cells C1:C3. The sample size, 120, is entered into cell C1. The COUNTIF function is used in cell C2 to compute the number of Yes responses in the sample. The sample proportion is computed by dividing the number of Yes responses in the sample (in cell C2) by the total number of responses (in cell C1).

The level of significance, .05, is entered into cell C5. Because this is a two-tailed test, we must compute a critical value for the lower tail and a critical value for the upper tail of the sampling distribution. We compute the lower-tail critical value by entering the formula =NORMSINV(C5/2) into cell C6. We compute the upper-tail critical value by entering the formula =NORMSINV(1-C5/2) into cell C7.

Next, the hypothesized value of the population proportion, .5, is entered into cell C9. We obtain an estimate of the standard error of the proportion in cell C10 by entering the formula =SQRT(C3*(1-C3)/C1). The value of the test statistic z is computed in cell C11 by dividing the difference between the sample proportion and the hypothesized population proportion by the standard error. The p-value is computed by entering the formula =2*(1-NORMSDIST(C11)) into cell C12.

Finally, if the p-value is less than α, we reject H_0; otherwise we do not reject H_0. Hence, we enter the formula =IF(C12<C5,"Reject","Do Not Reject") into cell C13. Similarly, if the test statistic, z, is less than the lower-tail critical value or is greater than the upper-tail critical value, we reject H_0. Hence, we could have entered the formula =IF(C11<C6,"Reject",IF(C11>C7,"Reject","Do Not Reject")) into cell C13. Either approach will yield the same conclusion.

Formula Worksheet:

	A	B	C
1	**Drunk Driving**	**Sample Size**	120
2	No	**Number of "Yes"**	=COUNTIF(A2:A121,"Yes")
3	Yes	**Sample Proportion**	=C2/C1
4	No		
5	Yes	**Lev. of Signif.**	0.05
6	No	**Crit. Value (lower)**	=NORMSINV(C5/2)
7	Yes	**Crit. Value (upper)**	=NORMSINV(1-C5/2)
8	Yes		
9	No	**Hypoth. Value**	0.5
10	No	**Standard Error**	=SQRT(C3*(1-C3)/C1)
11	Yes	**Test Statistic**	=(C3-C8)/C9
12	Yes	**p-Value**	=2*(1-NORMSDIST(C11))
13	Yes	**Conclusion**	=IF(C12<C5,"Reject","Do Not Reject")

Note: Rows 14-121 are not shown.

We see in the resulting worksheet below that the value of the test statistic, the p-value, and the test conclusion agree with the results from our earlier, manual calculations.

Value Worksheet:

	A	B	C
1	**Drunk Driving**	Sample Size	120
2	No	Number of "Yes"	67
3	Yes	Sample Proportion	0.5583
4	No		
5	Yes	Lev. of Signif.	0.05
6	No	Crit. Value (lower)	-1.960
7	Yes	Crit. Value (upper)	1.960
8	Yes		
9	No	Hypoth. Value	0.5
10	No	Standard Error	0.0456
11	Yes	Test Statistic	1.278
12	Yes	p-Value	0.201
13	Yes	Conclusion	Do Not Reject

Note: Rows 14-121 are not shown.

 **EXERCISES**

EXERCISE 1

One-Tailed Test about a Population Mean: Large n

A radio talk show host in Brockdale has complained that the average monthly rent for a studio apartment in that city is $500 or more. The Brockdale Landlords Association (BLA) believes that this claim is an exaggeration. BLA takes a random sample of 70 studio apartments in the city, inquiring about the monthly rent charged for each. The data, in dollars, collected from the 70-apartment sample is presented below.

```
440 575 580 435 600 435 435 600 615 425
440 515 525 445 525 445 445 550 570 450
450 485 490 450 490 460 460 500 500 465
480 480 480 475 475 475 472 470 470 465
510 500 500 490 480 465 460 450 450 450
510 440 440 525 445 535 549 445 450 615
575 440 435 590 435 600 600 430 430 570
```

Conduct a hypothesis test with $\alpha = .05$ and draw your conclusion using both the test statistic and p value approaches.

EXERCISE 2

Two-Tailed Test about a Population Mean: Large *n*

Fast 'n Clean operates 12 laundromats on the east side of the city. All of Fast 'n Clean's clothes dryers have a label stating "20 minutes for $1.00." You question the accuracy of the dryers' clocks and decide to conduct an observational study. You randomly select 36 dryers in several different Fast 'n Clean locations, put $1.00 in each and time the drying cycle. The sample mean drying time is 20 minutes and 25 seconds. The standard deviation for the sample is 1 minute and 10 seconds.

Using the sample data and α = .05, test the validity of the label on the dryers. Apply the *p*-value, test statistic, and confidence interval methodologies in conducting the hypothesis test.

EXERCISE 3

One-Tailed Test about a Population Mean: Small *n*

Laura Naples, Manager of Heritage Inn, periodically collects and tabulates information about a sample of the hotel's overnight guests. This information aids her in pricing and scheduling decisions she must make. The table below lists data on ten randomly selected hotel registrants, collected as the registrants checked out. The data listed are:
- Number of people in the group
- Hotel's shuttle service used: yes or no
- Total telephone charges incurred
- Reason for stay: business or personal

Name of Registrant	Number in Group	Shuttle Used	Telephone Charges ($)	Reason for Stay
Adam Sandler	1	yes	0.00	personal
Michelle Pepper	2	no	8.46	business
Claudia Shepler	1	no	3.20	business
Annette Rodriquez	2	no	2.90	business
Tony DiMarco	1	yes	3.12	personal
Amy Franklin	3	yes	4.65	business
Tammy Roberts	2	no	6.35	personal
Edward Blackstone	4	yes	2.10	personal
Mary Silverman	1	no	1.85	business
Todd Atherton	1	no	5.80	business

Before cellular telephones became so common, the average telephone charge per registered group was at least $5.00. Laura suspects that the average has dropped. Test H_0: $\mu \geq 5$ and H_a: $\mu < 5$ using a .05 level of significance. Use both the test statistic and *p*-value approaches to hypothesis testing.

EXERCISE 4

Two-Tailed Test about a Population Mean: Small *n*

Refer to the Heritage Inn data in Exercise 3. In the past, Laura has made some important managerial decisions based on the assumption that the average number of people in a registered group is 2.5. Now she wonders if the assumption is still valid. Test the assumption with $\alpha = .05$ and use both the test statistic and *p*-value approaches.

EXERCISE 5

Test about a Population Proportion: Large *n*

The board of directors of a corporation has agreed to allow the human resources manager to move to the step in planning day care service for employees' children if he can prove that at least 25% of the employees have interest in using the service.

The HR manager polls 300 employees and 90 say they would seriously consider utilizing the service. At the $\alpha = .10$ level of significance, is there enough interest in the service to move to the next planning step?

SELF-TEST

TRUE/FALSE

____ 1. The *p*-value and the corresponding test statistic will always provide the same hypothesis testing conclusion.

____ 2. Hypothesis testing is proof by contradiction.

____ 3. A Type I error is not rejecting H_0 when H_a is true.

____ 4. The larger the *p*-value, the less likely it is that the sample results came from a population where the null hypothesis is true.

____ 5. Generally, the research hypothesis is the null hypothesis.

FILL-IN-THE-BLANK

1. By never directly accepting H_0, the statistician avoids the risk of making a

_____ .

2. A manufacturer's claim is usually given the benefit of the doubt and stated as the _____ hypothesis.

3. If the cost of making a Type I error is high, a small value should be chosen for the
_____.

4. When the rejection region is in the lower tail of the sampling distribution, the
_____ is the area under the curve less than or equal to the test statistic.

5. The z-value that establishes the boundary of the rejection region is called the
_____.

MULTIPLE CHOICE

____ 1. Reducing the risk of a Type I error in a hypothesis test would result from doing any one of the following except
    a) increasing the sample size
    b) increasing the value of α
    c) decreasing the confidence coefficient
    d) decreasing the level of significance

____ 2. In tests about a population proportion, p_0 represents the
    a) hypothesized population proportion
    b) observed sample proportion
    c) observed p-value
    d) probability of $p - \bar{p} = 0$

____ 3. For small-sample hypothesis tests involving population proportions, the sampling distribution of $\bar{p}$ follows

    a) a normal probability distribution
    b) a binomial probability distribution
    c) an exponential probability distribution
    d) a Poisson probability distribution

____ 4. Which one of the following is an improper form of the null and alternative hypotheses?
    a) $H_0 : \mu \le \mu_0$ and $H_a : \mu > \mu_0$
    b) $H_0 : \mu = \mu_0$ and $H_a : \mu \ne \mu_0$
    c) $H_0 : \mu < \mu_0$ and $H_a : \mu \ge \mu_0$
    d) $H_0 : \mu \ge \mu_0$ and $H_a : \mu < \mu_0$

____ 5. For a two-tailed hypothesis test about μ, we can use any of the following approaches except
    a) compare the confidence interval estimate of μ to the hypothesized value of μ
    b) compare the p-value to the value of α
    c) compare the value of the test statistic to the critical value
    d) compare the level of significance to the confidence coefficient

ANSWERS

EXERCISES

1) $t = -1.406 > -1.645$ and p-value $= .0798 > .05$; do not reject H_0: $\mu \geq 500$

2) $z = 2.14 > 1.96$, p-value $= .0324 < .05$, 20.04 to 20.80 does not include 20.00; Reject H_0: $\mu = 20$

3) p-value $= .0877 > .05$, $t = -1.471 > -1.833$; Do not reject H_0: $\mu \geq 5$

4) p-value $= .0607 > .05$, $t = -2.1433 > -2.2622$; Do not reject H_0: $\mu = 2.5$

5) p-value $= .0228 < .05$, $z = 2.00 > 1.645$; Reject H_0: $p \leq .25$; move to next step

TRUE/FALSE

1) True
2) True
3) False
4) False
5) False

FILL-IN-THE-BLANK

1) Type II error
2) null
3) level of significance
4) p-value
5) critical value

MULTIPLE CHOICE

1) d
2) a
3) b
4) c
5) d

CHAPTER 10

Statistical Inferences About Means and Proportions For Two Populations

Estimation of the Difference Between the
Means of Two Populations: Independent Samples

Hypothesis Tests About the Difference Between the
Means of Two Populations: Independent Samples

Inferences About the Difference Between the
Means of Two Populations: Matched Samples

Inferences About the Difference Between the
Proportions of Two Populations

LEARNING OBJECTIVES

1. Be able to develop interval estimates and conduct hypothesis tests about the difference between the means of two populations.

2. Know the properties of the sampling distribution of the difference between two means $(\bar{x}_1 - \bar{x}_2)$.

3. Be able to use the t distribution to conduct statistical inferences about the difference between the means of two normal populations with equal variances.

4. Understand the concept and use of a pooled variance estimate.

5. Learn how to analyze the difference between the means of two populations when the samples are independent and when the samples are matched.

6. Be able to develop interval estimates and conduct hypothesis tests about the difference between the proportions of two populations.

7. Know the properties of the sampling distribution of the difference between two proportions $(\bar{p}_1 - \bar{p}_2)$.

REVIEW

Estimation of the Difference Between the Means of Two Populations
- Let μ_1 = the mean of population 1 and μ_2 = the mean of population 2.
- The difference between the two population means is $\mu_1 - \mu_2$.
- To estimate $\mu_1 - \mu_2$, we select a simple random sample of n_1 items from population 1 and n_2 items from population 2.
- Let $\bar{x}_1$ = the sample mean for the n_1 items and $\bar{x}_2$ = the sample mean for the n_2 items.
- The point estimator of the difference between the means of two populations is:
$$\bar{x}_1 - \bar{x}_2$$

Sampling Distribution of $\bar{x}_1 - \bar{x}_2$
- The sampling distribution of $\bar{x}_1 - \bar{x}_2$ has the following properties:
  - The <u>expected value</u> is:
  $$E(\bar{x}_1 - \bar{x}_2) = \mu_1 - \mu_2$$
  - The <u>standard deviation</u> is:
  $$\sigma_{\bar{x}_1-\bar{x}_2} = \sqrt{\frac{\sigma_1^2}{n_1} + \frac{\sigma_2^2}{n_2}}$$
  where: σ_1 = standard deviation of population 1
  σ_2 = standard deviation of population 2
  - The <u>distribution form</u> is approximately normally distributed if the sample sizes are both large ($n_1 \geq 30$ and $n_2 \geq 30$).

Interval Estimate of $\mu_1 - \mu_2$: Large-Sample Case

- With σ_1 and σ_2 known, the interval estimate is:

$$\bar{X}_1 - \bar{X}_2 \pm z_{\alpha/2}\sigma_{\bar{x}_1-\bar{x}_2}$$

where $1 - \alpha$ is the confidence coefficient

- With σ_1 and σ_2 unknown, the interval estimate is:

$$\bar{X}_1 - \bar{X}_2 \pm z_{\alpha/2}s_{\bar{x}_1-\bar{x}_2}$$

where

$$s_{\bar{x}_1-\bar{x}_2} = \sqrt{\frac{s_1^2}{n_1} + \frac{s_2^2}{n_2}}$$

Using Excel: Large-Sample Case

Assuming the data for sample 1 and sample 2, values for n_1 and n_2, and the confidence coefficient have already been entered in the worksheet, the general steps for computing the interval estimate are as follows:

- The <u>AVERAGE</u> function is used to compute the sample means, $\bar{x}_1$ and $\bar{x}_2$.
- The <u>STDEV</u> function is used to compute the sample standard deviation, s_1 and s_2.
- The level of significance, α, is computed by formula using the confidence coefficient.
- The <u>NORMSINV</u> function (with α as input) is used to compute the appropriate z value.
- The estimated standard error of the difference in the two sample means, $s_{\bar{x}_1} - s_{\bar{x}_2}$, is computed by formula using s_1, s_2, n_1 and n_2.
- The margin of error is computed by formula using z and $s_{\bar{x}_1} - s_{\bar{x}_2}$.
- The point estimate of the difference in the population means is computed by formula using $\bar{x}_1$ and $\bar{x}_2$.
- The upper and lower limits of the confidence interval are computed by formula using the point estimate of the difference in the population means and the margin of error.

Interval Estimate of $\mu_1 - \mu_2$: Small-Sample Case

- With σ_1 and σ_2 known, the interval estimate is:

$$\bar{X}_1 - \bar{X}_2 \pm z_{\alpha/2}\sigma_{\bar{x}_1-\bar{x}_2}$$

where $1 - \alpha$ is the confidence coefficient

- With σ_1 and σ_2 unknown, the interval estimate is:

$$\bar{X}_1 - \bar{X}_2 \pm t_{\alpha/2}s_{\bar{x}_1-\bar{x}_2}$$

where:

$$s^2 = \frac{(n_1 - 1)s_1^2 + (n_2 - 1)s_2^2}{n_1 + n_2 - 2}$$

$$s_{\bar{x}_1-\bar{x}_2} = \sqrt{s^2(\frac{1}{n_1} + \frac{1}{n_2})}$$

and the t value is based on the t distribution with $(n_1 + n_2 - 2)$ d.f.

Using Excel: Small-Sample Case

Assuming the data for sample 1 and sample 2, values for n_1 and n_2, and the confidence coefficient have already been entered in the worksheet, the general steps for computing the interval estimate are as follows:

- The AVERAGE function is used to compute the sample means, $\bar{x}_1$ and $\bar{x}_2$.
- The STDEV function is used to compute the sample standard deviation, s_1 and s_2.
- The level of significance, α, is computed by formula using the confidence coefficient.
- The degrees of freedom is computed by formula using n_1 and n_2.
- The TINV function (with α and the degrees of freedom as input) is used to compute the appropriate t value.
- The pooled estimate of variance, s^2, is computed by formula using s_1, s_2, n_1 and n_2.
- The standard error is computed by formula using n_1, n_2, and the pooled estimate of variance.
- The margin of error is computed by formula using t and the standard error.
- The point estimate of the difference in the population means is computed by formula using $\bar{x}_1$ and $\bar{x}_2$.
- The upper and lower limits of the confidence interval are computed by formula using the point estimate of the difference in the population means and the margin of error.

Hypothesis Tests about the Difference Between the Mean of Two Populations: Independent Samples

Hypothesis Tests about $\mu_1 - \mu_2$: Large-Sample Case

- Hypotheses:
  - Upper-tailed:

$$H_0: \mu_1 - \mu_2 \leq 0 \text{ and } H_a: \mu_1 - \mu_2 > 0$$

  - Lower-tailed:

$$H_0: \mu_1 - \mu_2 \geq 0 \text{ and } H_a: \mu_1 - \mu_2 < 0$$

  - Two-tailed:

$$H_0: \mu_1 - \mu_2 = 0 \text{ and } H_a: \mu_1 - \mu_2 \neq 0$$

- Test statistic:

$$z = \frac{(\bar{X}_1 - \bar{X}_2) - (\mu_1 - \mu_2)}{\sqrt{\sigma_1^2 / n_1 + \sigma_2^2 / n_2}}$$

- Rejection rule:
  - Upper-tailed:

$$\text{Reject } H_0 \text{ if } z > z_\alpha$$

  - Lower-tailed:

$$\text{Reject } H_0 \text{ if } z < -z_\alpha$$

  - Two-tailed:

$$\text{Reject } H_0 \text{ if } z < -z_{\alpha/2} \text{ or } z > z_{\alpha/2}$$

Using Excel: Large-Sample Case
Assuming the data for sample 1 and sample 2 have already been entered in the worksheet, the general steps for computing the hypothesis test are as follows:

- The <u>VAR</u> function is used to compute the sample variances, s_1^2 and s_2^2.
- Select the <u>Tools</u> pull-down menu, choose the <u>Data Analysis</u> option, and choose <u>z-Test: Two Sample for Means</u> tool.
- The <u>z-Test: Two Sample for Means</u> tool handles the remainder of the computation with a some input (α and hypothesized mean difference, for example) from you.
- The ouput of this tool includes values for: test statistic, critical z (both one- and two-tailed), and p-value (both one- and two-tailed).

Hypothesis Tests about $\mu_1 - \mu_2$: Small-Sample Case
- <u>Hypotheses</u>:
  - Upper-tailed:

$$H_0: \mu_1 - \mu_2 \leq 0 \text{ and } H_a: \mu_1 - \mu_2 > 0$$

  - Lower-tailed:

$$H_0: \mu_1 - \mu_2 \geq 0 \text{ and } H_a: \mu_1 - \mu_2 < 0$$

  - Two-tailed:

$$H_0: \mu_1 - \mu_2 = 0 \text{ and } H_a: \mu_1 - \mu_2 \neq 0$$

- <u>Test statistic</u>:

$$t = \frac{(\overline{x}_1 - \overline{x}_2) - (\mu_1 - \mu_2)}{\sqrt{s^2(\frac{1}{n_1} + \frac{1}{n_2})}}$$

- <u>Rejection rule</u>:
  - Upper-tailed:

$$\text{Reject } H_0 \text{ if } t > t_\alpha$$

  - Lower-tailed:

$$\text{Reject } H_0 \text{ if } t < -t_\alpha$$

  - Two-tailed:

$$\text{Reject } H_0 \text{ if } t < -t_{\alpha/2} \text{ or } t > t_{\alpha/2}$$

Using Excel: Small-Sample Case
Assuming the data for sample 1 and sample 2 have already been entered in the worksheet, the general steps for computing the hypothesis test are as follows:

- Select the <u>Tools</u> pull-down menu, choose the <u>Data Analysis</u> option, and choose <u>t-Test: Two Sample Assuming Equal Variances</u> tool.
- The <u>t-Test: Two Sample Assuming Equal Variances</u> tool handles the remainder of the computation with a some input (α and hypothesized mean difference, for example) from you.
- The ouput of this tool includes values for: test statistic, critical t (both one- and two-tailed), and p-value (both one- and two-tailed).

Inferences about the Difference Between the Mean of Two Populations: Matched Samples
- With a <u>matched-sample design</u> each sampled item provides a pair of data values.
- The matched-sample design can be referred to as <u>blocking</u>.
- This design often leads to a <u>smaller sampling error</u> than the independent-sample design because variation between sampled items is eliminated as a source of sampling error.
- The key to this analysis is to realize that we consider only the <u>*n* differences</u>.
- The <u>sample mean</u> is:

$$\bar{d} = \frac{\sum d_i}{n}$$

- The <u>sample standard deviation</u> is:

$$s_d = \sqrt{\frac{\sum(d_i - \bar{d})^2}{n-1}}$$

Hypothesis Tests about $\mu_1 - \mu_2$: Matched Samples
- <u>Hypotheses</u>:
  - Upper-tailed:

  $$H_0: \mu_d \leq 0 \text{ and } H_a: \mu_d > 0$$

  - Lower-tailed:

  $$H_0: \mu_d \geq 0 \text{ and } H_a: \mu_d < 0$$

  - Two-tailed:

  $$H_0: \mu_d = 0 \text{ and } H_a: \mu_d \neq 0$$
  where: μ_d = the mean of the <u>difference</u> values

- <u>Test statistic</u>:

$$t = \frac{\bar{d} - \mu_d}{s_d / \sqrt{n}}$$

- <u>Rejection rule</u>:
  - Upper-tailed:

  Reject H_0 if $t > t_\alpha$

  - Lower-tailed:

  Reject H_0 if $t < -t_\alpha$

  - Two-tailed:

  Reject H_0 if $t < -t_{\alpha/2}$ or $t > t_{\alpha/2}$

Using Excel: Matched Samples
Assuming the data for sample 1 and sample 2 have already been entered in the worksheet, the general steps for computing the hypothesis test are as follows:
- Select the <u>Tools</u> pull-down menu, choose the <u>Data Analysis</u> option, and choose <u>*t*-Test: Paired Two Sample for Means</u> tool.
- The <u>*t*-Test: Paired Two Sample for Means</u> tool handles the remainder of the computation with a some input (α and hypothesized mean difference, for example) from you.
- The ouput of this tool includes values for: test statistic, critical t (both one- and two-tailed), and p-value (both one- and two-tailed).

Inference about the Difference Between the Proportions of Two Populations

- The difference between the two population proportions is given by $p_1 - p_2$.
- The point estimator of $p_1 - p_2$ is the difference between the two sample proportions.

Sampling Distribution of $\bar{p}_1 - \bar{p}_2$

- The sampling distribution of a point estimator provides the basis for developing interval estimates and in testing hypotheses about parameters of interest.
- The <u>expected value</u> is:

$$E(\bar{p}_1 - \bar{p}_2) = p_1 - p_2$$

- The standard deviation is:

$$\sigma_{\bar{p}_1 - \bar{p}_2} = \sqrt{\frac{p_1(1 - p_1)}{n_1} \frac{p_2(1 - p_2)}{n_2}}$$

  where: n_1 = sample size for the simple randon sample from population 1
  n_2 = sample size for the simple randon sample from population 2

- If the sample sizes are large ($n_1 p_1$, $n_1(1 - p_1)$, $n_2 p_2$, and $n_2(1 - p_2)$ are all greater than or equal to 5), the sampling distribution of $\bar{p}_1 - \bar{p}_2$ can be approximated by a normal probability distribution.

Interval Estimation of $p_1 - p_2$

- Computing $\sigma_{\bar{p}_1 - \bar{p}_2}$ requires knowing the values of p_1 and p_2, which will not be known in practice. So, a point estimator of $\sigma_{\bar{p}_1 - \bar{p}_2}$ is used.

- Point estimator of $\sigma_{\bar{p}_1 - \bar{p}_2}$:

$$s_{\bar{p}_1 - \bar{p}_2} = \sqrt{\frac{\bar{p}_1(1 - \bar{p}_1)}{n_1} + \frac{\bar{p}_2(1 - \bar{p}_2)}{n_2}}$$

- Interval Estimate of the Difference Between the Proportions of Two Populations:

$$\bar{p}_1 - \bar{p}_2 \pm z_{\sigma/2} s_{\bar{p}_1 - \bar{p}_2}$$

Hypothesis Tests about $p_1 - p_2$

- The possible <u>hypotheses</u> are:
  - $H_0 : p_1 - p_2 \geq 0$, $H_a : p_1 - p_2 < 0$ (left-tailed test)
  - $H_0 : p_1 - p_2 \leq 0$, $H_a : p_1 - p_2 > 0$ (right-tailed test)
  - $H_0 : p_1 - p_2 = 0$, $H_a : p_1 - p_2 \neq 0$ (two-tailed test)
  - The subsequent steps for the two-tailed test are outlined below.

- To compute the <u>test statistic</u> for the two-tailed test we must first make two other calculations.
  - We "pool" the two sample proportions to provide one estimate of p given by $\bar{p}$.

$$\bar{p} = \frac{n_1\bar{p}_1 + n_2\bar{p}_2}{n_1 + n_2}$$

  - Then we use $\bar{p}$ to compute the point estimator of $\sigma_{\bar{p}_1-\bar{p}_2}$.

$$s_{\bar{p}_1-\bar{p}_2} = \sqrt{\bar{p}(1-\bar{p})(\frac{1}{n_1}+\frac{1}{n_2})}$$

- Now we can compute the test statistic as:

$$z = \frac{(\bar{p}_1 - \bar{p}_2) - (p_1 - p_2)}{s_{\bar{p}_1-\bar{p}_2}}$$

- The <u>rejection rule</u> for the two-tailed test is:

Reject H_0 if $z < -z_{\alpha/2}$ or $z > z_{\alpha/2}$

KEY CONCEPTS

CONCEPT	EXAMPLES	EXERCISES
Interval Estimate of $\mu_1 - \mu_2$: Independent Samples		
Large-Sample Case	①	1
Small-Sample Case	②	2
Hypothesis Test about $\mu_1 - \mu_2$: Independent Samples		
Large-Sample Case	③	3
Small-Sample Case	④	4
Hypothesis Test about $\mu_1 - \mu_2$: Matched Samples	⑤	5
Interval Estimation of $p_1 - p_2$	⑥	6
Hypothesis Test about $p_1 - p_2$	⑦	7

◯ Excel Used

 **EXAMPLES**

EXAMPLE 1

Interval Estimate of $\mu_1 - \mu_2$: Large-Sample

Par, Inc. is a manufacturer of golf equipment and has developed a new golf ball that has been designed to provide "extra distance." In a test of driving distance using a mechanical driving device, a sample of Par golf balls was compared with a sample of golf balls made by Rap, Ltd., a competitor. The sample data is below.

	Sample #1	Sample #2
Sample Size	n_1 = 120 balls	n_2 = 80 balls
Mean	$\bar{x}$ = 235 yards	$\bar{x}$ = 218 yards
Standard Deviation	s_1 = 15 yards	s_2 = 20 yards

a) What is the point estimate of the difference between the two population means?

b) Provide a 90% confidence interval for the difference between the two population means.

SOLUTION 1

Using Excel's *NORMSINV* Function

a) The point estimate of the difference between the two population means is the difference between the two sample means.

Let: μ_1 = mean distance for the population of Par, Inc. golf balls
μ_2 = mean distance for the population of Rap, Ltd. golf balls

Point estimate of $\mu_1 - \mu_2 = \bar{x}_1 - \bar{x}_2$ = 235 - 218 = 17 yards.

b) We do not know the population standard deviations (σ_1 and σ_2). Substituting the sample standard deviations for the population standard deviation, we can compute a point estimate of $\sigma_{\bar{x}_1} - \sigma_{\bar{x}_2}$ as follows:

$$s_{\bar{x}_1} - s_{\bar{x}_2} = \sqrt{\frac{s_1^2}{n_1} + \frac{s_2^2}{n_2}} = \sqrt{\frac{(15)^2}{120} + \frac{(20)^2}{80}} = 2.622$$

With $z_{\alpha/2} = z_{.05} = 1.645$, a 90% confidence interval is computed as:

$$\bar{x}_1 - \bar{x}_2 \pm z_{\alpha/2}\sqrt{\frac{\sigma_1^2}{n_1} + \frac{\sigma_2^2}{n_2}} = 17 \pm 1.645\sqrt{\frac{(15)^2}{120} + \frac{(20)^2}{80}}$$

$$= 17 \pm 4.3132 \text{ or } 12.69 \text{ yards to } 21.31 \text{ yards.}$$

We are 90% confident that the difference between the mean driving distances of Par, Inc. balls and Rap, Ltd. balls lies in the interval of 12.69 to 21.31 yards.

Excel can be used to develop an interval estimate of the difference in two population means.

Enter Data: Column A contains the driving distances for the 120 Par golf balls sampled. Column B contains the driving distances for the 80 Rap golf balls sampled.

Enter Functions and Formulas: The descriptive statistics needed to compute the interval estimate are provided in cells D2:E4. The confidence coefficient is entered into cell D6 and the corresponding level of significance is computed in cell D7. In cell D8 we use the NORMSINV function to compute the z value needed to develop the interval.

Using the two sample standard deviations and sample sizes, a point estimate of the standard error of the difference in the two sample means is computed by entering the following formula into cell D10:

$$=SQRT(D4\wedge2/D2+E4\wedge2/E2)$$

The margin of error is computed in cell D11 by multiplying the z value times the standard error.

In cell D13 the difference in the sample means is used to compute the point estimate of the difference in the two population means. The lower limit of the confidence interval is computed in cell D14 and the upper limit is computed in cell D15.

We see in the resulting worksheet below that the 90% confidence interval estimate developed here agrees with our earlier, manual calculations.

Formula Worksheet:

	A	B	C	D	E
1	Par	Rap		Par, Inc.	Rap, Ltd.
2	195	226	Sample Size	120	80
3	230	198	Mean	=AVERAGE(A2:A121)	=AVERAGE(A2:A81)
4	254	203	Stand. Dev.	=STDEV(A2:A121)	=STDEV(A2:A81)
5	205	237			
6	260	235	Confid. Coeff.	0.90	
7	222	204	Lev. of Signif.	=1-D6	
8	241	199	z Value	=NORMSINV(1-D7/2)	
9	217	202			
10	228	240	Std. Error	=SQRT(D4^2*/D2+E4^2/E2)	
11	255	221	Marg. of Error	=D8*D10	
12	209	206			
13	251	201	Pt. Est. of Diff.	=D3-E3	
14	229	233	Lower Limit	=D13-D11	
15	220	194	Upper Limit	=D13+D11	

Note: Rows 16-121 are not shown.

Value Worksheet:

	A	B	C	D	E
1	Par	Rap		Par, Inc.	Rap, Ltd.
2	195	226	Sample Size	120	80
3	230	198	Mean	235	218
4	254	203	Stand. Dev.	15	20
5	205	237			
6	260	235	Confid. Coeff.	0.90	
7	222	204	Lev. of Signif.	0.10	
8	241	199	z Value	1.645	
9	217	202			
10	228	240	Std. Error	2.622	
11	255	221	Marg. of Error	4.313	
12	209	206			
13	251	201	Pt. Est. of Diff.	17	
14	229	233	Lower Limit	12.69	
15	220	194	Upper Limit	21.31	

Note: Rows 16-121 are not shown.

EXAMPLE 2

Interval Estimate of $\mu_1 - \mu_2$: Small-Sample

Specific Motors of Detroit has developed a new vehicle known as the M-car. 12 M-cars and 8 J-cars (from Japan) were road tested to compare miles-per-gallon (mpg) performance. The sample statistics are shown below.

	Sample #1 M-Cars	Sample #2 J-Cars
Sample Size	$n_1 = 12$ cars	$n_2 = 8$ cars
Mean	$\bar{x} = 29.8$ mpg	$\bar{x} = 27.3$ mpg
Standard Deviation	$s_1 = 2.56$ mpg	$s_2 = 1.81$ mpg

Provide a 95% confidence interval for the difference between the two population means.

SOLUTION 2

Using Excel's *TINV* Function

The point estimate of the difference between the two population means is the difference between the two sample means.
Let:

μ_1 = mean miles-per-gallon for the population of M-cars
μ_2 = mean miles-per-gallon for the population of J-cars

Point estimate of $\mu_1 - \mu_2 = \bar{x}_1 - \bar{x}_2 = 29.8 - 27.3 = 2.5$ mpg.

We will make the following assumptions:
- The miles per gallon rating must be normally distributed for both the M-car and the J-car.
- The variance in the miles per gallon rating must be the same for both the M-car and the J-car.

Using the t distribution with $n_1 + n_2 - 2 = 18$ degrees of freedom, the appropriate t value is $t_{.025} = 2.101$. We will use a weighted average of the two sample variances as the pooled estimator of σ^2.

$$s^2 = \frac{(n_1 - 1)s_1^2 + (n_2 - 1)s_2^2}{n_1 + n_2 - 2} = \frac{11(2.56)^2 + 7(1.81)^2}{12 + 8 - 2} = 5.28$$

$$\bar{x}_1 - \bar{x}_2 \pm t_{.025}\sqrt{s^2(\frac{1}{n_1} + \frac{1}{n_2})} = 2.5 \pm 2.101\sqrt{5.28(\frac{1}{12} + \frac{1}{8})}$$

$$= 2.5 \pm 2.2 \text{ or } .3 \text{ to } 4.7 \text{ miles per gallon.}$$

We are 95% confident that the difference between the mean mpg ratings of the two car types is from .3 to 4.7 mpg (with the M-car having the higher mpg).

Excel can be used to develop a interval estimate of the difference in two population means.

Enter Data: Column A contains the mpg performance for the 12 M-cars sampled. Column B contains the mpg performance for the 8 J-cars sampled.

Enter Functions and Formulas: The descriptive statistics needed to compute the interval estimate are provided in cells D2:E4. The confidence coefficient is entered into cell D6 and the corresponding level of significance is computed in cell D7. The degrees of freedom were computed in cell D8, and the TINV function is used in cell D9 to compute the t value needed to develop the interval estimate.

Using the two sample standard deviations and sample sizes, the pooled estimate of the population variance is computed by entering the following formula into cell D11:

=((D2-1)*D4^2+(E2-1)*E4^2)/D8

A point estimate of the standard error of the difference in the two population means is computed by entering the following formula into cell D12:

=SQRT(D11*(1/D2+1/E2))

The margin of error is computed in cell D13 by multiplying the t value times the standard error.

In cell D15 the difference in the sample means is used to compute the point estimate of the difference in the two population means. The lower limit of the confidence interval is computed in cell D16 and the upper limit is computed in cell D17.

Formula Worksheet:

	A	B	C	D	E
1	M Car	J Car		M-Car	J-Car
2	25.1	25.6	Sample Size	12	8
3	32.2	28.1	Mean	=AVERAGE(A2:A13)	=AVERAGE(B2:B9)
4	31.7	27.9	Stand. Dev.	=STDEV(A2:A13)	=STDEV(B2:B9)
5	27.6	25.3			
6	28.5	30.1	Confid. Coeff.	0.95	
7	33.6	27.5	Lev. of Signif.	=1-D6	
8	30.8	25.1	Deg. Freed.	=D2+E2-2	
9	26.2	28.8	*t* Value	=TINV(D7,D8)	
10	29.0				
11	31.0		Pool.Est.Var.	=((D2-1)*D4^2+(E2-1)*E4^2)/D8	
12	31.7		Std. Error	=SQRT(D11*(1/D2+1/E2))	
13	30.0		Marg. of Error	=D9*D12	
14					
15			Pt. Est. of Diff.	=D3-E3	
16			Lower Limit	=D15-D13	
17			Upper Limit	=D15+D13	

We see in the resulting worksheet below that the 95% confidence interval estimate developed here agrees with our earlier, manual calculations.

Value Worksheet:

	A	B	C	D	E
1	M Car	J Car		M-Car	J-Car
2	25.1	25.6	Sample Size	12	8
3	32.2	28.1	Mean	29.8	27.3
4	31.7	27.9	Stand. Dev.	2.56	1.81
5	27.6	25.3			
6	28.5	30.1	Confid. Coeff.	0.95	
7	33.6	27.5	Lev. of Signif.	0.05	
8	30.8	25.1	Deg. Freed.	18	
9	26.2	28.8	*t* Value	2.101	
10	29.0				
11	31.0		Pool.Est.Var.	5.2765	
12	31.7		Std. Error	1.0485	
13	30.0		Marg. of Error	2.2027	
14					
15			Pt. Est. of Diff.	2.4833	
16			Lower Limit	0.2806	
17			Upper Limit	4.6861	

EXAMPLE 3

Hypothesis Test about $\mu_1 - \mu_2$: Large Sample

Refer to the golf equipment problem in Example 1. Can we conclude, using a .01 level of significance, that the mean driving distance of Par, Inc. golf balls is greater than the mean driving distance of Rap, Ltd. golf balls?

SOLUTION 3

Excel's z-TEST: TWO SAMPLE FOR MEANS Tool

This problem calls for a hypothesis test about the difference between two population means. Specifically, we are conducting a one-tailed test to determine if the mean of one population (Par golf balls) is greater than the mean of the other population (Rap golf balls).

Step 1: Determine the null and alternative hypotheses

H_0: $\mu_1 - \mu_2 \leq 0$ The mean driving distance of Par golf balls is less than or equal to the mean driving distance of Rap golf balls.

H_a: $\mu_1 - \mu_2 > 0$ The mean driving distance of Par golf balls is greater than the mean driving distance of Rap golf balls.

where: μ_1 = mean distance for the population of Par, Inc. golf balls
         μ_2 = mean distance for the population of Rap, Ltd. golf balls

Step 2: Select the test statistic to be used to decide whether to reject H_0

$$z = \frac{(\overline{X}_1 - \overline{X}_2) - (\mu_1 - \mu_2)}{\sqrt{\dfrac{\sigma_1^2}{n_1} + \dfrac{\sigma_2^2}{n_2}}}$$

Step 3: Specify the level of significance α

α = .01

Step 4: Develop the rejection rule based on the level of significance

Reject H_0 if $z > 2.33$

Step 5: Collect the data and compute the value of the test statistic

$$z = \frac{(\overline{X}_1 - \overline{X}_2) - (\mu_1 - \mu_2)}{\sqrt{\dfrac{\sigma_1^2}{n_1} + \dfrac{\sigma_2^2}{n_2}}} = \frac{(235 - 218) - 0}{\sqrt{\dfrac{(15)^2}{120} + \dfrac{(20)^2}{80}}} = \frac{17}{2.62} = 6.49$$

Step 6: a) Compare the value of the test statistic to the critical value(s)

$z = 6.49 > 2.33$

or b) <u>Compute the *p*-value and compare it to α</u>

With $z = 6.49$, the upper tail area $= .5000 - .4999 = .0001$ (approximately)

$p = .0001 < .01$

Step 7: <u>State your conclusion regarding H_0</u>

Reject H_0. We are 99% confident that Par golf balls have a mean driving distance greater than the mean driving distance of Rap golf balls.

Excel "z-Test: Two Sample for Means" Tool can be used to conduct a hypothesis test about the difference between the means of two populations. We will continue with the worksheet we developed in Example 1.

Enter Data: The data is already entered in columns A and B (see Solution 1).

Enter Functions and Formulas: To use Excel's z-Test: Two Sample for Means tool we need to compute the sample variance for both samples. To compute the variance for the 120 Par golf balls, we enter the formula =VAR(A2:A121) into cell E2. Then, to compute the variance for the 80 Rap golf balls, we enter the formula =VAR(B2:B81) into cell F2. The value worksheet below shows the sample variance for Par balls is 225 and that the sample variance for Rap balls is 400.

Apply Tools: Now we use Excel "z-Test: Two Sample for Means" Tool to conduct the hypothesis test about the difference between the population means in the golf ball study.

<u>Excel's "z-Test: Two Sample for Means" Tool</u>

Step 1 Select the **Tools** pull-down menu
Step 2 Choose the **Data Analysis** option
Step 3 Choose **z-Test: Two Sample for Means** from the list of Analysis Tools
Step 4 When the z-Test: Two Sample for Means dialog box appears:
        Enter A1:A121 in the **Variable 1 Range** box
        Enter B1:A81 in the **Variable 2 Range** box
        Enter 0 in the **Hypothesized Mean Difference** box
        Enter 225 in the **Variable 1 Variance (known)** box
        Enter 400 in the **Variable 2 Variance (known)** box
        Select **Labels**
        Enter .01 in the **Alpha** box
        Select **Output Range**
        Enter D4 in the **Output Range** box (any upper left-hand corner cell
        Indicating where the output is to begin may be entered)
        Select **OK**

Value Worksheet:

	A	B	C	D	E	F
1	Par	Rap			**Par, Inc.**	**Rap, Ltd.**
2	195	226		**Sample Variance**	225	400
3	230	198				
4	254	203		z-Test: Two Sample for Means		
5	205	237				
6	260	235			Par, Inc.	Rap, Ltd.
7	222	204		Mean	235	218
8	241	199		Known Variance	225	400
9	217	202		Observations	120	80
10	228	240		Hypothesized Mean Difference	0	
11	255	221		z	6.483545607	
12	209	206		P(Z<=z) one-tail	4.50145E-11	
13	251	201		z Critical one-tail	2.326341928	
14	229	233		P(Z<=z) two-tail	9.00291E-11	
15	220	194		z Critical two-tail	2.575834515	

Note: Rows 16-121 are not shown.

The value of the test statistic, 6.48, is shown in cell E11 of the worksheet above. The critical value 2.33, labeled z Critical one-tail, is shown in cell E13. Because $z = 6.48$ is in the rejection region, we can conclude that the mean driving distance of Par golf balls is greater than the mean driving distance of Rap golf balls.

Alternatively, we can use the p-value to make the hypothesis-testing decision. The p-value, labeled P(Z < z) one-tail, is shown in cell E12. Because the p-value is less than the level of significance, $\alpha = .01$, we have sufficient statistical evidence to reject the null hypothesis.

EXAMPLE 4

Hypothesis Test about $\mu_1 - \mu_2$: Small Sample

Refer to the Specific Motors problem in Example 2. Can we conclude, using a .05 level of significance, that the miles-per-gallon (mpg) performance of M-cars is greater than the miles-per-gallon performance of J-cars?

SOLUTION 4

Excel's *t*-TEST: TWO SAMPLE ASSUMING EQUAL VARIANCES Tool

This problem calls for a hypothesis test about the difference between two population means. Specifically, we are conducting a one-tailed test to determine if the mean of one population (M-cars) is greater than the mean of the other population (J-cars). Our approach will be similar to that of Example 3, but here we are dealing with a small-sample case.

Step 1: Determine the null and alternative hypotheses

H_0: $\mu_1 - \mu_2 \leq 0$ The mean miles-per-gallon of M-cars is less than or equal to the mean miles-per-gallon of J-cars.

H_a: $\mu_1 - \mu_2 > 0$ The mean miles-per-gallon of M-cars is greater than the mean miles-per-gallon of J-cars..

where: μ_1 = mean miles-per-gallon for the population of M-cars
μ_2 = mean miles-per-gallon for the population of J-cars

Step 2: Select the test statistic to be used to decide whether to reject H_0

$$t = \frac{(\bar{X}_1 - \bar{X}_2) - (\mu_1 - \mu_2)}{\sqrt{s^2(1/n_1 + 1/n_2)}}$$

where:

$$s^2 = \frac{(n_1 - 1)s_1^2 + (n_2 - 1)s_2^2}{n_1 + n_2 - 2}$$

Step 3: Specify the level of significance α

α = .05

Step 4: Develop the rejection rule based on the level of significance

Reject H_0 if $t > 1.734$ (α = .05, d.f. = 18)

Step 5: Collect the data and compute the value of the test statistic

$$t = \frac{(\bar{X}_1 - \bar{X}_2) - (\mu_1 - \mu_2)}{\sqrt{s^2(1/n_1 + 1/n_2)}} = 2.369$$

Step 6: a) Compare the value of the test statistic to the critical value(s)

$t = 2.369 > 1.734$

or b) Compute the *p*-value and compare it to α

(It is difficult to determine a precise *p*-value from the *t* Distribution table.)

Step 7: State your conclusion regarding H_0

Reject H_0. We are 95% confident that M-cars have a mean mpg greater than the mean mpg of J-cars.

Excel "*t*-Test: Assuming Equal Variances" tool can be used to conduct a hypothesis test about the difference between the means of two populations when the samples are small. We will continue with the worksheet we developed in Example 2.

Enter Data: The data is already entered in columns A and B (see Solution 2).

Apply Tools: The following steps describe how to use Excel "*t*-Test: Assuming Equal Variances" tool.

Excel's "*t*-Test: Two Sample Assuming Equal Variances" Tool

Step 1 Select the **Tools** pull-down menu

Step 2 Choose the **Data Analysis** option

Step 3 Choose *t*-Test: **Two Sample Assuming Equal Variances** from the list of Analysis Tools

Step 4 When the t-Test: Two Sample Assuming Equal Variances dialog box appears:

Enter A1:A13 in the **Variable 1 Range** box

Enter B1:B9 in the **Variable 2 Range** box

Enter 0 in the **Hypothesized Mean Difference** box

Select **Labels**

Enter .01 in the **Alpha** box

Select **Output Range**

Enter D1 in the **Output Range** box (any upper left-hand corner cell indicating where the output is to begin may be entered)

Select **OK**

The value of the test statistic, 2.369, is shown in cell E10 of the worksheet below. The critical value 1.734, labeled t Critical one-tail, is shown in cell E12. Because $t = 2.369$ is in the rejection region ($2.369 > 1.734$), we can conclude that the mean mpg of M-cars is greater than the mean mpg of J-cars.

Alternatively, we can use the *p*-value to make the hypothesis-testing decision. The *p*-value, labeled P(T < t) one-tail, is shown in cell E11. Because the *p*-value (.0146) is less than the level of significance, $\alpha = .05$, we have sufficient statistical evidence to reject the null hypothesis.

Value Worksheet:

	A	B	C	D	E	F
1	M Car	J Car		t-Test: Two-Sample Assuming Equal Variances		
2	25.1	25.6				
3	32.2	28.1			M Car	J Car
4	31.7	27.9		Mean	29.78333	27.3
5	27.6	25.3		Variance	6.556061	3.265714
6	28.5	30.1		Observations	12	8
7	33.6	27.5		Pooled Variance	5.276481	
8	30.8	25.1		Hypothesized Mean Diff.	0	
9	26.2	28.8		df	18	
10	29.0			t Stat	2.368555	
11	31.0			P(T<=t) one-tail	0.014626	
12	31.7			t Critical one-tail	1.734063	
13	30.0			P(T<=t) two-tail	0.029251	
14				t Critical two-tail	2.100924	

EXAMPLE 5

Hypothesis Test about $\mu_1 - \mu_2$: Matched Samples

A Chicago-based firm has documents that must be quickly distributed to district offices throughout the U.S. The firm must decide between two delivery services, UPX (United Parcel Express) and INTEX (International Express), to transport its documents. In testing the delivery times of the two services, the firm sent two reports to a random sample of ten district offices with one report carried by UPX and the other report carried by INTEX.

Do the data that follow indicate a difference in mean delivery times for the two services?

	Delivery Time (Hours)		
District Office	UPX	INTEX	Difference
Seattle	32	25	7
Los Angeles	30	24	6
Boston	19	15	4
Cleveland	16	15	1
New York	15	13	2
Houston	18	15	3
Atlanta	14	15	-1
St. Louis	10	8	2
Milwaukee	7	9	-2
Denver	16	11	5

SOLUTION 5

Excel's *t*-TEST: PAIRED TWO SAMPLE FOR MEANS Tool

This problem calls for a hypothesis test about the difference between two population means based on matched samples. Specifically, we are conducting a two-tailed test to determine if the mean delivery time for UPX is equal to the mean delivery time for Intex.

Step 1: Determine the null and alternative hypotheses

> Let μ_d = the mean of the <u>difference</u> values for the two
> delivery services for the population of district offices.
>
> H_0: μ_d = 0
> H_a: $\mu_d \neq 0$

Step 2: Select the test statistic to be used to decide whether to reject H_0

$$t = \frac{(\bar{x}_1 - \bar{x}_2) - (\mu_1 - \mu_2)}{\sqrt{s^2(1/n_1 + 1/n_2)}}$$

where:

$$s^2 = \frac{(n_1 - 1)s_1^2 + (n_2 - 1)s_2^2}{n_1 + n_2 - 2}$$

Step 3: Specify the level of significance α

$\alpha = .05$

Step 4: Develop the rejection rule based on the level of significance

> Assuming the population of difference values is approximately normally distributed, the t distribution with n - 1 degrees of freedom applies. With $\alpha = .05$, $t_{.025} = 2.262$ (9 degrees of freedom).
>
> Reject H_0 if $t < -2.262$ or if $t > 2.262$

Step 5: Collect the data and compute the value of the test statistic

$$\bar{d} = \frac{\sum d_i}{n} = \frac{(7 + 6 + ... + 5)}{10} = 2.7$$

$$s_d = \sqrt{\frac{\sum(d_i - \bar{d})^2}{n-1}} = \sqrt{\frac{76.1}{9}} = 2.9$$

$$t = \frac{\bar{d} - \mu_d}{s_d/\sqrt{n}} = \frac{2.7 - 0}{2.9/\sqrt{10}} = 2.94$$

<u>Step 6</u>: a) <u>Compare the value of the test statistic to the critical value(s)</u>

$t = 2.94 > 2.262$

or b) <u>Compute the *p*-value and compare it to α</u>

(It is difficult to determine a precise *p*-value from the *t* Distribution table.)

<u>Step 7</u>: <u>State your conclusion regarding H_0</u>

Reject H_0. We are 95% confident that there is a difference between the mean delivery times for the two services.

Excel "*t*-Test: Paired Two Sample for Means" tool can be used to conduct a hypothesis test about the difference between the means of two populations when the samples are matched.

<u>Excel's "*t*-Test: Paired Two Sample for Means" Tool</u>

Step 1 Select the **Tools** pull-down menu

Step 2 Choose the **Data Analysis** option

Step 3 Choose *t*-**Test: Paired Two Sample for Means** from the list of Analysis Tools

Step 4 When the *t*-Test: Paired Two Sample for Means dialog box appears:

Enter B1:B11 in the **Variable 1 Range** box

Enter C1:C11 in the **Variable 2 Range** box

Enter 0 in the **Hypothesized Mean Difference** box

Select **Labels**

Enter .05 in the **Alpha** box

Select **Output Range**

Enter E2 (your choice) in the **Output Range** box

Select **OK**

The value of the test statistic, 2.936, is shown in cell E11 of the worksheet below. The critical value 2.262, labeled <u>t Critical two-tail</u>, is shown in cell E15. Because *t* = 2.936 is in the rejection region (2.936 > 2.262), we can conclude that the mean delivery times for the two services are not equal.

Alternatively, we can use the *p*-value to make the hypothesis-testing decision. The *p*-value, labeled <u>P(T < t) two-tail</u>, is shown in cell E14. Because the *p*-value is less than the level of significance, $\alpha = .05$, we have sufficient statistical evidence to reject the null hypothesis.

Value Worksheet:

	A	B	C	D	E	F	G
1	Office	UPX	INTEX				
2	Seattle	32	25		t-Test: Paired Two Sample for Means		
3	Los Angeles	30	24				
4	Boston	19	15			*UPX*	*INTEX*
5	Cleveland	16	15		Mean	17.7	15
6	New York	15	13		Variance	62.011	31.778
7	Houston	18	15		Observations	10	10
8	Atlanta	14	15		Pearson Correlation	0.9612	
9	St. Louis	10	8		Hypothesized Mean Difference	0	
10	Milwaukee	7	9		df	9	
11	Denver	16	11		t Stat	2.9362	
12					P(T<=t) one-tail	0.0083	
13					t Critical one-tail	1.8331	
14					P(T<=t) two-tail	0.0166	
15					t Critical two-tail	2.2622	

EXAMPLE 6

Interval Estimation of $p_1 - p_2$

MRA (Market Research Associates) is conducting research to evaluate the effectiveness of a client's new advertising campaign. Before the new campaign began, a telephone survey of 150 households in the test market area was conducted. Each household was asked if they were aware of the client's product and the Yes or No response was recorded. The new campaign was initiated with TV and newspaper advertisements for three weeks and then a second survey, involving 250 households, was conducted. Again, each household was asked if they were aware of the client's product and the Yes or No response was recorded.

MRA tallied the survey data and found there were 60 Yes responses in the first study and 120 Yes responses in the second study. Do these results support the position that the advertising campaign has provided an increased awareness of the client's product? Develop an interval estimate of the difference between the proportions of the two populations, using a .05 level of significance, as the basis for your decision.

SOLUTION 6

Using Excel's COUNTIF and NORMSINV Functions

Let us solve this problem manually, to demonstrate the mathematical operations, and then we will use Excel. The first step is to determine a point estimate of the difference in the proportions of the two populations, $p_1 - p_2$.

$$p_1 - p_2 = \bar{p}_1 - \bar{p}_2 = \frac{120}{250} - \frac{60}{150} = .48 - .40 = .08$$

where: p_1 = proportion of the population of households
"aware" of the product <u>after</u> the new campaign

p_2 = proportion of the population of households
"aware" of the product <u>before</u> the new campaign

$\bar{p}_1$ = sample proportion of households "aware" of
the product <u>after</u> the new campaign

$\bar{p}_2$ = sample proportion of households "aware" of
the product <u>before</u> the new campaign

The point estimate, .08, <u>suggests</u> that the percentage of households aware of the product after the campaign is 8 percentage points greater than the percentage before the campaign. However, we should not base our decision on a suggestion that ignores the possible impact of sampling error.

The interval estimate of the difference between the proportions of "aware" households before and after the advertising campaign is computed as:

$$\bar{p}_1 - \bar{p}_2 \pm z_{\alpha/2} \sqrt{\frac{\bar{p}_1(1-\bar{p}_1)}{n_1} + \frac{\bar{p}_2(1-\bar{p}_2)}{n_2}}$$

For $\alpha = .05$, $z_{.025} = 1.96$:

$$.48 - .40 \pm 1.96 \sqrt{\frac{.48(.52)}{250} + \frac{.40(.60)}{150}}$$

$$.08 \pm 1.96(.0510)$$
$$.08 \pm .10$$
$$\text{or} \quad -.02 \text{ to } +.18$$

At a 95% confidence level, the interval estimate of the difference between the proportion of households aware of the client's product before and after the new advertising campaign is -.02 to +.18. Notice that the interval ranges from a <u>slight decrease</u> in awareness to a <u>significant increase</u> in awareness. On the basis of the interval estimate, the data does not support the position that the advertising campaign has provided an increased awareness of the client's product.

Now we will use Excel to develop an interval estimate of $p_1 - p_2$. Keep in mind that we are defining population 1 as household <u>after</u> the campaign.

Enter Data: A label and the 250 responses from the later survey are entered into cells A1:A251. A label and the 10 responses from the earlier survey are entered into cells B1:A151.

Enter Functions and Formulas: The descriptive statistics needed to compute the interval estimate are provided in cells D2:E4. The COUNTIF function is used in cells D3 and E3 to count the number of Yes responses from each population. Formulas are then entered into cells D4 and E4 to compute the sample proportions. The confidence coefficient is entered into cell D6 (.95) and the corresponding level of significance is computed in cell D7. In cell D8 we use the NORMSINV function to compute the z value needed.

The standard error of the difference in the two sample proportions is computed by entering the following formula into cell D10:

$$=SQRT(D4*(1-D4)/D2+E4*(1-E4)/E2)$$

The margin of error is computed in cell D11 by multiplying the z value times the standard error.

The point estimate of the difference in the two population proportions is computed by entering the formula =D4-E4 into cell D13. To compute the lower limit of the confidence interval, the formula =D13-D11 is entered into cell D14. The upper limit of the interval is computed by entering the formula =D13+D11 into cell D15.

Formula Worksheet:

	A	B	C	D	E
	Late Surv.	Early Surv.		Later Survey (from Population 1)	Earlier Survey (from Population 2)
1					
2	No	Yes	Sample Size	250	150
3	Yes	No	No. of "Yes"	=COUNTIF(A2:A251,"Yes")	=COUNTIF(B2:B151,"Yes")
4	Yes	Yes	Samp. Propor.	=D3/D2	=E3/E2
5	No	Yes			
6	Yes	No	Confid. Coeff.	0.95	
7	No	No	Lev. Of Signif.	=1-D6	
8	No	Yes	z Value	=NORMSINV(1-D7/2)	
9	Yes	No			
10	No	No	Std. Error	=SQRT(D4*(1-D4)/D2+E4*(1-E4)/E2)	
11	Yes	Yes	Marg. of Error	=D8*D10	
12	Yes	No			
13	Yes	Yes	Pt. Est. of Diff.	=D4-E4	
14	No	Yes	Lower Limit	=D13-D11	
15	Yes	Yes	Upper Limit	=D13+D11	

Note: Rows 16-251 are not shown.

We see in the resulting worksheet below that the 95% confidence interval estimate of the difference in the two population proportions is -.02 to .18. These numbers agree with the results of our manual calculations earlier.

Value Worksheet:

	A	B	C	D	E
1	Late Surv.	Early Surv.		**Later Survey** (from Population 1)	**Earlier Survey** (from Population 2)
2	No	Yes	Sample Size	250	150
3	Yes	No	No. of "Yes"	120	60
4	Yes	Yes	Samp. Propor.	0.48	0.40
5	No	Yes			
6	Yes	No	Confid. Coeff.	0.95	
7	No	No	Lev. Of Signif.	0.05	
8	No	Yes	z Value	1.960	
9	Yes	No			
10	No	No	Std. Error	0.0510	
11	Yes	Yes	Marg. of Error	0.0999	
12	Yes	No			
13	Yes	Yes	Pt. Est. of Diff.	0.080	
14	No	Yes	Lower Limit	-0.020	
15	Yes	Yes	Upper Limit	0.180	

Note: Rows 16-251 are not shown.

EXAMPLE 7

Hypothesis Test about $p_1 - p_2$

Refer to the Market Research Associates problem in Example 6. Can we conclude, using a .05 level of significance, that the proportion of households aware of the client's product increased after the new advertising campaign?

SOLUTION 7

Using Excel's NORMSINV and NORMSDIST Functions

Let us solve this problem manually, to demonstrate the mathematical operations, and then we will use Excel. The first step is to define our notation. Let:

p_1 = proportion of the population of households
    "aware" of the product <u>after</u> the new campaign
p_2 = proportion of the population of households
    "aware" of the product <u>before</u> the new campaign

Hypotheses:

H_0: $p_1 - p_2 \leq 0$
H_a: $p_1 - p_2 > 0$

Rejection Rule: Reject H_0 if $z > 1.645$

Test Statistic:

$$\bar{p} = \frac{250(.48) + 150(.40)}{250 + 150} = \frac{180}{400} = .45$$

$$s_{\bar{p}_1 - \bar{p}_2} = \sqrt{.45(.55)(\tfrac{1}{250} + \tfrac{1}{150})} = .0514$$

$$z = \frac{(.48 - .40) - 0}{.0514} = \frac{.08}{.0514} = 1.56$$

Conclusion: Do not reject H_0. The test statistic value, 1.56, is less than the critical value, 1.645. Our confidence in rejecting the null hypothesis is less than 95%.

Now we will use Excel to conduct a hypothesis test about the difference between the population proportions.

Enter Data: A label and the 250 responses from the later survey are entered into cells A1:A251. A label and the 150 responses from the earlier survey are entered into cells B1:A151.

Enter Functions and Formula: The descriptive statistics needed to perform the hypothesis test are provided in cells D2:E4. The COUNTIF function is used in cells D3 and E3 to count the number of Yes responses from each population. Formulas are then entered into cells D4 and E4 to compute the sample proportions. The level of significance (.05) is entered into cell D6. In cell D7 we use the NORMSINV function to compute the upper critical tail value.

In cell D9 the difference in the sample proportions is used to compute a point estimate of the difference in the two population proportions. The hypothesized value of the difference in the two population proportions (0) is entered into cell D10. Using the two sample proportions and sample sizes, a pooled estimate of the population proportion p is computed by entering the following formula into cell D12:

=(D2*D4+E2*E4)/(D2+E2)

Then, using the pooled estimate of p, the standard error of the difference in the two sample proportions is computed by entering the following formula into cell D13:

=SQRT(D12*(1-D12)*(1/D2+1/E2))

The formula =(D9-D10)/D13 is entered into cell D14 to compute the test statistic z. The NORMSDIST function is used in cell D15 to compute the corresponding p-value. Finally, to determine whether to reject the null hypothesis we enter the following formula into cell D16:

=IF(D15<D6,"Reject","Do Not Reject")

The above formula is stating: If the p-value in cell D15 is less than the level of significance value in D6, enter the label Reject into cell D16; otherwise enter the label Do Not Reject into cell D16.

Formula Worksheet:

	A	B	C	D	E
1	Late Surv.	Early Surv.		Later Survey (from Population 1)	Earlier Survey (from Population 2)
2	No	Yes	Sample Size	250	150
3	Yes	No	No. of "Yes"	=COUNTIF(A2:A251,"Yes")	=COUNTIF(B2:B151,"Yes")
4	Yes	Yes	Samp. Propor.	=D3/D2	=E3/E2
5	No	Yes			
6	Yes	No	Lev of Signif.	0.05	
7	No	No	Crit.Val. (upper)	=NORMSINV(1-D7)	
8	No	Yes			
9	Yes	No	Pt. Est. of Diff.	=D4-E4	
10	No	No	Hypoth. Value	0	
11	Yes	Yes			
12	Yes	No	Pool. Est. of p	=(D2*D4+E2*E4)/(D2+E2)	
13	Yes	Yes	Standard Error	=SQRT(D12*(1-D12)*(1/D2+1/E2))	
14	No	Yes	Test Statistic	=(D9-D10)/D13	
15	Yes	Yes	p-Value	=1-NORMSDIST(D14)	
16	Yes	No	Conclusion	=IF(D15<D6,"Reject","Do Not Reject")	

Looking at the results in the value worksheet below, we see that the *p*-value (.06) is greater than the level of significance (.05) and the test statistic (1.557) is less than the critical value (1.645). Our conclusion is to <u>not</u> reject the null hypothesis. This result is consistent, as it should be, with the result of our manual calculations.

Value Worksheet:

	A	B	C	D	E
1	Late Surv.	Early Surv.		Later Survey (from Population 1)	Earlier Survey (from Population 2)
2	No	Yes	Sample Size	250	150
3	Yes	No	No. of "Yes"	120	60
4	Yes	Yes	Samp. Propor.	0.48	0.40
5	No	Yes			
6	Yes	No	Lev of Signif.	0.05	
7	No	No	Crit.Val. (upper)	1.645	
8	No	Yes			
9	Yes	No	Pt. Est. of Diff.	0.08	
10	No	No	Hypoth. Value	0	
11	Yes	Yes			
12	Yes	No	Pool. Est. of p	0.450	
13	Yes	Yes	Standard Error	0.0514	
14	No	Yes	Test Statistic	1.557	
15	Yes	Yes	p-Value	0.060	
16	Yes	No	Conclusion	Do Not Reject	

EXERCISES

EXERCISE 1

Interval Estimate of $\mu_1 - \mu_2$: Large-Sample

Starting annual salaries for business school graduates majoring in finance and management information systems (MIS) were collected in two independent random samples. Use the following data to develop a 95% confidence interval estimate of the difference between the starting salaries for the two majors.

Finance	MIS
$n_1 = 60$	$n_2 = 50$
$\overline{x}_1 = \$43,200$	$\overline{x}_2 = \$46,500$
$s_1 = \$2,100$	$s_2 = \$2,600$

EXERCISE 2

Interval Estimate of $\mu_1 - \mu_2$: Small-Sample

A manager is thinking of providing, on a regular basis, in-house training for employees preparing for an inventory management certification exam. In the past, some employees received the in-house training before taking the exam, while others did not. Independent random samples taken from the company's records provided the following exam scores for 10 workers who did not receive in-house training and 8 workers who did receive training.

No Training	Training
76	80
80	66
60	71
91	79
73	94
77	74
82	83
68	78
75	
86	

Develop a 95% confidence interval estimate for the difference between the average test scores for the two populations of employees.

EXERCISE 3

Hypothesis Test about $\mu_1 - \mu_2$: Large Sample

Refer to the starting salary statistics in Exercise 1. Using $\alpha = .10$, test to determine if the average starting salary for an MIS graduate is $4,000 more than the starting salary for a finance graduate. Use both the test statistic and p-value approaches to hypothesis testing. (Hint: the null hypothesis is H_0: $\mu_1 - \mu_2 = \$4,000$, where μ_1 is the average starting salary of MIS graduates.)

EXERCISE 4

Hypothesis Test about $\mu_1 - \mu_2$: Small Sample

Refer to the certification exam score data in Exercise 2. Using $\alpha = .05$, test for any difference between the average test scores for the two populations of employees.

EXERCISE 5

Hypothesis Test about $\mu_1 - \mu_2$: Matched Samples

A survey was recently conducted to determine if consumers spend more on computer-related purchases via the Internet or store visits. Assume a sample of 8 respondents provided the following data on their computer-related purchases during a 30-day period. Using a .05 level of significance, can we conclude that consumers spend more on computer-related purchases by way of the Internet than by visiting stores?

Respondent	Expenditures (dollars)	
	In-Store	Internet
1	132	225
2	90	24
3	119	95
4	16	55
5	85	13
6	248	105
7	64	57
8	49	0

EXERCISE 6

Interval Estimation of $p_1 - p_2$

A movie based on a best-selling novel was recently released. Six hundred viewers of the movie, 235 of whom had previously read the novel, were asked to rate the quality of the movie. The survey showed that 141 of the novel readers gave the movie a rating of excellent, while 248 of the non-readers gave the movie an excellent rating.

Develop an interval estimate of the difference between the proportions of the two populations, using a .05 level of significance, as the basis for your decision.

EXERCISE 7

Hypothesis Test about $p_1 - p_2$

Refer to Exercise 6. Can we conclude, on the basis of a hypothesis test about $p_1 - p_2$, that the proportion of the non-readers of the novel who thought the movie was excellent is greater than the proportion of readers of the novel who thought the movie was excellent? Use a .05 level of significance. (Hint: this is a one-tailed test.)

SELF-TEST

TRUE/FALSE

_____ 1. The independent-sample design generally leads to a smaller sampling error than the matched-sample design.

_____ 2. In a two-tailed hypothesis test, the *p*-value is found by doubling the area in the tail corresponding to the value of the test statistic.

_____ 3. When making comparisons of population means using an independent sample design, the sizes of the samples do not have to be equal.

_____ 4. If the appropriate confidence interval estimate contains the hypothesized difference in two population means, we can reject the null hypothesis.

_____ 5. The sampling distribution of the difference between the means of two large independent samples will be approximately normal.

FILL-IN-THE-BLANK

1. The process of combining the results of two independent random samples to provide one estimate of σ^2 is referred to as _____.

2. The formula for the point estimate of the difference between the proportions of two populations is _____.

3. The d in the notation s_d and $\bar{d}$ is a reminder that the matched sample provides _____ data.

4. The null hypothesis H_0: $\mu_d = 0$ is appropriate for a test of the difference between two population means using a _____ design.

5. The _____ distribution of a point estimator provides the basis for developing interval estimates and in testing hypotheses about parameters of interest.

MULTIPLE CHOICE

____ 1. Which one of the following is an improper form of the null hypothesis in a test about the difference between the means of two populations?
   a) $H_0 : \mu_1 - \mu_2 = 0$
   b) $H_0 : \mu_1 - \mu_2 \leq 0$
   c) $H_0 : \mu_1 - \mu_2 > 0$
   d) $H_0 : \mu_1 - \mu_2 \geq D_0$

____ 2. In conducting a hypothesis test about $p_1 - p_2$, any of the following approaches can be used except
   a) comparing the observed frequencies to the expected frequencies
   b) comparing the p-value to α
   c) comparing the hypothesized difference to the confidence interval
   d) comparing the test statistic to the critical value

____ 3. The sampling distribution of $\bar{p}_1 - \bar{p}_2$ can be approximated by a normal probability distribution if $n_1 p_1$, $n_1(1 - p_1)$, $n_2 p_2$, and $n_2(1 - p_2)$ are all greater than or equal to
   a) 5
   b) 10
   c) 20
   d) 30

____ 4. The sampling distribution of $\bar{x}_1 - \bar{x}_2$ can be approximated by a normal probability distribution if
   a) $(n_1 + n_2) \geq 30$
   b) $n_1(n_2) \geq 30$
   c) $n_1 \geq 30$ and $n_2 \geq 30$
   d) $n_1 \geq 30$ or $n_2 \geq 30$

_____ 5. The t distribution used to compute an interval estimate of the difference between the means of two populations (that are normally distributed and have equal variances) will have how many degrees of freedom?

    a) $n_1 + n_2 - 1$

    b) $n_1 + n_2 - 2$

    c) $(n_1 - 1)(n_2 - 1)$

    d) $n_1 (1 - n_2)$

ANSWERS

EXERCISES

1) MIS is higher by $2,404.62 to $4,195.38

2) -11.1 to 5.9 (thus, the difference in avg. scores could be 0)

3) $z = -1.53 > -1.645$; do not reject H_0

4) $t = -0.643 > -2.120$, p-value $= .53 > .05$; do not reject H_0: $\mu_1 - \mu_2 = 0$

5) $t = 1.12 < 1.89$, p-value $= .15 > .05$; do not reject H_0: $\mu_d \leq 0$

6) .0118 to .1690 (note that 0 is not in the interval)

7) H_0: $p_{NR} - p_R \leq 0$, $z = 2.274 > 1.645$, p-value $= .0115 < .05$; reject H_0

TRUE/FALSE

1) False
2) True
3) True
4) False
5) True

FILL-IN-THE-BLANK

1) pooling
2) $\bar{p}_1 - \bar{p}_2$
3) difference
4) matched sample
5) sampling

MULTIPLE CHOICE

1) c
2) a
3) a
4) c
5) b

CHAPTER 11

Inferences About Population Variances

Inferences About a Population Variance

Inferences About the
Variances of Two Populations

LEARNING OBJECTIVES

1. Understand the importance of variance in a decision-making situation.

2 Understand the role of statistical inference in developing conclusions about the variance of a single population.

3. Know that the sampling distribution of $(n - 1)\,s^2/\sigma^2$ has a chi-square distribution and be able to use this result to develop a confidence interval estimate of σ^2.

4. Know how to test hypotheses involving σ^2.

5. Understand the role of statistical inference in developing conclusions about the variances of two populations.

6. Know that the sampling distribution of s_1^2 / s_2^2 has an F distribution and be able to use this result to test hypotheses involving the variances of two populations.

REVIEW

Inferences about a Population Variance
- In many manufacturing applications, controlling the process variance, and in particular lowering the process variance, is extremely important in maintaining quality.
- As the point estimator of the population variance σ^2 we use:

$$s^2 = \frac{\sum (x_i - \bar{x})^2}{n - 1}$$

- In using the sample variance as a basis for making inferences about the population variance, the sampling distribution of $(n - 1)s^2/\sigma^2$ is helpful.

Sampling Distribution of $(n - 1)s^2/\sigma^2$
- The sampling distribution of $(n - 1)s^2/\sigma^2$ is known to have a chi-square distribution with $n - 1$ degrees of freedom whenever a simple random sample of size n is selected from a normal population.
- The chi-square distribution can be used to develop interval estimates and conduct hypothesis tests about a population variance.

Interval Estimation of σ^2
- We use the notation χ_α^2 to denote the value for the chi-square distribution that provides an area or probability of α to the right of the stated χ_α^2 value.
- For example, there is a $1 - \alpha$ probability of obtaining a χ^2 value such that:

$$\chi_{(1-\alpha/2)}^2 \leq \chi^2 \leq \chi_{\alpha/2}^2$$

- Because $(n-1)s^2/\sigma^2$ follows a chi-square distribution, we can substitute $(n-1)s^2/\sigma^2$ for the χ^2 and write:

$$\chi^2_{(1-\alpha/2)} \leq (n-1)s^2/\sigma^2 \leq \chi^2_{\alpha/2}$$

- After some algebraic manipulation, the <u>interval estimate of a population variance</u> is:

$$\frac{(n-1)s^2}{\chi^2_{\alpha/2}} \leq \sigma^2 \leq \frac{(n-1)s^2}{\chi^2_{(1-\alpha/2)}}$$

Using Excel to Construct a Confidence Interval

- Excel's <u>CHIINV function</u> is used to compute the lower and upper tail chi-square values.
- The general form of the CHIINV function is <u>CHIINV(upper-tail probability, degrees of freedom)</u>.
- The upper-tail chi-square value $\chi^2_{\alpha/2}$ is found by CHIINV($\alpha/2$, $n-1$).
- The lower-tail chi-square value $\chi^2_{(1-\alpha/2)}$ is found by CHIINV(1 - $\alpha/2$, $n-1$).
- NOTE: These upper and lower chi-square values are <u>not</u> the interval limits.

Hypothesis Tests about a Population Variance

One-Tailed Test: Rejection Region in Upper Tail

- <u>Hypotheses</u>: $H_0 : \sigma^2 \leq \sigma_0^2$ and $H_a : \sigma^2 > \sigma_0^2$

    where σ_0^2 is the hypothesized value for the population variance

- <u>Test Statistic</u>: $\chi^2 = (n-1)s^2 / \sigma_0^2$
- <u>Rejection Rule</u>:

    Using p-value: Reject H_0 if p-value $< \alpha$

    Using test statistic: Reject H_0 if $\chi^2 > \chi_\alpha^2$

    where χ_α^2 is based on a chi-square distribution
    with $n-1$ degrees of freedom

One-Tailed Test: Rejection Region in Lower Tail

- <u>Hypotheses</u>: $H_0 : \sigma^2 \geq \sigma_0^2$ and $H_a : \sigma^2 < \sigma_0^2$

    where σ_0^2 is the hypothesized value for the population variance

- <u>Test Statistic</u>: $\chi^2 = (n-1)s^2 / \sigma_0^2$
- <u>Rejection Rule</u>:

    Using p-value: Reject H_0 if p-value $< \alpha$

    Using test statistic: Reject H_0 if $\chi^2 < \chi^2_{(1-\alpha)}$

    where $\chi^2_{(1-\alpha)}$ is based on a chi-square distribution
    with $n-1$ degrees of freedom

Two-Tailed Test: Reject Region in Both Tails
- <u>Hypotheses</u>: $H_0 : \sigma^2 = \sigma_0^2$ and $H_a : \sigma^2 \neq \sigma_0^2$

  where σ_0^2 is the hypothesized value for the population variance
- <u>Test Statistic</u>: $\chi^2 = (n-1)s^2 / \sigma_0^2$
- <u>Rejection Rule</u>:

  Using *p*-value: Reject H_0 if *p*-value $< \alpha$

  Using test statistic: Reject H_0 if $\chi^2 < \chi_{(1-\alpha/2)}^2$ or $\chi^2 > \chi_{\alpha/2}^2$

  where $\chi_{(1-\alpha/2)}^2$ and $\chi_{\alpha/2}^2$ are based on a chi-square

  distribution with $n - 1$ degrees of freedom

Using Excel to Conduct a Hypothesis Test
- The sample data are entered into the worksheet.
- The <u>COUNT function</u> is used to compute the sample size *n*.
- The <u>VAR function</u> is used to compute the sample variance s^2.
- The hypothesized value of the population variance σ_0^2 is entered.
- The test statistic χ^2 is computed using the sample size, sample variance, and hypothesized population variance.
- The degrees of freedom are computed using the sample size.
- The <u>CHIDIST function</u> is used to compute the *p*-value (lower tail), *p*-value (upper tail), and *p*-value (two tails).
- The form of the CHIDIST function is: <u>CHIDIST(test statistic, degrees of freedom)</u>.

Inferences About the Variances of Two Populations
- Practical applications include comparing the variances in:
  - <u>Product quality</u> resulting from two different production processes.
  - <u>Assembly times</u> for two assembly methods
  - <u>Temperatures</u> for two heating devices
- Data is collected from two independent random samples, one from population 1 and another from population 2.
- The two sample variances s_1^2 and s_2^2 will be the basis for making inferences about the two population variances σ_1^2 and σ_2^2.

Sampling Distribution of s_1^2 / s_2^2 When $\sigma_1^2 = \sigma_2^2$
- Whenever independent random samples of sizes n_1 and n_2 are selected from two normal populations with equal variances, the sampling distribution of s_1^2 / s_2^2 has an <u>*F* distribution</u> with $n_1 - 1$ degrees of freedom for the numerator and $n_2 - 1$ degrees of freedom for the denominator.
- Characteristics of the *F* distribution:
  - The shape of any particular *F* distribution depends on its numerator and denominator degrees of freedom.
  - The *F* distribution is <u>not symmetric</u>.
  - The *F* values <u>can never be negative</u>.

Hypothesis Tests About the Variances of Two Populations

Two-Tailed Test
- <u>Hypotheses</u>: $H_0 : \sigma_1^2 = \sigma_2^2$ and $H_a : \sigma_1^2 \neq \sigma_2^2$
   Denote the population providing the larger
   sample variance as population 1
- <u>Test Statistic</u>: $F = s_1^2 / s_2^2$
- <u>Rejection Rule</u>:
   Using p-value: Reject H_0 if p-value $< \alpha$
   Using test statistic: Reject H_0 if $F > F_{\alpha/2}$
   where $F_{\alpha/2}$ is based on an F distribution with
   $n_1 - 1$ degrees of freedom for the numerator and
   $n_2 - 1$ degrees of freedom for the denominator

One-Tailed Test
- <u>Hypotheses</u>: $H_0 : \sigma_1^2 \leq \sigma_2^2$ and $H_a : \sigma_1^2 > \sigma_2^2$
   Denote the population with the larger
   variance In H_a as population 1
- <u>Test Statistic</u>: $F = s_1^2 / s_2^2$
- <u>Rejection Rule</u>:
   Using p-value: Reject H_0 if p-value $< \alpha$
   Using test statistic: Reject H_0 if $F > F_\alpha$
   where F_α is based on an F distribution with
   $n_1 - 1$ degrees of freedom for the numerator and
   $n_2 - 1$ degrees of freedom for the denominator

Using Excel to Conduct a Hypothesis Test
- The sample data for each population are entered into the worksheet.
- Use the <u>F-Test Two-Sample for Variances</u> tool as follows:
  - Step 1: Select the <u>Tools</u> pull-down menu.
  - Step 2: Choose the <u>Data Analysis</u> option.
  - Step 3: Choose <u>F-Test Two-Sample for Variances</u>.
  - Step 4: Complete the F-Test Two-Sample for Variances dialog box.

KEY CONCEPTS

<u>CONCEPT</u>	<u>EXAMPLES</u>	<u>EXERCISES</u>
Interval Estimation of a Population Variance	①	1
Hypothesis Test about a Population Variance	②	2
Hypothesis Test about the Variances of Two Populations	③	3
	◯ Excel Used	

EXAMPLES

EXAMPLE 1

Interval Estimation of a Population Variance

Buyer's Digest rates thermostats manufactured for home temperature control. In a recent test, 10 thermostats manufactured by ThermoRite were selected and placed in a test room that was maintained at a temperature of 68°F. The temperature readings of the ten thermostats are listed below.

Thermostat	1	2	3	4	5	6	7	8	9	10
Temperature	67.4	67.8	68.2	69.3	69.5	67.0	68.1	68.6	67.9	67.2

a) Develop a 95% confidence interval estimate of the population variance (i.e., the temperature variance for ThermoRite thermostats).

b) Develop a 95% confidence interval estimate of the population standard deviation.

SOLUTION 1

Using Excel to Construct a Confidence Interval

a) First, we will manually compute the interval estimate of the temperature variance for ThermoRite thermostats.

The sample variance is:

$$s^2 = \frac{\sum(x_i - \bar{x})^2}{n-1} = \frac{6.3}{9} = .70$$

With $\alpha = .05$, $\chi^2_{\alpha/2} = \chi^2_{.025}$ and $\chi^2_{(1-\alpha/2)} = \chi^2_{.975}$. Knowing that $n - 1 = 10 - 1 = 9$ degrees of freedom, we can find in a chi-square distribution table that $\chi^2_{.025} = 19.0228$ and $\chi^2_{.975} = 2.7004$.

The interval estimate of a population variance is:

$$\frac{(n-1)s^2}{\chi^2_{\alpha/2}} \le \sigma^2 \le \frac{(n-1)s^2}{\chi^2_{(1-\alpha/2)}}$$

$$\frac{(10-1).70}{19.0228} \le \sigma^2 \le \frac{(10-1).70}{2.7004}$$

$$0.3312 \le \sigma^2 \le 2.3330$$

Excel can be used to construct a 95% confidence interval of the population variance.

Enter Data: Column A in the formula worksheet below shows the temperature for each of the 10 thermostats in the sample.

Enter Functions and Formulas: The sample size is computed in cell D3 using the COUNT function. The sample variance is computed in cell D4 using the VAR function.

The confidence coefficient is entered into cell D6 and the level of significance (α) is computed in cell D7 by entering the formula 1 - D6.

Excel's CHIINV function is used to compute the lower and upper tail chi-square values. The formula =CHIINV(1 – D7/2,D3 – 1) is entered into cell D8 to compute the lower-tail chi-square value. The formula =CHIINV(D7/2,D3 – 1) is entered into cell D9 to compute the upper-tail chi-square value.

To compute the lower limit of the 95% confidence interval, the formula =((D3 – 1)*D4)/D9 is entered into cell D12. Similarly, to compute the upper limit of the 95% confidence interval, the formula =((D3 – 1)*D4)/D8 is entered into cell D13.

Formula Worksheet:

	A	B	C	D
1	Temp.		Interval Estimate of a Population Variance	
2	67.4			
3	67.8		Sample Size	=COUNT(A2:A11)
4	68.2		Variance	=VAR(A2:A11)
5	69.3			
6	69.5		Confidence Coefficient	0.95
7	67.0		Level of Significance (alpha)	=1-D6
8	68.1		Chi-Square Value (lower tail)	=CHIINV(1-D7/2,D3-1)
9	68.6		Chi-Square Value (upper tail)	=CHIINV(D7/2,D3-1)
10	67.9			
11	67.2		Point Estimate	=D4
12			Lower Limit	=((D3-1)*D4)/D9
13			Upper Limit	=((D3-1)*D4)/D8

We see in the value worksheet below that the results of our manual calculations agree with the interval limits found using Excel.

$$0.3312 \le \sigma^2 \le 2.3330$$

b) The interval estimate of a population standard deviation is found by computing the square roots of the lower limit and upper limit of the interval for the population variance.

$$\sqrt{.3312} \le \sigma \le \sqrt{2.3330}$$

$$0.5755 \le \sigma \le 1.5274$$

Value Worksheet:

	A	B	C	D
1	Temp.		**Interval Estimate of a Population Variance**	
2	67.4			
3	67.8		Sample Size	10
4	68.2		Variance	0.7
5	69.3			
6	69.5		Confidence Coefficient	0.95
7	67.0		Level of Significance (alpha)	0.05
8	68.1		Chi-Square Value (lower tail)	2.7004
9	68.6		Chi-Square Value (upper tail)	19.0228
10	67.9			
11	67.2		Point Estimate	0.7
12			Lower Limit	0.3312
13			Upper Limit	2.3330

EXAMPLE 2

Hypothesis Test about a Population Variance

Refer again to the ThermoRite thermostat problem in Example 1 above. Buyer's Digest gives an "acceptable" rating to a thermostat with a temperature variance of 0.5 or less. Conduct a hypothesis test (with $\alpha = .10$) to determine whether the ThermoRite thermostat's temperature variance is "acceptable".

The temperature readings of the ten thermostats are listed again below.

Thermostat	1	2	3	4	5	6	7	8	9	10
Temperature	67.4	67.8	68.2	69.3	69.5	67.0	68.1	68.6	67.9	67.2

SOLUTION 2

Using Excel to Conduct a Hypothesis Test

This is a one-tail hypothesis test with the rejection region in the upper tail.

Hypotheses: $H_0 : \sigma^2 \le 0.5$ and $H_a : \sigma^2 > 0.5$

Rejection Rule: Reject H_0 if $\chi^2 > 14.6837$

                      (using 9 degrees of freedom and .10 area in upper tail)

Test Statistic: $\chi^2 = (n-1)s^2 / \sigma_0^2 = (10-1)(.7)/0.5 = 12.6$

Conclusion: Do not reject H_0. (The test statistic χ^2 is less than χ_α^2.)

                      There is insufficient evidence to conclude that the temperature variance for ThermoRite thermostats is unacceptable.

We will now use Excel to conduct the same hypothesis test about a population variance.

Enter Data: Column A in the formula worksheet below shows the temperature for each of the 10 thermostats in the sample.

Enter Functions and Formulas: The sample size is computed in cell D3 using the COUNT function. The sample variance is computed in cell D4 using the VAR function.

The hypothesized value for the population variance is entered into cell D6. The formula =((D3 – 1)*D4)/D6 is entered into cell D8 to compute the χ^2 test statistic. The formula =D3 – 1 is entered into cell D9 to compute the degrees of freedom associated with the test statistic.

Excel's CHIDIST function is used to compute the p-values in cells D11:D13. The formula =1 - CHIDIST(D8,D9) is entered into cell D11 to compute the p-value for a one-tail test in which the rejection region is in the lower tail. The formula =CHIDIST(D8,D9) is entered into cell D12 to compute the p-value for a one-tail test in which the rejection region is in the upper tail. The formula =2*MIN(D11,D12) is entered into cell D13 to compute the p-value for a two-tailed test.

Formula Worksheet:

	A	B	C	D
1	Temp.		Hypothesis Test about a Population Variance	
2	67.4			
3	67.8		Sample Size	=COUNT(A2:A11)
4	68.2		Variance	=VAR(A2:A11)
5	69.3			
6	69.5		Hypothesized Value	0.5
7	67.0			
8	68.1		Test Statistic	=((D3-1)*D4)/D6
9	68.6		Degrees of Freedom	=D3-1
10	67.9			
11	67.2		p-Value (lower tail)	=1-CHIDIST(D8,D9)
12			p-Value (upper tail)	=CHIDIST(D8,D9)
13			p-Value (two tail)	=2*MIN(D11,D12)

The rejection region for our ThermoRite thermostats problem is in the upper tail; thus, we see in the value worksheet below that the appropriate p-value is .18156. At a .10 level of significance, we cannot reject H_0 because .18156 > .10. Hence, the sample variance of $s^2 = 0.7$ is insufficient evidence to conclude that the temperature variance is not meeting the "acceptable" criterion.

Value Worksheet:

	A	B	C	D
1	Temp.		**Hypothesis Test about a Population Variance**	
2	67.4			
3	67.8		Sample Size	10
4	68.2		Variance	0.7
5	69.3			
6	69.5		Hypothesized Value	0.5
7	67.0			
8	68.1		Test Statistic	12.6
9	68.6		Degrees of Freedom	9
10	67.9			
11	67.2		*p*-Value (lower tail)	0.81844
12			*p*-Value (upper tail)	0.18156
13			*p*-Value (two tail)	0.36311

EXAMPLE 3

Hypothesis Test about the Variances of Two Populations

Buyer's Digest rates thermostats manufactured for home temperature control. In a recent test, 10 thermostats manufactured by ThermoRite and 10 thermostats produced by TempKing were selected and placed in a test room that was maintained at a temperature of 68^OF. The temperature readings of the twenty thermostats are listed below.

Conduct a hypothesis test with $\alpha = .10$ to see if the variances are equal for ThermoRite's thermostats and TempKing's thermostats.

ThermoRite	67.4	67.8	68.2	69.3	69.5	67.0	68.1	68.6	67.9	67.2
TempKing	66.4	67.8	68.2	70.3	69.5	68.0	68.1	68.6	67.9	66.2

SOLUTION 3

Using Excel to Conduct a Hypothesis Test

This is a two-tail hypothesis test about the variances of two populations.

Hypotheses: $H_0: \sigma_1^2 = \sigma_2^2$ (TempKing and ThermoRite thermostats
                            have same temperature variance)

$H_0: \sigma_1^2 \neq \sigma_2^2$ (Their variances are not equal)

Rejection Rule: Reject H_0 if $F > 3.18$

   ($F_{.05} = 3.18$ using $\alpha = .10$, 9 degrees of freedom for the numerator,
    and 9 degrees of freedom for the denominator)

Test Statistic: TempKing's sample variance is 1.52.
ThermoRite's sample variance is .70.

$$F = \frac{s_1^2}{s_2^2} = 1.52/.70 = 2.17$$

Conclusion: We <u>cannot</u> reject H_0. There is insufficient evidence to conclude that the population variances differ for the two thermostat brands.

We will now use Excel to conduct the same hypothesis test about the variances of two populations.

Enter Data: Columns A and B in the formula worksheet below show the temperatures for each of the 10 TempKing thermostats and each of the 10 ThermoRite thermostats.

Apply Tools: The following steps describe how to use Excel's F-Test Two-Sample for Variances tool.

Excel's F-Test Two-Sample for Variances Tool
    Step 1:   Select the **Tools** pull-down menu
    Step 2:   Choose the **Data Analysis** option
    Step 3:   When the Data Analysis dialog box appears:
                Choose **F-Test Two Sample for Variances**
                Select **OK**
    Step 4:   When the F-Test Two-Sample for Variances dialog box appears:
                Enter A1:A11 in the **Variable 1 Range** box
                Enter B1:B11 in the **Variable 2 Range** box
                Select **Labels**
                Enter .05 in the **Alpha** box
                Select **Output Range**
                Enter C1 in the **Output Range** box
                Click **OK**

Value Worksheet:

	A	B	C	D	E
1	Temp-King	Therm-oRite	F-Test Two-Sample for Variances		
2	66.4	67.4			
3	67.8	67.8		*Temp-King*	*Therm-oRite*
4	68.2	68.2	Mean	68.1	68.1
5	70.3	69.3	Variance	1.5222	0.7000
6	69.5	69.5	Observations	10	10
7	68.0	67.0	df	9	9
8	68.1	68.1	F	2.1746	
9	68.6	68.6	P(F<=f) one-tail	0.1314	
10	67.9	67.9	F Critical one-tail	3.1789	
11	66.2	67.2			

The output labeled "P(F<=f) one-tail", 0.1314, can be used to determine the p-value for the hypothesis test. Because our test is a two-tailed test, we must multiply this value by 2 to obtain the correct p-value. Thus, the two-tailed p-value we are looking for is 2(.1314) = .2628.

Because .2628 > α = .10, we <u>cannot</u> reject the null hypothesis that the two population variances are equal. There is insufficient evidence to conclude that the population variances differ for the two thermostat brands.

 **EXERCISES**

EXERCISE 1

Interval Estimation of a Population Variance

The State Highway Patrol (SHP) periodically samples vehicle speeds at Milepost 92 on Interstate 17. The SHP is concerned about the dispersion of speeds of vehicles sharing the same highway because significant difference in speed is a known cause of accidents. The speeds of a random sample of 16 vehicles are shown below.

Vehicle	1	2	3	4	5	6	7	8
Speed	69.6	73.5	74.1	64.4	66.3	68.7	69.0	65.2
Vehicle	9	10	11	12	13	14	15	16
Speed	71.1	70.8	64.6	67.4	69.9	66.3	68.3	70.6

a) Develop a 90% confidence interval estimate of the population variance (i.e., the speed variance of vehicles at Milepost 92 on Interstate 17).

b) Develop a 90% confidence interval estimate of the population standard deviation.

EXERCISE 2

Hypothesis Test about a Population Variance

Refer again to the State Highway Patrol problem in Exercise 1 above. The SHP's policy is to position a patrol car at Milepost 92 on Interstate 17 if the vehicle speed variance at that location is believed to be greater than 6 miles per hour.

Conduct a hypothesis test (with α = .15) to determine whether the speed variance for all vehicles passing Milepost 92 exceeds 6 mph.

EXERCISE 3

Hypothesis Test about the Variances of Two Populations

Specific Motors of Detroit has developed a new vehicle known as the M-car. 12 M-cars and 8 J-cars (from Japan) were road tested to compare miles-per-gallon (mpg) performance. The sample data are shown below.

M-Car	1	2	3	4	5	6	7	8	9	10	11	12
MPG	25.1	32.2	31.7	27.6	28.5	33.6	30.8	26.2	29.0	31.0	31.7	30.0

J-Car	1	2	3	4	5	6	7	8
MPG	25.6	28.1	27.9	25.3	30.1	27.5	25.1	28.8

Conduct a hypothesis test with $\alpha = .10$ to determine if the variance of M-car mpg performance is greater than the variance of J-car mpg performance.

SELF-TEST

TRUE/FALSE

_____ 1. A confidence interval for a population standard deviation can be found by computing the square roots of the lower limit and upper limit of the confidence interval for the population variance.

_____ 2. A test hypothesis about two population variances can be formulated so that the rejection region is always in the upper tail of the distribution.

_____ 3. The F distribution is not symmetric and the F values can never be negative.

_____ 4. Both the chi-square and F distributions are based on sampling from normal distributions.

_____ 5. As the degrees of freedom increases, the value of χ_α^2 decreases.

FILL-IN-THE-BLANK

1. The _____ value for the population variance is denoted by σ_0^2.

2. The F distribution is based on sampling from two _____ populations.

3. A two-tailed hypothesis test places an area of _____ in each tail of the distribution to establish the two critical values for the test.

4. When testing for the difference between two population variances with sample sizes of $n_1 = 20$ and $n_2 = 24$, the degrees of freedom for the _____ are 23.

5. We can use the _____ distribution to develop interval estimates and conduct hypothesis tests about a population variance.

MULTIPLE CHOICE

___ 1. In a hypothesis test about two population variances, the test statistic F is computed as
   a) $1/(s_1^2/s_2^2)$
   b) s_1^2/s_2^2
   c) $1/(\sigma_1^2/\sigma_2^2)$
   d) σ_1^2/σ_2^2

___ 2. Which of the following rejection rules is proper?
   a)   Reject H_0 if p-value $> F_\alpha$
   b)   Reject H_0 if p-value $< \chi_\alpha^2$
   c)   Reject H_0 if p-value $> \chi_{\alpha/2}^2$
   d)   Reject H_0 if p-value $< \alpha$

___ 3. There is a .90 probability of obtaining a χ^2 value such that
   a) $\chi_{.05}^2 \leq \chi^2 \leq \chi_{.95}^2$
   b) $\chi_{.10}^2 \leq \chi^2 \leq \chi_{.90}^2$
   c) $\chi_{.90}^2 \leq \chi^2 \leq \chi_{.10}^2$
   d) $\chi_{.95}^2 \leq \chi^2 \leq \chi_{.05}^2$

___ 4. $\chi_{.975}^2 = 8.9066$ indicates that
   a)   97.5% of the chi-square values are to the right of 8.9066.
   b)   97.5% of the chi-square values are to the left of 8.9066.
   c)   2.5% of the chi-square values are to the right of 8.9066.
   d)   5% of the chi-square values are more than 8.9066 from the mean.

___ 5. In practice, the most frequently encountered hypothesis test about a population variance is a
   a)   one-tailed test, with rejection region in lower tail
   b)   one-tailed test, with rejection region in upper tail
   c)   two-tailed test, with equal-size rejection regions
   d)   two-tailed test, with unequal-size rejection regions

ANSWERS

EXERCISES

1) a) 90% confidence interval estimate of population variance is from 6.4358 to 22.1553

b) 90% confidence interval estimate of population std. deviation is from 2.537 to 4.707

	A	B	C	D
1	Vehicle Speed		**Interval Estimate of a Population Variance**	
2	69.6			
3	73.5		**Sample Size**	16
4	74.1		**Sample Variance**	10.7246
5	64.4			
6	66.3		**Confidence Coefficient**	0.90
7	68.7		**Level of Significance (alpha)**	0.10
8	69.0		**Chi-Square Value (lower tail)**	7.2609
9	65.2		**Chi-Square Value (upper tail)**	24.9958
10	71.1			
11	70.8		**Point Estimate**	10.7246
12	64.6		**Lower Limit**	6.4358
13	67.4		**Upper Limit**	22.1553

2) H_0: $\sigma^2 \leq 6.0$ and H_a: $\sigma^2 > 6.0$
Reject H_0 because p-value $< \alpha$ (that is, .12 < .15)

	A	B	C	D
1	Vehicle Speed		**Hypothesis Test about a Population Variance**	
2	69.6			
3	73.5		**Sample Size**	16
4	74.1		**Sample Variance**	8.6145
5	64.4			
6	66.3		**Hypothesized Value**	6
7	68.7			
8	69.0		**Test Statistic**	21.5363
9	65.2		**Degrees of Freedom**	15
10	71.1			
11	70.8		*p*-**Value (lower tail)**	0.8794
12	64.6		*p*-**Value (upper tail)**	0.120552991
13	67.4		*p*-**Value (two tail)**	0.241105982

3) H_0: $\sigma_1^2 \leq \sigma_2^2$ (M-car mpg variance is less than or equal to J-car mpg variance)
H_0: $\sigma_1^2 > \sigma_2^2$ (M-car mpg variance is greater than J-car mpg variance)

Do not reject H_0 because *p*-value is not < α (that is, .1823 > .10)

	A	B	C	D	E
1	**M-Car**	**J-Car**	F-Test Two-Sample for Variances		
2	25.1	25.6			
3	32.2	28.1		*M-Car*	*J-Car*
4	31.7	27.9	Mean	29.783333	27.3
5	27.6	25.3	Variance	6.5560606	3.26571429
6	28.5	30.1	Observations	12	8
7	33.6	27.5	df	11	7
8	30.8	25.1	F	2.0075426	
9	26.2	28.8	P(F<=f) one-tail	0.1822991	
10	29.0		F Critical one-tail	3.6030343	
11	31.0				

TRUE/FALSE

1) True
2) True
3) True
4) True
5) False

FILL-IN-THE-BLANK

1) hypothesized
2) normal
3) $\alpha/2$
4) denominator
5) chi-square

MULTIPLE CHOICE

1) b
2) d
3) d
4) a
5) b

CHAPTER 12

Tests of Goodness of Fit and Independence

Goodness of Fit Test:
A Multinomial Population

Test of Independence

Goodness of Fit Test:
Poisson Distribution

Goodness of Fit Test:
Normal Distribution

LEARNING OBJECTIVES

1. Know how to conduct a goodness of fit test.

2. Know how to use sample data to test for independence of two variables.

3. Understand the role of the chi-square distribution in conducting tests of goodness of fit and independence.

4. Be able to conduct a goodness of fit test for cases where the population is hypothesized to have either a multinomial, a Poisson, or a normal probability distribution.

5. For a test of independence, be able to set up a contingency table, determine the observed and expected frequencies, and determine if the two variables are independent.

REVIEW

Hypothesis Test for Proportions of a Multinomial Population
*   Here we are concerned with the proportion of elements in a population belonging to each of <u>several classes or categories</u>.
*   The multinomial probability distribution can be viewed as an <u>extension of the binomial distribution</u> to the case of three or more categories of outcomes.
*   Here, conducting a hypothesis test involves performing a <u>goodness of fit test</u>.
*   The goodness of fit test is based on a <u>comparison</u> of the sample of <u>observed results</u> with the <u>expected results</u> under the assumption that the null hypothesis is true.
*   The test for goodness of fit is always a <u>one-tailed test</u> with the rejection region located in the <u>upper tail</u> of the chi-square distribution.

Multinomial Distribution Goodness of Fit Test: A Summary
*   Set up the <u>null and alternative hypotheses</u>:
    * H_0: The population follows a multinomial probability distribution with specified probabilities for each of k categories.
    * H_a: The population <u>does not</u> follow a multinomial probability distribution with specified probabilities for each of k categories.
*   Select a random sample and record the <u>observed frequencies</u> f_i for each category.
*   Assuming the null hypothesis is true, determine the <u>expected frequency e_i</u> in each category by multiplying the category probability by the sample size.
*   Compute the value of the <u>test statistic</u>:

$$\chi^2 = \sum_{i=1}^{k} \frac{(f_i - e_i)^2}{e_i}$$

*   <u>Rejection rule</u>:
    Using p-value: Reject H_0 if p-value $< \alpha$
    Using test statistic: Reject H_0 if $\chi^2 > \chi^2_\alpha$
    where: α is the level of significance for the test
    and there are $k - 1$ degrees of freedom.

Using Excel to Conduct a Goodness of Fit Test
- First, the sample observations are entered into the worksheet.
- The COUNTIF function is used to count the number of sample observations (determine the observed frequency) in each category.
- The SUM function is used to compute the total frequency.
- For each category:
  - A formula is entered to compute the expected frequency.
  - A formula is entered to compute the difference between the observed frequency and the expected frequency.
  - A formula is entered to compute the squared difference.
  - A formula is entered to compute the squared difference divided by the expected frequency.
- The SUM function is used to compute the test statistic, which is the sum of the squared differences divided by the expected frequencies.
- The number of categories is entered into the worksheet.
- The degrees of freedom are computed by subtracting 1 from the number of categories.
- The CHIDIST function is used to compute the *p*-value.

Test of Independence
- A test of independence addresses the question of whether one variable is independent of another variable.
- The test of independence uses the contingency table format (cross-tabulation) and for that reason is sometimes referred to as the contingency table test.

Test of Independence: A Summary
- Set up the null and alternative hypotheses:
  H_0: The column variable is independent of the row variable
  H_a: The column variable is not independent of the row
- Select a random sample and record the observed frequencies for each cell of the contingency table.
- Compute the expected frequency e_{ij} for each cell:
$$e_{ij} = \frac{(\text{Row } i \text{ Total})(\text{Column } j \text{ Total})}{\text{Sample Size}}$$
- Compute the value of the χ^2 test statistic:
$$\chi^2 = \sum_i \sum_j \frac{(f_{ij} - e_{ij})^2}{e_{ij}}$$

where: f_{ij} = observed frequency for contingency table category
in row *i* and column *j*
e_{ij} = expected frequency for contingency table category in
row *i* and column *j* based on the assumption of independence

- Rejection rule:
  Using the *p*-value: Reject H_0 if *p*-value < α
  Using the test statistic: Reject H_0 if $\chi^2 > \chi_\alpha^2$

where α is the level of significance; *n* rows and *m* columns
providing $(n-1)(m-1)$ degrees of freedom.

Using Excel to Conduct a Test of Independence
- First, the two-variable observation for each element in the sample is entered into the worksheet.
- The <u>PivotTable tool</u> is used to develop a $n \times m$ crosstabulation of observed frequencies.
- Formulas are entered to develop a $n \times m$ crosstabulation of expected frequencies.
- The <u>CHIINV function</u> is used to compute the chi-square test statistic.
- The <u>CHITEST function</u> is used to compute the p-value for the test.

Goodness of Fit Test: Poisson Distribution
- The goodness of fit test can be used with almost <u>any hypothesized probability distribution</u>.
- We might want to test the assumption that a population follows a Poisson distribution.
- For example, some waiting line analysis models are based on the assumption that the number of customer arriving during a specified period of time is Poisson distributed.

Poisson Distribution Goodness of Fit Test: A Summary
- Set up the <u>null and alternative hypotheses</u>:
    - H_0: The population has a Poisson probability distribution
    - H_a: The population does not have a Poisson probability distribution
- Select a random sample and
    - Record the <u>observed frequency</u> f_i for each value of the Poisson random variable.
    - Compute the <u>expected frequency</u> of occurrences e_i for each value of the Poisson random variable (by multiplying the sample size by the Poisson probability of occurrence for each value of the Poisson random variable). If there are fewer than 5 expected occurrences for some values, combine adjacent values and reduce the number of categories as necessary.
- Compute the value of the χ^2 <u>test statistic</u>:

$$\chi^2 = \sum_{i=1}^{k} \frac{(f_i - e_i)^2}{e_i}$$

  where: f_i = observed frequency for Poisson random variable value i
  e_i = expected frequency for Poisson random variable value i

- <u>Rejection rule</u>:
    Using the p-value: Reject H_0 if p-value $< \alpha$
    Using the test statistic: Reject H_0 if $\chi^2 > \chi_\alpha^2$

    where α is the level of significance and
    there are $k - 2$ degrees of freedom.

Using Excel to Conduct a Goodness of Fit Test
- For each of the k Poisson random variable values:
    - The observed frequency is entered directly into the worksheet.
    - The <u>POISSON function</u> is used to compute the expected frequency.
    - A formula is entered to compute the <u>difference between the observed frequency and the expected frequency</u>.
    - Formulas are entered to compute the <u>squared difference</u> and <u>squared difference divided by the expected frequency</u>.
- The <u>SUM function</u> is used to compute the <u>test statistic</u>, which is the sum of the squared differences divided by the expected frequencies.

- The number of Poisson random variable values k is entered into the worksheet.
- The degrees of freedom are computed by subtracting 2 from k.
- The CHIDIST function is used to compute the p-value.

Goodness of Fit Test: Normal Distribution

- The goodness of fit test for a normal probability distribution is also based on the use of the chi-square distribution.
- Because the normal probability distribution is continuous, we must modify the way the categories are defined and how the expected frequencies are computed.

Normal Distribution Goodness of Fit Test: A Summary

- Set up the null and alternative hypotheses:

  H_0: The population has a normal probability distribution

  H_a: The population does not have a normal probability distribution
- Select a random sample and:
  - Compute the sample mean and sample standard deviation.
  - Define intervals of values so that the expected frequency is at least 5 for each interval. (Using equal probability intervals is a good approach.)
  - Record the observed frequency of data values f_i in each interval defined.
- Compute the expected number of occurrences e_i for each interval of values defined. Multiply the sample size by the probability of a normal variable being in the interval.
- Compute the value of the χ^2 test statistic:

$$\chi^2 = \sum_{i=1}^{k} \frac{(f_i - e_i)^2}{e_i}$$

  where: f_i = observed frequency for normal random variable interval i

  e_i = expected frequency for normal random variable interval i
- Rejection rule:

  Using the p-value: Reject H_0 if p-value $< \alpha$

  Using the test statistic: Reject H_0 if $\chi^2 > \chi_\alpha^2$

  where α is the level of significance and
  there are $k - 3$ degrees of freedom.

Using Excel to Conduct a Goodness of Fit Test

- For each of the k Poisson random variable values:
  - The observed and expected frequencies are entered directly into the worksheet.
  - A formula is entered to compute the difference between the observed frequency and the expected frequency.
  - Formulas are entered to compute the squared difference and squared difference divided by the expected frequency.
- The SUM function is used to compute the test statistic, which is the sum of the squared differences divided by the expected frequencies.
- The number of normal random variable intervals k is entered into the worksheet.
- The degrees of freedom are computed by subtracting 3 from k.
- The CHIDIST function is used to compute the p-value.

KEY CONCEPTS

CONCEPT	EXAMPLES	EXERCISES
Goodness of Fit Test: A Multinomial Population	(1)	1
Test of Independence	(2)	2
Goodness of Fit Test: Poisson Distribution	(3)	3
Goodness of Fit Test: Normal Distribution	(4)	4

◯ Excel Used

EXAMPLES

EXAMPLE 1

Goodness of Fit Test: A Multinomial Population

Finger Lakes Homes manufactures four styles of prefabricated homes, a two-story colonial, a ranch, a split-level, and an A-frame. To help in production planning, management would like to determine if previous customer purchases indicate that there is a preference in the style selected.

The number of homes sold of each style for 100 sales over the past two years is shown below.

Style:	Colonial	Ranch	Split-Level	A-Frame
# Sold:	30	20	35	15

Use α = .05 to determine if there is a preference in the home style selected by customers. In other words, determine if there are any differences in the proportion of home styles among all the styles sold.

SOLUTION 1

Using Excel's CHIINV and CHITEST Functions

This problem calls for a multinomial distribution goodness of fit test. Let us perform the test manually, to demonstrate the mathematical operations, and then we will use Excel. The first step is to define our notation. Let:

p_C = population proportion that purchase a colonial style
p_R = population proportion that purchase a ranch style
p_S = population proportion that purchase a split-level style
p_A = population proportion that purchase an A-frame style

Hypotheses:

$$H_0: p_C = p_R = p_S = p_A = .25$$
H_a: The population proportions are not
$$p_C = .25, \ p_R = .25, \ p_S = .25, \text{ and } p_A = .25$$

Expected Frequencies:

$$e_1 = .25(100) = 25 \qquad e_2 = .25(100) = 25$$
$$e_3 = .25(100) = 25 \qquad e_4 = .25(100) = 25$$

Test Statistic:

$$\chi^2 = \frac{(30-25)^2}{25} + \frac{(20-25)^2}{25} + \frac{(35-25)^2}{25} + \frac{(15-25)^2}{25}$$
$$= 1 + 1 + 4 + 4$$
$$= 10$$

Rejection Rule:

Reject H_0 if $\chi^2 > 7.815$

(based on $\alpha = .05$ and $k - 1 = 4 - 1 = 3$ degrees of freedom)

Conclusion:

Reject the null hypothesis

The test statistic value (10) is greater than the critical value (7.815). Therefore, we reject the assumption there is no home style preference, at the .05 level of significance. The sample strongly suggests that there is a preference in home style selected by customers.

Now we will use Excel to conduct a multinomial distribution goodness of fit test.

Enter Data: A label and the home styles of the 100 homes in the sample are entered into cells A1:A101. The hypothesized proportions (.25, .25, .25, and .25) are entered into cells D3:D6, and the total number of observations (100) is entered into cell E7. The value of the specified level of significance (.05) is entered into cell E9.

Enter Functions and Formulas: The COUNTIF function is used to compute the number of customers that preferred the Colonial style home by entering the following formula into cell E3:

=COUNTIF(A2:A101,"Col")

The number of customers that preferred each of the other home styles is computed in the same manner; we simply replace the second argument of the function with the appropriate home style such as "Ran", and so on.

To compute the expected frequency of the Colonial home style, the formula =D3*$E$7 is entered into cell F3. Similar formulas are entered into cell F4:F6 to compute the expected frequencies for the other home styles.

At this point we have the observed frequencies and expected frequencies in cells E3:E6 and F3:F6, respectively. Now, to compute the p-value associated with this goodness of fit test, we enter the following formula into cell E11:

=CHITEST(E3:E6,F3:F6)

Finally, to determine whether to reject the null hypothesis we enter the following formula into cell E12:

=IF(E11<E9,"Reject","Do Not Reject")

The above formula is stating: If the *p*-value in cell E11 is less than the level of significance value in E9, enter the label Reject into cell E12; otherwise enter the label Do Not Reject into cell E12.

Lastly, if we are interested in knowing the value of the test statistic, we can use the CHIINV function to translate the *p*-value into a χ^2 value. We do this by entering the following formula into cell E10:

=CHIINV(E11,3)

The first argument in the CHIINV function is the cell address for the *p*-value (upper tail area), and the second argument is the degrees of freedom value ($k - 1 = 4 - 1 = 3$).

Formula Worksheet:

	A	B	C	D	E	F
1	**Style**			**Hypothesized**	**Observed**	**Expected**
2	Col		**Category**	**Proportion**	**Frequency**	**Frequency**
3	Ran		**Colonial**	0.25	=COUNTIF(A2:A101,"Col")	=D3*$E$7
4	Ran		**Ranch**	0.25	=COUNTIF(A2:A101,"Ran")	=D4*$E$7
5	Afr		**Split-Level**	0.25	=COUNTIF(A2:A101,"Spl")	=D5*$E$7
6	Col		**A-Frame**	0.25	=COUNTIF(A2:A101,"Afr")	=D6*$E$7
7	Spl			**Total**	100	
8	Afr					
9	Col			**Lev.of Signif.**	0.05	
10	Afr			**Chi-Square**	=CHIINV(E11,3)	
11	Ran			**p-Value**	=CHITEST(E3:E6,F3:F6)	
12	Spl			**Conclusion**	=IF(E11<E9,"Reject","Do Not Reject")	

Looking at the results in the value worksheet below, we see the *p*-value (.0186) is less than the level of significance (.05). Therefore, our conclusion is to reject the null hypothesis. This result is consistent, as it should be, with the result of our manual calculations.

Value Worksheet:

	A	B	C	D	E	F
1	Style			Hypothesized	Observed	Expected
2	Col		Category	Proportion	Frequency	Frequency
3	Ran		Colonial	0.25	30	25
4	Ran		Ranch	0.25	20	25
5	Afr		Split-Level	0.25	35	25
6	Col		A-Frame	0.25	15	25
7	Spl			Total	100	
8	Afr					
9	Col			Lev.of Signif.	0.05	
10	Afr			Chi-Square	10.000	
11	Ran			*p*-Value	0.0186	
12	Spl			Conclusion	Reject	

Note: Rows 13-101 are not shown.

EXAMPLE 2

Test of Independence

Finger Lakes Homes manufactures prefabricated homes. Each home sold can be classified according to price and to style. The Finger Lakes Homes manager would like to determine if the price of the home and the style of the home are independent variables.

The number of homes sold for each style and price for the past two years is shown below. For convenience, the price of the home is listed as either *$99,000 or less* or *more than $99,000*.

Price	Colonial	Ranch	Split-Level	A-Frame
≤ $99,000	18	6	19	12
> $99,000	12	14	16	3

Conduct a test of independence using α = .05 to address the question of whether the home price preference is independent of the home style preference.

SOLUTION 2

Using Excel's PIVOT TABLE REPORT Tool and Excel's CHIINV and CHITEST Functions

Let us perform the test of independence manually, to demonstrate the mathematical operations, and then we will use Excel.

Hypotheses:

H_0: Price of the home is independent of the style of the home that is purchased

H_a: Price of the home is not independent of the style of the home that is purchased

Expected Frequencies:

Price	Colonial	Ranch	Split-Level	A-Frame	Total
$\leq$ \$99K	18	6	19	12	55
$>$ \$99K	12	14	16	3	45
Total	30	20	35	15	100

Test Statistic:

$$\chi^2 = \frac{(18-16.5)^2}{16.5} + \frac{(6-11)^2}{11} + \ldots + \frac{(3-6.75)^2}{6.75}$$

$$= .1364 + 2.2727 + \ldots + 2.0833$$

$$= 9.1486$$

Rejection Rule:

Reject H_0 if $\chi^2 > 7.81$

(based on $\alpha = .05$ and $(2-1)(4-1) = 3$ degrees of freedom)

Conclusion:

Reject H_0. We reject the assumption that the price of the home is independent of the style of the home that is purchased.

Now we will use Excel to conduct a test of independence.

Enter Data: Column A is used to identify each of the 100 sold homes in the study. Column B shows the price and column C shows the style of each home sold.

Data Worksheet:

	A	B	C	D	E	F	G
1	Home	Price (\$)	Style				
2	1	>99K	Colonial				
3	2	<=99K	Ranch				
4	3	>99K	Ranch				
5	4	<=99K	A-Frame				
6	5	<=99K	Colonial				

Note: Rows 7-101 are not shown.

Apply Tools: Next, we use Excel's PivotTable Report tool to develop a crosstabulation. The steps involved are as follows:

Using the PivotTable Report

Step 1 Select the **Data** pull-down menu

Step 2 Choose the **PivotTable and PivotChart Report**

Step 3 When the **PivotTable and PivotChart Wizard Step 1 of 3** dialog box appears:
Choose **Microsoft Excel list or database**
Choose **PivotTable**
Select **Next >**

Step 4 When the **PivotTable and PivotChart Wizard Step 2 of 3** dialog box appears:
Enter A1:C101 in the **Range** box
Select **Next >**

Step 5 When the **PivotTable and PivotChart Wizard Step 3 of 3** dialog box appears:
Select **New Worksheet**
Click on the **Layout** button
When the **PivotTable and PivotChart Wizard – Layout** diagram appears:
Drag the **Price ($)** field button to the **ROW** section of the diagram
Drag the **Style** field button to the **COLUMN** section of the diagram
Drag the **Home** field button to the **DATA** section of the diagram
Double click the **Sum of Home** field button in the data section
When the **PivotTable Field** dialog box appears:
Choose **Count** under **Summarized by**:
Select **OK**
Select **OK**
When the **PivotTable and PivotChart Wizard Step 3 of 3** dialog box reappears:
Select **Finish >**

Value Worksheet:

D	E	F	G	H	I	J
1	Count of Home	Style				
2	Price ($)	Colonial	Ranch	Split-Lev.	A-Frame	Grand Tot.
3	<=99K	18	6	19	12	55
4	>99K	12	14	16	3	45
5	Grand Total	30	20	35	15	100

Note: Columns A-C and rows 6-101 are not shown.

Enter Functions and Formulas: Now we ready to compute the expected frequencies for the Finger Lakes Homes contingency table under the assumption of independence. To compute the expected number of homes sold that are a Colonial style and priced at $\leq$ 99,000, we enter the formula =F5*J3/J5 into cell F9. To compute the expected number of homes sold that are a Colonial style and priced at > 99,000, we enter the formula =F5*J4/J5 into cell F10. Similar formulas are entered into cells G9:I10 to compute the expected frequencies for the remaining style-price combinations.

At this point we have the observed frequencies and expected frequencies in cells F3:E4 and F9:F10, respectively. Now, to compute the *p*-value associated with this test of independence, we enter the following formula into cell G13:

=CHITEST(F3:I4,F9:I10)

Lastly, if we are interested in knowing the value of the test statistic, we can use the CHIINV function to translate the p-value into a χ^2 value. We do this by entering the formula =CHIINV(G13,3) into cell G12. The first argument in the CHIINV function is the cell address for the p-value (upper tail area), and the second argument is the degrees of freedom value, $(r-1)(c-1) = (2-1)(3-1) = 3$.

Formula Worksheet:

D	E	F	G	H	I	J
1	Count of Home	Style				
2	Price ($)	Colonial	Ranch	Split-Lev.	A-Frame	Grand Tot.
3	<=99K	18	6	19	12	55
4	>99K	12	14	16	3	45
5	Grand Total	30	20	35	15	100
6						
7	Expected Frequencies					
8		Colonial	Ranch	Split-Lev.	A-Frame	
9	<=99K	=F5*J3/J5	=G5*J3/J5	=H5*J3/J5	=I5*J3/J5	
10	>99K	=F5*J4/J5	=G5*J4/J5	=H5*J4/J5	=I5*J4/J5	
11						
12			Chi-Sq.	=CHIINV(G13,3)		
13			p-Value	=CHITEST(F3:I4,F9:I10)		

We see below that the p-value (.0274) is less than the level of significance (.05). Therefore, our conclusion is to reject the null hypothesis. We are 95% confident that the two variables, home price and home style, are not independent.

Value Worksheet:

D	E	F	G	H	I	J
1	Count of Home	Style				
2	Price ($)	Colonial	Ranch	Split-Lev.	A-Frame	Grand Tot.
3	<=99K	18	6	19	12	55
4	>99K	12	14	16	3	45
5	Grand Total	30	20	35	15	100
6						
7	Expected Frequencies					
8		Colonial	Ranch	Split-Lev.	A-Frame	
9	<=99K	16.50	11.00	19.25	8.25	
10	>99K	13.50	9.00	15.75	6.75	
11						
12			Chi-Sq.	9.1486		
13			p-Value	0.0274		

EXAMPLE 3

Goodness of Fit Test: Poisson Distribution

In studying the need for an additional entrance to a Troy city parking garage, a consultant has recommended an analysis approach that is applicable only in situations where the number of cars entering during a specified time period follows a Poisson distribution.

A random sample of 100 one-minute intervals resulted in the customer arrivals listed below.

Arrivals	0	1	2	3	4	5	6	7	8	9	10	11	12
Frequency	0	1	4	10	14	20	12	12	9	8	6	3	1

Conduct a goodness of fit test, at the .05 level of significance, to determine if the assumption of a Poisson distribution is reasonable for the number of arrivals in a one-minute interval.

SOLUTION 3

Using Excel's POISSON and CHIDIST Functions

Let us perform the goodness of fit test manually, to demonstrate the mathematical operations, and then we will use Excel.

Hypotheses:

H_0: Number of cars entering the garage during a one-minute interval is Poisson distributed

H_a: Number of cars entering the garage during a one-minute interval is _not_ Poisson distributed

Total Arrivals = 0(0) + 1(1) + 2(4) + 3(10) . . . + 12(1) = 600
Total Time Periods = 100
Estimate of μ = 600/100 = 6
Hence,

$$f(x) = \frac{6^x e^{-6}}{x!}$$

x	f(x)	nf(x)	i	f_i	e_i	$f_i - e_i$	$(f_i - e_i)^2$	$(f_i - e_i)^2 / e_i$
0	.0025	.25						
1	.0149	1.49						
2	.0446	4.46	0, 1, or 2	5	6.20	-1.20	1.4325	0.2312
3	.0892	8.92	3	10	8.92	1.08	1.1588	0.1299
4	.1339	13.39	4	14	13.39	0.61	0.3779	0.0282
5	.1606	16.06	5	20	16.06	3.94	15.5054	0.9653
6	.1606	16.06	6	12	16.06	-4.06	16.5024	1.0274
7	.1377	13.77	7	12	13.77	-1.77	3.1248	0.2270
8	.1033	10.33	8	9	10.33	-1.33	1.7577	0.1702
9	.0688	6.88	9	8	6.88	1.12	1.2458	0.1810
10	.0413	4.13	10 or more	10	8.39	1.62	2.5844	0.3079
11	.0225	2.25						
12+	.0201	2.01						
Total	1.0000	100.00						3.2681

Test Statistic:

$$\chi^2 = \frac{(-1.20)^2}{6.20} + \frac{(1.08)^2}{8.92} + \ldots + \frac{(1.62)^2}{8.38} = 3.268$$

Rejection Rule: Reject H_0 if $\chi^2 > 14.07$
where $\alpha = .05$ and $k - p - 1 = 9 - 1 - 1 = 7$ degrees of freedom
(k = number of categories and p = number
of population parameters estimated)

Conclusion: We cannot reject H_0.
There's no reason to doubt the assumption of a Poisson distribution.

Now we will use Excel to conduct the goodness of fit test.

Enter Data: The nine categories of arrivals and their observed frequencies are entered in Columns A and B. The expected frequencies are computed in Column C using the POISSON function. (Note that in the cases of "0, 1, or 2" and "10 or more" arrivals, we have the POISSON function return a <u>cumulative</u> probability.)

Columns D and E are used to compute the χ^2 test statistic. The degrees of freedom are computed in cell C15 as $k - 2$. The p-value is computed in cell C16 using the CHIDIST function.

Formula Worksheet:

	A	B	C	D	E
1	Number	Observed	Expected	Sq'd.	Sq.Diff./
2	of Arriv.	Frequency	Frequency	Differ.	Exp.Freq.
3	0, 1, or 2	5	=POISSON(2,6,TRUE)*B12	=(B3-C3)^2	=D3/C3
4	3	10	=POISSON(3,6,FALSE)*B12	=(B4-C4)^2	=D4/C4
5	4	14	=POISSON(4,6,FALSE)*B12	=(B5-C5)^2	=D5/C5
6	5	20	=POISSON(5,6,FALSE)*B12	=(B6-C6)^2	=D6/C6
7	6	12	=POISSON(6,6,FALSE)*B12	=(B7-C7)^2	=D7/C7
8	7	12	=POISSON(7,6,FALSE)*B12	=(B8-C8)^2	=D8/C8
9	8	9	=POISSON(8,6,FALSE)*B12	=(B9-C9)^2	=D9/C9
10	9	8	=POISSON(9,6,FALSE)*B12	=(B10-C10)^2	=D10/C10
11	10 or more	10	=(1-POISSON(9,6,TRUE))*B12	=(B11-C11)^2	=D11/C11
12	Total	=SUM(B3:B11)			=SUM(E3:E11)
13	Categories	9			
14	Test Statistic	=E12			
15	Degrees of Freedom	=C13-2			
16	p-Value	=CHIDIST(C14,C15)			

The value worksheet below shows a *p*-value of .8591. With .8591 > α = .05, we <u>cannot</u> reject the null hypothesis that the number of cars entering the garage during a one-minute interval is Poisson distributed.

Value Worksheet:

	A	B	C	D	E
1	Number	Observed	Expected	Sq'd.	Sq.Diff./
2	of Arriv.	Frequency	Frequency	Differ.	Exp.Freq.
3	0, 1, or 2	5	6.197	1.433	0.2312
4	3	10	8.924	1.159	0.1299
5	4	14	13.385	0.378	0.0282
6	5	20	16.062	15.505	0.9653
7	6	12	16.062	16.502	1.0274
8	7	12	13.768	3.125	0.2270
9	8	9	10.326	1.758	0.1702
10	9	8	6.884	1.246	0.1810
11	10 or more	10	8.392	2.584	0.3079
12	Total	100	100.000		3.2681
13	Categories	9			
14	Test Statistic	3.2681			
15	Degrees of Freedom	7			
16	p-Value	0.8591			

EXAMPLE 4

Goodness of Fit Test: Normal Distribution

Victor Computers manufactures and sells a general purpose microcomputer. As part of a study to evaluate sales personnel, management wants to determine if the monthly sales volume (number of units sold by a salesperson) follows a normal probability distribution.

A simple random sample of 30 of the salespeople was taken. The number of units each salesperson sold in a month are listed below. The sample mean is 71 and the sample standard deviation is 18.54.

33	43	44	45	52	52	56	58	63	64
64	65	66	68	70	72	73	73	74	75
83	84	85	86	91	92	94	98	102	105

Conduct a goodness of fit test, at a .05 significance level, to determine if the population of computers sold in a month by the salespeople is normally distributed with a mean of 71 units and a standard deviation of 18.54 units.

SOLUTION 4

Using Excel's CHIDIST Function

Let us perform the goodness of fit test manually, to demonstrate the mathematical operations, and then we will use Excel.

Hypotheses: H_0: The population of number of units sold has a normal distribution
                   with mean 71 and standard deviation 18.54.
              H_a: The population of number of units sold does not have a normal
                   distribution with mean 71 and standard deviation 18.54.

Interval Definition: To satisfy the requirement of an expected frequency of at least 5 in
                   each interval we will divide the normal distribution into 30/5 = 6 equal
                   probability intervals.

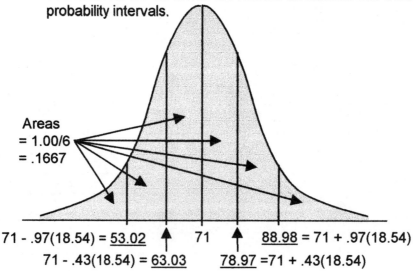

Areas
= 1.00/6
= .1667

71 - .97(18.54) = <u>53.02</u>   71   <u>88.98</u> = 71 + .97(18.54)
71 - .43(18.54) = <u>63.03</u>   <u>78.97</u> =71 + .43(18.54)

i	f_i	e_i	$f_i - e_i$
Less than 53.02	6	5	1
53.02 to 63.03	3	5	-2
63.03 to 71.00	6	5	1
71.00 to 78.97	5	5	0
78.97 to 88.98	4	5	-1
More than 88.98	6	5	1
Total	30	30	

Test Statistic:

$$\chi^2 = \frac{(1)^2}{5} + \frac{(-2)^2}{5} + \frac{(1)^2}{5} + \frac{(0)^2}{5} + \frac{(-1)^2}{5} + \frac{(1)^2}{5} = 1.60$$

Rejection Rule: Reject H_0 if $\chi^2 > 7.81$
(with $\alpha = .05$ and $k - p - 1 = 6 - 2 - 1 = 3$ degrees of freedom)

Conclusion: We <u>cannot</u> reject H_0 because $\chi^2 < \chi^2_\alpha$ (That is, $1.60 < 7.81$).
There is little evidence to support rejecting the assumption that
the population is normally distributed with $\mu = 71$ and $\sigma = 18.54$.

Now we will use Excel to conduct the goodness of fit test.

Enter Data: The six categories of sales, their observed frequencies, and their expected frequencies are entered in Columns A, B, and C. Columns D and E are used to compute the χ^2 test statistic. The degrees of freedom are computed in cell C12 as $k - 3$. The p-value is computed in cell C13 using the CHIDIST function.

Formula Worksheet:

	A	B	C	D	E
1	**Number of**	**Observed**	**Expected**	**Sq'd.**	**Sq.Differ./**
2	**Units Sold**	**Frequency**	**Frequency**	**Differ.**	**Exp.Freq.**
3	Less than 53.02	6	5	=(B3-C3)^2	=D3/C3
4	53.02 to 63.03	3	5	=(B4-C4)^2	=D4/C4
5	63.03 to 71.00	6	5	=(B5-C5)^2	=D5/C5
6	71.00 to 78.97	5	5	=(B6-C6)^2	=D6/C6
7	78.97 to 88.98	4	5	=(B7-C7)^2	=D7/C7
8	88.98 and Over	6	5	=(B8-C8)^2	=D8/C8
9	Total	=SUM(B3:B8)			=SUM(E3:E8)
10		Categories	6		
11		Test Statistic	=E9		
12		Degrees of Freedom	=C10-3		
13		p-Value	=CHIDIST(C11,C12)		

The value worksheet below shows a *p*-value of .6594. With .6594 > α = .05, we <u>cannot</u> reject the assumption that the number of units sold by a salesperson follows a normal distribution. This conclusion is consistent with the result of our manually computations.

Value Worksheet:

	A	B	C	D	E
1	**Number of**	**Observed**	**Expected**	**Sq'd.**	**Sq.Differ./**
2	**Units Sold**	**Frequency**	**Frequency**	**Differ.**	**Exp.Freq.**
3	Less than 53.02	6	5	1.000	0.2000
4	53.02 to 63.03	3	5	4.000	0.8000
5	63.03 to 71.00	6	5	1.000	0.2000
6	71.00 to 78.97	5	5	0.000	0.0000
7	78.97 to 88.98	4	5	1.000	0.2000
8	88.98 and Over	6	5	1.000	0.2000
9	**Total**	30			1.6000
10	**Categories**	6			
11	**Test Statistic**	1.6000			
12	**Degrees of Freedom**	3			
13	***p*-Value**	0.6594			

EXERCISES

EXERCISE 1

<u>Goodness of Fit Test: A Multinomial Population</u>

Employee panel preferences for three proposed company logo designs follow.

<u>Design A</u>	<u>Design B</u>	<u>Design C</u>
78	59	66

Use α = .05 and test to determine any difference in preference among the three logo designs.

EXERCISE 2

<u>Test of Independence</u>

City planners are evaluating three proposed alternatives for relieving the growing traffic congestion on a north-south highway in a booming city. The proposed alternatives are: (1) designate high-occupancy vehicle (HOV) lanes on the existing highway, (2) construct a new, parallel highway, and (3) construct a light (passenger) rail system.

In an analysis of the three proposals, a citizen group has raised the question of whether preferences for the three alternatives differ among residents near the highway and non-residents. A test of independence will address this question, with the hypotheses being:

H_0: Proposal preference is independent of the residency status of the individual
H_a: Proposal preference is not independent of the residency status of the individual

A simple random sample of 500 individuals has been selected. The crosstabulation of the residency statuses and proposal preferences of the individuals sampled is shown below.

| | Proposal | | |
Residency Status	HOV Lanes	New Highway	Light Rail
Nearby resident	110	45	70
Distant resident	140	75	60

Conduct a test of independence using $\alpha = .05$ to address the question of whether residency status is independent of the proposal preference.

EXERCISE 3

Goodness of Fit Test: Poisson Distribution

The supervisor in charge of staffing the university's computer help desk is studying the occurrence of Incoming calls for assistance. The calls occur randomly and independently; the probability of a call is the same for any two time periods of equal length.

A random sample of 75 fifteen-minute intervals resulted in the call frequencies listed below.

Incoming Calls	0	1	2	3	4	5	6	7	8	9	10
Frequency	1	5	11	19	16	9	7	4	2	1	0

Conduct a goodness of fit test, at the .05 level of significance, to determine if the assumption of a Poisson distribution is reasonable for the number of calls in a 15-minute interval.

EXERCISE 4

Goodness of Fit Test: Normal Distribution

Nada Walker is a fairly serious runner. She runs nearly every day, although her distance varies due to weather, how she feels, and available spare time. The distances (in miles) she has run per month for the last 30 months are listed below. The sample mean is 63 miles and the sample standard deviation is 6.95 miles.

62.0	62.0	62.0	62.0	62.0	62.0	62.0	62.0	62.0	62.0
58.4	58.4	58.4	58.4	58.4	58.4	58.4	58.4	58.4	58.4
60.5	60.5	60.5	60.5	60.5	60.5	60.5	60.5	60.5	60.5

Conduct a goodness of fit test, at a .025 significance level, to determine if the population of miles run in a month by Nada is normally distributed with a mean of 63 miles and a standard deviation of 6.95 miles.

SELF-TEST

TRUE/FALSE

___ 1. The test of independence is always a one-tailed test.

___ 2. If we reject the null hypothesis H_0 in a test of independence, we are concluding that the variables are independent.

___ 3. The purpose of the hypothesis test for proportions of a multinomial population is to determine whether the proportions are equal (follow a discrete uniform distribution).

___ 4. For a chi-square goodness of fit test, if the expected number in some category is less than the required minimum, adjacent categories can be combined to increase the expected number.

___ 5. If we conclude by means of the test of independence that the variables are not independent, we can then determine from the test results exactly how the dependence comes about.

FILL-IN-THE-BLANK

1. The _____ used in the test of independence is an example of crosstabulation.

2. For the normal distribution goodness of fit test, it is a good approach to define the intervals of values in a way that the intervals have _____.

3. Both the hypothesis test for proportions of a multinomial population and the test of independence focus on the differences between the observed frequencies and the

   _____.

4. The _____ probability distribution can be thought of as an extension of the binomial distribution to the case of three or more categories of outcomes.

5. Both the hypothesis test for proportions of a multinomial population and the test of independence employ a _____ test.

MULTIPLE CHOICE

____ 1. The test statistic for the chi-square tests in this chapter requires, for each category, an expected frequency of at least
   a) 2
   b) 5
   c) 10
   d) 30

____ 2. For the Poisson and normal distribution goodness of fit tests, the variable p in the degrees of freedom equation $k - p - 1$ represents
   a) the number of population parameters estimated from the sample data
   b) the critical p-value
   c) the significance level stated as a percentage
   d) the number of categories (partitions) used

____ 3. In the case of the test of independence, the number of degrees of freedom for the appropriate chi-square distribution is computed as
   a) $k - 1$
   b) $k - p - 1$
   c) $n - m - 1$
   d) $(n - 1)(m - 1)$

____ 4. The properties of a multinomial experiment include all of the following <u>except</u>
   a) the experiment consists of a sequence of n identical trials
   b) three or more outcomes are possible on each trial
   c) the probability of each outcome can change from trial to trial
   d) the trials are independent

____ 5. The test of independence presented in the chapter requires that there be
   a) two variables, each having two outcomes
   b) two variables, each having two or more outcomes
   c) two or more variables, each having two outcomes
   d) two or more variables, each having two or more outcomes

ANSWERS

EXERCISES

1) p-value = .2667 > .05; do not reject H_0 (no apparent preferences)

2) p-value = .0277 < .05; reject H_0 (they are not independent)

3) Do <u>not</u> reject H_0. *p*-value is much greater than α. Little evidence to suggest that call arrivals are <u>not</u> Poisson distributed.

	A	B	C	D	E
1	Number	Observed	Expected	Sq'd.	Sq.Diff./
2	of Arriv.	Frequency	Frequency	Differ.	Exp.Freq.
3	0 or 1	6	7.802	3.248	0.4163
4	2	11	11.885	0.783	0.0659
5	3	19	15.213	14.342	0.9427
6	4	16	14.604	1.948	0.1334
7	5	9	11.216	4.911	0.4379
8	6	7	7.178	0.032	0.0044
9	7 or more	7	7.101	0.010	0.0014
10	Total	75	75.000		2.0021
11	Categories	7			
12	Test Statistic	2.0021			
13	Degrees of Freedom	5			
14	*p*-Value	0.8489			

4) Reject H_0 because $\chi^2 = 10.4 > \chi^2_\alpha = 9.3484$ (or because *p*-value $= .0155 < \alpha = .025$). The population does <u>not</u> have a normal distribution with $\mu = 63$ and $\sigma = 6.95$.

	A	B	C	D	E
1	Number of	Observed	Expected	Sq'd.	Sq.Differ./
2	Units Sold	Frequency	Frequency	Differ.	Exp.Freq.
3	Less than 56.26	3	5	4.000	0.8000
4	56.26 to 60.01	2	5	9.000	1.8000
5	60.01 to 63.00	10	5	25.000	5.0000
6	63.00 to 65.99	7	5	4.000	0.8000
7	65.99 to 69.74	6	5	1.000	0.2000
8	69.74 and Over	2	5	9.000	1.8000
9	Total	30			10.4000
10	Categories	6			
11	Test Statistic	10.4000			
12	Degrees of Freedom	3			
13	*p*-Value	0.0155			

TRUE/FALSE

1) True
2) False
3) False
4) True
5) False

FILL-IN-THE-BLANK

1) contingency table
2) equal probability
3) expected frequencies
4) multinomial
5) chi-square goodness of fit

MULTIPLE CHOICE

1) b
2) a
3) d
4) c
5) b

CHAPTER 13

Analysis of Variance and Experimental Design

Introduction to Analysis of Variance

Analysis of Variance: Testing for the Equality of k Population Means

Multiple Comparison Procedures

Introduction to Experimental Design

Completely Randomized Designs

Randomized Block Design

Factorial Experiments

LEARNING OBJECTIVES

1. Understand how the analysis of variance procedure can be used to determine if the means of more than two populations are equal.

2. Know the assumptions necessary to use the analysis of variance procedure.

3. Understand the use of the *F* distribution in performing the analysis of variance procedure.

4. Know how to set up an ANOVA table and interpret the entries in the table.

5. Be able to use output from computer software packages to solve analysis of variance problems.

6. Know how to use Fisher's least significant difference (LSD) procedure and Fisher's LSD with the Bonferroni adjustment to conduct statistical comparisons between pairs of populations means.

7. Understand the difference between a completely randomized design, a randomized block design, and factorial experiments.

8. Know the definition of the following terms:

comparisonwise Type I error rate	replication
experimentwise Type I error rate	partitioning
factor	blocking
level	main effect
treatment	interaction

REVIEW

Introduction to Analysis of Variance
- Analysis of Variance (ANOVA) can be used to test for the equality of three or more population means using data obtained from observational or experimental studies.
- We want to use the sample results to test the following hypotheses.

$$H_0: \ \mu_1 = \mu_2 = \mu_3 = \cdots = \mu_k$$
$$H_a: \text{ Not all population means are equal}$$

- If H_0 is rejected, we cannot conclude that all population means are different.
- Rejecting H_0 means that at least two population means have different values.
- Terminology:
  - The response variable is the dependent variable.
  - The factor is the independent variable.
  - The treatments are the levels of the factor.

Assumptions for Analysis of Variance
- For each population, the response variable is normally distributed. (This is not a concern if the sample sizes are equal.)
- The variance of the response variable, denoted s^2, is the same for all of the populations.
- The observations must be independent.

Analysis of Variance: Testing the Equality of k Population Means
- The <u>notation</u> is:

$$x_{ij} = \text{value of observation } i \text{ for treatment } j$$
$$n_j = \text{number of observations for treatment } j$$
$$\bar{x}_j = \text{sample mean for treatment } j$$
$$s_j^2 = \text{sample variance for treatment } j$$
$$s_j = \text{sample standard deviation for treatment } j$$

- The <u>sample mean for treatment j</u> is:

$$\bar{x}_j = \frac{\sum_{i=1}^{n_j} x_{ij}}{n_j}$$

- The <u>sample variance for treatment j</u> is:

$$s_j^2 = \frac{\sum_{i=1}^{n_j} (x_{ij} - \bar{x}_j)^2}{n_j - 1}$$

- The <u>overall sample mean</u> is:

$$\bar{\bar{x}} = \frac{\sum_{j=1}^{k} \sum_{i=1}^{n_j} x_{ij}}{n_T}$$

Between-Treatments Estimate of Population Variance
- The <u>sum of squares due to treatments</u> is:

$$\text{SSTR} = \sum_{j=1}^{k} n_j (\bar{x}_j - \bar{\bar{x}})^2$$

- The <u>mean of squares due to treatments</u> is:

$$\text{MSTR} = \frac{\text{SSTR}}{k-1}$$

Within-Treatments Estimate of Population Variance
- The <u>sum of squares due to error</u> is:

$$\text{SSE} = \sum_{j=1}^{k} (n_j - 1) s_j^2$$

- The <u>mean of squares due to error</u> is:

$$\text{MSE} = \frac{\text{SSE}}{n_T - k}$$

Comparing the Variance Estimates: The *F* Test
- If the null hypothesis is true and the ANOVA assumptions are valid, the sampling distribution of MSTR/MSE is an *F* distribution with MSTR d.f. equal to $k - 1$ and MSE d.f. equal to $n_T - k$.
- If the means of the *k* populations are not equal, the value of MSTR/MSE will be inflated because MSTR overestimates s^2.
- Hence, we will reject H_0 if the resulting value of MSTR/MSE appears to be too large to have been selected at random from the appropriate *F* distribution.
- <u>Hypotheses</u>:

$$H_0: \ \mu_1 = \mu_2 = \mu_3 = \cdots = \mu_k$$
$$H_a: \ \text{Not all population means are equal}$$

- <u>Test statistic</u>:

$$F = \text{MSTR/MSE}$$

- <u>Rejection rule</u>:

Reject H_0 if $F > F_\alpha$
where the value of F_α is based on an *F* distribution
with $k - 1$ numerator degrees of freedom and
$n_T - 1$ denominator degrees of freedom.

ANOVA Table
- An ANOVA table is used to summarize the analysis of variance computations and results.
- The general form of the table is:

Source of Variation	Sum of Squares	Degrees of Freedom	Mean Square	F
Treatments	SSTR	$k - 1$	MSTR	MSTR/MSE
Error	SSE	$n_T - k$	MSE	
Total	SST	$n_T - 1$		

Using Excel to Test for the Equality of *k* Population Means
Assuming the data for samples 1 to *k* have already been entered in the worksheet, the general steps for computing the hypothesis test are as follows:
- Select the <u>Tools</u> pull-down menu, choose the <u>Data Analysis</u> option, and choose <u>Anova: Single Factor</u> tool.
- The <u>Anova: Single Factor</u> tool handles the remainder of the computation with some input (α, for example) from you.
- The ouput of this tool includes values for: test statistic, critical *F*, and *p*-value.

Multiple Comparison Procedures
- Anova can only tell us whether the means of *k* populations are equal.
- We may want to determine where the differences among means occur.
- <u>Multiple comparison procedures</u> can be used to conduct statistical comparisons between pairs of population means.

Fisher's LSD Procedure

- <u>Fisher's least significant difference (LSD)</u> procedure can be used to determine where the differences occur between population means.
- <u>Hypotheses</u>:

$$H_0: \ \mu_i = \mu_j$$

$$H_a: \ \mu_i \neq \mu_j$$

- <u>Test statistic</u>:

$$t = \frac{\bar{x}_i - \bar{x}_j}{\sqrt{MSE\left(\frac{1}{n_i} + \frac{1}{n_j}\right)}}$$

- <u>Rejection rule</u>:

Using *p*-value: Reject H_0 if *p*-value $< \alpha$

Using test statistic: Reject H_0 if $t < -t_{\alpha/2}$ or $t > t_{\alpha/2}$
where the value of $t_{\alpha/2}$ is based on a t distribution
with $n_T - k$ degrees of freedom.

Fisher's LSD Procedure Based on the Test Statistic $\bar{x}_i - \bar{x}_j$

- Another approach is to determine how large the difference between the sample means must be to reject H_0.
- <u>Hypotheses</u>:

$$H_0: \ \mu_i = \mu_j$$

$$H_a: \ \mu_i \neq \mu_j$$

- <u>Test statistic</u>:

$$\bar{x}_i - \bar{x}_j$$

- <u>Rejection rule</u>:

Reject H_0 if $|\bar{x}_i - \bar{x}_j| > \text{LSD}$

where

$$\text{LSD} = t_{\alpha/2}\sqrt{MSE\left(\frac{1}{n_i} + \frac{1}{n_j}\right)}$$

Confidence Interval Estimate Using Fisher's LSD Procedure

- Fisher's LSD can also be used to develop a confidence interval estimate of the difference between the means of two populations.
- The confidence interval estimate can be used to test the hypotheses stated above.
- If the confidence interval includes the value zero, we cannot reject the hypothesis that the two population means are equal.
- <u>Confidence Interval Estimate</u>: $\bar{x}_i - \bar{x}_j \pm \text{LSD}$

Type I Error Rate
- The comparisonwise Type I error rate α indicates the level of significance associated with a single pairwise comparison.
- The experimentwise Type I error rate α_{ew} indicates the probability of committing a Type I error on at least one of the pairwise comparisons.
- The experimentwise Type I error rate gets larger for problems with more populations.
- One alternative for controlling the experimentwise Type I error rate involves using a smaller comparisonwise error rate for each test.

Introduction to Experimental Design
- Statistical studies are classified as being either experimental or observational.
- In an observational study:
  - No attempt is made to control the variables.
  - A survey is a common type of observational study.
- In an experimental study:
  - One or more independent variables of interest, called factors, are identified.
  - One or more factors are controlled so that data can be obtained about how the factors influence the dependent or response variables.
  - Treatments refer to the different levels of a factor.
  - The primary statistical objective of the experiment is to determine whether the mean value of the response variable is the same for all of the populations.
  - Obtaining a sample size greater than one for each treatment is called replication.
  - Each item in a sample is an experimental unit.
  - Randomization is the process of assigning the treatments to the experimental units at random.

Completely Randomized Designs
- The hypotheses we want to test are:
  H_0: $\mu_1 = \mu_2 = \mu_3$
  H_a: Not all the means are equal
- ANOVA requires the calculation of two independent estimates of the population variance σ^2.

Between-Treatments Estimate of Population Variance
- The between-treatments estimate of σ^2 is referred to as the mean square due to treatments and is denoted MSTR.

$$MSTR = \frac{SSTR}{k-1} = \frac{\sum_{j=1}^{k} n_j (\bar{x}_j - \bar{\bar{x}})^2}{k-1}$$

- The numerator is called the sum of squares between or sum of squares due to treatments and is denoted SSTR.
- The denominator $k - 1$ represents the degrees of freedom associated with SSTR.

Within-Treatments Estimate of Population Variance
- The between-treatments estimate of σ^2 is referred to as the <u>mean square due to error</u> and is denoted <u>MSE</u>.

$$\text{MSE} = \frac{\text{SSE}}{n_T - k} = \frac{\sum_{j=1}^{k}(n_j - 1)s_j^2}{n_T - k}$$

- The numerator is called the sum of squares within or <u>sum of squares due to error</u> and is denoted <u>SSE</u>.
- The denominator $n_T - k$ represents the <u>degrees of freedom</u> associated with MSE.

Comparing the Variance Estimates: The F Test
- If the null hypothesis is true and the ANOVA assumptions are valid, the <u>sampling distribution of MSTR/MSE is an F distribution</u> with $k - 1$ numerator degrees of freedom and $n_T - k$ denominator degrees of freedom.
- If the null hypothesis is not true, the value of MSTR/MSE will be inflated because MSTR overestimates σ^2.
- Hence, we will reject H_0 if the resulting value of MSTR/MSE appears to be too large to have selected at random from an F distribution with $k - 1$ and $n_T - k$ degrees of freedom.

Using Excel's Anova: Single Factor Tool
Assuming the data for samples 1 to k have already been entered in the worksheet, the general steps for computing the hypothesis test are as follows:
- Select the <u>Tools</u> pull-down menu, choose the <u>Data Analysis</u> option, and choose <u>Anova: Single Factor</u> tool.
- The <u>Anova: Single Factor</u> tool handles the remainder of the computation with some input (α, for example) from you.
- The ouput of this tool includes values for: test statistic, critical F, and p-value.

Randomized Block Design
- A problem can arise whenever differences due to factors not considered in the experiment cause the MSE term in the MSTR/MSE ratio to become large.
- In such cases, the F value can become small, signaling no difference among treatment means when in fact such a difference exists.
- A completely randomized design is useful when the experimental units are homogeneous.
- When the experimental units are not homogeneous, <u>blocking</u> is useful to form homogeneous groups.
- This design tends to provide a better estimate of the true error variance MSE.
- Blocking in experimental design is similar to stratification in sampling.
- The *randomized* aspect of the randomized block design is the random order in which the treatments are assigned to the experimental units.

ANOVA Procedure

- The ANOVA procedure partitions the sum of squares total (SST) into three groups:
  - Sum of squares due to treatments (SSTR)
  - Sum of squares due to blocks (SSBL)
  - Sum of squares due to error (SSE)

$$SST = SSTR + SSBL + SSE$$

- Also, the $n_T - 1$ total degrees of freedom are partitioned into three groups:
  - $k - 1$ degrees of freedom go to treatments
  - $b - 1$ degrees of freedom go to blocks
  - $(k - 1)(b - 1)$ go to the error term
- The ANOVA table is:

Source of Variation	Sum of Squares	Degrees of Freedom	Mean Square	F
Treatments	SSTR	$k - 1$	MSTR = SSTR/$(k - 1)$	MSTR/MSE
Blocks	SSBL	$b - 1$	MSBL = SSBL/$(b - 1)$	
Error	SSE	$(k - 1)(b - 1)$	MSE = SSE/$[(k - 1)(b - 1)]$	
Total	SST	$n_T - 1$		

ANOVA Computations

- Total sum of squares:

$$SST = \sum_{i=1}^{b} \sum_{j=1}^{k} (x_{ij} - \bar{\bar{x}})^2$$

- Sum of squares due to treatments:

$$SSTR = b \sum_{j=1}^{k} (\bar{x}_{\cdot j} - \bar{\bar{x}})^2$$

- Sum of squares due to blocks:

$$SSBL = k \sum_{i=1}^{b} (\bar{x}_{i \cdot} - \bar{\bar{x}})^2$$

- Sum of squares due to error:

$$SSE = SST - SSTR - SSBL$$

Using Excel's Anova: Two-Factor Without Replication Tool

Assuming the n_t observations have already been entered in the worksheet, the general steps for conducting the ANOVA are as follows:

- Select the Tools pull-down menu, choose the Data Analysis option, and choose Anova: Two-Factor Without Replication tool.
- The Anova: Two-Factor Without Replication tool handles the remainder of the computation with some input (α, for example) from you.
- The ouput of this tool includes an ANOVA table similar to the one above, but the "Treatments" label is replaced with "Rows" and the "Blocks " label is replaced with "Columns".
- The Excel output also includes critical F values and p-values for treatments and blocks.

Factorial Experiments
- In some experiments we want to draw <u>simultaneous conclusions</u> about more than one variable or factor.
- In <u>factorial experiments</u>, the experimental conditions include <u>all possible combinations of the factors</u>.
- <u>Interaction</u> is a new effect that we can now study as a result of using a factorial experiment.

ANOVA Procedure
- The ANOVA procedure partitions the sum of squares total (SST) into four groups:
  - <u>Sum of squares due to factor A</u> (SSA)
  - <u>Sum of squares due to factor B</u> (SSB)
  - <u>Sum of squares due to interaction</u> (SSAB)
  - <u>Sum of squares due to error</u> (SSE)

$$SST = SSA + SSB + SSAB + SSE$$

- Also, the $n_T - 1$ total degrees of freedom are partitioned into three groups:
  - $a - 1$ degrees of freedom go to factor A, where a is the number of levels of factor A
  - $b - 1$ degrees of freedom go to factor B, where b is the number of levels of factor B
  - $(a - 1)(b - 1)$ go to interaction
  - $ab(r - 1)$ go to the error term, where r is the number of replications
- The <u>ANOVA table</u> is:

Source of Variation	Sum of Squares	Degrees of Freedom	Mean Square	F
Factor A	SSA	$a - 1$	$MSA = SSA/(a - 1)$	MSA/MSE
Factor B	SSB	$b - 1$	$MSB = SSB/(b - 1)$	MSB/MSE
Interaction	SSAB	$(a - 1)(b - 1)$	$MSAB = SSAB/[(a - 1)(b - 1)]$	MSAB/MSE
Error	SSE	$ab(r - 1)$	$MSE = SSE/[ab(r - 1)]$	
Total	SST	$n_T - 1$		

ANOVA Computations
- <u>Total sum of squares</u>:

$$SST = \sum_{i=1}^{a} \sum_{j=1}^{b} \sum_{k=1}^{r} (X_{ijk} - \bar{\bar{x}})^2$$

- <u>Sum of squares due to factor A</u>:

$$SSA = br \sum_{i=1}^{a} (\bar{x}_{i.} - \bar{\bar{x}})^2$$

- <u>Sum of squares due to factor B</u>:

$$SSB = ar \sum_{j=1}^{b} (\bar{x}_{.j} - \bar{\bar{x}})^2$$

- <u>Sum of squares due to interaction</u>:

$$SSAB = r \sum_{i=1}^{a} \sum_{j=1}^{b} (\bar{x}_{ij} - \bar{x}_{i.} - \bar{x}_{.j} + \bar{\bar{x}})^2$$

- <u>Sum of squares due to error</u>:

$$SSE = SST - SSA - SSB - SSAB$$

Using Excel's Anova: Two-Factor With Replication Tool
Assuming the n_t observations have already been entered in the worksheet, the general steps for conducting the ANOVA are as follows:

- Select the Tools pull-down menu, choose the Data Analysis option, and choose Anova: Two-Factor With Replication tool.
- The Anova: Two-Factor With Replication tool handles the remainder of the computation with some input from you, such as α and r (number of replications).
- The ouput of this tool includes an ANOVA table similar to the one above, but with the following differences:
- "Factor A" label is replaced with "Sample"
- "Factor B " label is replaced with "Columns"
- "Error" label is replaced with "Within"
- The Excel output also includes critical F values and p-values for "Sample", "Columns", and "Interaction".

KEY CONCEPTS

CONCEPT	EXAMPLES	EXERCISES
Test for the Equality of k Population Means	①	1
Multiple Comparison Procedure: Fisher's LSD	②	2
Completely Randomized Design	③	3
Randomized Block Design	④	4
Factorial Experiment	⑤	5
	◯ Excel Used	

EXAMPLES

EXAMPLE 1

Test for the Equality of k Population Means

J. R. Reed would like to know if the mean number of hours worked per week is the same for the department managers at her three manufacturing plants (Buffalo, Pittsburgh, and Detroit).

A simple random sample of 5 managers from each of the three plants was taken and the number of hours worked by each manager for the previous week is shown below.

	Plant 1	Plant 2	Plant 3
Observation	Buffalo	Pittsburgh	Detroit
1	48	73	51
2	54	63	63
3	57	66	61
4	54	64	54
5	62	74	56
Sample Mean	55	68	57
Sample Variance	26.0	26.5	24.5

Using $\alpha = .05$, test for any significant difference in hours worked at the three plants.

SOLUTION 1

Using Excel's ANOVA: SINGLE FACTOR Tool

In this problem we are using analysis of variance to test for the equality of the mean number of hours worked at three plants.

Step 1: Determine the null and alternative hypotheses

H_0: $\mu_1 = \mu_2 = \mu_3$
H_a: Not all the means are equal

where:
μ_1 = mean number of hours worked per week by the managers at Plant 1
μ_2 = mean number of hours worked per week by the managers at Plant 2
μ_3 = mean number of hours worked per week by the managers at Plant 3

Step 2: Select the test statistic to be used to decide whether to reject H_0

F = MSTR/MSE

Step 3: Specify the level of significance α

$\alpha = .05$

Step 4: Develop the rejection rule based on the level of significance

Assuming $\alpha = .05$, $F_{.05} = 3.89$ (2 d.f. numerator, 12 d.f. denominator).
Reject H_0 if $F > 3.89$ (found in the F Distribution table in the textbook)

Step 5: Collect the data and compute the value of the test statistic

Mean Square Treatment (MSTR) is found by:
$x = (55 + 68 + 57)/3 = 60$
$SSTR = 5(55 - 60)^2 + 5(68 - 60)^2 + 5(57 - 60)^2 = 490$
$MSTR = 490/(3 - 1) = 245$

Mean Square Error (MSE) is found by:
$SSE = 4(26.0) + 4(26.5) + 4(24.5) = 308$
$MSE = 308/(15 - 3) = 25.667$

F = MSTR/MSE = 245/25.667 = 9.55

Step 6: a) <u>Compare the value of the test statistic to the critical value(s)</u>

$F = 9.55 > 3.89$

or b) <u>Compute the *p*-value and compare it to α</u>

(It is difficult to determine a precise *p*-value of the *F* Distribution table.)

Step 7: <u>State your conclusion regarding H_0</u>

$F = 9.55 > F_{.05} = 3.89$, so we reject H_0. The mean number of hours worked per week by department managers is <u>not</u> the same at all of the plant.

Excel "Anova: Single Factor" tool can be used to conduct a hypothesis test about the difference between the means of three populations.

Enter Data: Column A is used to identify the observations at each of the plants. Columns B, C, and D contain the hours worked data for the managers at the three plants.

Apply Tools: The following steps describe how to use Excel's Anova: Single Factor tool.

<u>Excel's "Anova: Single Factor" Tool</u>

Step 1 Select the **Tools** pull-down menu
Step 2 Choose the **Data Analysis** option
Step 3 Choose **Anova: Single Factor** from the list of Analysis Tools
Step 4 When the Anova: Single Factor dialog box appears:
  Enter B1:D6 in the **Input Range** box
  Select Grouped By **Columns**
  Select **Labels in First Row**
  Enter .05 in the **Alpha** box
  Select **Output Range**
  Enter A8 (your choice) in the **Output Range** box
  Select **OK**

Value Worksheet:

	A	B	C	D	E	F	G
1	Observation	**Buffalo**	**Pittsb.**	**Detroit**			
2	1	48	73	51			
3	2	54	63	63			
4	3	57	66	61			
5	4	54	64	54			
6	5	62	74	56			
7							
8	Anova: Single Factor						
9							
10	SUMMARY						
11	*Groups*	*Count*	*Sum*	*Average*	*Variance*		
12	Buffalo	5	275	55	26		
13	Pittsburgh	5	340	68	26.5		
14	Detroit	5	285	57	24.5		
15							
16							
17	ANOVA						
18	*Source of Variation*	*SS*	*df*	*MS*	*F*	*P-value*	*F crit*
19	Between Groups	490	2	245	9.54545	0.00331	3.88529
20	Within Groups	308	12	25.6667			
21							
22	Total	798	14				

The value of the test statistic, 9.55, is shown in cell E19 of the worksheet below. The critical value of F, 3.89, is shown in cell G19. Because $F = 9.55$ is in the rejection region (9.55 > 3.89), we can conclude that the mean number of hours worked at the three plants are not all equal. Alternatively, we can use the p-value to make the test decision. The p-value, .0033, is shown in cell F19. Because the p-value is less than the level of significance, $\alpha = .05$, we have sufficient statistical evidence to reject the null hypothesis.

EXAMPLE 2

Multiple Comparison Procedure: Fisher's LSD

Refer again to the J.R. Reed manufacturing plants problem in Example 1. Analysis of variance provided statistical evidence to reject the null hypothesis of equal population means. In other words, it was concluded that the mean number of hours worked at the three plants were not all equal.

Apply Fisher's least significant difference (LSD) procedure to determine where the differences occur.

SOLUTION 2

The value of LSD is:

$$LSD = t_{\alpha/2}\sqrt{MSE\left(\frac{1}{n_1} + \frac{1}{n_2}\right)}$$

With $\alpha = .05$ and $n_T - k = 15 - 3 = 12$ degrees of freedom, $t_{\alpha/2} = 2.179$.
MSE $= 25.667$ is taken from the ANOVA table in Solution 1.

$$LSD = 2.179\sqrt{25.667\left(\frac{1}{5} + \frac{1}{5}\right)} = 6.982$$

First, we will determine whether there is a significant difference between the means of Plants 1 and 2. Then, we'll do the same for Plants 1 and 3. Finally, we'll focus on Plants 2 and 3.

Plants 1 and 2

Hypotheses:	H_0: $\mu_1 = \mu_2$ and H_a: $\mu_1 \neq \mu_2$
Rejection Rules:	Reject H_0 if $\left\|\bar{x}_1 - \bar{x}_2\right\| > 6.982$
	Reject H_0 if $t < -2.179$ or $t > 2.179$
	Reject H_0 if p-value $< .05$
Test Statistic:	$\left\|\bar{x}_1 - \bar{x}_2\right\| = \left\|55 - 68\right\| = 13$

$$t = \frac{\bar{x}_1 - \bar{x}_2}{\sqrt{MSE\left(\frac{1}{n_1} + \frac{1}{n_2}\right)}} = \frac{13}{\sqrt{25.667\left(\frac{1}{5} + \frac{1}{5}\right)}} = 4.0572$$

Conclusion: Reject H_0 because $\left|\bar{x}_1 - \bar{x}_2\right| = 13 > 6.982$
or because $t = 4.057 > 2.179$
or because (using Excel) p-value $= .00159 < .05$

.00159	=TDIST(4.0572,12,2)

The mean number of hours worked at Plant 1 is
<u>not equal</u> to the mean number worked at Plant 2.

Plants 1 and 3

Hypotheses:	H_0: $\mu_1 = \mu_3$ and H_a: $\mu_1 \neq \mu_3$
Rejection Rule:	Reject H_0 if $\left\|\bar{x}_1 - \bar{x}_3\right\| > 6.982$
	Reject H_0 if $t < -2.179$ or $t > 2.179$
	Reject H_0 if p-value $< .05$
Test Statistic:	$\left\|\bar{x}_1 - \bar{x}_3\right\| = \left\|55 - 57\right\| = 2$

$$t = \frac{\bar{x}_1 - \bar{x}_3}{\sqrt{MSE\left(\frac{1}{n_1} + \frac{1}{n_3}\right)}} = \frac{2}{\sqrt{25.667\left(\frac{1}{5} + \frac{1}{5}\right)}} = 0.6242$$

Conclusion: Do not reject H_0 because $|\bar{x}_1 - \bar{x}_3| = 2 < 6.982$ or because

$t = 0.6242 < 2.179$ or because (using Excel) p-value = .54418 > .05

.54418	=TDIST(0.6242,12,2)

We cannot conclude that the mean number of hours worked at Plant 1 is different than the mean number worked at Plant 3.

Plants 2 and 3

Hypotheses: H_0: $\mu_2 = \mu_3$ and H_a: $\mu_2 \neq \mu_3$

Rejection Rule: Reject H_0 if $|\bar{x}_2 - \bar{x}_3| > 6.982$

Reject H_0 if $t < -2.179$ or $t > 2.179$

Reject H_0 if p-value < .05

Test Statistic: $|\bar{x}_2 - \bar{x}_3| = |68 - 57| = 11$

$$t = \frac{\bar{x}_2 - \bar{x}_3}{\sqrt{MSE\left(\dfrac{1}{n_2} + \dfrac{1}{n_3}\right)}} = \frac{11}{\sqrt{25.667\left(\dfrac{1}{5} + \dfrac{1}{5}\right)}} = 3.4330$$

Conclusion: Reject H_0. $|\bar{x}_2 - \bar{x}_3| = 11 > 6.982$ or because $t = 3.4330 > 2.179$

or because p-value = .00496 < .05

.00496	=TDIST(3.433,12,2)

The mean number of hours worked at Plant 2 is not equal to the mean number worked at Plant 3.

EXAMPLE 3

Completely Randomized Design

Home Products, Inc. is considering marketing a long-lasting car wax. Three different waxes (Type 1, Type 2, and Type 3) have been developed.

In order to test the durability of these waxes, 5 new cars were waxed with Type 1, 5 with Type 2, and 5 with Type 3. Each car was then repeatedly run through an automatic carwash until the wax coating showed signs of deterioration. The number of times each car went through the carwash is shown below. Are the three waxes equally effective?

Observation	Wax Type 1	Wax Type 2	Wax Type 3
1	27	33	29
2	30	28	28
3	29	31	30
4	28	30	32
5	31	30	31
Sample Mean	29.0	30.4	30.0
Sample Variance	2.5	3.3	2.5

SOLUTION 3

Using Excel's ANOVA: SINGLE FACTOR Tool

First, we will manually conduct the completely-randomized-design ANOVA to determine if the three waxes have equal means. Then, we will use Excel to do the same.

Hypotheses: H_0: $\mu_1 = \mu_2 = \mu_3$
                   H_a: Not all the means are equal
                   where:
                      μ_1 = mean number of washes for Type 1 wax
                      μ_2 = mean number of washes for Type 2 wax
                      μ_3 = mean number of washes for Type 3 wax

Mean Square Between Treatments:
         Because the sample sizes are all equal:
         $x = (x_1 + x_2 + x_3)/3 = (29 + 30.4 + 30)/3 = 29.8$
         SSTR $= 5(29-29.8)^2 + 5(30.4-29.8)^2 + 5(30-29.8)^2 = 5.2$
         MSTR $= 5.2/(3 - 1) = 2.6$

Mean Square Error:
         SSE $= 4(2.5) + 4(3.3) + 4(2.5) = 33.2$
         MSE $= 33.2/(15 - 3) = 2.77$

Rejection Rule:
         Using test statistic: Reject H_0 if $F > 3.89$
         Using p-value: Reject H_0 if p-value $< .05$
         (where $F_{.05} = 3.89$ is based on an F distribution
         with 2 numerator degrees of freedom and
         12 denominator degrees of freedom)

Test Statistic: F = MSTR/MSE $= 2.6/2.77 = .939$

ANOVA Table:

Source of Variation	Sum of Squares	Degrees of Freedom	Mean of Squares	F
Treatments	5.2	2	2.60	.9398
Error	33.2	12	2.77	
Total	38.4	14		

Conclusion: Since $F = .939 < F_{.05} = 3.89$, we cannot reject H_0.
                There is insufficient evidence to conclude that the mean number
                of washes for the three wax types are not all the same.

Now we will use Excel's ANOVA: Single Factor tool

Enter Data: Column A is used to identify the observations at each of the plants. Columns B, C, and D contain the number of hours worked for the three plants.

Apply Tools: The following steps describe how to use Excel's ANOVA: Single Factor tool.

Step 1: Select the **Tools** pull-down menu
Step 2: Choose the **Data Analysis** option
Step 3: Choose **Anova: Single Factor** from the list of Analysis Tools
Step 4: When the Anova: Single Factor dialog box appears:
        Enter B1:D6 in the **Input Range** box
        Select Grouped By **Columns**
        Select **Labels**
        Enter .05 in the **Alpha** box
        Select **Output Range**
        Enter A8 in the **Output Range** box
        Click **OK**

Value Worksheet:

	A	B	C	D	E	F	G
1	Observation	Wax Type 1	Wax Type 2	Wax Type 3			
2	1	27	33	29			
3	2	30	28	28			
4	3	29	31	30			
5	4	28	30	32			
6	5	31	30	31			
7							
8	Anova: Single Factor						
9							
10	SUMMARY						
11	*Groups*	*Count*	*Sum*	*Average*	*Variance*		
12	Wax Type 1	5	145	29	2.5		
13	Wax Type 2	5	152	30.4	3.3		
14	Wax Type 3	5	150	30	2.5		
15							
16	ANOVA						
17	*Source of Variation*	*SS*	*df*	*MS*	*F*	*P-value*	*F crit*
18	Between Groups	5.2	2	2.6	0.939759	0.41768	3.88529
19	Within Groups	33.2	12	2.76667			
20							
21	Total	38.4	14				

Conclusion Using the *p*-Value:
    The value worksheet shows a *p*-value of .418. Because .418 > .05,
    we cannot reject H_0. There is insufficient evidence to conclude that the
    mean number of washes for the three wax types are not all the same.

EXAMPLE 4

Randomized Block Design

Eastern Oil has developed three new blends of gasoline and must decide which blend or blends to produce and distribute. A study of the miles per gallon ratings of the three blends must be conducted to determine if the mean ratings are the same for the three blends.

Five automobiles have been tested using each of the three gasoline blends and the miles per gallon ratings are shown below.

| | Type of Gasoline | | |
Automobile	Blend X	Blend Y	Blend Z
1	31	30	30
2	30	29	29
3	29	29	28
4	33	31	29
5	26	25	26

Do the sample results justify the conclusion that the mean ratings for the three gasoline blends differ?

SOLUTION 4

Using Excel's ANOVA: TWO-FACTOR WITHOUT REPLICATION Tool

First, we will manually conduct the randomized-block-design ANOVA to determine if the three gasoline blends have equal ratings. Then, we will use Excel to do the same.

| Automobile | Type of Gasoline (Treatment) | | | Block |
(Block)	Blend X	Blend Y	Blend Z	Means
1	31	30	30	30.333
2	30	29	29	29.333
3	29	29	28	28.667
4	33	31	29	31.000
5	26	25	26	25.667
Treatment Means	29.8	28.8	28.4	

Mean Square Due to Treatments:
The overall sample mean is 29. Thus,
$$SSTR = 5[(29.8 - 29)^2 + (28.8 - 29)^2 + (28.4 - 29)^2] = 5.2$$
$$MSTR = 5.2/(3 - 1) = 2.6$$

Mean Square Due to Blocks:

SSBL = $3[(30.333 - 29)^2 + \ldots + (25.667 - 29)^2] = 51.33$

MSBL = $51.33/(5 - 1) = 12.8$

Mean Square Due to Error:

SSE = $62 - 5.2 - 51.33 = 5.47$

MSE = $5.47/[(3 - 1)(5 - 1)] = .68$

Rejection Rule:

Using test statistic: Reject H_0 if $F > 4.46$

Using p-value: Reject H_0 if p-value $< .05$

($F_{.05} = 4.46$, assuming $\alpha = .05$ and 2 d.f. numerator and 8 d.f. denominator)

Test Statistic: $F = MSTR/MSE = 2.6/.68 = 3.82$

Conclusion: Since $3.82 < 4.46$, we <u>cannot</u> reject H_0.

There is not sufficient evidence to conclude that the miles per gallon ratings differ for the three gasoline blends.

Now we will use Excel's ANOVA: Single Factor tool

Enter Data: Column A is used to identify the observations for each of the gasoline blends. Columns B, C, and D contain the number of hours worked for the three plants.

Apply Tools: The following steps describe how to use Excel's ANOVA: Two Factor Without Replication tool.

Step 1   Select the **Tools** pull-down menu
Step 2   Choose the **Data Analysis** option
Step 3   Choose **Anova: Two Factor Without Replication** from the list of Analysis Tools
Step 4   When the Anova: Two Factor Without Replication dialog box appears:
        Enter A1:D6 in the **Input Range** box
        Select **Labels**
        Enter .05 in the **Alpha** box
        Select **Output Range**
        Enter A8 (your choice) in the Output Range box
        Click **OK**

Conclusion Using the p-Value:

The value worksheet shows that the p-value is .06899. We <u>cannot</u> reject H_0 because the p-value = .06899 $> \alpha = .05$. There is not sufficient evidence to conclude that the miles per gallon ratings differ for the three gasoline blends.

Value Worksheet:

	A	B	C	D	E	F	G
1	Automobile	Blend X	Blend Y	Blend Z			
2	1	31	30	30			
3	2	30	29	29			
4	3	29	29	28			
5	4	33	31	29			
6	5	26	25	26			
7							
8	Anova: Two-Factor Without Replication						
9							
10	SUMMARY	Count	Sum	Average	Variance		
11	1	3	91	30.3333	0.33333		
12	2	3	88	29.3333	0.33333		
13	3	3	86	28.6667	0.33333		
14	4	3	93	31	4		
15	5	3	77	25.6667	0.33333		
16							
17	Blend X	5	149	29.8	6.7		
18	Blend Y	5	144	28.8	5.2		
19	Blend Z	5	142	28.4	2.3		
20							
21	ANOVA						
22	Variation	SS	df	MS	F	P-value	F crit
23	Rows	51.3333	4	12.8333	18.7805	0.0004	3.83785
24	Columns	5.2	2	2.6	3.80488	0.06899	4.45897
25	Error	5.46667	8	0.68333			
26	Total	62	14				

EXAMPLE 5

Factorial Experiment

The hourly wages for a sample of workers in two industries at three locations in Ohio are shown below. Part of the purpose of the wage survey was to determine if differences exist in both industry type and location.

Industry	Cincinnati	Cleveland	Columbus
Fast Food	5.50	5.10	5.90
Fast Food	5.80	5.00	6.20
Fast Food	6.10	5.50	6.10
Light Mfg.	6.40	5.80	6.50
Light Mfg.	6.50	6.00	6.00
Light Mfg.	6.00	5.60	6.10

Use the ANOVA procedure for factorial designs to test for any significant effects due to type of industry, location, or interaction. Use $\alpha = .05$.

SOLUTION 5

Using Excel's ANOVA: TWO-FACTOR WITH REPLICATION Tool

This is a two-factor experiment. One factor is the industry type, which has two treatments: fast food and light manufacturing. The second factor is location, which has three treatments: Cincinnati, Cleveland, and Columbus. We will have a total of 2 X 3 = 6 treatment combinations. The sample size of three for each treatment combination indicates that we have three replications. ANOVA computations will provide answers to the following:

Main effect (factor A): Do the industry types differ in terms of effect on wages?
Main effect (factor B): Do the locations differ in terms of effect on wages?
Interaction effect (factors A and B): Do workers in one industry earn more in some locations whereas workers in another industry earn more in other locations?

Because of the computational effort involved in even this modest-size experiment, we will rely on Excel to perform and summarize the ANOVA calculations.

Enter Data: Column A is used to identify each of the industry types (Factor A) in the study. Columns B, C, and D contain the wages for the Cincinnati, Cleveland, and Columbus workers, respectively.

Apply Tools: The following steps describe how to use Excel's ANOVA: Two Factor With Replication tool.

    Step 1 Select the **Tools** pull-down menu
    Step 2 Choose the **Data Analysis** option
    Step 3 Choose Anova: Two Factor With Replication from the list of Analysis Tools
    Step 4 When the Anova: Two Factor With Replication dialog box appears:
            Enter A1:D7 in the Input Range box
            Enter 3 in the **Rows per sample** box
            Enter .05 in the **Alpha** box
            Select **Output Range**
            Enter A9 (your choice) in the **Output Range** box
            Click **OK**

The resulting worksheet appears on the next page.

Conclusions: (Both test statistic and *p*-value approaches used)

    Industries: $F = 12.7 > F_\alpha = 4.75$
                    p-value = .004 < α = .05
                    Mean wages differ by industry type

    Locations: $F = 11.8 > F_\alpha = 3.89$
                    p-value = .0015 < α = .05
                    Mean wages differ by location

Interaction: $F = 1.5 < F_\alpha = 3.89$
p-value = .263 > α = .05
Interaction is not significant

Value Worksheet:

	A	B	C	D	E	F	G
1		Cincin.	Clevel.	Columb.			
2	**Fast Food**	5.50	5.10	5.90			
3		5.80	5.00	6.20			
4		6.10	5.50	6.10			
5	**Light Mfg.**	6.40	5.80	6.50			
6		6.50	6.00	6.00			
7		6.00	5.60	6.10			
8							
9	Anova: Two-Factor With Replication						
10							
11	SUMMARY	Cincin.	Clevel.	Columb.	Total		
12	*Fast Food*						
13	Count	3	3	3	9		
14	Sum	17.4	15.6	18.2	51.2		
15	Average	5.8	5.2	6.06667	5.68889		
16	Variance	0.09	0.07	0.02333	0.19361		
17							
18	*Light Mfg.*						
19	Count	3	3	3	9		
20	Sum	18.9	17.4	18.6	54.9		
21	Average	6.3	5.8	6.2	6.1		
22	Variance	0.07	0.04	0.07	0.0975		
23							
24	SUMMARY	Cincin.	Clevel.	Columb.			
25	*Total*						
26	Count	6	6	6			
27	Sum	36.3	33	36.8			
28	Average	6.05	5.5	6.13333			
29	Variance	0.139	0.152	0.04267			
30							
31	ANOVA						
32	*Var. Source*	SS	df	MS	F	P-value	F crit
33	Sample	0.76056	1	0.76056	12.5596	0.00404	4.74722
34	Columns	1.42111	2	0.71056	11.7339	0.0015	3.88529
35	Interaction	0.18111	2	0.09056	1.49541	0.26311	3.88529
36	Within	0.72667	12	0.06056			
37							
38	Total	3.08944	17				

EXERCISES

EXERCISE 1

Test for the Equality of k Population Means

Regional Manager Sue Collins would like to know if the mean number of telephone calls made per 8-hour shift is the same for the telemarketers at her three call centers (Austin, Las Vegas, and Albuquerque).

A simple random sample of 6 telemarketers from each of the three call centers was taken and the number of telephone calls made in eight hours by each observed employee is shown below.

Observation	Center 1 Austin	Center 2 Las Vegas	Center 3 Albuquerque
1	82	72	71
2	68	63	81
3	77	74	73
4	80	60	68
5	69	70	76
6	78	73	80
Sample Mean	75.667	68.667	74.833
Sample Variance	33.867	33.467	26.167

Using $\alpha = .10$, test for any significant difference in number of telephone calls made at the three call centers.

EXERCISE 2

Multiple Comparison Procedure: Fisher's LSD

Refer again to the telephone call center problem in Exercise 1. ANOVA revealed that not all three call center means are equal. Apply Fisher's least significant difference (LSD) procedure to determine where the differences occur. Use $\alpha = .05$.

EXERCISE 3

Completely Randomized Design

To test whether the time required to fully load a standard delivery truck is the same for three work shifts (day, evening, and night), NatEx obtained the following data on the time (in minutes) needed to pack a truck. Use these data to test whether the population mean times for loading a truck differ for the three work shifts. Use $\alpha = .05$.

Observation	Day Shift	Evening Shift	Night Shift
1	92	83	89
2	81	93	97
3	103	79	95
4	77	102	88
5	82	84	106
Sample Mean	75.667	68.667	74.833
Sample Variance	33.867	33.467	26.167

EXERCISE 4

Randomized Block Design

Orange Freight Ltd. must decide which of three tire brands to purchase for its 1,400 trailers. The criterion that Orange Freight uses in choosing a tire brand is its useful life (in miles). A study of the miles attained by the three brands must be conducted to determine if the mean mileages are the same for the three brands.

Five trailers have been tested using each of the three tire brands and the mileage (in thousands) attained are shown below.

Trailer	Tire Brand GY	Tire Brand GR	Tire Brand FS
1	33	40	36
2	40	39	37
3	37	44	42
4	40	41	34
5	36	38	38

At α = .05, is there a sufficient difference in the mean mileage of the three tire brands?

EXERCISE 5

Factorial Experiment

Refer again to the Orange Freight trailer tire problem in Exercise 4. Todd, the manager of the trailer fleet designed a factorial experiment to determine whether the mileage of the three tire brands differed and if the mileage of the tires also depended on whether the tires were used on short trailers or long trailers. The following data give the mileage (in thousands) attained in the experiment.

Trailer Size	Tire Brand GY	Tire Brand GR	Tire Brand FS
Short	41	44	40
	40	39	37
	38	46	40
Long	39	36	35
	40	34	36
	38	35	38

Using a = .05, test for any significant effect due to trailer size, tire brand, and interaction.

SELF-TEST

TRUE/FALSE

____ 1. If we reject the hypothesis H_0: $\mu_1 = \mu_2 = \mu_3$, we can conclude that all three population means are different.

____ 2. Analysis of variance can be used to test for the equality of two or more population means.

____ 3. In *factorial experiments*, the term *factorial* is used because the experimental conditions include all possible combinations of the factors.

____ 4. Fisher's LSD can be used to develop a confidence interval estimate of the difference between the means of two population means.

____ 5. Cause-and-effect relationships are easier to establish in observational studies than in experimental studies.

FILL-IN-THE-BLANK

1. The process of allocating the total sum of squares and degrees of freedom to the various components is referred to as _____.

2. _____ is the process of using the same or similar experimental units for all treatments in order to remove a source of variation from the error term.

3. In analysis of variance, the levels of the factor (independent variable) are called the _____.

4. The independent variable of interest is called the _____.

5. The dependent variable is also called the _____ variable.

MULTIPLE CHOICE

___ 1. In making three pairwise comparisons, what is the experimentwise Type I error rate α_{ew} if the comparisonwise Type I error rate α is .10?
   a) .001
   b) .081
   c) .271
   d) .300

___ 2. The test statistic F is the ratio
   a) MSE/MST
   b) MSTR/MSE
   c) SSTR/SSE
   d) SSTR/SSE

___ 3. In testing for the equality of k population means, the number of treatments is
   a) k
   b) $k - 1$
   c) n_T
   d) $n_T - k$

___ 4. The within-treatments estimate of σ^2 is called the
   a) sum of squares due to error
   b) mean square due to error
   c) sum of squares due to treatments
   d) mean square due to treatments

___ 5. If we are testing for the equality of 3 population means, we should use the
   a) test statistic F
   b) test statistic t
   c) test statistic z
   d) test statistic χ^2

ANSWERS

EXERCISES

1) Reject H_0, because $F = 2.815 > 2.695$ (or because p-value = .092 < α = .10).
   Conclusion: Not all call center means are equal.

ANOVA

Source of Variation	SS	df	MS	F	P-value	F crit
Between Groups	175.444	2	87.722	2.814637	0.091645	2.69517
Within Groups	467.500	15	31.167			
Total	642.944	17				

2) <u>Centers 1 & 2</u>: Reject H_0
  Using $|\bar{x}_i - \bar{x}_j|$ 7.000 > 6.869
  Using t: 2.172 > 2.1317
  Using p-value   .0463 < .05
  <u>Centers 1 & 3</u>: Do <u>not</u> reject H_0
  Using $|\bar{x}_i - \bar{x}_j|$ 0.834 < 6.869
  Using t: 0.259 < 2.1317
  Using p-value   .7992 > .05
  <u>Centers 2 & 3</u>: Do <u>not</u> reject H_0
  Using $|\bar{x}_i - \bar{x}_j|$ 6.166 < 6.869
  Using t: 1.913 < 2.1317
  Using p-value   .0750 > .05

3) We <u>cannot</u> reject H_0: $\mu_1 = \mu_2 = \mu_3$ because $F = 2.073 < F_\alpha = 3.885$ (or p-value = .17 > $\alpha - .05$). Conclusion: There Is little evidence of a difference in the three shifts' mean loading times.

ANOVA

Source of Variation	SS	df	MS	F	P-value	F crit
Between Groups	260.8	2	130.4	2.073132	0.168521	3.88529
Within Groups	754.8	12	62.9			
Total	1015.6	14				

4) Reject H_0: $\mu_1 = \mu_2 = \mu_3$ because $F = 6.43 > F_\alpha = 4.54$ (or p-value = .06 < α = .10). Conclusion: Not all tire brand mean mileage are equal.

ANOVA

Source of Variation	SS	df	MS	F	P-value	F crit
Rows	42.4	4	10.6	3.02857	0.15426	4.10725
Columns	22.5	1	22.5	6.42857	0.06429	4.54477
Error	14	4	3.5			
Total	78.9	9				

5) <u>Trailer Size</u>: We <u>can</u> reject the hypothesis that there is no difference between the tire mileage on short trailers and tire mileage on long trailers (because $F = 17 > F_\alpha = 4.75$ or because p-value = .0014 < α = .05).
  <u>Tire Brand</u>: We <u>cannot</u> reject the hypothesis that there is no difference the tire mileage among the three brands (because $F = 1.235 < F_\alpha = 3.885$ or because p-value = .3252 > α = .05).
  <u>Interaction</u>: We <u>can</u> reject the hypothesis that there is no interaction between trailer size and tire brand on tire mileage (because $F = 5.706 > F_\alpha = 3.885$ or because p-value = .018 < α = .05).

ANOVA

Source of Variation	SS	df	MS	F	P-value	F crit
Sample	64.2222	1	64.2222	17	0.001413	4.74722
Columns	9.3333	2	4.6667	1.235294	0.325215	3.88529
Interaction	43.1111	2	21.5556	5.705882	0.018134	3.88529
Within	45.3333	12	3.7778			
Total	162	17				

TRUE/FALSE

1) False
2) True
3) True
4) True
5) False

FILL-IN-THE-BLANK

1) partitioning
2) Blocking
3) treatments
4) factor
5) response

MULTIPLE CHOICE

1) c
2) b
3) a
4) b
5) a

CHAPTER 14

Simple Linear Regression

Simple Linear Regression Model

Least Squares Method

Coefficient of Determination

Model Assumptions

Testing for Significance

Excel's Regression Tool

Using the Estimated Regression Equation
for Estimation and Prediction

Residual Analysis:
Validating Model Assumptions

Outliers and Influential Observations

LEARNING OBJECTIVES

1. Understand how regression analysis can be used to develop an equation that estimates mathematically how two variables are related.

2. Understand the differences between the regression model, the regression equation, and the estimated regression equation.

3. Know how to fit an estimated regression equation to a set of sample data based upon the least-squares method.

4. Be able to determine how good a fit is provided by the estimated regression equation and compute the sample correlation coefficient from the regression analysis output.

5. Understand the assumptions necessary for statistical inference and be able to test for a significant relationship.

6. Learn how to use a residual plot to make a judgement as to the validity of the regression assumptions, recognize outliers, and identify influential observations.

7. Know how to develop confidence interval estimates of y given a specific value of x in both the case of a mean value of y and an individual value of y.

8. Be able to compute the sample correlation coefficient from the regression analysis output.

9. Know the definition of the following terms:

independent and dependent variable	prediction interval
simple linear regression	residual plot
regression model	standardized residual plot
regression equation and estimated regression equation	
scatter diagram	outlier
coefficient of determination	influential observation
standard error of the estimate	leverage
confidence interval	

REVIEW

Regression Analysis
*   Managerial decisions often are based on the relationship between two or more variables.
*   A statistical procedure called <u>regression analysis</u> can be used to develop an equation showing how the variables are related.
*   The variable being predicted is called the <u>dependent variable</u>.
*   The variable(s) being used to predict the value of the dependent variable are called the <u>independent variables</u>.

Simple Linear Regression
- Regression analysis involving one independent variable and one dependent variable, in which a straight line approximates the relationship between the variables, is called <u>simple linear regression</u>.

Simple Linear Regression Model
- The equation that describes how y is related to x and an error term is called the <u>regression model</u>.
- The regression model used in simple linear regression is:
$$y = \beta_0 + \beta_1 x + \varepsilon$$
- β_0 and β_1 are referred to as the <u>parameters of the model</u>.
- ε is a random variable referred to as the <u>error term</u>.
- The error term accounts for the variability in y that cannot be explained by the linear relationship between x and y.

Simple Linear Regression Equation
- One of the assumptions made here is that the <u>mean or expected value of ε is zero</u>.
- As a result of the above assumption, the mean or expected value of y, denoted $E(y)$, is equal to $\beta_0 + \beta_1 x$.
- The equation that describes how the mean value of y is related to x is called the <u>simple linear regression equation</u>.
$$E(y) = \beta_0 + \beta_1 x$$
- The graph of the simple linear regression equation is a straight line.
- β_0 is the y intercept of the regression equation; β_1 is the slope.
- $E(y)$ is the expected value of y for a given value of x.

Estimated Regression Equation
- The values of the parameters β_0 and β_1 are not known in practice and must be estimated by using sample data.
- The <u>sample statistics b_0 and b_1</u> are computed as estimates of β_0 and β_1.
- The <u>estimated simple linear regression equation</u> is:
$$\hat{y} = b_0 + b_1 x$$
where: $\hat{y}$ = the estimated value of y for a given value of x

b_0 = the y intercept

b_1 = the slope

Scatter Diagram
- A <u>scatter diagram</u> (introduced in Chapter 2) enables us to <u>observe the data graphically</u> and to <u>draw preliminary conclusions</u> about the possible relationship between the independent and dependent variables.
- The <u>independent variable x is on the horizontal axis</u> and the <u>dependent variable y is on the vertical axis</u>.
- We hope to observe that the relationship between the two variables appears to be <u>approximated by a straight line</u>.

Least Squares Method

- The <u>least squares method</u> is a procedure for using sample data to compute an estimated regression equation, specifically values for b_0 and b_1.
- Values are found for b_0 and b_1 that minimize the <u>sum of the squares of the deviations</u> between the observed values of y_i and the estimated values $\hat{y}_i$.
- The <u>least squares criterion</u> is:

$$\min \sum (y_i - \hat{y}_i)^2$$

where:

y_i = <u>observed</u> value of the dependent variable for the i th observation

$\hat{y}_i$ = <u>estimated</u> value of the dependent variable for the i th observation

Slope for the Estimated Regression Equation

$$b_1 = \frac{\sum x_i y_i - (\sum x_i \sum y_i)/n}{\sum x_i^2 - (\sum x_i)^2/n}$$

y-Intercept for the Estimated Regression Equation

$$b_0 = \bar{y} - b_1 \bar{x}$$

where:

x_i = value of independent variable for i th observation

y_i = value of dependent variable for i th observation

$\bar{x}$ = mean value for independent variable

$\bar{y}$ = mean value for dependent variable

n = total number of observations

Applying the Estimated Regression Equation

- If we believe the least squares estimated regression equation adequately describes the relationship between x and y, it probably is reasonable to <u>use the equation to predict the value of y</u> for a given value of x.
- Plugging into the equation an x value outside the range of the x data with which the equation was developed should be done with caution because we cannot be sure the same relationship is valid.

Using Excel to Develop a Scatter Diagram
and to Compute the Estimated Regression Equation

- Excel's <u>Chart Wizard</u> can be used to develop a scatter diagram.
- The <u>XY (Scatter)</u> chart type should be chosen.
- After the chart appears and you have edited it to your satisfaction, select the <u>Add Trendline</u> option in the Chart Menu.
- Select <u>Linear</u> as the trendline type and select <u>Display Equation on Chart</u>.

Coefficient of Determination
- The <u>coefficient of determination</u> provides a <u>measure of the goodness of fit</u> for the estimated regression equation.
- It can also be used to measure of the goodness of fit involving relationships that are nonlinear or have two or more independent variables.

Sum of Squares Due to Error (SSE)
- The SSE is a measure of the error in using the estimated regression equation to estimate the values of the dependent variable in the sample.
- The formula for the SSE is:

$$SSE = \sum (y_i - \hat{y}_i)^2$$

Total Sum of Squares (SST)
- The SST is a measure of the error involved if we had used the average value of y, $\bar{y}$, to estimate y.
- The formula for the SSE is:

$$SST = \sum (y_i - \bar{y})^2$$

Sum of Squares Due to Regression (SSR)
- The SSR is a measure of how much the $\hat{y}$ values on the estimated regression line deviate from $\bar{y}$.
- The formula for the SSR is:

$$SSR = \sum (\hat{y}_i - \bar{y})^2$$

Relationship Among SST, SSR, and SSE
- SST = SSR + SSE
- SSR can be thought of as the <u>explained</u> portion of SST.
- SSE can be thought of as the <u>unexplained</u> portion of SST.
- If the regression equation provided a perfect fit, $y_i - \hat{y}_i$ would be zero for each observation, resulting in SSE = 0 and SSR/SST = 1.
- The ratio <u>SSR/SST</u>, which will be <u>between 0 and 1</u>, is used to evaluate the <u>goodness of fit</u> for the estimated regression equation.
- The coefficient of determination, r^2, is:

$$r^2 = SSR/SST$$

Using Excel to Compute the Coefficient of Determination
- Assuming you have developed a scatter diagram using Excel's <u>Chart Wizard</u>, the next step is to select the <u>Add Trendline</u> option in the Chart menu.
- On the Options tab of the Add Trendline dialog box, select <u>Display R-Squared Value on Chart</u>.

Correlation Coefficient

- The correlation coefficient is a <u>measure of the strength of linear association between two variables</u>, x and y. (Note – only <u>linear</u> association, and only <u>two</u> variables)
- Values of the correlation coefficient are always between –1 and +1.
- A value of +1 indicates that the two variables x and y are perfectly related in a positive linear sense (all data points are on a straight line that has a positive slope).
- A value of -1 indicates that the two variables x and y are perfectly related in a negative linear sense (all data points are on a straight line that has a negative slope).
- Values close to zero indicate that x and y are not linearly related.
- The sign for the sample correlation coefficient is positive if the estimated regression equation has a positive slope ($b_1 > 0$). The sign is negative if $b_1 < 0$.
- If the coefficient of determination, r^2, has been computed, the correlation coefficient is easily computed as follows:

$$r_{xy} = (\text{sign of } b_1)\sqrt{r^2}$$

Testing for Significance

- Determining the <u>appropriateness of a model</u> includes testing for the significance of the relationship.
- The tests for significance are based on the following <u>assumptions about the error term</u> ε:
  - The error ε is a random variable with mean of zero.
  - The variance of ε, denoted by σ^2, is the same for all values of the independent variable.
  - The values of ε are independent.
  - The error ε is a normally distributed random variable.
  - To test for significance we must conduct a hypothesis test to determine whether the value of β_1 is zero. Two tests often used are the t test and F test.
  - Both the t and F tests require an estimate of σ^2, the variance of ε in the regression model.

An Estimate of σ^2

- The <u>mean square error</u> (an estimate of σ^2) is denoted s^2 and computed as:

$$s^2 = \text{MSE} = \text{SSE}/(n-2)$$

- The <u>standard error of the estimate</u> (an estimate of σ) is denoted s and computed as:

$$s = \sqrt{\text{MSE}} = \sqrt{\frac{\text{SSE}}{n-2}}$$

t Test

- The t test can be summarized as follows:
  - <u>Hypotheses</u>:

$$H_0 : \beta_1 = 0$$
$$H_a : \beta_1 \neq 0$$

  - <u>Test statistic</u>:

$$t = \frac{b_1}{s_{b_1}}$$

- Rejection rule:
  Reject H_0 if $t < -t_{\alpha/2}$ or if $t > t_{\alpha/2}$
  where $t_{\alpha/2}$ is based on a t distribution with $n - 2$ degrees of freedom

Confidence Interval for β_1

- We can use a confidence interval for β_1 to test the hypotheses used above in the t test.
- H_0 is rejected if the hypothesized value of β_1 is not within the confidence interval for β_1.
- The form of the confidence interval is:

$$b_1 \pm t_{\alpha/2} s_{b_1}$$

F Test

- The F test can be summarized as follows:
  - Hypotheses:

$$H_0 : \beta_1 = 0$$
$$H_a : \beta_1 \neq 0$$

  - Test statistic:

$$F = MSR/MSE$$

  - Rejection rule:

  Reject H_0 if $F > F_\alpha$
  where F_α is based on an F distribution with
  1 d.f. in the numerator and $n - 2$ d.f. in the denominator

Interpretation of Significance Tests

- Rejecting the null hypothesis in the t or F test and concluding the relationship between x and y is significant does not prove a cause-and-effect relationship is present between x and y.
- Rejecting the null hypothesis in the t or F test does not enable us to conclude that the relationship between x and y is linear.

Excel's Regression Tool

- Excel's Regression Tool in its Data Analysis package performs a complete regression analysis, including statistical tests of significance.
- The resulting Summary Output has three sections:
  - Regression Statistics
  - ANOVA (Analysis of Variance)
  - Estimated Regression Equation Output – estimated regression coefficients and more
- The Regression Statistics section contains summary statistics, including the coefficient of determination, sample correlation coefficient, standard deviation of the error term ε, and number of observations.
- The ANOVA section is a relatively standard ANOVA table showing, most importantly, the test statistic F and the critical value of F.
- The Estimated Regression Equation Output section (it's not labeled) provides information about the y intercept and slope of the estimated regression line. This information can be used to conduct hypothesis tests for significance and develop confidence interval estimates.

Using the Estimated Regression Equation for Estimation and Prediction

Point Estimation
- The estimated regression equation can be used to compute a point estimate of the <u>mean</u> value of *y* for a particular value of *x* or to predict an <u>individual</u> value of *y* for a given value of *x*. (Either way the question is stated, the results are the same.)

Interval Estimation
- Point estimates do not provide any information on the precision of the estimates.
- One type of interval estimate, a <u>confidence interval estimate</u>, is an interval estimate of the <u>mean value of *y*</u> for a given *x*.
- Another type of interval estimate, a <u>prediction interval estimate</u>, is an interval estimate of an <u>individual value of *y*</u> corresponding to a given value of *x*.

Confidence Interval Estimate of the Mean Value of *y*
- The estimate of the standard deviation of $\hat{y}_p$ is:

$$s_{\hat{y}_p} = s\sqrt{\frac{1}{n} + \frac{(x_p - \overline{x})^2}{\sum(x_i - \overline{x})^2}}$$

    where: x_p = the given value of the independent variable *x*
    s = the standard error of the estimate
- The confidence interval estimate of $E(y_p)$ is:

$$\hat{y}_p \pm t_{\alpha/2}s_{\hat{y}_p}$$

    where: the confidence coefficient is $1 - \alpha$ and $t_{\alpha/2}$ is based
    on a *t* distribution with $n - 2$ degrees of freedom

Prediction Interval Estimate of an Individual Value of *y*
- The estimate of the standard deviation of an individual value of y_p is:

$$s_{ind} = s\sqrt{1 + \frac{1}{n} + \frac{(x_p - \overline{x})^2}{\sum(x_i - \overline{x})^2}}$$

    where: x_p = the given value of the independent variable *x*
    s = the standard error of the estimate
- The prediction interval estimate of y_p is:

$$\hat{y}_p \pm t_{\alpha/2}s_{ind}$$

    where: the confidence coefficient is $1 - \alpha$ and $t_{\alpha/2}$ is based
    on a *t* distribution with $n - 2$ degrees of freedom

Using Excel to Develop Confidence and Prediction Interval Estimates
- Excel's Regression tool does not have an option for computing confidence and prediction intervals.
- For simple linear regression, these intervals can be computed using formulas along with the output of the Regression tool.
- The general expression for a confidence or prediction interval is:
         point estimate $\pm$ margin of error

Residual Analysis: Validating Model Assumptions

- The <u>residual</u> for observation I is the difference between the observed value (y_i) and the estimated value ($\hat{y}_i$) of the dependent variable.
- Residual analysis is the primary tool for determining whether the assumed regression model is appropriate because:
  - The residuals provide the best information about ε.
  - It is important to determine whether the assumptions about ε are appropriate.

Residual Plot against *x*

- A residual plot against *x* is, as it sounds, a graph with residuals (represented by the vertical axis) corresponding to the independent variable (represented by the horizontal axis) plotted.
- The plotted points should give an overall impression of a <u>horizontal band of points</u> if:
  - The assumption that the variance of ε is the same for all values of *x*.
  - The assumed regression model is an adequate representation of the relationship between the two variables.

Using Excel's Regression Tool to Construct a Residual Plot

- The steps to obtain the regression output are performed with one additional selection.
- When the Regression dialog box appears, we must also select the <u>Residual Plot</u> option.
- The output will include two new items:
  - A plot of the residuals against the independent variable.
  - A list of predicted values of *y* and the corresponding residual values.

Standardized Residual Plot

- A residual is standardized by dividing it by its standard deviation.
- The standard deviation of the *i* th residual is:

$$s_{y_i-\hat{y}_i} = s\sqrt{1-h_i}$$

  where: s = the standard error of the estimate

$$h_i = \frac{1}{n} + \frac{(x_i - \overline{x})^2}{\sum(x_i - \overline{x})^2}$$

- The standardized residual for observation *i* is:

$$\frac{y_i - \hat{y}_i}{s_{y_i-\hat{y}_i}}$$

- If the error term ε has a normal distribution, we should expect to see roughly 95% of the standardized residuals between −2 and +2.

Using Excel's Scatter Diagram Tool to Construct a Standardized Residual Plot
- The steps to obtain the regression output are performed with one additional selection.
- When the Regression dialog box appears, we must select the <u>Standardized Residuals</u> option.
- The output will contain a list of:
  - Predicted values of *y*
  - Residuals
  - Standardized residuals
- Then, move the data and the standardized residuals to adjacent columns and plot these two variables in a scatter diagram.

Normal Probability Plot
- This is another approach for determining the validity of the assumption that the error term has a normal distribution.
- Normal scores are on the horizontal axis.
- The corresponding standardized residuals are on the vertical axis.
- The plotted points should cluster closely around a 45-degree line passing through the origin if the standardized residuals are normally distributed.

Outliers and Influential Observations

Detecting Outliers
- An <u>outlier</u> is a data point that does not fit the trend shown by the remaining data.
- Outliers are suspect and warrant careful examination.
- They may be erroneous data ⟶ if so, they should be corrected.
- They may signal a violation of model assumptions ⟶ if so, another model should be considered
- They may simply be unusual values that have occurred by chance ⟶ if so, they should be retained.
- The standardized residuals can be used to identify outliers.
- A standardized residual less than –2 or greater than +2 might be considered an outlier.

Detecting Influential Observations
- An <u>influential observation</u> is one that has a strong influence on the regression results.
- It may correspond to a somewhat off-trend *y* value, somewhat extreme *x* value, or both.
- Observations with extreme values for the independent variables are called <u>high leverage points</u>.
- The <u>leverage</u> of an observation is determined by how far the value of the independent variable is from its mean value.
- Leverage of observation *i* is:

$$h_i = \frac{1}{n} + \frac{(x_i - \overline{x})^2}{\sum (x_i - \overline{x})^2}$$

- Minitab identifies observations as having high leverage if $h_i > 6/n$.
- Data points having high leverage are often influential.
- Excel does not have built-in capabilities for identifying outliers and high-leverage points.

KEY CONCEPTS

CONCEPT	EXAMPLES	EXERCISES
Scatter Diagram Approach		
Estimated Regression Equation	①	1,2,3,4
Coefficient of Determination	②	5
Correlation Coefficient	②	5
Testing for Significance		
t Test for β_1	3	6
Confidence Interval for β_1	3	6
F Test for β_1	3	6
Analysis of Variance Table	3	6
Excel's *Regression* Tool		
Interpretation of Output	④	7
Using the Estimated Regression Equation		
Confidence Interval Estimate of $E(y_p)$	⑤	8
Prediction Interval Estimate of y_p	⑤	8
Residual Analysis	⑥	9

◯ Excel Used

EXAMPLES

EXAMPLE 1

Estimated Regression Equation

Reed Auto periodically has a special week-long sale. As part of the advertising campaign Reed runs one or more television commercials during the weekend preceding the sale. Data from a sample of 5 previous sales are shown below.

Number of TV Ads	Number of Cars Sold
1	14
3	24
2	18
1	17
3	27

a) Develop a scatter diagram for these data.

b) Develop the estimated regression equation by computing the values of b_0 and b_1.

c) Use the estimated regression equation to predict the number of cars sold when two television ads are run.

SOLUTION 1

Using Excel's *Scatter Diagram* and *Trendline* Tools

a) See the application of Excel below for the scatter diagram.

b) Slope for the estimated regression equation:

$$b_1 = \frac{\sum(x_i - \bar{x})(y_i - \bar{y})}{\sum(x_i - \bar{x})^2} \quad \text{or} \quad b_1 = \frac{\sum x_i y_i - (\sum x_i \sum y_i)/n}{\sum x_i^2 - (\sum x_i)^2 /n}$$

$$b_1 = \frac{220 - (10)(100)/5}{24 - (10)^2/5} = \frac{20}{4} = 5$$

y-Intercept for the estimated regression equation:

$$b_0 = \bar{y} - b_1 \bar{x} = 20 - 5(2) = 10$$

Estimated regression equation:

$$\hat{y} = 10 + 5x$$

c) $\hat{y} = 10 + 5x = 10 + 5(2) = 10 + 10 = 20$ cars sold

Excel's Chart Wizard can be used to construct a scatter diagram. Once the scatter diagram has been developed, Excel's Chart menu provides options for computing the estimated regression equation and displaying the regression line.

Enter Data: The labels Week, TV Ads, and Cars Sold are entered into cells A1:C1 of the worksheet. To identify each of the 5 observations, we enter the number 1 through 5 into cells A2:A6. The sample data are entered into cells B2:C6.

Data Worksheet:

	A	B	C	D	E	F
1	Week	TV Ads	Cars Sold			
2	1	1	14			
3	2	3	24			
4	3	2	18			
5	4	1	17			
6	5	3	27			
7						

Enter Functions and Formulas: There are none to be entered.

Apply Tools: First we will produce the scatter diagram using Chart Wizard and then we will add the trend line. The steps are as follows:

<u>Producing a Scatter Diagram</u>

Step 1 Select cells B1:C6
Step 2 Select the **Chart Wizard**
Step 3 When the **Chart Type** dialog box appears:
　　　　Choose **XY (Scatter)** in the Chart type list
　　　　Choose **Scatter** from the Chart sub-type display
　　　　Select **Next >**
Step 4 When the **Chart Source Data** dialog box appears
　　　　Select **Next >**
Step 5 When the **Chart Options** dialog box appears:
　　　　Select the **Titles** tab and then
　　　　　　Delete **Cars Sold** in the Chart title box
　　　　　　Enter **TV Ads** in the **Value (X)** axis box
　　　　　　Enter **Cars Sold** in the **Value (Y)** axis box
　　　　Select the **Legend** tab and then
　　　　　　Remove the check in the **Show Legend** box
　　　　　　Select **Next >**
Step 6 When the **Chart Location** dialog box appears:
　　　　Specify the location for the new chart
　　　　Select **Finish** to display the scatter diagram

<u>Adding the Trendline</u>

Step 1 Position the mouse pointer over any data point
　　　　and right click to display the **Chart** menu
Step 2 Select the **Add Trendline** option
Step 3 When the **Add Trendline** dialog box appears:
　　　　On the **Type** tab select **Linear**
　　　　On the **Options** tab select the **Display equation on chart** box
　　　　Select **OK**

Scatter Diagram with Regression Line and Regression Equation:

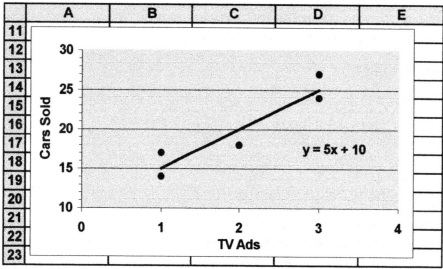

EXAMPLE 2

Coefficient of Determination and Correlation Coefficient

Refer to the Reed Auto problem in Example 1. The estimated regression equation for these data is $\hat{y} = 10 + 5x$.

a) Compute SSE, SST, and SSR.

b) Compute the coefficient of determination r^2. Comment on the goodness of fit.

c) Compute the correlation coefficient.

SOLUTION 2

Using Excel's to Compute the Coefficient of Determination

a) SST = SSR + SSE = $\sum(y_i - \bar{y})^2 = \sum(\hat{y}_i - \bar{y})^2 + \sum(y_i - \hat{y}_i)^2$ = 100 + 14 = 114
   SSE = 14, SST = 114, and SSR = 100

b) r^2 = SSR/SST = 100/114 = .8772
   An r^2 = .8772 indicates that almost 88 % of the total sum of squares can be explained by using the estimated regression equation $\hat{y} = 10 + 5x$ to predict the number of cars sold.

c) r_{xy} = (sign of b_1) $\sqrt{r^2}$ = (+)$\sqrt{.8772}$ = .9366

Excel's Chart menu provides an option for computing the coefficient of determination. We will continue with the worksheet we developed for Example 1.

Enter Data: The data and labels are already entered (see Solution 1).

Enter Functions and Formulas: There are none to be entered.

Apply Tools: We produce the scatter diagram, added the trend line, and displayed the estimated regression equation already (see Solution 1). The additional steps required to compute the coefficient of determination are as follows:

Producing r^2

Step 1 Position the mouse pointer over any data point in the diagram and right click
Step 2 When the Chart menu appears:
    Select the **Add Trendline** option
Step 3 When the Add Trendline dialog box appears:
    On the **Options** tab, select the **Display R-squared value on chart** box
    Select **OK**

r^2 **Value Displayed on Scatter Diagram:**

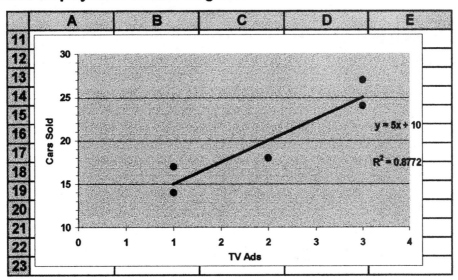

EXAMPLE 3

Testing for Significance

Refer to the Reed Auto problem in Example 1. The estimated regression equation for these data is $\hat{y} = 10 + 5x$.

a) Compute the mean square error MSE.

b) Compute the standard error of the estimate.

c) Compute the estimated standard deviation of b_1.

d) Use the t test to test the following hypotheses ($\alpha = .05$):

$$H_0 : \beta_1 = 0$$
$$H_a : \beta_1 \neq 0$$

e) Develop a 95% confidence interval estimate for β_1 to test the hypotheses in part (d).

f) Use the F test to test the hypotheses in part (d) at a .05 level of significance. Present the results in an analysis of variance table format.

SOLUTION 3

a) $MSE = s^2 = SSE/(n - 2) = 14/(5 - 2) = 14/3 = 4.667$
(SSE = 14 was computed in Solution 2.)

b) $s = \sqrt{MSE} = \sqrt{4.667} = 2.1603$

c) $s_{b_1} = \dfrac{s}{\sqrt{\sum(x_i - \overline{x})^2}} = \dfrac{2.1603}{\sqrt{4}} = \dfrac{2.1603}{2} = 1.08$

d) t Test for Significance

Step 1: Determine the null and alternative hypotheses

$H_0 : \beta_1 = 0$ The mean value of y does not depend on x.
The number of TV ads run and the number of cars sold are <u>not</u> linearly related.

$H_a : \beta_1 \neq 0$ The number of TV ads run and the number of cars sold are linearly related.

where: β_1 = the slope of the simple linear regression equation.

Step 2: Select the test statistic to be used to decide whether to reject H_0

$$t = \frac{b_1}{s_{b_1}}$$

Step 3: Specify the level of significance α

$\alpha = .05$

Step 4: Develop the rejection rule based on the level of significance

Reject H_0 if $t < -t_{\alpha/2}$ or if $t > t_{\alpha/2}$
Reject H_0 if $t < -3.182$ or if $t > 3.182$ (based on 3 d.f.)

Step 5: Collect the data and compute the value of the test statistic

$$t = \frac{b_1}{s_{b_1}} = \frac{5}{1.08} = 4.63$$

Step 6: a) Compare the value of the test statistic to the critical value(s)

$t = 4.63 > 3.182$

or b) Compute the *p*-value and compare it to α

Precise *p*-values are difficult to determine from the Student *t* Table.

Step 7: State your conclusion regarding H_0

Reject H_0. We are 95% confident that the mean value of *y* depends on *x* (that the number of TV ads run and the number of cars sold are linearly related).

e) 95% Confidence Interval Estimate for β_1

We can use a 95% confidence interval for β_1 to test the hypotheses just used in the *t* test. H_0 is rejected if the hypothesized value of β_1 is not included in the confidence interval for β_1.

Rejection Rule

Reject H_0 if 0 is not included in the confidence interval for β_1.

95% Confidence Interval for β_1

$$b_1 \pm t_{\alpha/2} s_{b_1} = 5 \pm 3.182(1.08) = 5 \pm 3.44 = 5 +/- 3.182(1.08) = 5 +/- 3.44 = 1.56 \text{ to } 8.44$$

Conclusion

Reject H_0.   0 is not in the 95% confidence interval estimate of 1.56 to 8.44.

f) *F* Test

Step 1: Determine the null and alternative hypotheses

$H_0 : \beta_1 = 0$ The mean value of *y* does not depend on *x*.
The number of TV ads run and the number of cars sold are <u>not</u> linearly related.

$H_a : \beta_1 \neq 0$ The number of TV ads run and the number of cars sold are linearly related.

where: β_1 = the slope of the simple linear regression equation.

Step 2: Select the test statistic to be used to decide whether to reject H_0

$F = MSR/MSE$

Step 3: Specify the level of significance α

$\alpha = .05$

Step 4: Develop the rejection rule based on the level of significance

Reject H_0 if $F > F_\alpha$

Reject H_0 if $F > 10.13$

where F_α is based on an F distribution with 1 d.f.
in the numerator and $n - 2$ d.f. in the denominator

Step 5: Collect the data and compute the value of the test statistic

$F = 100/4.667 = 21.43$

Step 6: a) Compare the value of the test statistic to the critical value(s)

$F = 21.43 > 10.13$

or b) Compute the p-value and compare it to α

Precise p-values are difficult to determine from the Student t Table.

Step 7: State your conclusion regarding H_0

Reject H_0. We are 95% confident that the mean value of y depends on x (that the number of TV ads run and the number of cars sold are linearly related).

ANALYSIS OF VARIANCE TABLE

Source of Variation	Sum of Squares	Degrees of Freedom	Mean Square	F
Regression	100	1	100	21.43
Residual	14	3	4.67	
Total	114	4		

EXAMPLE 4

Interpretation of Excel's Regression Output

Refer to the Reed Auto problem in Example 1. Use Excel's Regression tool to perform a complete regression analysis. Interpret the output.

SOLUTION 4

Using Excel's *Regression* Tool

Excel has a comprehensive tool in its Data Analysis package called Regression that can be used to perform a complete regression analysis. All of the analysis we performed in Examples 1, 2, and 3 will automatically be performed using the Regression tool.

Enter Data: The data and labels are already entered (see Solution 1).

Enter Functions and Formulas: There are none to be entered.

Apply Tools: The following steps describe how to use Excel's Regression tool:

Performing the Regression Analysis

       Step 1 Select the **Tools** pull-down menu
       Step 2 Choose the **Data Analysis** option
       Step 3 Choose **Regression** from the list of Analysis Tools
       Step 4 When the Regression dialog box appears:
               Enter C1:C6 in the **Input Y Range** box
               Enter B1:B6 in the **Input X Range** box
               Select **Labels**
               Select **Confidence Level**
               Enter 95 in the Confidence Level box
               Select **Output Range**
               Enter A9 (any cell) in the **Ouput Range** box
               Select **OK** to begin the regression analysis

Value Worksheet:

	A	B	C	D	E	F	G	H	I
1	Week	TV Ads	Cars Sold						
2	1	1	14						
3	2	3	24						
4	3	2	18						
5	4	1	17						
6	5	3	27						
7									
8	SUMMARY OUTPUT								
9									
10	*Regression Statistics*								
11	Multiple R	0.93658581							
12	R Square	0.87719298							
13	Adjusted R Sq.	0.83625731							
14	Standard Error	2.1602469							
15	Observations	5							
16									
17	ANOVA								
18		*df*	*SS*	*MS*	*F*	*Signific. F*			
19	Regression	1	100	100	21.4286	0.01898623			
20	Residual	3	14	4.66667					
21	Total	4	114						
22									
23		*Coeffic.*	*Std. Error*	*t Stat*	*P-value*	*Low. 95%*	*Up. 95%*	*Low. 95.0%*	*Up. 95.0%*
24	Intercept	10	2.36643191	4.22577	0.02424	2.46895044	17.5310496	2.46895044	17.5310496
25	TV Ads	5	1.08012345	4.6291	0.01899	1.56256189	8.43743811	1.56256189	8.43743811
26									

     We see above that the regression output, titled SUMMARY OUTPUT, begins with row 8. The first section of the output, titled *Regression Statistics*, contains summary statistics such as the coefficient of determination (R Square). The second section, titled ANOVA, contains the analysis of variance table. The third section, which is not titled, contains the estimated regression coefficients and related information.

     The values you solved for in Examples 1, 2, and 3 can be found in the worksheet above among the output generated by Excel's Regression tool.

Items to note in the *Regression Statistics* section shown below:
- The MULTIPLE R value of .9366 in cell B11 is the sample correlation coefficient value we calculated in Example 2, part (c).
- The R Square value of .8872 in cell B12 is the coefficient of determination value we calculated in Example 2, part (b).
- The Standard Error value of 2.16 in cell B14 is the standard error of the estimate value we calculated in Example 3, part (b).

Regression Statistics Ouput:

	A	B	C	D	E	F
9						
10	*Regression Statistics*					
11	Multiple R	0.93658581				
12	R Square	0.87719298				
13	Adjusted R Sq.	0.83625731				
14	Standard Error	2.1602469				
15	Observations	5				
16						

Items to note in the ANOVA section shown below:
- The ANOVA table generated by Excel is virtually the same as the table we constructed in Example 3, part (f).
- The label in cell A20 is Residual, whereas the textbook uses the label Error.
- The degrees of freedom (*df*) and sum of squares (*SS*) columns are in reverse order here compared with the table in the textbook.
- The values in cells C19:C21 correspond to the SSR, SSE, and SST values we computed in Example 2, part (a).
- The *F* value in cell E19 is the test statistic value we computed in Example 3, part (f).
- The *Signific. F* value in cell F19 is the *p*-value for the *F* test. When we compare the *p*-value .019 with the level of significance .05, we clearly have overwhelming reason to reject the null hypothesis.

ANOVA Output:

	A	B	C	D	E	F
16						
17	ANOVA					
18		*df*	*SS*	*MS*	*F*	*Signific. F*
19	Regression	1	100	100	21.4286	0.01898623
20	Residual	3	14	4.66667		
21	Total	4	114			
22						

Items to note in the Estimated Regression Equation (unlabeled) section shown below:
- The *Coeffic.* Values in cells B24 and B25 are the b_0 and b_1 values we computed in Example 1, part (b).

- The *Std. Error* value of 1.08 in cell C25 is the estimated standard deviation of b_1 value we computed in Example 3, part (c).
- The *t Stat* value of 4.23 in cell D24 is the *t* value we computed in Example 3, part (d).
- The values 1.56 and 8.44 in cells H25 and I24 are the lower and upper limits of the confidence interval estimate for β_1 that we computed in Example 3, part (e).

Estimated Regression Equation Output:

	A	B	C	D	E	F	G	H	I
22									
23		Coeffic.	Std. Error	t Stat	P-value	Low. 95%	Up. 95%	Low. 95.0%	Up. 95.0%
24	Intercept	10	2.36643191	4.22577	0.02424	2.46895044	17.5310496	2.46895044	17.5310496
25	TV Ads	5	1.08012345	4.6291	0.01899	1.56256189	8.43743811	1.56256189	8.43743811
26									

EXAMPLE 5

Confidence and Prediction Interval Estimates

Refer to the Reed Auto problem in Example 1.

a) Develop a 95% confidence interval estimate of the mean number of cars sold when 3 TV ads are run.

b) Develop a 95% prediction interval estimate for the number of cars sold when 3 TV ads are run.

SOLUTION 5

Using Excel's *DEVSQ* Function

The general expression for a confidence or prediction interval is:

Point Estimate +/- Margin of Error

Excel's Regression tool does not have an option for computing confidence and prediction intervals. However, formulas can be designed to compute these intervals along with the output provided by the Regression tool.

Enter Data: The data (cells B2:C6) and regression output (A8:I25) that were developed in Example 4 are used as a starting point here.

Confidence Interval Estimate

Enter Functions and Formulas: We enter the value 3 for x_p into cell F2. The AVERAGE function is used to compute $\bar{x}$ in cell F3. The formula =F2-F3 is entered into cell F4 to compute the value of $x_p - \bar{x}$. The formula =F4^2 is entered into cell F5 to compute the value of $(x_p - \bar{x})^2$. The DEVSQ function is used to compute $\Sigma(x_i - \bar{x})^2$ by entering the formula =DEVSQ(B2:B6) into cell F6.

We can now compute $s_{\hat{y}_p}^2$ by entering the formula =D20*(1/B15+F5/F6) into cell F7. We then enter the formula =SQRT(F7) into cell F8 to compute $s_{\hat{y}_p}$. To compute the t value required, we enter the formula =TINV(0.05,3) into cell F9. Finally, the margin of error is computed by entering the formula =F9*F8 into cell F10.

To compute the point estimate, we enter the formula =B24+B25*F2 into cell F11. The lower and upper limits of the 95% confidence interval are then computed by entering the formulas =F11-F10 and =F11+F10 into cells F12 and F13, respectively.

Formula Worksheet:

	D	E	F
1		CONFIDENCE INTERVAL	
2		x_p	3
3		x bar	=AVERAGE(B2:B6)
4		x_p-x bar	=F2-F3
5		$(x_p$-x bar$)^2$	=F4^2
6		$\Sigma(x_p$-x bar$)^2$	=DEVSQ(B2:B6)
7		Variance of y hat	=D20*(1/B15+F5/F6)
8		Std. Dev of y hat	=SQRT(F7)
9		t Value	=TINV(0.05,3)
10		Margin of Error	=F9*F8
11		Point Estimate	=B24+B25*F2
12		Lower Limit	=F11-F10
13		Upper Limit	=F11+F10

We see in the resulting worksheet below that the 95% confidence interval estimate of the mean number of cars sold when 3 TV ads are run is 20.39 to 29.61 cars.

Value Worksheet:

	D	E	F
1		CONFIDENCE INTERVAL	
2		x_p	3
3		x bar	2.0
4		x_p-x bar	1.0
5		$(x_p$-x bar$)^2$	1.0
6		$\Sigma(x_p$-x bar$)^2$	4.0
7		Variance of y hat	2.1000
8		Std. Dev of y hat	1.4491
9		t Value	3.1824
10		Margin of Error	4.6118
11		Point Estimate	25.0
12		Lower Limit	20.39
13		Upper Limit	29.61

Prediction Interval Estimate

Enter Functions and Formulas: To compute $s_{ind}^2 = s^2 + s_{\hat{y}_p}^2$ we enter the formula =D20+F7 into cell I2. Then, in cell I3 we enter the formula =SQRT(I2) to compute s_{ind}. To compute the margin of error the formula =F9*I3 is entered into cell I4. The formulas =F11-I4 and =F11+I4 are entered into cells I5 and I6 respectively to compute the lower and upper limits of the prediction interval.

Formula Worksheet:

	H	I
1	PREDICTION INTERVAL	
2	Variance of y ind	=D20+F7
3	Std. Dev. of y ind	=SQRT(I2)
4	Margin of Error	=F9*I3
5	Lower Limit	=F11-I4
6	Upper Limit	=F11+I4
7		

We see in the resulting worksheet below that the 95% prediction interval estimate for the number of cars sold when 3 TV ads run is 16.72 to 33.28 cars.

Value Worksheet:

	H	I
1	PREDICTION INTERVAL	
2	Variance of y ind	6.76667
3	Std. Dev. of y ind	2.60128
4	Margin of Error	8.27845
5	Lower Limit	16.72
6	Upper Limit	33.28
7		

EXAMPLE 6

Residual Analysis

Refer to the Reed Auto problem in Example 1. Develop a plot of the residuals against the independent variable, number of TV ads run. Do the assumptions about the error terms seem to be satisfied?

SOLUTION 6

Using Excel's *Regression* Tool for Residual Plot

The steps outlined earlier in Example 4 to obtain the regression output are performed with one change. When the Regression dialog box appears, we must also select the **Residual Plot** option. The output will include two new items:
- a plot of the residuals against the independent variable, and
- a list of predicted values of *y* and the corresponding residual values.

Residual Plot:

Residual Ouput:

	A	B	C
28			
29	RESIDUAL OUTPUT		
30			
31	*Observation*	*Predicted Cars Sold*	*Residuals*
32	1	15	-1
33	2	25	-1
34	3	20	-2
35	4	15	2
36	5	25	2

If the assumption that the variance of the error term is the same for all values of x, the residual plot should give an overall impression of a horizontal band of points, which is what we see in the Residual Plot above.

On the other hand, if the absolute value of the residuals is greater for larger values of x, the assumption of a constant variance of ε is violated. Fortunately, this is not true here. We see that when x is smallest (15) the error is 2 and when x is the largest (25) the error is 2 again. We conclude that the assumed regression model is an adequate representation of the relationship between the number of TV ads run and the number of cars sold.

EXERCISES

EXERCISE 1

Estimated Regression Equation

Connie Harris, in charge of office supplies at First Capital Mortgage Corp., would like to predict the quantity of paper used in the office photocopying machines per month. She believes that the number of loans originated in a month influence the volume of photocopying performed. She has compiled the following recent monthly data:

Number of Loans Originated in Month	Sheets of Photocopy Paper Used (000's)
45	22
25	13
50	24
60	25
40	21
25	16
35	18
40	25

a) Develop the least-squares estimated regression equation that relates sheets of photocopy paper used to loans originated.

b) Use the regression equation developed in part (a) to forecast the amount of paper used in a month when 42 loan originations are expected.

EXERCISE 2

Estimated Regression Equation

Four months ago, the Bank Drug Company introduced Jeffrey William brand designer bandages. Advertised using the slogan, "What the best dressed cuts are wearing", weekly sales for this period (in 1000's) have been as follows:

Week	Sales	Week	Sales	Week	Sales
1	12.8	7	20.6	12	23.8
2	14.6	8	18.5	13	25.1
3	15.2	9	19.9	14	24.7
4	16.1	10	23.6	15	26.5
5	15.8	11	24.2	16	28.9
6	17.2				

a) Plot a graph of sales vs. weeks. Does linear trend appear reasonable?

b) Assuming linear trend, forecast sales for weeks 17, 18, 19, and 20.

EXERCISE 3

Estimated Regression Equation

At a local car dealership the following is a record of sales for the past 12 months:

Month	Sales	Month	Sales
Jan	36	Jul	25
Feb	34	Aug	22
Mar	28	Sep	26
Apr	30	Oct	22
May	27	Nov	21
Jun	24	Dec	19

a) Using the method of least squares, determine a trend line for forecasting future sales.

b) Using your model in part (a), determine how long it will be before zero sales are forecasted.

c) Consider your answer to part (b). What will be the forecasted sales for the month after that? Does this make sense? Comment on the validity of the model. What assumption about the model appears to be in error?

EXERCISE 4

Estimated Regression Equation

Scott Bell Builders would like to predict the total number of labor hours spent framing a house based on the square footage of the house. The following data has been compiled on ten houses recently built.

Square Footage (100's)	Framing Labor Hours	Square Footage (100's)	Framing Labor Hours
20	195	27	225
21	170	29	240
23	220	31	225
23	200	32	275
26	230	35	260

a) Develop the least-squares estimated regression equation that relates framing labor hours to house square footage.

b) Use the regression equation developed in part (a) to predict framing labor hours when the house size is 3350 square feet.

EXERCISE 5

Coefficient of Determination and Correlation Coefficient

Refer to the First Capital Mortgage Corp. problem in Exercise 1.

a) Compute SSE, SST, and SSR.

b) Compute the coefficient of determination r^2. Comment on the goodness of fit.

c) Compute the correlation coefficient.

EXERCISE 6

Testing for Significance

Refer to the First Capital Mortgage Corp. problem in Exercise 1.

a) Compute the mean square error MSE.

b) Compute the standard error of the estimate.

c) Compute the estimated standard deviation of b_1.

d) Use the t test to test the following hypotheses ($\alpha = .05$):

$$H_0 : \beta_1 = 0$$
$$H_0 : \beta_1 \neq 0$$

e) Develop a 95% confidence interval estimate for β_1 to test the hypotheses in part (d).

f) Use the F test to test the hypotheses in part (d) at a .05 level of significance. Present the results in an analysis of variance table format.

EXERCISE 7

Interpretation of Excel's Regression Output

Refer to the Scott Bell Builders problem in Exercise 4. Use Excel's Regression tool to perform a complete regression analysis. Interpret the output.

EXERCISE 8

Confidence and Prediction Interval Estimates

Refer to the First Capital Mortgage Corp. problem in Exercise 1.

a) Develop a 95% confidence interval estimate of the mean number of sheets of paper used when 38 mortgages are originated.

b) Develop a 95% prediction interval estimate for the number of sheets of paper used when 38 mortgages are originated.

EXERCISE 9

Residual Analysis

Refer to the First Capital Mortgage Corp. problem in Exercise 1. Develop a plot of the residuals against the independent variable, number of mortgages originated. Do the assumptions about the error terms seem to be satisfied?

SELF-TEST

TRUE/FALSE

___ 1. Rejecting the null hypothesis H_0: $\beta_1 = 0$ as the result of a t test enables us to conclude that a cause-and-effect relationship is present between x and y.

___ 2. In the context of simple linear regression, the t test and the F test provide the same conclusion regarding β_1.

___ 3. Residuals represent the difference between the actual y values and the mean of the y values.

___ 4. A correlation coefficient (r) value of −1 indicates a perfect linear relationship between x and y.

___ 5. If the sign of the sample correlation coefficient is negative, we know the estimated regression equation has a negative slope.

FILL-IN-THE-BLANK

1. The _____ is a measure of the strength of the linear relationship between two variables.

2. The interval estimate of the mean value of y for a given value of x is the _____ interval estimate..

3. A scatter diagram is constructed with the values of the _____ variable on the horizontal axis.

4. In every ANOVA table the total sum of squares is the sum of the regression sum of squares and the _____.

5. The _____ variable is the variable doing the predicting or explaining.

MULTIPLE CHOICE

___ 1. The proportion of the variation in the dependent variable y that is explained by the estimated regression equation is measured by the
   a) correlation coefficient
   b) standard error of the estimate
   c) coefficient of determination
   d) confidence interval estimate

___ 2. The least squares criterion is
   a) min $\sum(x_i - y_i)^2$
   b) min $\sum(y_i - \bar{y})^2$
   c) min $(\sum y_i - \hat{y}_i)^2$
   d) min $\sum(y_i - \hat{y}_i)^2$

___ 3. In a residual plot that does <u>not</u> suggest we should challenge the assumptions of our regression model, we would expect to see
   a) a horizontal band of points centered near zero
   b) a widening band of points
   c) a band of points having a slope consistent with that of the regression equation
   d) a parabolic band of points

___ 4. The difference between the observed value of the dependent variable and the value predicted by using the estimated regression equation is the
   a) standard error
   b) residual
   c) prediction interval
   d) variance

___ 5. As the goodness of fit for the estimated regression equation increases,
   a) the absolute value of the regression equation's slope increases
   b) the value of the regression equation's y intercept decreases
   c) the value of the coefficient of determination increases
   d) the value of the correlation coefficient increases

ANSWERS

EXERCISES

1) a) $\hat{y} = 7.5 + .325x$
   b) $\hat{y} = 21{,}150$ sheets.

2) a) Yes
   b) Week 17: 29.0; Week 18: 30.0;
      Week 19: 31.0; Week 20: 32.0

3) a) $F_t = 34.80 - 1.329t$
   b) 26 months
   c) After 27 months sales will be approximately -1 cars; this is clearly impossible;
      the assumption of a continued linear decline is inappropriate.

4) a) $\hat{y} = 80.8757 + 5.3605(x)$
   b) $\hat{y} = 260.45245$ hours

5) a) 32.38, 138.00, 105.63
   b) $r^2 = .7654$; very good fit
   c) $r = .8749$

6) a) 5.3958
   b) 2.3229
   c) 0.0735
   d) p-value = .0045; Reject H_0
   e) .145 to .505; Reject H_0
   f) $F = 19.575$

7) $r^2 = .7608$; very good fit
   p-value = .001; Reject H_0
   Confid. Interval = 2.91 to 7.81; Reject H_0

8) a) 17.83 to 21.87
   b) 13.82 to 25.88

9) Residual range: -2.6 to 4.5;
   Approx. horizontal band of pts; yes

10) a) $\hat{y} = -47.34160 + 6.020214x_1 + 23.03526x_2 + 27.02864x_3$
    b) $r^2 = .807$; very good fit
    c) $12{,}040.43
    d) $23{,}035.26
    e) $27{,}028.64
    f) $282{,}410.92

TRUE/FALSE

1) False
2) True
3) False
4) True
5) True

FILL-IN-THE-BLANK

1) correlation coefficient
2) confidence
3) independent
4) error sum of squares
5) independent

MULTIPLE CHOICE

1) c
2) d
3) a
4) b
5) c

CHAPTER 15

Multiple Regression

Multiple Regression Model

Least Squares Method

Multiple Coefficient of Determination

Model Assumptions

Testing for Significance

Using the Estimated Regression Equation
for Estimation and Prediction

Qualitative Independent Variables

Residual Analysis

LEARNING OBJECTIVES

1. Understand how multiple regression analysis can be used to develop relationships involving one dependent variable and several independent variables.

2. Be able to interpret the coefficients in a multiple regression analysis.

3. Know the assumptions necessary to conduct statistical tests involving the hypothesized regression model.

4. Understand the role of Excel in performing multiple regression analysis.

5. Be able to interpret and use Excel's Regression tool output to develop the estimated regression equation.

6. Be able to determine how good a fit is provided by the estimated regression equation.

7. Be able to test for the significance of the regression equation.

8. Understand how multicollinearity affects multiple regression analysis.

9. Know how residual analysis can be used to make a judgement as to the appropriateness of the model, identify outliers, and determine which observations are influential.

REVIEW

Regression Analysis
- Managerial decisions often are based on the relationship between two or more variables.
- A statistical procedure called <u>regression analysis</u> can be used to develop an equation showing how the variables are related.
- The variable being predicted is called the <u>dependent variable</u>.
- The variable(s) being used to predict the value of the dependent variable are called the <u>independent variables</u>.

Multiple Regression
- Multiple regression analysis is the study of how <u>one dependent variable</u> is related to <u>two or more independent variables</u>.
- Multiple regression analysis enables us to consider more factors and thus obtain better estimates than are possible with simple linear regression.

Multiple Regression Model
- The equation that describes how y is related to the independent variables x_1, x_2, . . x_p and an error term is called the <u>regression model</u>.
- The <u>multiple regression model</u> is:
$$y = \beta_0 + \beta_1 x_1 + \beta_2 x_2 + \ldots + \beta_p x_p + \varepsilon$$
where: p = number of independent variables
- β_0, β_1, . . . β_p are re referred to as the <u>parameters of the model</u>.
- The error term ε accounts for the variability in y that cannot be explained by the linear effect of the p independent variables.

Multiple Regression Equation
- One of the assumptions made here is that the <u>mean or expected value of ε is zero</u>.
- As a result of the above assumption, the mean or expected value of y, denoted $E(y)$, is equal to $\beta_0 + \beta_1 x_1 + \beta_2 x_2 + \ldots + \beta_p x_p$.
- The <u>multiple regression equation</u> is:
$$E(y) = \beta_0 + \beta_1 x_1 + \beta_2 x_2 + \ldots + \beta_p x_p$$
- The values of β_0, β_1, β_2, ... β_p are not known, so we take a simple random sample and compute sample statistics b_0, b_1, b_2, . . . b_p that are used as point estimators.

Estimated Multiple Regression Equation
- The <u>estimated multiple regression equation</u> is:
$$\hat{y} = b_0 + b_1 x_1 + b_2 x_2 + \ldots + b_p x_p$$
where: $\hat{y}$ = estimated value of the dependent variable

b_0, b_1, b_2, . . . b_p are the estimates of β_0, β_1, β_2, ... β_p

Least Squares Method
- The <u>least squares method</u> is a procedure for using sample data to compute an estimated regression equation, specifically values for b_0, b_1, b_2, . . . b_p.
- Values are found for b_0, b_1, b_2, . . . b_p that minimize the <u>sum of the squares of the deviations</u> between the observed values of y_i and the estimated values $\hat{y}_i$.
- The <u>least squares criterion</u> is:
$$\min \sum (y_i - \hat{y}_i)^2$$
where:

y_i = <u>observed</u> value of the dependent variable for the i th observation

$\hat{y}_i$ = <u>estimated</u> value of the dependent variable for the i th observation
- The formulas for the regression coefficients b_0, b_1, b_2, . . . b_p involve the use of matrix algebra. We will rely on Excel to perform the calculations.

Excel's Regression Tool
- Excel's Regression Tool in its Data Analysis package performs a <u>complete regression analysis, including statistical tests of significance</u>.
  - Select the *Tools* pull-down menu.
  - Choose the *Data Analysis* option.
  - Choose *Regression* from the list of Analysis Tools.
  - Then, complete the Regression dialog box.

- The resulting <u>Summary Output</u> has three sections:
  - Regression Statistics
  - ANOVA (Analysis of Variance)
  - Estimated Regression Equation Output
- The <u>Regression Statistics section</u> contains summary statistics, including the coefficient of determination, sample correlation coefficient, standard deviation of the error term ε, and number of observations.
- The <u>ANOVA section</u> is a relatively standard ANOVA table showing, most importantly, the test statistic F and the critical value of F.
- The <u>Estimated Regression Equation Output section</u> (it's not labeled) provides information about the y intercept and slope of the estimated regression line. This information can be used to conduct hypothesis tests for significance and develop confidence interval estimates.

Note on Interpretation of Coefficients
- In multiple regression, we must be careful when interpreting the regression coefficients.
- We interpret each coefficient as follows: b_i represents an estimate of the change in y corresponding to a one-unit increase in x_i <u>when all other independent variables are held constant</u>.

Multiple Coefficient of Determination
- The multiple coefficient of determination provides a <u>measure of the goodness of fit</u> for the estimated regression equation.
- R^2 is the proportion of the variability in the dependent variable that can be explained by the estimated regression equation.
- The <u>multiple coefficient of determination</u>, R^2, is computed using the same formula as is used in simple regression:

$$R^2 = SSR/SST$$

  where:

$$SST = \sum (y_i - \bar{y})^2 = \text{total sum of squares}$$
$$SSR = \sum (\hat{y}_i - \bar{y})^2 = \text{sum of squares due to regression}$$
$$SSE = \sum (y_i - \hat{y}_i)^2 = \text{sum of squares due to error}$$

Relationship Among SST, SSR, and SSE
- SST = SSR + SSE
- SSR can be thought of as the <u>explained</u> portion of SST.
- SSE can be thought of as the <u>unexplained</u> portion of SST.
- If the regression equation provided a perfect fit, $y_i - \hat{y}_i$ would be zero for each observation, resulting in SSE = 0 and SSR/SST = 1.
- The ratio <u>SSR/SST</u>, which will be <u>between 0 and 1</u>, is used to evaluate the <u>goodness of fit</u> for the estimated regression equation.

Adjusted Multiple Coefficient of Determination

- If a variable is added to the model, $R2$ becomes larger even if the variable added is not statistically significant.
- The <u>adjusted multiple coefficient of determination</u> compensates for the number of independent variables in the model.
- The <u>adjusted multiple coefficient of determination</u> is computed as follows:

$$R_a^2 = 1 - (1 - R^2)\frac{n-1}{n-p-1}$$

where: n = number of observations

p = number of independent variables

Assumptions About the Error Term ε

- The error ε is a random variable with mean or expected value of zero. $E(\varepsilon) = 0$.
- The variance of ε is denoted by σ^2 and is the same for all values of the independent variables.
- The values of ε are independent.
- The error ε is a normally distributed random variable reflecting the deviation between the y value and the expected value of y given by $\beta_0 + \beta_1 x_1 + \beta_2 x_2 + \ldots + \beta_p x_p$.

Testing for Significance

- In multiple regression, the t and the F test have different purposes.
- The F test determines whether there is a significant relationship between the dependent variable and the <u>set of all</u> independent variables. (a test for <u>overall</u> significance)
- A separate t test is conducted for <u>each</u> of the independent variables. (a test for <u>individual</u> significance)

- F Test
  - <u>Hypotheses</u>: H_0: $\beta_1 = \beta_2 = \ldots = \beta_p = 0$
    H_a: One or more of the parameters is not equal to zero
  - <u>Test Statistic</u>: F = MSR/MSE
  - <u>Rejection Rule</u>:   Using test statistic: Reject H_0 if $F > F_\alpha$
    where F_α is based on an F distribution with p d.f. in the numerator and $(n - p - 1)$ d.f. in the denominator.
    Using p-value: Reject H_0 if p-value $< \alpha$

- t Test
  - <u>Hypotheses</u>: $H_0 : \beta_i = 0$
    $H_a : \beta_i \neq 0$
  - <u>Test Statistic</u>:

    $$t = \frac{b_i}{s_{b_i}}$$

  - <u>Rejection Rule</u>:   Using test statistic: Reject H_0 if $t < -t_{\alpha/2}$ or $t > t_{\alpha/2}$
    where $t_{\alpha/2}$ is based on a t distribution
    with $(n - p - 1)$ degrees of freedom
    Using p-value: Reject H_0 if p-value $< \alpha$

Multicollinearity

- Most independent variables in a multiple regression problem are correlated to some degree with one another.
- Multicollinearity refers to the correlation among the independent variables.
- When the independent variables are highly correlated, it is not possible to determine the separate effect of any particular independent variable on the dependent variable.
- Every attempt should be made to avoid including independent variables that are highly correlated.
- Multicollinearity is a potential problem if the absolute value of the sample correlation coefficient exceeds .7 for any two independent variables.

Point Estimation

- Estimating the mean value of *y* and an individual value of *y* in multiple regression is similar to that in simple regression. The given values of each of the independent variables are substituted into the estimated regression equation and the corresponding value of $\hat{y}$ is the point estimate.

Interval Estimation

- The estimated multiple regression equation can be used to make two interval estimates:
  - a confidence interval estimate of the mean value of *y*
  - a prediction interval estimate of an individual value of *y*
- The formulas required for these estimates are beyond the scope of the textbook.
- Excel's Regression tool does not have this capability, but the PredInt.xls macro included on the data disk will produce these estimates.

Qualitative Independent Variables

- A qualitative variable can be represented as one or more quantitative variables.
- In this case, the quantitative variable is called a dummy or indicator variable.
- If a qualitative variable has *k* levels, *k* – 1 dummy variables are required.
- Each dummy variable is coded as 0 or 1.
- A qualitative variable with 3 levels - high, medium, and low – can be represented by 2 dummy variables, x_1 and x_2.
  - High could be coded $x_1 = 0$ and $x_2 = 0$.
  - Medium could be coded $x_1 = 1$ and $x_2 = 0$.
  - Low could be coded $x_1 = 0$ and $x_2 = 1$.
- Care must be taken in defining and interpreting the dummy variables.

Residual Analysis

- The residual for observation I is the difference between the observed value (y_i) and the estimated value ($\hat{y}_i$) of the dependent variable.
- Residual analysis is the primary tool for determining whether the assumed regression model is appropriate because:
  - The residuals provide the best information about ε.
  - It is important to determine whether the assumptions about ε are appropriate.

a) <u>Compute</u> the multiple coefficient of determination R^2 using the SSR and SST values provided by Excel's Regression tool. Compare your answer with the R^2 value provided by Excel.

b) <u>Compute</u> the adjusted coefficient of determination R_a^2. Compare your answer with the R_a^2 value provided by Excel.

c) Comment on the goodness of fit. Does the model appear to explain a large amount of variability in the data?

SOLUTION 3

The Summary Output and ANOVA Table portions of the Excel Regression output are relevant here.

Summary Output:

	A	B	C	D	E	F	G
23							
24	SUMMARY OUTPUT						
25							
26	*Regression Statistics*						
27	Multiple R	0.91333					
28	R Square	0.83418					
29	Adj. R Sq.	0.81467					
30	Std. Error	2.41876					

ANOVA Table:

	A	B	C	D	E	F	G
32							
33	ANOVA						
34		df	SS	MS	F	Signif. F	
35	Regression	2	500.329	250.16	42.7601	2.3E-07	
36	Residual	17	99.457	5.8504			
37	Total	19	599.786				
38							

a) The SSR and SST values appear in cells C35 and C37 of the ANOVA Table above.

$$R^2 = SSR/SST = 500.329/599.786 = .83418$$

This result agrees with the R^2 value appearing in cell B28 of the Summary Output above.

b) $R_a^2 = 1 - (1 - R^2)\dfrac{n-1}{n-p-1}$

where n = number of observations, and p = number of independent variables.

$$R_a^2 = 1 - (1 - .83418)\frac{20 - 1}{20 - 2 - 1} = .81467$$

This result agrees with the R_a^2 value appearing in cell B29 of the Summary Output above.

c) Goodness of Fit:

Based on the R^2 value, 83.42% of the variability in programmer salaries is explained by the estimated multiple regression equation with experience and test score as the independent variables. Even after adjusting the coefficient of determination for the number of independent variables in the model, the % of variability explained by the model is high (81.47%). On this basis (without performing residual analysis) we can say that the estimated multiple regression equation fits well.

EXAMPLE 4

Testing for Significance

In Example 1, the following estimated multiple regression equation was presented.

$$\hat{y} = 3.174 + 1.404x_1 + 0.2509x_2$$

where: $\hat{y}$ = estimated annual salary ($000) for a programmer
            x_1 = years of programming experience
            x_2 = score on programmer aptitude test

a) Compute the mean square due to regression (MSR) and mean square error (MSE) using the SSR and SSE values provided by Excel.

b) Compute F and perform the appropriate F test. Use $\alpha = .05$.

c) Perform a t test for the significance of β_1. Use $\alpha = .05$.

d) Perform a t test for the significance of β_2. Use $\alpha = .05$.

SOLUTION 4

The Summary Output and ANOVA Table portions of the Excel output are relevant here.

a) MSR = SSR/p = 500.329/2 = 250.1645
   MSE = SSE/($n - p - 1$) = 99.457/(20 - 2 - 1) = 5.8504
   where: n = number of observations, and p = number of independent variables

b) F = MSR/MSE = 250.1645/5.8504 = 42.7602

   F Test for Overall Significance:

      $H_0 : \beta_1 = \beta_2 = 0$
      $H_a : \beta_1$ and/or β_2 is not equal to zero

Reject H_0 if $F > F_\alpha$ or p-value $< \alpha$
where F_α is based on an F distribution with p degrees of freedom in the numerator and $n - p - 1$ degrees of freedom in the denominator

F_α = 3.59 is found in Appendix B of the textbook.
p-value = 2.3E-07 is found in cell F35 of the ANOVA Table output

Using the F or p-value approach, we reject H_0.
(42.7602 > 3.59 and 2.3E-07 < .05)
β_1 and/or β_2 is not equal to zero.

c) t Test for Significance of β_1

$H_0 : \beta_1 = 0$
$H_a : \beta_1 \neq 0$

Reject H_0 if $t < -t_{\alpha/2}$ or $t > t_{\alpha/2}$ or p-value $< \alpha$
where $t_{\alpha/2}$ is based on a t distribution with $n - p - 1$ degrees of freedom

$t = \dfrac{b_1}{s_{b_1}}$ = 1.4039/.1986 = 7.0702

where s_{b_1} = .1986 is found in cell C41 of the Regression Equation output

$t_{.025}$ = 2.11 is found in Appendix B of the textbook (using 17 deg. of freedom)
p-value = 1.9E-06 is found in cell E41 of the Regression Equation output

Using the t or p-value approach, we reject H_0.
(7.0702 > 2.11 and 1.9E-06 < .05)
β_1 is not equal to zero.

d) t Test for Significance of β_2

$H_0 : \beta_2 = 0$
$H_a : \beta_2 \neq 0$

Reject H_0 if $t < -t_{\alpha/2}$ or $t > t_{\alpha/2}$ or p-value $< \alpha$
where $t_{\alpha/2}$ is based on a t distribution with $n - p - 1$ degrees of freedom

$t = \dfrac{b_2}{s_{b_2}}$ = 0.25089/.07735 = 3.2436

where s_{b_2} = .07735 is found in cell C42 of the Regression Equation output

$t_{.025}$ = 2.11 is found in Appendix B of the textbook (using 17 deg. of freedom)
p-value = .00478 is found in cell E42 of the Regression Equation output

Using the t or p-value approach, we reject H_0.
(3.2436 > 2.11 and .00478 < .05)
β_2 is not equal to zero.

EXAMPLE 5

Qualitative Variables

Refer again to the Cortland Software problem in Example 1. As an extension of the problem, suppose that management also believes that the annual salary is related to whether the individual has a graduate degree in computer science or information systems.

The years of experience, the score on the programmer aptitude test, whether or not the individual has a relevant graduate degree, and the annual salary ($000) for each of the sampled 20 programmers are shown below.

Exper.	Test Score	Degree	Salary	Exper.	Test Score	Degree	Salary
4	78	No	24.0	9	88	Yes	38.0
7	100	Yes	43.0	2	73	No	26.6
1	86	No	23.7	10	75	Yes	36.2
5	82	Yes	34.3	5	81	No	31.6
8	86	Yes	35.8	6	74	No	29.0
10	84	Yes	38.0	8	87	Yes	34.0
0	75	No	22.2	4	79	No	30.1
1	80	No	23.1	6	94	Yes	33.9
6	83	No	30.0	3	70	No	28.2
6	91	Y	33.0	3	89	No	30.0

a) Develop the estimated multiple regression equation to predict the programmer's salary given the number of years of experience, score on the aptitude test, and presence or absence of a relevant graduate degree.

b) Interpret the coefficients of the regression equation.

c) Estimate the salary for a programmer with 5 years of experience, a score of 88 on the aptitude test, and a relevant graduate degree.

SOLUTION 5

Using Excel's *Regression* Tool for Multiple Regression

a) $\hat{y} = b_0 + b_1x_1 + b_2x_2 + b_3x_3$

where: $\hat{y}$ = estimated annual salary ($000)
  x_1 = years of programming experience
  x_2 = score on programmer aptitude test
  x_3 = 0 if individual <u>does not</u> have a graduate degree
       1 if individual <u>does</u> have a graduate degree

To develop the estimated multiple regression equation, we will use Excel's Regression tool. (The calculations involve matrix algebra and are beyond the scope of the textbook.)

Enter Data: We can modify the worksheet we developed for Example 1. A new column for the Graduate Degree data is inserted between the columns containing the Test Score and Salary data.

Data Worksheet:

	A	B	C	D	E	F
1	Program-mer	Exper-ience	Test Score	Grad. Degree	Salary ($K)	
2	1	4	78	0	24.0	
3	2	7	100	1	43.0	
4	3	1	86	0	23.7	
5	4	5	82	1	34.3	
6	5	8	86	1	35.8	
7	6	10	84	1	38.0	
8	7	0	75	0	22.2	
9	8	1	80	0	23.1	

Note: Rows 10-21 are not shown.

Enter Functions and Formulas: There are none to enter.

Apply Tools: The following steps describe how to use the Regression tool for multiple regression analysis:

<u>Performing the Multiple Regression Analysis</u>

Step 1 Select the **Tools** pull-down menu
Step 2 Choose the **Data Analysis** option
Step 3 Choose **Regression** from the list of Analysis Tools
Step 4 When the Regression dialog box appears:
      Enter E1:E21 in the **Input Y Range** box
      Enter B1:D21 in the **Input X Range** box
      Select **Labels**
      Select **Confidence Level**
      Enter 95 (for now) in the **Confidence Level** box
      Select **Output Range** and enter A24 in the **Output Range** box
      Select **OK**

Regression Equation Output:

	A	B	C	D	E	F	G	H	I
38									
39		Coeffic.	Std. Err.	t Stat	P-value	Lo. 95%	Up. 95%	Lo. 95.0%	Up. 95.0%
40	Intercept	7.9448	7.3808	1.0764	0.2977	-7.7017	23.5914	-7.7017	23.5914
41	Experience	1.1476	0.2976	3.8561	0.0014	0.5167	1.7785	0.5167	1.7785
42	Test Score	0.1969	0.0899	2.1905	0.0436	0.0063	0.3875	0.0063	0.3875
43	Grad. Degr.	2.2804	1.9866	1.1479	0.2679	-1.9310	6.4918	-1.9310	6.4918
44									

The values for b_0, b_1, b_2, and b_3 in the estimated multiple regression equation are found in cells B40:B43 of the Excel output shown above.

$$\hat{y} = 7.945 + 1.148x_1 + 0.197x_2 + 2.280x_3$$

That is, Estimated Salary = 7.945 + 1.148(Exper) + 0.197(Score) + 2.280(Degree). Note that estimated salary will be in thousands of dollars.

b) Interpretation of coefficients:

b_1: With each additional year of experience, salary is expected to increase by $1,148.00, when the aptitude test score is held constant.

b_2: With each additional point scored on the aptitude test, salary is expected to increase by $197.00, when the years of experience is held constant.

B_3: The salary of a programmer with a relevant graduate degree is, on average, $2,280.00 higher than the salary of a programmer without the advanced degree.

c) The estimated salary $\hat{y}$ for a programmer with 5 years of experience, a test score of 88, and a relevant graduate degree is:
$$\hat{y} = 7.945 + 1.148(5) + 0.197(88) + 2.280(1) = 33.30100 \text{ or } \$33,301.00$$

EXAMPLE 6

Residual Analysis

Refer again to the Cortland Software problem in Example 5.

a) Plot the residuals against $\hat{y}$. Does the residual plot support the assumptions about the error term ε? Explain.

b) Plot the standardized residuals against $\hat{y}$. Do there appear to be any outliers in these data? Explain. residual plot support the assumptions about ε? Explain.

SOLUTION 6

Using Excel's *Regression* Tool and *Chart Wizard* for Residual Analysis

Excel's Regression tool provides plots of residuals against one independent variable at a time, but not a plot of residuals or standardized residuals against $\hat{y}$. To accomplish the latter, we will use the Scatter Diagram tool after generating the residuals.

The steps to obtain the regression output are performed with two additional selections. When the Regression dialog box appears, we must select the Residuals option. While we are at it, we'll select the Standardized Residuals option (for part b of this problem). The output will contain a list of predicted values of y, residuals, and standardized residuals as shown below.

Residual Ouput:

	A	B	C	D
29	RESIDUAL OUTPUT			
30				
31	Observation	Predicted Salaries	Residuals	Standard Residuals
32	1	27.89626	-3.89626	-1.77171
33	2	37.95204	5.04796	2.29541
34	3	26.02901	-2.32901	-1.05905
35	4	32.11201	2.18799	0.99492
36	5	36.34251	-0.54251	-0.24669
37	6	38.24380	-0.24380	-0.11086
38	7	22.71512	-0.51512	-0.23424
39	8	24.84739	-1.74739	-0.79457
40	9	31.17611	-1.17611	-0.53480
41	10	35.03203	-2.03203	-0.92400
42	11	37.88396	0.11604	0.05276
43	12	24.61641	1.98359	0.90198
44	13	36.47136	-0.27136	-0.12339
45	14	29.63465	1.96535	0.89368
46	15	29.40368	-0.40368	-0.18356
47	16	36.53944	-2.53944	-1.15474
48	17	28.09320	2.00680	0.91253
49	18	35.62284	-1.72284	-0.78341
50	19	25.17318	3.02682	1.37635
51	20	28.91499	1.08501	0.49338

a) To plot the residuals against $\hat{y}$, follow these steps:

    Step 1 Select cells B31:C51

    Step 2 Select the **Chart Wizard**

    Step 3 When the **Chart Type** dialog box appears:

            Choose **XY (Scatter)** in the Chart type list

            Choose **Scatter** from the Chart sub-type display

            Select **Next >**

    Step 4 When the **Chart Source Data** dialog box appears

            Select **Next >**

    Step 5 When the **Chart Options** dialog box appears:

            Select the **Titles** tab and then

                Enter **Plot of Residuals Against y-hat** in the Chart title box

                Enter **Predicted Salaries** in the **Value (X)** axis box

                Enter **Residuals** in the **Value (Y)** axis box

            Select the **Legend** tab and then

                Remove the check in the **Show Legend** box

            Select **Next >**

Step 6 When the **Chart Location** dialog box appears:
Specify the location for the new chart
Select **Finish** to display the scatter diagram

Residual Plot Against $\hat{y}$

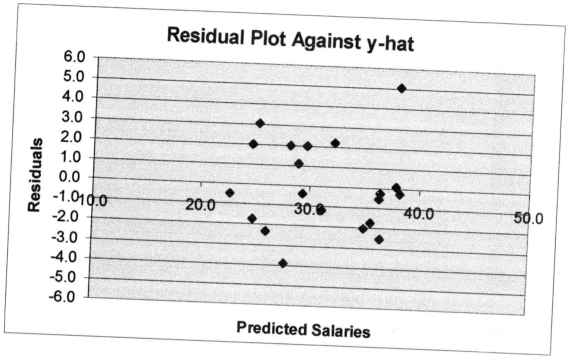

If the assumption that the variance of the error term is the same for all values of $\hat{y}$, the residual plot should give an overall impression of a horizontal band of points. We see in the Residual Plot above that an approximately horizontal band of points is present.

If on the other hand, the absolute value of the residuals is greater for larger values of $\hat{y}$, the assumption of a constant variance of ε is violated. Our conclusion is that the assumed regression model is an adequate representation of the relationship between a programmer's salary and the three independent variables.

b) Now, move the predicted salaries and standardized residuals to adjacent columns and plot these two variables in a scatter diagram.

Standardized Residual Plot Against ŷ

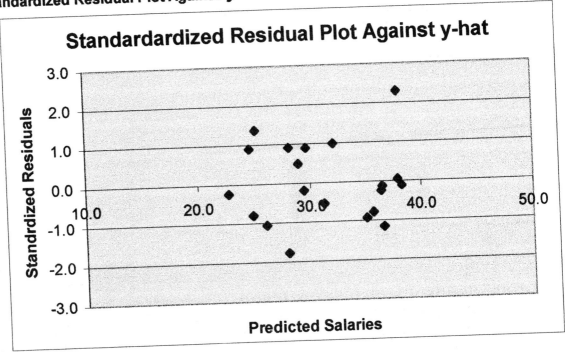

Note that the pattern of the standardized residual plot against $\hat{y}$ is the same as the pattern of the residual plot against $\hat{y}$ shown in part (a). But, the standardized residual plot enables us to check for outliers and determine if the assumption of normality for the regression model is reasonable.

In the plot above there is one standardized residual out of 20 (or 5%) that has a value less than –2 or more than +2. So, it appear that the errors are normally distributed and the model assumptions are satisfied.

EXERCISES

EXERCISE 1

Estimated Multiple Regression Equation

Tony Zamora, a real estate investor, has just moved to Clarksville and wants to learn about the city's residential real estate market. Tony has randomly selected 25 house-for-sale listings from the Sunday newspaper and collected the data listed below.

a) Use square footage, number of bedrooms, and number of bathrooms as three independent variables and selling price as the dependent variable. What is the estimated multiple regression equation?

b) A house in Clarksville is advertised as having 2,600 square feet, four bedrooms, and three bathrooms. Use the results in part (a) to predict the selling price for the house.

Segment of City	Selling Price ($000)	House Size (00 sq. ft.)	Number of Bedrooms	Number of Bathrooms	Garage Size (cars)
Northwest	290	21	4	2	2
South	95	11	2	1	0
Northeast	170	19	3	2	2
Northwest	375	38	5	4	3
West	350	24	4	3	2
South	125	10	2	2	0
West	310	31	4	4	2
West	275	25	3	2	2
Northwest	340	27	5	3	3
Northeast	215	22	4	3	2
Northwest	295	20	4	3	2
South	190	24	4	3	2
Northwest	385	36	5	4	3
West	430	32	5	4	2
South	185	14	3	2	1
South	175	18	4	2	2
Northeast	190	19	4	2	2
Northwest	330	29	4	4	3
West	405	33	5	4	3
Northeast	170	23	4	2	2
West	365	34	5	4	3
Northwest	280	25	4	2	2
South	135	17	3	1	1
Northeast	205	21	4	3	2
West	260	26	4	3	2

EXERCISE 2

Interpretation of Coefficients

Refer again to the Clarksville real estate problem in Exercise 1. Interpret the coefficients b_1, b_2, and b_3 in the estimated multiple regression equation.

a) How much does an additional 200 square feet add to the predicted selling price of a house? Assume this additional space will not be used for a bedroom or bathroom.

b) How much does an additional bedroom add to the predicted selling price of a home? Assume the new bedroom space will come, through remodeling, from existing space in the house.

c) How much does an additional bathroom add to the predicted selling price of a house? Assume the new bathroom space will come, through remodeling, from existing space in the house.

EXERCISE 3

Multiple Coefficient of Determination

Refer again to the Clarksville real estate problem in Exercise 1.

a) Compute the multiple coefficient of determination R^2 using the SSR and SST values provided by Excel's Regression tool. Compare your answer with the R^2 value provided by Excel.

b) Compute the adjusted coefficient of determination R_a^2. Compare your answer with the R_a^2 value provided by Excel.

c) Comment on the goodness of fit. Does the model appear to explain a large amount of variability in the data?

EXERCISE 4

Testing for Significance

Refer again to the Clarksville real estate problem in Exercise 1.

a) Compute the mean square due to regression (MSR) and mean square error (MSE) using the SSR and SSE values provided by Excel.

b) Compute F and perform the appropriate F test. Use $\alpha = .05$.

c) Perform a t test for the significance of β_1. Use $\alpha = .05$.

d) Perform a t test for the significance of β_2. Use $\alpha = .05$.

e) Perform a t test for the significance of β_3. Use $\alpha = .05$.

f) Does there appear to be a correlation among the independent variables?

EXERCISE 5

Qualitative Variables

Refer again to the Clarksville real estate problem in Exercise 1. As an extension of the problem, suppose that Tony Zamora also believes that the selling price of a house in Clarksville is related to the segment of the city in which the house is located.

a) Develop the estimated multiple regression equation to predict the selling price of a house given the square footage, number of bedrooms, number of bathrooms, and segment of the city in which it is located.

b) Estimate the selling price of a house having 1800 square feet, 3 bedrooms, and 1.5 bathrooms and located in the South segment of Clarksville.

EXERCISE 6

Residual Analysis

Refer again to the Clarksville real estate problem in Exercise 5.

a) Plot the residuals against $\hat{y}$. Does the residual plot support the assumptions about the error term ε? Explain.

b) Plot the standardized residuals against $\hat{y}$. Do there appear to be any outliers in these data? Explain.

SELF-TEST

TRUE/FALSE

____ 1. Rejecting the null hypothesis $H_0: \beta_1 = \beta_2 = \ldots = \beta_p = 0$ as the result of a F test enables us to conclude that the overall relationship between y and the set of independent variables is significant.

____ 2. If a qualitative variable has k levels, $k + 1$ dummy variables are required.

____ 3. Multiple regression analysis involves two or more dependent variables.

____ 4. The value of the adjusted multiple coefficient of determination will always be greater than the value of the unadjusted multiple coefficient of determination.

____ 5. If an independent variable is added to the multiple regression model, R^2 becomes larger even if the variable added is not statistically significant.

FILL-IN-THE-BLANK

1. The _____ can be interpreted as the proportion of the variability in the dependent variable that can be explained by the estimated multiple regression eqution.

2. Correlation among the independent variables is known as _____.

3. The standardized residual plot is useful in identifying _____.

4. In every ANOVA table the total sum of squares is the sum of the regression sum of squares and the _____.

5. In multiple regression analysis, b_i represents an estimate of the change in y corresponding to a one-unit change in x_i when _____.

MULTIPLE CHOICE

___ 1. The multiple coefficient of determination is computed as
   a) SSR/SSE
   b) SSE/SSR
   c) SSR/SST
   d) SSE/SST

___ 2. The least squares criterion is
   a) min $\sum(x_i - y_i)^2$

   b) min $\sum(y_i - \bar{y})^2$

   c) min $(\sum y_i - \hat{y}_i)^2$

   d) min $\sum(y_i - \hat{y}_i)^2$

___ 3. In a residual plot that does <u>not</u> suggest we should challenge the assumptions of our regression model, we would expect to see
   a) a horizontal band of points centered near zero
   b) a widening band of points
   c) a band of points having a slope consistent with that of the regression equation
   d) a parabolic band of points

___ 4. The difference between the observed value of the dependent variable and the value predicted by using the estimated regression equation is the
   a) standard error
   b) residual
   c) prediction interval
   d) variance

___ 5. As the goodness of fit for the estimated multiple regression equation increases,
   a) the absolute value of the regression equation's slope increases
   b) the value of the regression equation's y intercept decreases
   c) the value of the coefficient of determination increases
   d) the value of the correlation coefficient increases

ANSWERS

EXERCISES

1)

	Coeffic.	Std. Error	t Stat	P-value
Intercept	-47.3416	44.34672	-1.06753	0.29785
Square Feet	6.020214	2.94446	2.044591	0.053633
Bedrooms	23.03526	20.8229	1.106247	0.281132
Bathrooms	27.02864	18.36005	1.472144	0.155811

a) $\hat{y}$ = -47.34160 + 6.020214x_1 + 23.03526x_2 + 27.02864x_3

b) $282,410.92

2) a) b_1: With each additional 100 square feet, selling price is expected to increase by $6,020.21, when number of bedrooms and bathrooms are held constant. An additional 200 sq. ft. raises the estimated selling price by $12,040.42.

b) b_2: With each additional bedroom, selling price is expected to increase by $23,035.26, when the square footage and number of bathrooms are held constant.

c) b_3: With each additional bathroom, selling price is expected to increase by $27,028.64, when the square footage and number of bedrooms are held constant.

3)

Regression Statistics	
Multiple R	0.89813
R Square	0.806638
Adj. R Square	0.779015
Standard Error	44.94059
Observations	25

ANOVA

	df	SS	MS	F	Signif. F
Regression	3	176931.2	58977.07	29.20153	1.1E-07
Residual	21	42412.79	2019.657		
Total	24	219344			

a) R^2 = SSR/SST = 176,931.2/219,344 = .806638

b) $R_a^2 = 1 - (1 - .806638)\dfrac{25 - 1}{25 - 3 - 1} = .779015$

c) Based on the R^2 value, 80.7% of the variability in house selling prices is explained by the estimated multiple regression equation with square footage, bedrooms, and bathrooms as the independent variables. After adjusting the coefficient of determination for the number of independent variables in the model, the % of variability explained by the model is still high (77.9%). On this basis (without performing residual analysis) we can say that the estimated multiple regression equation fits well.

4) a) $MSR = SSR/p = 176,931.2/3 = 58,977.07$
   $MSE = SSE/(n-p-1) = 42,412.79/(25-3-1) = 2,019.657$

   b) $F = MSR/MSE = 58,977.07/2,019.657 = 29.20153$; $F_\alpha = 3.07$
   Reject $H_0 : \beta_1 = \beta_2 = \beta_3 = 0$

   c) $t = \dfrac{b_1}{s_{b_1}} = 6.020214/2.94446 = 2.045$; $t_{.025} = 2.080$; Do not reject H_0

   β_1 is not statistically significant.

   d) $t = \dfrac{b_2}{s_{b_2}} = 23.03526/20.8229 = 1.106$; $t_{.025} = 2.080$; Do not reject H_0

   β_2 is not statistically significant.

   e) $t = \dfrac{b_3}{s_{b_3}} = 27.02864/18.36005 = 1.472$; $t_{.025} = 2.080$; Do not reject H_0

   β_3 is not statistically significant.

   f) Yes, because the F test indicates a relationship between the dependent variable and the set of independent variables. However, the t tests indicate no relationships between the dependent variable and the individual independent variables.

5) a) $\hat{y} = -2.0035 + .0042x_1 + 35.5549x_2 + 23.6697x_3 + 97.8948x_4 + 110.4917x_5 + 2.7117x_6$

	Coeffic.	Std. Error	t Stat	P-value
Intercept	-2.0035	33.78591	-0.0593	0.953367
Square Feet	0.004212	1.954649	0.002155	0.998304
Bedrooms	35.55493	12.9314	2.749503	0.013186
Bathrooms	23.66965	10.83255	2.18505	0.04235
Northwest	97.89483	17.40063	5.625938	2.45E-05
West	110.4917	18.82655	5.868929	1.48E-05
South	2.7117	17.23321	0.157353	0.876718

   b) $\hat{y} = -2.0035 + .0042(1800) + 35.5549(3) + 23.6697(1.5) + 2.7117(1) = \$150,437.45$

6) a) Residuals appear to grow larger as the selling price increases. Assumption of a constant variance for ε is violated.

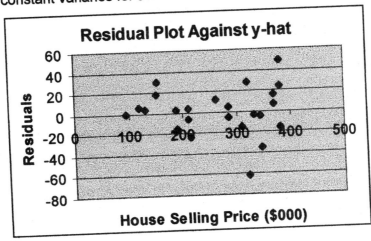

b) Two outliers (10% of residuals) suggest that errors might not be normally distributed.

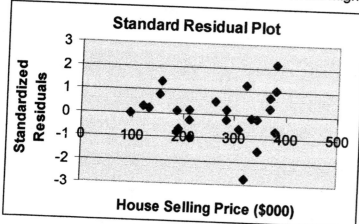

TRUE/FALSE

1) True
2) False
3) False
4) False
5) True

FILL-IN-THE-BLANK

1) multiple coefficient of determination
2) multicollinearity
3) outliers
4) error sum of squares
5) all other independent variables are held constant

MULTIPLE CHOICE

1) c
2) d
3) a
4) b
5) c

CHAPTER 16

Regression Analysis:
Model Building

General Linear Model

Determining When to Add or Delete Variables

Analysis of a Larger Problem

Variable Selection Procedures

Residual Analysis

Multiple Regression Approach to
Analysis of Variance and Experimental Design

LEARNING OBJECTIVES

1. Learn how the general linear model can be used to model problems involving curvilinear relationships.

2. Understand the concept of interaction and how it can be accounted for in the general linear model.

3. Understand how an *F* test can be used to determine when to add or delete one or more variables.

4. Develop an appreciation for the complexities involved in solving larger regression analysis problems.

5. Understand how variable selection procedures can be used to choose a set of independent variables for an estimated regression equation.

6. Know how the Durban-Watson test can be used to test for autocorrelation.

7. Learn how analysis of variance and experimental design problems can be analyzed using a regression model.

REVIEW

Regression Analysis: Model Building

- Model building is the process of developing an estimated regression equation that describes the relationship between a dependent variable and one or more independent variables.
- The major issues in model building are:
  - Finding the proper functional form of the relationship
  - Selecting the independent variables to be included in the model

General Linear Model

- The general linear model involving *p* independent variables is:

$$y = \beta_0 + \beta_1 z_1 + \beta_2 z_2 + \ldots + \beta_p z_p + \varepsilon$$

- In the above equation, each of the independent variables z_j is a function of $x_1, x_2, \ldots, x_k$.
- In some cases, z_j may be a function of only one *x* variable.
- The simplest case is when we have just one independent variable x_1 and want to estimate *y* by using the following straight-line relationship:

$$y = \beta_0 + \beta_1 x + \varepsilon$$

- This model is called a simple first-order model with one predictor variable.

Modeling Curvilinear Relationships

- Even though a linear relationship explains a high percentage of the variability in the dependent variable, the standardized residual plot might suggest a curvilinear relationship is present.
- To account for a <u>curvilinear relationship</u>, we might set $z_1 = x_1$ and $z_2 = x_1^2$ to obtain the model:

$$y = \beta_0 + \beta_1 x_1 + \beta_2 x_1^2 + \varepsilon$$

- This model is called a <u>second-order model with one predictor variable</u>.
- In multiple regression analysis, the word "<u>linear</u>" in the term "general linear model" refers only to the fact that β_0, β_1, . . . , β_p all have <u>exponents of one</u>.
- "Linear" does not imply that the relationship between y and the x_j variables is linear.

Interaction

- <u>Interaction</u> is the effect of <u>two variables acting together</u>.
- When interaction between two variables is present, we cannot study the effect of one variable on the response y independently of the other variable.
- Meaningful conclusions can be developed only if we consider the <u>joint effect</u> that both variables have on the response.
- To account for the effect of interaction, we might use this model:

$$y = \beta_0 + \beta_1 x_1 + \beta_2 x_2 + \beta_3 x_1 x_2 + \varepsilon$$

Transformations Involving the Dependent Variable

- Often, the problem of nonconstant variance can be corrected by transforming the dependent variable to a <u>different scale</u>.
- If we work with the <u>logarithm</u> of the dependent variable, the effect will be to compress its values and diminish the effects of constant variance.
- Two common transformations involve using the <u>base 10</u> (common logarithm) and the <u>base $e = 2.71828$</u>... (natural logarithm).
- Another approach, called a <u>reciprocal transformation</u>, is to use $1/y$ as the dependent variable instead of y.
- There is no way to know whether a logarithmic transformation or a reciprocal transformation will perform best without actually trying each of them.

<u>Nonlinear Models that are Intrinsically Linear</u>

- The <u>exponential model</u> involves the following regression equation:

$$E(y) = \beta_0 \beta_1^x$$

- This model is appropriate when y increases or decreases by a <u>constant percentage</u>, instead of a fixed amount, as x increases.
- We can transform this nonlinear model to a linear model by taking the logarithm of both sides of the above equation.

$$\log E(y) = \log \beta_0 + x \log \beta_1$$

- This leads to the following estimated regression equation:

$$\hat{y}' = b_0' + b_1' x$$

- The <u>antilog</u> of $\hat{y}'$ would be our prediction of y, or the expected value of y.
- Many nonlinear models cannot be transformed into an equivalent linear model.

Determining When to Add or Delete Variables

- An <u>F test</u> can be used to determine whether it is advantageous to add one or more variables to a multiple regression model.
- This test is based on a determination of the amount of reduction in the error sum of squares resulting from adding one or more independent variables to the model.
- The <u>test statistic F</u> is:

$$F = \frac{\dfrac{\text{SSE(reduced) - SSE(full)}}{\text{number of extra terms}}}{\text{MSE(full)}}$$

- This computed F value is compared with the table F value with numerator degrees of freedom equal to the number of extra terms being added and denominator degrees of freedom equal to (n – total number of terms – 1).
- Computing <u>all possible regressions</u> in order to find an estimated regression equation that will do the best job given the data available involves a great amount of computation.

Variable Selection Procedures

- Four variable selection procedures are: <u>stepwise regression</u>, <u>forward selection</u>, <u>backward elimination</u>, and <u>best-subsets regression</u>.
- <u>Stepwise regression</u>, <u>forward selection</u>, and <u>backward elimination</u> are iterative; at each step a single independent variable is added or deleted based on the F statistic and the new model is evaluated.
- There is no guarantee that the best model for a given number of variables will be found using these iterative procedures.

Stepwise Regression

- This procedure begins each step by determining whether any of the variables already in the model should be removed.
  - An F statistic and corresponding p-value is computed for each independent variable in the model.
  - If the p-value for any independent variable is greater than <u>Alpha to remove</u> (a specified α value), the independent variable with the largest p-value is removed and a new step is begun.
- If no independent variable can be removed, the procedure attempts to enter another independent variable into the model.
  - An F statistic and corresponding p-value is computed for each independent variable <u>not</u> in the model.
  - If the p-value for any independent variable is less than <u>Alpha to enter</u> (a second specified α value), the independent variable with the smallest p-value is entered and a new step is begun.

Forward Selection
- This procedure starts with no independent variables in the model.
- It adds variables one at a time using the same procedure as stepwise regression uses.
- This procedure does not permit a variable to be removed from the model.
- This procedure stops when the p-value for each independent variable not in the model is less than the alpha to enter.

Backward Elimination
- This procedure starts with all independent variables entered into the model.
- It deletes variables one at a time using the same procedure as stepwise regression uses.
- This procedure does not permit a variable to be reentered once it has been removed.
- This procedure stops when none of the independent variables in the model have a p-value greater than alpha to remove.

Best-Subsets Regression
- Some statistical software packages have a procedure called best-subsets regression that enables the user to find:
  - Two best one-variable estimated regression equations
  - Two best two-variable estimated regression equations
  - Two best three-variable estimated regression equations, and so on
- The criterion used to determine which equations are the best is usually the coefficient of determination.

Autocorrelation
- Often, the data used in business regression studies are collected over time.
- Often, the value of y at time t is related to the value of y at previous time periods ($t - 1, t - 2$, etc.).
- In these cases, we call this autocorrelation (or serial correlation).
- First-order autocorrelation is present when y_t is related to y_{t-1}.
- Second-order autocorrelation is present when y_t is related to y_{t-2}.
- When autocorrelation is present, a model assumption is violated; the error terms are not independent.
- When autocorrelation is present, serious errors can be made in performing test of statistical significance.

Durbin-Watson Test for Autocorrelation
- Suppose the value of ε are not independent, but are related in this manner:

$$\varepsilon_t = p\varepsilon_{t-1} + z_t$$

where p = a parameter with an absolute value < 1
z_t = a normally distributed random variable
with a mean of 0 and a variance of σ^2

- The Durbin-Watson test for autocorrelation uses the residuals to determine whether $p = 0$.
- The null hypothesis is always that there is no autocorrelation: $H_0: p = 0$

- The <u>alternative hypothesis</u> to test for <u>positive autocorrelation</u>: $H_0: p > 0$
- The <u>alternative hypothesis</u> to test for <u>negative autocorrelation</u>: $H_0: p < 0$
- The <u>alternative hypothesis</u> to test for <u>positive or negative autocorrelation</u>: $H_0: p = 0$

Durbin-Watson test statistic:
- The <u>Durbin-Watson test statistic</u> is computed as follows:

$$d = \frac{\sum_{t=2}^{n}(e_t - e_{t-1})^2}{\sum_{t=1}^{n} e_t^2}$$

- The Durbin-Watson test statistic <u>ranges from zero to four</u>.
- A value of two indicates no autocorrelation is present.
- There are <u>Durbin-Watson tables</u> that show lower and upper bounds (d_l and d_u) for hypothesis tests.
- The appropriate (d_l and d_u) values depend on α (significance level), k (number of independent variables in model), and n (number of observations).
- A <u>minimum sample size of 15</u> is necessary (a minimum of 50 is recommended).

Test for Positive Autocorrelation
- If $d < d_L$, we reject H_0 and conclude that positive autocorrelation is present.
- If $d_L \leq d \leq d_U$, we say the test is inconclusive.
- If $d < d_U$, we conclude that there is no evidence of positive autocorrelation.

Test for Negative Autocorrelation
- If $d > 4 - d_L$, we reject H_0 and conclude that negative autocorrelation is present.
- If $4 - d_U \leq d \leq 4 - d_L$, we say the test is inconclusive.
- If $d < 4 - d_U$, we conclude that there is no evidence of negative autocorrelation.

Two-Sided Test for Autocorrelation
- If $d < d_L$ or $d > 4 - d_L$, we reject H_0 and conclude that autocorrelation is present.
- If $d_L \leq d \leq d_U$ or $4 - d_U \leq d \leq 4 - d_L$, we say the test is inconclusive.
- If $d_U < d < 4 - d_U$, we conclude that there is no evidence of autocorrelation.

Reducing or Removing Autocorrelation
- If significant autocorrelation is identified, one of the following should be tried:
  - We should investigate whether we have omitted one or more key independent variables that have time-ordered effects on the dependent variable.
  - We might include an independent variable that measures the time of the observation (for example: 1, 2, 3, ...).
  - We might transform the dependent or independent variables.

Multiple Regression Approach to ANOVA and Experimental Design

- If the factor being investigated involves k distinct levels or populations, we need to define $k-1$ dummy variables.
- For example, if we have 3 populations: A, B, and C:
  - To relate the expected value of y to a particular population, we use the function:

$$E(y) = \beta_0 + \beta_1 B + \beta_2 C$$

  - For population A: $E(y) = \beta_0$
  - For population B: $E(y) = \beta_0 + \beta_1$
  - For population C: $E(y) = \beta_0 + \beta_2$
- Next, we use Excel's REGRESSION tool to estimate $\beta_0, \beta_1, \ldots \beta_{k-1}$.
- Now, we use the Excel regression output to perform the ANOVA test on the difference in the means for the k populations.
- For example, if we have 3 populations (A, B, and C) and there is no difference in the means of the 3 populations, then:
  - $E(y)$ for B - $E(y)$ for B = 0 $\rightarrow$ $(\beta_0 + \beta_1) - \beta_0 = \beta_1$
  - $E(y)$ for C - $E(y)$ for A = 0 $\rightarrow$ $(\beta_0 + \beta_2) - \beta_0 = \beta_2$
  - We would conclude that there is no difference in the 3 means if) $\beta_1 = 0$ and $\beta_2 = 0$.
  - Hence, the null hypothesis is:

$$H_0: \beta_1 = \beta_2 = 0$$

- If the p-value associated with the F test for overall significance is $< \alpha$, we can reject H_0 and conclude that the means for the 3 populations are different.

KEY CONCEPTS

CONCEPT	EXAMPLES	EXERCISES
Variable Selection Procedures		
Forward Selection	①	1
Backward Selection	②	2
Multiple Regression Approach to ANOVA	③	3
	◯ Excel Used	

EXAMPLES

EXAMPLE 1

Variable Selection Procedures: Forward Selection

Cortland Software, Inc. collected the data shown below for a sample of 20 computer programmers. A suggestion was made that regression analysis could be used to determine if salary was related to years of experience, score on the firm's programmer aptitude test, and whether the programmer has a relevant graduate degree.

Experience	Test Score	Grad. Degree	Salary	Experience	Test Score	Grad. Degree	Salary
4	78	No	24.0	9	88	Yes	38.0
7	100	Yes	43.0	2	73	No	26.6
1	86	No	23.7	10	75	Yes	36.2
5	82	Yes	34.3	5	81	No	31.6
8	86	Yes	35.8	6	74	No	29.0
10	84	Yes	38.0	8	87	Yes	34.0
0	75	No	22.2	4	79	No	30.1
1	80	No	23.1	6	94	Yes	33.9
6	83	No	30.0	3	70	No	28.2
6	91	Y	33.0	3	89	No	30.0

Develop, using the forward selection procedure, a multiple regression model to predict the salary of a programmer. (Use *Alpha to enter* = .05)

SOLUTION 1

Using Excel's REGRESSION Tool

The estimated multiple regression equation will be of the following form:
$$\hat{y} = b_0 + b_1x_1 + b_2x_2 + b_3x_3$$

where: $\hat{y}$ = estimated annual salary ($000)

x_1 = years of programming experience

x_2 = score on programmer aptitude test

x_3 = 0 if individual <u>does not</u> have a graduate degree

       1 if individual <u>does</u> have a graduate degree

To develop the estimated multiple regression equation, we will use Excel's Regression tool. (The calculations involve matrix algebra and are beyond the scope of the textbook.)

Forward Selection Procedure

- This procedure starts with no independent variables in the model.
- It adds variables to the model one at a time.
- The independent variable with the smallest p-value is entered into the model (provided its p-value is less than *Alpha to enter*.
- This procedure does not permit a variable to be removed from the model.
- This procedure stops when the p-value for each independent variable not in the model is less than the *Alpha to enter*.

Iteration 1

p-value for EXPERIENCE = **1.54E-06**
p-value for TEST SCORE = 0.006316
p-value for GRAD DEGREE = 6.76E-0
EXPERIENCE has the smallest p-value < *Alpha to enter*, so put EXPERIENCE in model

Iteration 2

p-value for TEST SCORE = **0.004780**
p-value for GRAD DEGREE = 0.026371
TEST SCORE has the smallest p-value < *Alpha to enter*, so put TEST SCORE in model

Iteration 3

p-value for GRAD DEGREE = 0.267885
GRAD DEGREE's p-value > *alpha to enter*, so do <u>not</u> put GRAD DEGREE in model

Summary

Estimated multiple regression equation is:

Expected SALARY = 3.173936 + 1.403902(EXPERIENCE) + 0.250885(TEST SCORE)

Adjusted R^2 = .814671

EXAMPLE 2

Variable Selection Procedures: Backward Elimination

Tony Zamora, a real estate investor, has just moved to Clarksville and wants to learn about the city's residential real estate market. Tony has randomly selected 25 house-for-sale listings from the Sunday newspaper and collected the data listed below.

Develop, using the backward elimination procedure, a multiple regression model to predict the selling price of a house in Clarksville. (Use *Alpha to remove* = .05)

House Size (00 sq. ft.)	Number of Bedrooms	Number of Bathrooms	Garage Size (cars)	Selling Price ($000)
21	4	2	2	290
11	2	1	0	95
19	3	2	2	170
38	5	4	3	375
24	4	3	2	350
10	2	2	0	125
31	4	4	2	310
25	3	2	2	275
27	5	3	3	340
22	4	3	2	215
20	4	3	2	295
24	4	3	2	190
36	5	4	3	385
32	5	4	2	430
14	3	2	1	185
18	4	2	2	175
19	4	2	2	190
29	4	4	3	330
33	5	4	3	405
23	4	2	2	170
34	5	4	3	365
25	4	2	2	280
17	3	1	1	135
21	4	3	2	205
26	4	3	2	260

SOLUTION 2

Using Excel's REGRESSION Tool

The estimated multiple regression equation will be of the following form:

$$\hat{y} = b_0 + b_1x_1 + b_2x_2 + b_3x_3 + b_4x_4$$

where: $\hat{y}$ = estimated selling price of house ($1000s)

x_1 = house size (100s square feet)

x_2 = number of bedrooms

x_3 = number of bathrooms

x_4 = garage size (number of cars)

Backward Elimination Procedure

- This procedure begins with a model that includes all the independent variables.
- It then deletes one independent variable from the model at a time.
- The independent variable with the greatest p-value is removed from the model (provided its p-value is greater than *Alpha to remove*.
- This procedure does not permit a variable to be reentered once it has been removed.
- This procedure stops when none of the independent variables in the model have a p-value greater than *Alpha to remove*.

Iteration 1

p-value for HOUSE SIZE   = .058833
p-value for BEDROOMS   = .208122
p-value for BATHROOMS   = .175744
p-value for GARAGE SIZE   = .696804
GARAGE SIZE has the greatest p-value > *Alpha to remove*, so remove GARAGE from model

Iteration 2

p-value for HOUSE SIZE   = .053633
p-value for BEDROOMS   = .281132
p-value for BATHROOMS   = .155811
BEDROOMS has the greatest p-value > *Alpha to remove*, so remove BEDROOMS from model

Iteration 3

p-value for HOUSE SIZE   = .003039
p-value for BATHROOMS   = .109738
BATHROOMS has the greatest p-value > *alpha to remove*, so remove BATHROOMS from model

Summary

Estimated multiple regression equation is:

Expected SELLING PRICE = - 9.86687 + 11.33835(HOUSE SIZE)

Adjusted R^2 = .7595

EXAMPLE 3

Multiple Regression Approach to ANOVA

John Norr, Director of Athletics at Lakewood High School, is curious about whether a student's total number of absences in four years of high school is the same for students participating in no varsity sport, one varsity sport, and two varsity sports.

Number of absences data were available for 20 recent graduates and are listed below. Test for difference of means of the three populations using the multiple regression approach to ANOVA.. Use α = .10.

No Sport	1 Sport	2 Sports
13	18	12
16	12	22
6	19	9
27	7	11
20	15	15
14	20	21
	17	10

SOLUTION 3

Using Excel's REGRESSION Tool

First, the factor being investigated involves $k = 3$ distinct levels or populations, so we need to define $k - 1 = 3 - 1 = 2$ dummy variables. That is, $x_1 = 0$ and $x_2 = 0$ for No Sport; $x_1 = 1$ and $x_2 = 0$ for 1 Sport; and $x_1 = 0$ and $x_2 = 1$ for 2 Sports.

Next, we use Excel's REGRESSION tool to estimate b_1 and b_2.

	Coefficients
Intercept	16
One Sport	-0.57143
Two Sports	-1.71429

Segment of City	Estimate of E(Selling Price)
No Sport	$b_0 = 16$
One Sport	$b_0 + b_1 = 16 + (-0.57143) = 15.42857$
Two Sports	$b_0 + b_2 = 16 + (-1.71429) = 14.28571$

Then, we use the Excel regression output to perform the ANOVA test on the difference in the means for the k populations. The null hypothesis is:

H_0: The population means are equal ($\beta_1 = \beta_2 = 0$)
H_a: The population means are different

If the p-value associated with the F test for overall significance is $< \alpha$, we can reject H_0 and conclude that the means for the 3 populations are different.

ANOVA

	df	SS	MS	F	Significance F
Regression	2	10.05714	5.028571	0.157391	0.855601
Residual	17	543.1429	31.94958		
Total	19	553.2			

p-value → (points to 0.855601)

We cannot reject H_0 because the p-value is MUCH greater than $\alpha = .05$. There is insufficient evidence to conclude that the population means are not equal.

Residual Plot against $\hat{y}$

- A residual plot against the predicted values $\hat{y}$ represents the predicted value of the dependent variable $\hat{y}$ on the horizontal axis and the residual values on the vertical axis.
- The plotted points should give an overall impression of a <u>horizontal band of points</u> if:
  - The assumption that the variance of ε is the same for all values of the x variables.
  - The assumed regression model is an adequate representation of the relationship between the variables.

Standardized Residual Plot against $\hat{y}$

- A standardized residual plot against $\hat{y}$ can be used to:
  - Identify outliers (any standardized residual less than –2 or more than +2).
  - Provide that the error term ε has a normal distribution (only 5% of standardized residuals should be less than –2 or more than +2).

Using Excel's Scatter Diagram Tool to Construct a Standardized Residual Plot

- The steps to obtain the regression output are performed with one additional selection.
- When the Regression dialog box appears, we must select the <u>Standardized Residuals</u> option.
- The output will contain a list of:
  - (1) Predicted values of y
  - (2) Residuals
  - (3) Standardized residuals
- Then, move the data and the standardized residuals to adjacent columns and plot these two variables (1) and (3) in a scatter diagram.

KEY CONCEPTS

CONCEPT	EXAMPLES	EXERCISES
Estimated Multiple Regression Equation	①	1
Interpretation of Coefficients	2	2
Coefficient of Determination	③	3
F Test for Overall Significance	④	4
t Test for Individual Significance	④	4
Qualitative Variables	⑤	5
Residual Analysis	⑥	6

◯ Excel Used

EXAMPLES

EXAMPLE 1

Estimated Multiple Regression Equation

Cortland Software, Inc. collected data for a sample of 20 computer programmers. A suggestion was made that regression analysis could be used to determine if salary was related to the years of experience and the score on the firm's programmer aptitude test. The years of experience, score on the aptitude test, and corresponding annual salary ($1000s) for a sample of 20 programmers are shown below.

Experience	Test Score	Salary	Experience	Test Score	Salary
4	78	24.0	9	88	38.0
7	100	43.0	2	73	26.6
1	86	23.7	10	75	36.2
5	82	34.3	5	81	31.6
8	86	35.8	6	74	29.0
10	84	38.0	8	87	34.0
0	75	22.2	4	79	30.1
1	80	23.1	6	94	33.9
6	83	30.0	3	70	28.2
6	91	33.0	3	89	30.0

Suppose we believe that salary (y) is related to the years of experience (x_1) and the score on the programmer aptitude test (x_2) by the following regression model:

$$y = b_0 + b_1x_1 + b_2x_2 + e$$

where:

y = annual salary ($000) for a programmer
x_1 = years of programming experience
x_2 = score on programmer aptitude test

Use years of experience and test score as two independent variables and salary as the dependent variable.

a) What is the estimated multiple regression equation?

b) Estimate the salary for a programmer with 4.5 years of experience and a score of 82 on the aptitude test.

SOLUTION 1

Using Excel's *Regression* Tool for Multiple Regression

To develop the estimated multiple regression equation, we will use Excel's Regression tool. (The calculations involve matrix algebra and are beyond the scope of the textbook.)

a) The values for b_0, b_1, and b_2 in the estimated multiple regression equation are found in cells B40:B42 of the Excel output shown above.

$$\hat{y} = 3.174 + 1.404x_1 + 0.2509x_2$$

In other words, Estimated Salary = 3.174 + 1.404(Exper) + 0.2509(Score). Note that estimated salary will be in thousands of dollars.

b) The estimated salary $\hat{y}$ for a programmer with 4.5 years of experience and a test score of 82 is:

$$\hat{y} = 3.174 + 1.404(4.5) + 0.2509(82) = 30.0658 \text{ or } \$30,065.80$$

EXAMPLE 2

Interpretation of Coefficients

In Example 1, the following estimated multiple regression equation was presented.

$$\hat{y} = 3.174 + 1.404x_1 + 0.2509x_2$$

where: $\hat{y}$ = estimated annual salary ($000) for a programmer
x_1 = years of programming experience
x_2 = score on programmer aptitude test

Interpret the coefficients b_1 and b_2 in this estimated multiple regression equation.

SOLUTION 2

Interpretation of coefficients:

b_1: With each additional year of experience, salary is expected to increase by $1,404.00, when the aptitude test score is held constant.

b_2: With each additional point scored on the aptitude test, salary is expected to increase by $250.90, when the years of experience is held constant.

EXAMPLE 3

Multiple Coefficient of Determination

In Example 1, the following estimated multiple regression equation was presented.

$$\hat{y} = 3.174 + 1.404x_1 + 0.2509x_2$$

where: $\hat{y}$ = estimated annual salary ($000) for a programmer
x_1 = years of programming experience
x_2 = score on programmer aptitude test

Enter Data: The appropriate labels are entered into cells A1:D1 of the worksheet. To identify each of the 20 observations, we enter the number 1 through 20 into cells A2:A21. The sample data are entered into cells B2:D21.

Data Worksheet:

	A	B	C	D	E	F
1	Program-mer	Exper-ience	Test Score	Salary ($K)		
2	1	4	78	24.0		
3	2	7	100	43.0		
4	3	1	86	23.7		
5	4	5	82	34.3		
6	5	8	86	35.8		
7	6	10	84	38.0		
8	7	0	75	22.2		
9	8	1	80	23.1		

Note: Rows 10-21 are not shown.

Enter Functions and Formulas: There are none to enter.

Apply Tools: The following steps describe how to use the Regression tool for multiple regression analysis:

Performing the Multiple Regression Analysis

    Step 1 Select the **Tools** pull-down menu
    Step 2 Choose the **Data Analysis** option
    Step 3 Choose **Regression** from the list of Analysis Tools
    Step 4 When the Regression dialog box appears:
            Enter D1:D21 in the **Input Y Range** box
            Enter B1:C21 in the **Input X Range** box
            Select **Labels**
            Select **Confidence Level**
            Enter 95 (for now) in the **Confidence Level** box
            Select **Output Range** and enter A24 in the **Output Range** box
            Select **OK**

Regression Equation Output:

	A	B	C	D	E	F	G	H	I
38									
39		Coeffic.	Std. Err.	t Stat	P-value	Lo. 95%	Up. 95%	Lo. 95.0%	Up. 95.0
40	Intercept	3.17394	6.15607	0.5156	0.61279	-9.81425	16.1621	-9.814248	16.162
41	Experience	1.4039	0.19857	7.0702	1.9E-06	0.98496	1.82284	0.9849623	1.82284
42	Test Score	0.25089	0.07735	3.2433	0.00478	0.08768	0.41409	0.0876823	0.41408
43									

EXERCISE 1

Variable Selection Procedures: Forward Selection

The Professional Golfers Association keeps a variety of statistics regarding performance measures. Data include the average driving distance, percentage of drives that land in the fairway, percentage of greens hit in regulation, average number of putts, percentage of sand saves, and average score. Data from a sample of 25 golfers are shown below. (The variable names and definitions are shown below the data.)

Develop, using the forward selection procedure, a multiple regression model to predict the score of a golfer. (Use *Alpha to enter* = .05)

Drive	Fair	Green	Putt	Sand	Score
277.6	.681	.667	1.768	.550	69.10
259.6	.691	.665	1.810	.536	71.09
269.1	.657	.649	1.747	.472	70.12
267.0	.689	.673	1.763	.672	69.88
267.3	.581	.637	1.781	.521	70.71
255.6	.778	.674	1.791	.455	69.76
272.9	.615	.667	1.780	.476	70.19
265.4	.718	.699	1.790	.551	69.73
272.6	.660	.672	1.803	.431	69.97
263.9	.668	.669	1.774	.493	70.33
267.0	.686	.687	1.809	.492	70.32
266.0	.681	.670	1.765	.599	70.09
258.1	.695	.641	1.784	.500	70.46
255.6	.792	.672	1.752	.603	69.49
261.3	.740	.702	1.813	.529	69.88
262.2	.721	.662	1.754	.576	70.27
260.5	.703	.623	1.782	.567	70.72
271.3	.671	.666	1.783	.492	70.30
263.3	.714	.687	1.796	.468	69.91
276.6	.634	.643	1.776	.541	70.69
252.1	.726	.639	1.788	.493	70.59
263.0	.687	.675	1.786	.486	70.20
263.0	.639	.647	1.760	.374	70.81
253.5	.732	.693	1.797	.518	70.26
266.2	.681	.657	1.812	.472	70.96

Variable Names and Definitions

Drive: average length of a drive in yards
Fair: percentage of drives that land in the fairway
Green: percentage of greens hit in regulation
(a par-3 green is "hit in regulation" if the player's first shot lands on the green)
Putt: average number of putts for greens that have been hit in regulation
Sand: percentage of sand saves (landing in a sand trap and still scoring par or better)
Score: average score for an 18-hole round
Sample Data

EXERCISE 2

Variable Selection Procedures: Backward Elimination

Refer again to the Professional Golfers Association data in Exercise 1. Develop, using the backward elimination procedure, a multiple regression model to predict the score of a golfer. (Use *Alpha to remove* = .05)

EXERCISE 3

Multiple Regression Approach to ANOVA

Refer again to the Clarksville real estate data in Exercise 2. Tony Zamora wants to use the selling prices of the 25 houses he sampled to determine whether the mean selling prices are the same in each segment of the city. The 25 selling prices, sorted by segment of the city, are listed below.

Northeast	Northwest	West	South
170	290	350	95
215	375	310	125
190	340	275	190
170	295	430	185
205	385	405	175
	330	365	135
	280	260	

Use the multiple regression approach to analysis of variance to test for difference of means, with .05 level of significance. (HINT: Introduce 3 dummy variables x_5, x_6, and x_7 in order to code city segments. That is, x_5, x_6, and x_7 = 0,0,0 for Northeast; x_5, x_6, and x_7 = 1,0,0 for Northwest; x_5, x_6, and x_7 = 0,1,0 for West; and x_5, x_6, and x_7 = 0,0,1 for South.)

TRUE/FALSE

_____ 1. There is no guarantee that the best regression model for a given number of variables will be found using the iterative procedures presented in the textbook.

_____ 2. No more than one variable at a time should ever be dropped from a regression model on the basis of an F test.

_____ 3. Best-subsets regression is an iterative procedure that adds or deletes one variable at a time.

_____ 4. Reciprocal transformation involves transforming both the dependent variable and at least one independent variable.

_____ 5. Serial correlation is another name for autocorrelation.

FILL-IN-THE-BLANK

1. $\beta_0, \beta_1, \ldots, \beta_p$ all have exponents of one in a _____ model.

2. The Durbin-Watson test statistic ranges in value from zero to _____.

3. When _____ between two x variables is present, we cannot study the effect of one variable on the response y independently of the other variable.

4. At Step 1 of the backward elimination procedure, we first check to see whether the p-value for any independent variable is greater than _____.

5. A(n) _____ model is appropriate when y increases or decreases by a constant percentage, instead of a fixed amount, as x increases.

MULTIPLE CHOICE

_____ 1. Looking up the appropriate critical values for the Durbin-Watson test for autocorrelation requires knowing
   a) n, p
   b) α, z
   c) α, n, k
   d) α, χ^2

_____ 2. The Durbin-Watson test determines whether
   a) first-order autocorrelation is present
   b) first- or second-order autocorrelation is present
   c) interaction is present
   d) a curvilinear relationship exists

____ 3. We expect a positive residual in one period to be followed by a negative residual in the next period when
  a) positive autocorrelation is present
  b) negative autocorrelation is present
  c) a curvilinear relationship exists
  d) the error terms are independent

____ 4. The multiple regression approach to an ANOVA test on the difference in means for 3 populations would require how many dummy variables?
  a) 2
  b) 3
  c) 4
  d) 6

____ 5. The variable selection procedure that begins with all the available independent variables entered into the model is
  a) forward selection
  b) stepwise regression
  c) best-subsets regression
  d) backward selection

ANSWERS

EXERCISES

1) Iteration 1
  p-value for DRIVE   = .463777
  p-value for FAIR   = .033447
  p-value for GREEN   = **.003900**
  p-value for PUTT   = .212328
  p-value for SAND   = .179165
  GREEN has the smallest p-value < *Alpha to enter*, so enter GREEN into model
  Iteration 2
  p-value for DRIVE   = .312503
  p-value for FAIR   = .228931
  p-value for PUTT   = **.002643**
  p-value for SAND   = .185713
  PUTT has the smallest p-value < *Alpha to enter*, so enter PUTT into model
  Iteration 3
  p-value for DRIVE   = .432582
  p-value for FAIR   = .205456
  p-value for SAND   = .653614
  All p-values > *Alpha to enter*, so do not enter any more variables into model

Summary

Estimated multiple regression equation is:
Expected SCORE = 59.0665 - 17.2978(GREEN) + 12.7218(PUTT)
Adjusted R^2 = .3053

2) Iteration 1

p-value for DRIVE	= .004991
p-value for FAIR	= .003444
p-value for GREEN	= .010323
p-value for PUTT	= .007179
p-value for SAND	= **.696113**

SAND has the greatest p-value > *Alpha to remove*, so remove SAND from model

Iteration 2

p-value for DRIVE	= 9.37E-10
p-value for FAIR	= .004265
p-value for PUTT	= .002545
p-value for SAND	= .008766

There is no p-value > *Alpha to remove*, so the procedure comes to an end.

Summary

Estimated multiple regression equation is:
Expected Score = 74.678 − 0.0398(Drive) − 6.6858(Fair) − 10.3423(Green)
+9.8576(Putt)
Adjusted R^2 = .6685

3) H_0: The population means are equal ($\beta_1 = \beta_2 = 0$)
H_a: The population means are different

Segment of City	Estimate of E(Selling Price)
Northeast	$b_0 = 190$
Northwest	$b_0 + b_1 = 190 + 137.8571 = 327.8571$
West	$b_0 + b_2 = 190 + 152.1429 = 342.1429$
South	$b_0 + b_3 = 190 - 39.1667 = 150.8333$

ANOVA

	df	SS	MS	F	Significance F
Regression	3	175387.5	58462.48	27.93013	1.6E-07
Residual	21	43956.55	2093.169		
Total	24	219344			

p-value

We can reject H_0 because the p-value is MUCH less than $\alpha = .05$. There is sufficient evidence to conclude that the population means are not equal.

TRUE/FALSE

1) True
2) False
3) False
4) False
5) True

FILL-IN-THE-BLANK

1) first-order (or linear)
2) four
3) interaction
4) alpha to remove
5) exponential

MULTIPLE CHOICE

1) c
2) a
3) b
4) a
5) d

CHAPTER 17

Nonparametric Methods

Sign Test

Wilcoxin Signed-Rank Test

Mann-Whitney-Wilcoxin Test

Kruskal-Wallis Test

Rank Correlation

LEARNING OBJECTIVES

1. Learn the difference between parametric and nonparametric methods.

2. Know the particular advantages of nonparametric methods and when they are and when they are not applicable.

3. Learn how to use the sign test for the analysis of paired comparisons.

4. Be able to use the sign test to conduct hypothesis tests about a median.

5. Be able to use the Wilcoxon signed-rank test and the Mann-Whitney-Wilcoxon test to determine whether or not two populations have the same distribution.

6. Be able to use the Kruskal-Wallis tests for the comparison of k populations.

7. Be able to compute the Spearman rank correlation coefficient and test for a significant correlation between two sets of rankings.

8. Be able to use an Excel worksheet for nonparametric procedures.

REVIEW

Four scales of measurement
- Nominal scale:
  - Data are labels or categories used to define an attribute of an element.
  - Data may be numeric or nonnumeric.
  - Means, variances, standard deviations, and so on are inappropriate.
  - Nonnumeric Example: Baseball player's team: Braves, Mets, Cubs, ...
  - Numeric Example: Baseball player's number on his uniform
- Ordinal scale:
  - Data can be used to rank or order the observations.
  - Data may be numeric or nonnumeric.
  - Means, variances, standard deviations, and so on are inappropriate.
  - Nonnumeric Example: Clothing size: small, medium, large, ...
  - Numeric Example: Students' class rank of 1, 2, 3, ...
- Interval scale:
  - Data have the properties of ordinal data and the interval between observations is expressed in terms of a fixed unit of measure.
  - Data must be numeric.
  - Means, variances, standard deviations, and so on can be computed and analyzed.
  - Numeric Example: Measures of temperature: 88° F, 12° C, ...
- Ratio Scale:
  - Data have the properties of interval and the ratio of measures is meaningful.
  - There is an inherently defined zero point.
  - Data must be numeric.
  - Means, variances, standard deviations, and so on can be computed and analyzed.
  - Numeric Example: Measures of height, weight, distance, time, ...

Nonparametric Methods

- Nonparametric methods usually require:
  - <u>Less restrictive</u> assumptions about the level of data measurement,
  - <u>Fewer assumptions</u> about the form of the probability distributions for the populations being sampled.
- Nonparametric methods are often called <u>distribution-free methods</u>.
- For a statistical method to be classified as nonparametric, it must satisfy at least one of the following conditions:
  - The method can be used with nominal data.
  - The method can be used with ordinal data.
  - The method can be used with interval or ratio data when no assumption can be made about the population probability distribution.
- In cases where a parametric or nonparametric method can be used, the nonparametric method is almost as good or almost as powerful as the parametric method.
- Nonparametric methods include: the <u>sign test</u>, the <u>Wilcoxon signed-rank test</u>, the <u>Mann-Whitney-Wilcoxon test</u>, the <u>Kruskal-Wallis test</u>, and the <u>Spearman rank correlation</u>.

Sign Test

- A common application of the <u>sign test</u> involves using a sample of n potential customers to <u>identify a preference</u> for one of two brands of a product.
- The objective is to determine whether there is a difference in preference between the two items being compared.
- To record the preference data, we use a <u>plus sign</u> if the individual prefers one brand and a <u>minus sign</u> if the individual prefers the other brand.
- Because the data are recorded as plus and minus signs, this test is called the sign test.
- Letting p indicate the proportion of the population preferring one brand over another, the hypotheses are:

$$H_0 : p = .5$$
$$H_0 : p \neq .5$$

- Under the assumption that H_0 is true, the number of plus signs follows a <u>binomial probability distribution</u> with $p = .5$.
- The small sample case, using a binomial distribution, should be used whenever $n \leq 20$.
- Even when the sample size is greater than 20, a binomial approach is recommended if possible (i.e., a spreadsheet is available).

Large-Sample Case

- The normal approximation provides good results for <u>sample sizes > 20</u>.
  - <u>Mean</u>: $\mu = .50n$
  - <u>Standard deviation</u>: $\sigma = \sqrt{.25n}$
  - <u>Test statistic</u>: $z = (x - \mu)/\sigma$
  - <u>Rejection rule</u>:   Reject H_0 if $z < -z_{\alpha/2}$ or $z > z_{\alpha/2}$

Hypothesis Test About a Median
- In applying the sign test we:
  - Use a plus sign whenever the data in the sample are above the hypothesized value of the median.
  - Use a minus sign whenever the data in the sample are below the hypothesized value of the median.
  - Discard any data exactly equal to the hypothesized median.

Wilcoxon Signed-Rank Test
- This test is the nonparametric alternative to the parametric matched-sample test presented in an earlier chapter.
- The methodology of the parametric matched-sample analysis requires interval data, and the assumption that the population of differences between the pairs of observations is normally distributed.
- If the assumption of normally distributed differences is not appropriate, the Wilcoxon signed-rank test can be used.
- The <u>hypotheses</u> are: H_0: The populations are identical
  H_a: The populations are not identical

Preliminary Steps of the Test
- Compute the differences between the paired observations.
- Discard any differences of zero.
- Rank the absolute value of the differences from lowest to highest. Tied differences are assigned the average ranking of their positions.
- Give the ranks the sign of the original difference in the data.
- Sum the signed ranks. The sum is denoted T.

Test For Significance
- The test for significance involves determining whether T is significantly different from zero.
- The <u>sampling distribution of T</u> for identical populations:
  - Mean: $\mu_T = 0$
  - <u>Standard deviation</u>: $\sigma_T = \sqrt{\dfrac{n(n+1)(2n+1)}{6}}$
  - <u>Test statistic</u>: $z = (T - \mu_T)/\sigma_T$
- <u>Rejection rule</u>: Reject H_0 if $z < -z_{\alpha/2}$ or $z > z_{\alpha/2}$

Mann-Whitney-Wilcoxon Test
- This test is another nonparametric method for determining whether there is a difference between two populations.
- This test, unlike the Wilcoxon signed-rank test, is <u>not</u> based on a matched sample.
- This test does <u>not</u> require interval data or the assumption that both populations are normally distributed.
- The only requirement is that the measurement scale for the <u>data is at least ordinal</u>.
- Instead of testing for the difference between the means of two populations, this method tests to <u>determine whether the two populations are identical</u>.

- The small-sample case should be used whenever the sample sizes for <u>both populations are less than or equal to 10</u>.
- The <u>hypotheses</u> are:
  - H_0: The two populations are identical
  - H_a: The two populations are not identical

Preliminary Steps of the Test

- First, rank the <u>combined</u> data from the lowest to the highest values.
- Assign tied values the average of the tied rankings.
- Compute T, the sum of the ranks for the first sample.

Test of Significance: Small-Sample Case

- Look up the value of T_L in the <u>T_L Values for the MWW Test</u> table.
- Compute the value of T_U using: $T_U = n_1(n_1 + n_2 + 1) - T_L$
- Reject H_0 if $T < T_L$ or if $T > T_U$

Test of Significance: Large-Sample Case

- <u>Sampling distribution of T</u> for identical populations:

  - <u>Mean</u>: $\mu_T = \frac{1}{2} n_1(n_1 + n_2 + 1)$

  - <u>Standard Deviation</u>: $\sigma_T = \sqrt{\frac{1}{12} n_1 n_2 (n_1 + n_2 + 1)}$

  - <u>Test Statistic</u>: $z = \dfrac{T - \mu_T}{\sigma_T}$

  - <u>Rejection rule</u>: Reject H_0 if $z < -z_{\alpha/2}$ or $z > z_{\alpha/2}$

Kruskal-Wallis Test

- The Mann-Whitney-Wilcoxon test can be used to test whether two populations are identical.
- The MWW test has been extended by Kruskal and Wallis for cases of <u>3+ populations</u>.
- The Kruskal-Wallis test can be used with ordinal data as well as with interval or ratio data.
- Also, the Kruskal-Wallis test does not require the assumption of normally distributed populations.
- The <u>hypotheses</u> are: H_0: All populations are identical
   H_a: Not all populations are identical

Test of Significance

- First, rank the <u>combined</u> data from the lowest to the highest values.
- Assign tied values the average of the tied rankings.
- <u>Kruskal-Wallis test statistic</u>: $W = \left[\dfrac{12}{n_T(n_T + 1)} \sum_{i=1}^{k} \dfrac{R_i^2}{n_i} \right] - 3(n_T + 1)$
- Under the null hypothesis, the sampling distribution of W can be approximated by a <u>chi-square distribution</u> with $k - 1$ degrees of freedom.
- Reject H_0 if $W > \chi_\alpha^2$

Rank Correlation

- The Pearson correlation coefficient, r, is a measure of the linear association between two variables for which interval or ratio data are available.
- The <u>Spearman rank-correlation coefficient</u>, r_S, is a measure of association between two variables when only <u>ordinal data</u> are available.
- Values of r_S can range from -1.0 to $+1.0$, where
  - Values near 1.0 indicate a <u>strong positive association</u> between the rankings.
  - Values near -1.0 indicate a <u>strong negative association</u> between the rankings.
- Hypotheses being tested are: H_0: $p_s = 0$ (No rank correlation exists.)
$$H_a\text{: } p_s \neq 0 \quad \text{(Rank correlation exists.)}$$

Test of Significance

- Compute the differences between the paired sample 1 and sample 2 ratings.
- Square the differences.
- Sum the square differences.

- Compute the <u>Spearman rank-correlation coefficient</u>: $r_s = 1 - \dfrac{6\sum d_i^2}{n(n^2 - 1)}$

- Compute the test statistic:

  - <u>Mean</u> of r_s: $\mu_{r_s} = 0$

  - <u>Standard Deviation</u> of r_s: $\sigma_{r_s} = \sqrt{\dfrac{1}{n-1}}$

  - <u>Test Statistic</u>: $z = \dfrac{r_s - \mu_{r_s}}{\sigma_{r_s}}$

- <u>Rejection Rule</u>:
      Using test statistic: Reject H_0 if $z < -z_{\alpha/2}$ or $z > z_{\alpha/2}$

KEY CONCEPTS

CONCEPT	EXAMPLES	EXERCISES
Sign Test		
Large-Sample Case	①	1
Hypothesis Test About a Median	②	2
Wilcoxon Signed-Rank Test	③	3
Mann-Whitney-Wilcoxon Test		
Large-Sample Case	④	4
Kruskal-Wallis Test	5	5
Rank Correlation	⑥	6

○ Excel Used

EXAMPLES

EXAMPLE 1

Sign Test: Large-Sample Case

As part of a market research study, a sample of 36 consumers were asked to taste two brands of peanut butter and indicate a preference. Do the data shown below indicate a significant difference in the consumer preferences for the two brands? Use $\alpha = .05$.

> 19 preferred Hoppy Peanut Butter
> 11 preferred Pokey Peanut Butter
> 6 had no preference

SOLUTION 1

Using Excel's BINOMDIST Function

Hypotheses:
H_0: $p = .50$ (No preference for one brand over the other exists)
H_a: $p \neq .5$ (A preference for one brand over the other exists)

The analysis is based on a sample size of $19 + 11 = 30$. (The 6 no-preferences are not counted.) Arbitrarily assigning a "+" sign to Hoppy, we have 19 "+" signs and 11 " –" signs.

Rejection Rule:
Using normal approximation: Reject H_0 if $z < -1.96$ or $z > 1.96$
Using binomial distribution: Reject H_0 if the number of plus signs
is less than 10 or greater than 19
Using p-value: Reject H_0 if p-value $< .05$

Conclusion:
Using normal approximation: $\mu = .50n = .50(30) = 15$
$\sigma = \sqrt{.25n}$
$$z = \frac{x - \mu}{\sigma} = \frac{18 - 15}{2.74} = 1.095$$
Do not reject H_0. z is not > 1.96

Using binomial distribution: Do not reject H_0. Number of "+" signs
Is not greater than 20.

Using p-value: p-value $= 2(1 - P(x \leq 18)$
$= 2(1 - .899756)$
$= 2(.100244) = .200488$
Do not reject H_0 because p-value $> \alpha$

Now we will use Excel to conduct our large-sample sign test.

Enter Data: The brand preference data are entered in column A.

Enter Functions and Formulas: The descriptive statistics we need are computed in cells C2:C4. The COUNTA function is used in cell C2 to count the number of persons in the sample. Hoppy is entered into cell C3 to identify the response of interest (the one considered a +) and the COUNTIF function is used in cell C4 to count the number of people stating a preference for the response of interest. All that remains is to compute the *p*-value.

The p-value (lower tail) is computed in cell C6. Recall that the form of Excel's BINOMDIST function is BINOMDIST(x, *n*, *p*, cumulative). So we enter in cell C6 the formula BINOMDIST(C4, C2, 0.5, TRUE) to compute the cumulative probability of the number of successes shown in cell C4.

To compute the *p*-value (upper tail) we enter the formula =1-BINOMDIST(C4-1,C2, 0.5, TRUE) in cell C7. The p-value (two tail) is computed in cell C8 as twice the minimum of the two one-tail *p*-values.

Formula Worksheet:

	A	B	C
1	Brand Preference		
2	Hoppy	Sample Size	=COUNTA(A2:A31)
3	Hoppy	Response of Interest	Hoppy
4	Hoppy	Count of Response	=COUNTIF(A2:A31,C3)
5	Pokey		
6	Hoppy	*p*-Value (lower tail)	=BINOMDIST(C4,C2,0.5,TRUE)
7	Pokey	*p*-Value (upper tail)	=1-BINOMDIST(C4-1,C2,0.5,TRUE)
8	Pokey	*p*-Value (two tail)	=2*MIN(C6,C7)
9	Hoppy		

Note: Rows 10-31 are not shown.

We see in the value worksheet below that the two-tail *p*-value is .2005, which is greater than α = .05. Therefore, we cannot reject H_0. This conclusion is consistent with the results of our manual calculations. There is insufficient evidence in the sample to conclude that a difference in preference exists for the two brands of peanut butter.

Value Worksheet:

	A	B	C
1	Brand Preference		
2	Hoppy	Sample Size	30
3	Hoppy	Response of Interest	Hoppy
4	Hoppy	Count of Response	19
5	Pokey		
6	Hoppy	*p*-Value (lower tail)	0.95
7	Hoppy	*p*-Value (upper tail)	0.10
8	Pokey	*p*-Value (two tail)	0.200488422
9	Hoppy		

EXAMPLE 2

Sign Test: Hypothesis Test About a Median

A hypothesis test is being conducted about the median age of male members of the T Fitness Center.

H_0: Median Age = 34 years
H_a: Median Age ≠ 34 years

In a sample of 40 male members, 25 are older than 34, 14 are younger than 34, and 1 is 34. Is there sufficient evidence to reject H_0? Assume α = .05.

SOLUTION 2

Using Excel's BINOMDIST Function

Let us use the worksheet developed in Solution 1 as a template and modify it slightly to conduct the hypothesis test involving the median age of male members of T Fitness Center.

The sample size is 39 (we do not count the one 34-year-old in the sample) and 25 are older than the hypothesized median age of 34. We enter 39 into cell C2 and 24 into cell C4. We can enter into C3 as a matter of record our response of interest which is "Older than 34".

Formula Worksheet:

	A	B	C
1			
2		Sample Size	39
3		Response of Interest	Older than 34
4		Count of Response	25
5			
6		*p*-Value (lower tail)	=BINOMDIST(C4,C2,0.5,TRUE)
7		*p*-Value (upper tail)	=1-BINOMDIST(C4-1,C2,0.5,TRUE)
8		*p*-Value (two tail)	=2*MIN(C6,C7)
9			

Note that the *p*-value (two tail) = .1081. This is more than the level of significance specified for the test (α = .05), so we cannot reject H_0. There is insufficient evidence in the sample to conclude that the median age is <u>not</u> 34 for male members of the T Fitness Center.

Value Worksheet:

	A	B	C
1			
2		Sample Size	39
3		Response of Interest	Older than 34
4		Count of Response	25
5			
6		p-Value (lower tail)	0.97
7		p-Value (upper tail)	0.05
8		p-Value (two tail)	0.108129021
9			

EXAMPLE 3

Wilcoxon Signed-Rank Test

A firm has decided to select one of two express delivery services to provide next-day deliveries to the district offices.

To test the delivery times of the two services, the firm sends two reports to a sample of 10 district offices, with one report carried by OverNight and the other report carried by NiteFlite.

Do the data (delivery times in hours) shown below indicate a difference in the two services? Use $\alpha = .05$.

District Office	OverNight	NiteFlite
Seattle	32 hrs.	25 hrs.
Los Angeles	30	24
Boston	19	15
Cleveland	16	15
New York	15	13
Houston	18	15
Atlanta	14	15
St. Louis	10	8
Milwaukee	7	9
Denver	16	11

SOLUTION 3

Using Excel's NORMSDIST Function

Hypotheses:
    H_0: The delivery times of the two services are the same;
        neither offers faster service than the other.
    H_a: Delivery times differ between the two services;
        recommend the one with the smaller times.

Preliminary Steps of the Test:
1. Compute the differences between the paired observations.
2. Discard any differences of zero.
3. Rank the absolute value of the differences from lowest to highest.
   (Tied differences are assigned the average ranking of their positions.)
4. Give the ranks the sign of the original difference in the data.
5. Sum the signed ranks.

District Office	Difference	|Difference| Rank	Signed Rank
Seattle	7	10	+10
Los Angeles	6	9	+ 9
Boston	4	7	+ 7
Cleveland	1	1.5	+1.5
New York	2	4	+ 4
Houston	3	6	+ 6
Atlanta	-1	1.5	-1.5
St. Louis	2	4	+ 4
Milwaukee	-2	4	- 4
Denver	5	8	+ 8
Total			+44

Now we will determine whether the sum is significantly different from zero.

Rejection Rule:
    Using test statistic: Reject H_0 if $z < -1.96$ or $z > 1.96$
    Using p-value: Reject H_0 if p-value $< .05$

Test Statistic:
$$\mu_T = 0$$
$$\sigma_T = \sqrt{\frac{n(n+1)(2n+1)}{6}} = \sqrt{\frac{10(10+1)(2(10)+1)}{6}} = \sqrt{\frac{2,310}{6}} = 19.62142$$
$$z = \frac{T - \mu_T}{\sigma_T} = \frac{44 - 0}{19.62} = 2.24$$

Conclusion:

Reject H_0. $z > z_{\alpha/2}$. There is sufficient evidence in the sample to conclude that a difference exists in the delivery times provided by the two services. Recommend using the NiteFlite service.

Now we will use Excel to conduct our Wilcoxon signed-rank test. Excel does not provide any tools specifically designed for the WSR test, but a worksheet will be helpful in computing the signed ranks.

Enter Data: The data are entered into cells A1:C11.

	A	B	C	D
1	**District Office**	**OverNight**	**NiteFlite**	
2	Seattle	32	25	
3	Los Angeles	30	24	
4	Boston	19	15	
5	Cleveland	16	15	
6	New York	15	13	
7	Houston	18	15	
8	Atlanta	14	15	
9	St. Louis	10	8	
10	Milwaukee	7	9	
11	Denver	16	11	

Enter Functions and Formulas: The formulas in cells E2:E11 compute the differences in delivery times and Excel's ABS function is used in cells F2:F11 to compute the absolute value of the differences.

Excel's RANK function is used in column G to rank the absolute differences in ascending order. The arguments in the RANK function are: (1) the data value to be ranked, (2) the range of values for it to ranked among, and (3) the number one to indicate ascending order ranking. The RANK function does not assign an average rank to tied values, so we must modify the results provided by the function. We must type in the average values for ties in cells G5 and G8.

With the differences ranked, we use Excel's SIGN function in column H to assign each of the ranked differences their original sign from column E. The sum of the signed ranks is then computed in cell H12.

Now we are ready to compute the test statistic and the p-value. The effective sample size (after discarding any differences of zero) is computed in cell G14 using the COUNTA function. The standard deviation is computed in cell G15 and the test statistic is computed in cell G16.

The NORMSDIST function is used in cell G18:G19 to compute the lower-tail and upper-tail p-values, respectively. Then, p-value (two-tail) is computed in cell G20 as twice the minimum of the two one-tail p-values.

Formula Worksheet:

	E	F	G	H
1	Differ.	Abs. Val.	Rank	Signed Rank
2	=B2-C2	=ABS(E2)	=RANK(F2,$F$2:$F$11,1)	=SIGN(E2)*G2
3	=B3-C3	=ABS(E3)	=RANK(F3,$F$2:$F$11,1)	=SIGN(E3)*G3
4	=B4-C4	=ABS(E4)	=RANK(F4,$F$2:$F$11,1)	=SIGN(E4)*G4
5	=B5-C5	=ABS(E5)	1.5	=SIGN(E5)*G5
6	=B6-C6	=ABS(E6)	4	=SIGN(E6)*G6
7	=B7-C7	=ABS(E7)	=RANK(F7,$F$2:$F$11,1)	=SIGN(E7)*G7
8	=B8-C8	=ABS(E8)	1.5	=SIGN(E8)*G8
9	=B9-C9	=ABS(E9)	4	=SIGN(E9)*G9
10	=B10-C10	=ABS(E10)	4	=SIGN(E10)*G10
11	=B11-C11	=ABS(E11)	=RANK(F11,$F$2:$F$11,1)	=SIGN(E11)*G11
12			Total	=SUM(H2:H11)
13				
14		Effect. Sample Size	=COUNTA(A2:A11)	
15		Standard Deviation	=SQRT(G14*(G14+1)*(2*G14+1)/6)	
16		Test Statistic	=H12/G15	
17				
18		*p*-Value (lower tail)	=NORMSDIST(G16)	
19		*p*-Value (upper tail)	=1-NORMSDIST(G16)	
20		*p*-Value (two tail)	=2*MIN(G18,G19)	

We see in the value worksheet below that the two-tail *p*-value = .0249. Because .0249 < α = .05, we reject the null hypothesis of no difference between the two delivery services.

Value Worksheet:

	E	F	G	H
1	Differ.	Abs. Val.	Rank	Signed Rank
2	7	7	10	10
3	6	6	9	9
4	4	4	7	7
5	1	1	1.5	1.5
6	2	2	4	4
7	3	3	6	6
8	-1	1	1.5	-1.5
9	2	2	4	4
10	-2	2	4	-4
11	5	5	8	8
12			Total	44
13				
14	Effect. Sample Size		10	
15	Standard Deviation		19.6214	
16	Test Statistic		2.2424	
17				
18	p-Value (lower tail)		0.9875	
19	p-Value (upper tail)		0.0125	
20	p-Value (two tail)		0.0249	

EXAMPLE 4

Mann-Whitney-Wilcoxon Test: Large Sample Case

Manufacturer labels indicate the annual energy cost associated with operating home appliances such as freezers. The energy costs for a sample of 10 Westin freezers and a sample of 10 Easton freezers are shown below. Do the data indicate, using $\alpha = .10$, that a difference exists in the annual energy costs associated with the two brands of freezers?

Westin Freezers	Easton Freezers
$55.10	$56.10
54.50	54.70
53.20	54.40
53.00	55.40
55.50	54.10
54.90	56.00
55.80	55.50
54.00	55.00
54.20	54.30
55.20	57.00

SOLUTION 4

Using Excel's NORMSINV Function

Hypotheses:

H_0: Annual energy costs for Westin freezers and Easton freezers are the same.

H_a: Annual energy costs differ for the two brands of freezers.

First, rank the <u>combined</u> data from the lowest to the highest values, with tied values being assigned the average of the tied rankings. Then the sum the ranks for each sample.

Westin	Rank	Easton	Rank
$55.10	12	$56.10	19
54.50	8	54.70	9
53.20	2	54.40	7
53.00	1	55.40	14
55.50	15.5	54.10	4
54.90	10	56.00	18
55.80	17	55.50	15.5
54.00	3	55.00	11
54.20	5	54.30	6
55.20	13	57.00	20
Sum of Ranks	86.5	Sum of Ranks	123.5

Next, we can choose the sum of the ranks of either sample as our value of T. We will choose sample 1 and thus, $T = 86.5$.

Then, compare the observed value of T to the sampling distribution of T for identical populations. The value of the standardized test statistic z will provide the basis for deciding whether to reject H_0.

Rejection Rule:

Using test statistic: Reject H_0 if $z < -1.645$ or $z > 1.645$

Using p-value: Reject H_0 if p-value $< .10$

Mean:

$$\mu_T = \tfrac{1}{2} n_1 (n_1 + n_2 + 1) = \tfrac{1}{2} 10(10 + 10 + 1) = 105$$

Standard Deviation:

$$\sigma_T = \sqrt{\tfrac{1}{12} n_1 n_2 (n_1 + n_2 + 1)} = \sqrt{\tfrac{1}{12}(10)(10)(10 + 10 + 1)} = \sqrt{175} = 13.2288$$

Test Statistic:

$$z = \frac{T - \mu_T}{\sigma_T} = \frac{86.5 - 105}{13.2288} = -1.3985$$

Conclusion:

> Do not reject H_0. There is insufficient evidence in the sample data to conclude that there is a difference in the annual energy cost associated with the two brands of freezers.

We will now use Excel to conduct this Mann-Whitney-Wilcoxon test. Excel does not have any special tools for the M-W-W test, but we can a spreadsheet to rank the data, sum the ranks, compute the test statistic, and compute the p-value in the large-sample case. The approach is similar to the one used in Example 3 earlier.

Formula Worksheet:

	A	B	C
1	**Brand**	**Energy $**	**Rank**
2	Westin	55.10	=RANK(B2,$B$2:$B$21,1)
3	Westin	54.50	=RANK(B3,$B$2:$B$21,1)
4	Westin	53.20	=RANK(B4,$B$2:$B$21,1)
5	Westin	53.00	=RANK(B5,$B$2:$B$21,1)
6	Westin	55.50	15.5
7	Westin	54.90	=RANK(B7,$B$2:$B$21,1)
8	Westin	55.80	=RANK(B8,$B$2:$B$21,1)
9	Westin	54.00	=RANK(B9,$B$2:$B$21,1)
10	Westin	54.20	=RANK(B10,$B$2:$B$21,1)
11	Westin	55.20	=RANK(B11,$B$2:$B$21,1)
12	Easton	56.10	=RANK(B12,$B$2:$B$21,1)
13	Easton	54.70	=RANK(B13,$B$2:$B$21,1)
14	Easton	54.40	=RANK(B14,$B$2:$B$21,1)
15	Easton	55.40	=RANK(B15,$B$2:$B$21,1)
16	Easton	54.10	=RANK(B16,$B$2:$B$21,1)
17	Easton	56.00	=RANK(B17,$B$2:$B$21,1)
18	Easton	55.50	15.5
19	Easton	55.00	=RANK(B19,$B$2:$B$21,1)
20	Easton	54.30	=RANK(B20,$B$2:$B$21,1)
21	Easton	57.00	=RANK(B21,$B$2:$B$21,1)
22			
23		n_1	=COUNT(B2:B11)
24		n_2	=COUNT(B12:B21)
25			
26		Observed T	=SUM(C2:C11)
27		Expected T	=.5*C23*(C23+C24+1)
28		Std. Dev. T	=SQRT(1/12*C23*C24*(C23+C24+1))
29		Test Statistic z	=(C26-C27)/C28
30			
31		p-Value (low. tail)	=NORMSDIST(C29)
32		p-Value (up. tail)	=1-NORMSDIST(C29)
33		p-Value (two tail)	=2*MIN(C31,C32)

We see in the value worksheet below that the two-tail p-value in cell C33 is .1620. We cannot reject the null hypothesis that the freezer brands are identical because the p-value is greater than $\alpha = .10$.

Value Worksheet:

	A	B	C
1	**Brand**	**Energy \$**	**Rank**
2	Westin	55.10	12
3	Westin	54.50	8
4	Westin	53.20	2
5	Westin	53.00	1
6	Westin	55.50	15.5
7	Westin	54.90	10
8	Westin	55.80	17
9	Westin	54.00	3
10	Westin	54.20	5
11	Westin	55.20	13
12	Easton	56.10	19
13	Easton	54.70	9
14	Easton	54.40	7
15	Easton	55.40	14
16	Easton	54.10	4
17	Easton	56.00	18
18	Easton	55.50	15.5
19	Easton	55.00	11
20	Easton	54.30	6
21	Easton	57.00	20
22			
23		n_1	10
24		n_2	10
25			
26		**Observed** T	86.5
27		**Expected** T	105
28		**Std. Dev.** T	13.2288
29		**Test Statistic** z	-1.3985
30			
31		p**-Value (low. tail)**	0.0810
32		p**-Value (up. tail)**	0.9190
33		p**-Value (two tail)**	0.1620

EXAMPLE 5

Kruskal-Wallis Test

John Norr, Director of Athletics at Lakewood High School, is curious about whether a student's total number of absences in four years of high school is the same for students participating in no varsity sport, one varsity sport, and two varsity sports.

Number of absences data were available for 20 recent graduates and are listed below. Test whether the three populations are identical in terms of number of absences. Use α = .10.

No Sport	1 Sport	2 Sports
13	18	12
16	12	22
6	19	9
27	7	11
20	15	15
14	20	21
	17	10

SOLUTION 5

Using Excel's CHIDIST Function

First, we will manually conduct the Kruskal-Wallis test.

Hypotheses:
H_0: All populations are identical
H_a: Not all populations are identical

We must first rank all 20 data items. We will give the lowest number of absences (6) a 1 ranking and the greatest number of absences (27) a 20 ranking. Note that we assign the average ranking to tied items.

No Sport	Rank	1 Sport	Rank	2 Sports	Rank
13	8	18	14	12	6.5
16	12	12	6.5	22	19
6	1	19	15	9	3
27	20	7	2	11	5
20	16.5	15	10.5	15	10.5
14	9	20	16.5	21	18
		17	13	10	4
Total	66.5		77.5		66

Rejection Rule:

Using test statistic: Reject H_0 if $\chi^2 > 4.60517$ (2 degrees of freedom)
Using p-value: Reject H_0 if p-value < .10

Kruskal-Wallis Test Statistic::

$k = 3$ populations, $n_1 = 6$, $n_2 = 7$, $n_3 = 7$, $n_T = 20$

$$W = \left[\frac{12}{n_T(n_T + 1)} \sum_{i=1}^{k} \frac{R_i^2}{n_i} \right] - 3(n_T + 1)$$

$$= \left[\frac{12}{20(20 + 1)} \left[\frac{(66.5)^2}{6} + \frac{(77.5)^2}{7} \frac{(66.0)^2}{7} \right] \right] - 3(20 + 1) = .3532$$

Conclusion:

Do no reject H_0. There is <u>in</u>sufficient evidence to conclude that the populations are not identical. (W = .3532 < χ_α^2 = 4.6052)

EXAMPLE 6

Rank Correlation

Connor Investors provides a portfolio management service for its clients. Two of Connor's analysts ranked ten investments in terms of risk as shown below (with a 1 indicating minimal risk and 10 indicating maximal risk). Use rank correlation, with $\alpha = .10$, to comment on the agreement of the two analysts' rankings.

Investment	A	B	C	D	E	F	G	H	I	J
Analyst #1	1	4	9	8	6	3	5	7	2	10
Analyst #2	1	5	6	2	9	7	3	10	4	8

SOLUTION 6

Using Excel's CORREL and NORMSDIST Functions

First, we will manually conduct the rank correlation.

Hypotheses:

H_0: $p_s = 0$ (No rank correlation exists.)
H_a: $p_s \neq 0$ (Rank correlation exists.)

We compute the difference and then the square difference between the paired sample 1 and sample 2 ratings. Then, the squared differences are summed.

Investment (i)	Analyst #1 Rating (x_i)	Analyst #2 Rating (y_i)	Difference (d_i)	Difference^2 (d_i^2)
A	1	1	0	0
B	4	5	-1	1
C	9	6	3	9
D	8	2	6	36
E	6	9	-3	9
F	3	7	-4	16
G	5	3	2	4
H	7	10	-3	9
I	2	4	-2	4
J	10	8	2	4
			Sum =	92

Rejection Rule:

Using test statistic: Reject H_0 if $z < -1.645$ or $z > 1.645$

Using p-value: Reject H_0 if p-value $< .10$

Spearman Rank-Correlation Coefficient: $r_s = 1 - \dfrac{6 \sum d_i^2}{n(n^2 - 1)} = 1 - \dfrac{6(92)}{10(100 - 1)} = .4424$

Mean of r_s: $\mu_{r_s} = 0$

Standard Deviation of r_s: $\sigma_{r_s} = \sqrt{\dfrac{1}{n-1}} = \sqrt{\dfrac{1}{10-1}} = \sqrt{1/9} = .3333$

Test Statistic: $z = \dfrac{r_s - \mu_{r_s}}{\sigma_{r_s}} = \dfrac{.4424 - 0}{.3333} = 1.3273$

Conclusion:

Do no reject H_0. There is not a significant rank correlation. The two analysts are not showing agreement in their rating of the risk associated with the investments.

Now we will use Excel to conduct the Spearman rank-correlation test.

Enter Data: The data for the 10 investments are entered into cells B2:C11. The data in columns B and C are the ratings of analyst 1 and analyst 2, respectively.

Enter Functions and Formulas: Excel's CORREL function is used in cell C13 to compute the correlation coefficient for the correlation between the ranks in columns B and C. The standard error of the correlation coefficient is computed in cell C14. The test statistic z is computed in cell C15.

The NORMSDIST function is used in cell C17:C18 to compute the lower-tail and upper-tail p-values, respectively. Then, p-value (two-tail) is computed in cell C19 as twice the minimum of the two one-tail p-values.

Formula Worksheet:

	A	B	C
1	Investment	Analyst #1 Rating	Analyst #1 Rating
2	A	1	1
3	B	4	5
4	C	9	6
5	D	8	2
6	E	6	9
7	F	3	7
8	G	5	3
9	H	7	10
10	I	2	4
11	J	10	8
12			
13		Correlation (r_s)	=CORREL(B2:B11,C2:C11)
14		Std. Dev. of r_s	=SQRT(1/(COUNT(B2:B11)-1
15		Test Statistic	=C13/C14
16			
17		p-Value (lower tail)	=NORMSDIST(C15)
18		p-Value (upper tail)	=1-NORMSDIST(C15)
19		p-Value (two tail)	=2*MIN(C17,C18)

The two-tail p-value in cell C19 is .1844, which is greater than $\alpha = .10$. There is little evidence of a rank correlation between the two analysts' investment rankings.

Value Worksheet:

	A	B	C
1	Investment	Analyst #1 Rating	Analyst #1 Rating
2	A	1	1
3	B	4	5
4	C	9	6
5	D	8	2
6	E	6	9
7	F	3	7
8	G	5	3
9	H	7	10
10	I	2	4
11	J	10	8
12			
13		Correlation (r_s)	0.4424
14		Std. Dev. of r_s	0.3333
15		Test Statistic	1.3273
16			
17		p-Value (lower tail)	0.9078
18		p-Value (upper tail)	0.0922
19		p-Value (two tail)	0.1844

EXERCISES

EXERCISE 1

Sign Test: Large-Sample Case

Maria Gonzales is the supervisor responsible for scheduling telephone operators at a major call center. She is interested in determining whether her operators' preferences between the day shift (7 a.m. to 3 p.m.) and evening shift (3 p.m. to 11 p.m.) are different.

Maria randomly selected a sample of 35 operators who were asked to state a preference for the one of the two work shifts. The data collected from the sample is shown below.

11 preferred the day shift
21 preferred the evening shift
3 had no preference

Can Maria conclude, using a level of significance of $\alpha = .05$, that operator preferences are different for the two shifts. (Denote a preference for the day shift with a "+" sign.)

EXERCISE 2

Sign Test: Hypothesis Test About a Median

Terry Newton is accounts receivable supervisor for Zap Pest Control. He believes that the median duration of an outstanding customer bill is 24 days. His manager believes the duration is longer than 24 days.

Terry has randomly selected a sample of 50 paid customer bills and found the following:

31 paid in more than 24 days
17 paid in less than 24 days
2 paid in exactly 24 days

Who is correct, Terry or his manager? Use $\alpha = .05$ as the level of significance.

EXERCISE 3

Wilcoxon Signed-Rank Test

Tiffany Faust is attempting to determine whether her finished-product packagers are more productive with rock music or popular music playing in the background. A sample of 12 employees was selected. The number of units packaged by each employee in four hours was observed and recorded on two separate days, one day with rock music playing and a second day with popular music playing. The sample data are listed below.

Packager	Rock Music	Popular Music
1	42	45
2	30	37
3	32	35
4	41	40
5	32	32
6	36	39
7	47	49
8	44	50
9	35	38
10	37	42
11	36	36
12	31	34

Use a .025 level of significance to determine whether the type of music has an effect on the packagers' productivity

EXERCISE 4

Mann-Whitney-Wilcoxon Test: Large Sample Case

The print capacity of ink cartridges in computer printers is a concern to many buyers due to the cost of cartridges. The observed print capacities (in number of pages) of black ink cartridges in a sample of 12 Epsmark printers and a sample of 12 Lexson printers are shown below. Do the data indicate, using $\alpha = .10$, that a difference exists in the print capacities associated with the two brands of printers?

Epsmark	Lexson
912	855
854	912
903	877
909	893
878	922
866	874
934	866
881	859
890	880
898	897
906	909
905	882

EXERCISE 5

Kruskal-Wallis Test

Rebecca Roush, Manager of the Home Square (home improvement) store in Athens, would like to determine whether an employee's number of years practicing his/her trade prior to working in retail is the same for employees in the plumbing, electrical, and paint departments.

Data on the number of trade-practice years were available for 20 employees and are listed below. Test whether the three populations are identical in terms of number of years of trade-practical experience. Use $\alpha = .05$.

Plumbing	Electrical	Paint
13	17	11
9	22	5
21	14	8
17	9	17
8	18	10
11	28	6
16		12

EXERCISE 6

Rank Correlation

The Suburbia Health Department inspects restaurants for compliance to laws regulating the storage, preparation, and serving of food to the public. Two of the department's inspectors ranked ten restaurants in terms of cleanliness as shown below (with a 1 indicating cleanest and 10 indicating least clean). Use rank correlation, with $\alpha = .05$, to comment on the agreement of the two inspectors' rankings.

Restaurant	A	B	C	D	E	F	G	H	I	J
Inspector #1	3	6	10	4	1	5	2	8	7	9
Inspector #2	1	5	9	2	3	7	6	10	4	8

SELF-TEST

TRUE/FALSE

___ 1. Nominal and ordinal scales can provide quantitative data.

___ 2. When conducting a hypothesis test about a median, a plus sign must be assigned to sample values greater than the hypothesized median.

___ 3. The Spearman rank-correlation coefficient can take on values between 0 and 1.

___ 4. The larger the p-value, the more likely it is that the null hypothesis is true.

___ 5. The large-sample sign test is equivalent to the test of a population proportion with $p = .5$.

FILL-IN-THE-BLANK

1. Distribution-free methods are another name for _____ statistical methods.

2. Under the assumption that a sign test's H_0 is true, the number of plus signs follows a _____ probability distribution with $p = .50$.

3. When conducting a hypothesis test about a median, if a sample observation equals the _____, it is dropped from the analysis and the sample size is reduced by one.

4. The scale of measurement is _____ if the data are labels or categories used to define an attribute of an element.

5. Under the null hypothesis in which the populations are identical, the sampling distribution of the Kruskal-Wallis test statistic W can be approximated by a _____ distribution with $k - 1$ degrees of freedom.

MULTIPLE CHOICE

___ 1. The Wilcoxon signed-rank test is the nonparametric alternative to the parametric hypothesis test about the difference between the
   a) means of two populations with matched samples
   b) means of two populations with independent samples
   c) medians of two populations
   d) proportions of two populations

___ 2. All of the following describe the interval scale EXCEPT
    a) data must be numeric
    b) data have the properties of ordinal data
    c) ratios are meaningful
    d) interval between observations is expressed in terms of a fixed unit of measure

___ 3. Which of the following is the appropriate null hypothesis for the sign test?
    a) $H_0: p_s = 0$
    b) $H_0: p = .5$
    c) H_0: The two populations are identical
    d) H_0: All populations are identical

___ 4. A test that can be used with nominal data is
    a) sign test
    b) Wilcoxon signed-rank test
    c) Mann-Whitney-Wilcoxon test
    d) Kruskal-Wallis test

___ 5. If three values being ranked tie for the eighth position,
    a) all three are given a rank of 8
    b) all three are given a rank of 9
    c) (any) one is given a rank of 8, another is given 9, another is given 10
    d) (any) one is given a rank of 8, another is given 8 1/3, another is given 8 2/3

ANSWERS

EXERCISES

1) Using binomial distribution approach (results below), reject H_0 if number of + signs is less than 10 or more than 21. We cannot reject H_0. p-value = .11 > α = .05.

Sample Size	32
Response of Interest	Day
Count of Response	11
p-Value (lower tail)	0.06
p-Value (upper tail)	0.97
p-Value (two tail)	0.110184165

Using normal distribution approach, reject H_0 if $z < -1.96$ or $z > 1.96$. We cannot reject H_0 because $z = -1.77 > z_{\alpha/2} = -1.96$. (p-value = .0968.) Using either approach, there is insufficient evidence to conclude that the shift preferences are different.

2) We cannot reject H_0. p-value = .0595 > α = .0500. (We ALMOST rejected!)

Sample Size	48
Response of Interest	More than 24 days
Count of Response	31
p-Value (lower tail)	0.99
p-Value (upper tail)	0.03
p-Value (two tail)	0.059463375

3) T = -53, σ_T = 19.6214, z = 2.70. Reject H_0 because z = -2.70 < $z_{\alpha/2}$ = -2.24

Effect. Sample Size	10
Standard Deviation	19.6214
Test Statistic	2.2424
p-Value (lower tail)	0.9965
p-Value (upper tail)	0.0035
p-Value (two tail)	0.0069

4) p-value = .3408 > α = .10.   Do not reject H_0

Observed T	166.5
Expected T	150
Std. Dev. T	17.3205
Test Statistic z	0.9526
p-Value (low. tail)	0.8296
p-Value (up. tail)	0.1704
p-Value (two tail)	0.3408

5) R_1 = 74.5, R_2 = 88.5, R_3 = 47, W = 5.967.
We cannot reject H_0 because W = 5.9668 < χ_α^2 = 5.9915
(If α was equal to .10, we could reject H_0 because W = 5.9668 > χ_α^2 = 4.6052)

6) Reject H_0 because p-value = .0334 < α = .05 (There <u>is</u> a significant correlation.)

Correlation (r_s)	0.7091
Std. Dev. of r_s	0.3333
Test Statistic	2.1273
p-Value (lower tail)	0.9833
p-Value (upper tail)	0.0167
p-Value (two tail)	0.0334

TRUE/FALSE

1) False
2) False
3) False
4) True
5) True

FILL-IN-THE-BLANK

1) nonparametric
2) binomial
3) median
4) nominal
5) chi-square

MULTIPLE CHOICE

1) a
2) c
3) b
4) a
5) b

CHAPTER 18

Sample Survey

Terminology Used in Sample Surveys

Types of Surveys and Sampling Methods

Survey Errors

Simple Random Sampling

Stratified Simple Random Sampling

Cluster Sampling

Systematic Sampling

LEARNING OBJECTIVES

1. Learn what a sample survey is and how it differs from an experiment as a method of collecting data.

2. Know about the methods of data collection for a survey.

3. Know the difference between sampling and nonsampling error.

4. Learn about four sample designs: (1) simple random sampling, (2) stratified simple random sampling, (3) cluster sampling, and (4) systematic sampling.

5. Lean how to estimate a population mean, a population total, and a population proportion using the above sample designs.

6. Understand the relationship between sample size and precision.

7. Learn how to choose the appropriate sample size using stratified and simple random sampling.

8. Learn how to allocate the total sample to the various strata using stratified simple random sampling.

REVIEW

Terminology Used in Sample Surveys
- An <u>element</u> is the entity on which data are collected.
- A <u>population</u> is the set of all the elements of interest.
- Examining the entire population might be <u>time and/or cost prohibitive</u> or simply <u>not feasible</u>.
- Instead, we examine a sample taken from the population.
- A <u>sample</u> is a subset of the population.
- The <u>target population</u> is the population we want to make inferences about.
- The <u>sampled population</u> is the population from which the sample is actually selected.
- If inferences from a sample are to be valid, the sampled population must be representative of the target population.
- Before sampling, the population must be divided into <u>sampling units</u>.
- In some cases, the sampling units are simply the elements, while in other cases the sampling units are groups of the elements. (Example: sampling elements = engineers; sampling units = engineering firms)
- A list of the sampling units for a particular study is called a <u>frame</u>.
- The choice of a particular frame is often determined by the availability and reliability of a list.
- The development of the frame can be one of the most difficult and important steps in conducting a sample survey.

Types of Surveys

Surveys Involving Questionnaires
- Three common types are <u>mail surveys</u>, <u>telephone surveys</u>, and <u>personal interview surveys</u>.
- Survey cost are lower for mail and telephone surveys.
- With well-trained interviewers, higher response rates and longer questionnaires are possible with personal interviews.
- The design of the questionnaire is critical.
- Long questionnaires can lead to respondent and interviewer fatigue.

Surveys Not Involving Questionnaires
- Often, someone simply counts or measures the sampled items and records the results.
- An example is sampling a company's inventory of parts to estimate the total inventory value.

Sampling Methods

Nonprobabilistic Sampling
- The probability of obtaining each possible sample can be computed.
- Statistically valid statements cannot be made about the precision of the estimates.
- Sampling cost is lower and implementation is easier.
- Methods include <u>convenience</u> and <u>judgment sampling</u>.
- <u>Convenience sampling</u> is an example of nonprobabilistic sampling.
  - The units included in the sample are chosen because of accessibility.
  - In some cases, convenience sampling is the only practical approach.
  - <u>Advantage</u>: Sample selection and data collection are relatively easy.
  - <u>Disadvantage</u>: It is impossible to determine how representative of the population the sample is.
  - <u>Example</u>: A professor conducting research might use student volunteers to constitute a sample.
- <u>Judgment sampling</u> is another example of nonprobabilistic sampling.
  - A knowledgeable person selects sampling units that he/she feels are most representative of the population.
  - Generally, no statistical statement should be made about the precision of the result.
  - <u>Advantage</u>: It is a relatively easy way of selecting a sample.
  - <u>Disadvantage</u>: The quality of the sample results depends on the judgment of the person selecting the sample.
  - <u>Example</u>: A reporter might sample three or four senators, judging them as reflecting the general opinion of the senate.

Probabilistic Sampling
- The probability of obtaining each possible sample can be computed.
- Confidence intervals can be developed which provide bounds on the sampling error.
- Methods include <u>simple random</u>, <u>stratified simple random</u>, <u>cluster</u>, and <u>systematic sampling</u>.

Survey Errors
- Two types of errors can occur in conducting a survey, <u>sampling error</u> and <u>nonsampling error</u>.

Sampling Error
- It is defined as the magnitude of the difference between the point estimate, developed from the sample, and the population parameter.
- It occurs because not every element in the population is surveyed.
- It cannot occur in a census.
- It can not be avoided, but it can be controlled by proper choice of a sample design.

Nonsampling Error
- It can occur in both a census and a sample survey.
- Examples include <u>measurement error</u>, <u>errors due to nonresponse</u>, <u>errors due to lack of respondent knowledge</u>, <u>selection error</u>, and <u>processing error</u>.

Measurement Error
- Measuring instruments are not properly calibrated.
- People taking the measurements are not properly trained.

Errors Due to Nonresponse
- They occur when no data can be obtained, or only partial data are obtained, for some of the units surveyed.
- The problem is most serious when a bias is created.

Errors Due to Lack of Respondent Knowledge
- These errors on common in technical surveys.
- Some respondents might be more capable than others of answering technical questions.

Selection Error
- An inappropriate item is included in the survey.
- For example, in a survey of "small truck owners" some interviewers include SUV owners while other interviewers do not.

Processing Error
- Data is incorrectly recorded.
- Data is incorrectly transferred from recording forms to computer files.

Simple Random Sampling
- A <u>simple random sample from a finite population</u> of size N is a sample selected such that each possible sample of size n has the same probability of being selected.
- We begin by developing a frame or list of all elements in the sampled population.
- Then a selection procedure, based on the use of random numbers, is used to ensure that each element in the sampled population has the same probability of being selected.
- In large sampling projects, computer-generated <u>random numbers</u> are often used to automate the sample selection process.

Pont Estimates and Interval Estimates
- We will estimate the following population parameters: <u>population mean</u>, <u>population total</u>, and <u>population proportion</u>.
- In a sample survey it is common practice to provide an approximate <u>95% confidence interval</u> estimate of the population parameter.
- Assuming the sampling distribution of the point estimator can be approximated by a normal probability distribution, we use a value of <u>z = 2</u> for a 95% confidence interval.
- The interval estimate is:

  Point Estimator +/- 2(Estimate of the Standard Error of the Point Estimator)

- The <u>bound on the sampling error</u> is:

  2(Estimate of the Standard Error of the Point Estimator)

Population Mean
- <u>Point Estimator</u>:

$$\bar{x}$$

- <u>Estimate of the Standard Error of the Mean</u>:

$$s_{\bar{x}} = \sqrt{\frac{N-n}{N}} \left(\frac{s}{\sqrt{n}} \right)$$

$$\bar{x} \pm z_{\alpha/2} s_{\bar{x}}$$

- <u>Interval Estimate</u>:
- <u>Approximate 95% Confidence Interval Estimate</u>:

$$\bar{x} \pm 2 s_{\bar{x}}$$

Population Total
- <u>Point Estimator</u>:

$$\hat{X} = N\bar{x}$$

- <u>Estimate of the Standard Error of the Total</u>:

$$s_{\hat{x}} = N s_{\bar{x}}$$

- <u>Interval Estimate</u>:

$$N\bar{x} \pm z_{\alpha/2} s_{\hat{x}}$$

- <u>Approximate 95% Confidence Interval Estimate</u>:

$$N\bar{x} \pm 2 s_{\hat{x}}$$

Population Proportion
- <u>Point Estimator</u>:

$$\bar{p}$$

- <u>Estimate of the Standard Error of the Proportion</u>:

$$s_{\bar{p}} = \sqrt{\left(\frac{N-n}{n} \right) \left(\frac{\bar{p}(1-\bar{p})}{n-1} \right)}$$

- Interval Estimate:

$$\bar{p} \pm z_{\alpha/2} s_{\bar{p}}$$

- Approximate 95% Confidence Interval Estimate:

$$\bar{p} \pm 2 s_{\bar{p}}$$

Determining the Sample Size
- An important consideration in sample design is the choice of sample size.
- The best choice usually involves a tradeoff between cost and precision (size of the confidence interval).
- Larger samples provide greater precision, but are more costly.
- A budget might dictate how large the sample can be.
- A specified level of precision might dictate how small a sample can be.
- Smaller confidence intervals provide more precision.
- The size of the approximate confidence interval depends on the bound B on the sampling error.
- Choosing a level of precision amounts to choosing a value for B.
- Given a desired level of precision, we can solve for the value of n.
- Necessary Sample Size for Estimating the Population Mean:

$$n = \frac{Ns^2}{N\left(\dfrac{B^2}{4}\right) + s^2}$$

- Necessary Sample Size for Estimating the Population Total:

$$n = \frac{Ns^2}{\left(\dfrac{B^2}{4N}\right) + s^2}$$

- Necessary Sample Size for Estimating the Population Proportion:

$$n = \frac{N\bar{p}(1-\bar{p})}{N\left(\dfrac{B^2}{4}\right) + \bar{p}(1-\bar{p})}$$

Stratified Simple Random Sampling
- The population is first divided into H groups of elements called strata.
- The basis for forming the various strata depends on the judgment of the designer of the sample.
- Each element in the population belongs to one and only one stratum.
- Best results are obtained when the elements within each stratum are as much alike as possible (i.e. homogeneous group).
- Then from each stratum h a simple random sample of size n_k is taken.
- The data from the H simple random samples are combined to develop an estimate of a population parameter.

- Formulas are available for combining the stratum sample results into one population parameter estimate.
- <u>Advantage</u>: If strata are homogeneous, this method is as "precise" as simple random sampling but with a smaller total sample size (or more precise with the same total sample size).
- <u>Example</u>: The basis for forming the strata might be department, location, age, industry type, etc.

Population Mean
- <u>Point Estimator</u>:

$$\overline{x}_{st} = \sum_{h=1}^{H} \left(\frac{N_h}{N} \right) \overline{x}_h$$

where: H = number of strata
$\overline{x}_k$ = sample mean for stratum h
N_h = number of elements in the population in stratum h
N = total number of elements in the population (all strata)

- <u>Estimate of the Standard Error of the Mean</u>:

$$s_{\overline{x}_{st}} = \sqrt{\left(\frac{1}{N^2} \right) \sum_{h=1}^{3} N_h(N_h - n_h) \frac{s_h^2}{n_h}}$$

- <u>Interval Estimate</u>:

$$\overline{x}_{st} \pm z_{\alpha/2} s_{\overline{x}_{st}}$$

- <u>Approximate 95% Confidence Interval Estimate</u>:

$$\overline{x}_{st} \pm 2 s_{\overline{x}_{st}}$$

Population Total
- <u>Point Estimator</u>:

$$\hat{X} = N\overline{x}_{st}$$

- <u>Estimate of the Standard Error of the Total</u>:

$$s_{\hat{x}} = N s_{\overline{x}_{st}}$$

- <u>Interval Estimate</u>:

$$N\overline{x}_{st} \pm z_{\alpha/2} s_{\hat{x}}$$

- <u>Approximate 95% Confidence Interval Estimate</u>:

$$N\overline{x}_{st} \pm 2 s_{\hat{x}}$$

Population Proportion
- <u>Point Estimator</u>:

$$\overline{p}_{st} = \sum_{h=1}^{H} \left(\frac{N_h}{N} \right) \overline{p}_h$$

where: H = number of strata

$\bar{p}_k$ = sample proportion for stratum h

N_h = number of elements in the population in stratum h

N = total number of elements in the population (all strata)

- <u>Estimate of the Standard Error of the Proportion</u>:

$$s_{\bar{p}_{st}} = \sqrt{\left(\frac{1}{N^2}\right) \sum_{h=1}^{H} N_h (N_h - n_h) \frac{\bar{p}_h (1 - \bar{p}_h)}{n_h - 1}}$$

- <u>Interval Estimate</u>:

$$\bar{p}_{st} \pm z_{\alpha/2} s_{\bar{p}_{st}}$$

- <u>Approximate 95% Confidence Interval Estimate</u>:

$$\bar{p}_{st} \pm 2 s_{\bar{p}_{st}}$$

Determining the Sample Size

- We can think of choosing a <u>sample size</u> as a two-step process.
- First, an overall sample size n is found.
- Second, an allocation is found that will provide the necessary precision for the overall population parameter of interest.
- Then, if the sample sizes in some of the strata are not large enough to provide the necessary precision for the estimates within the strata, those sample sizes are adjusted upward.
- Important factors in allocation of the total sample size are:
  - The number of elements in each stratum (larger stratum ... larger sample)
  - The variance of the elements within each stratum (larger variance ... larger sample)
  - The cost of selecting elements within each stratum (higher cost ... smaller sample)
- <u>Necessary Total Sample Size for Estimating the <u>Population Mean</u></u>:

$$n = \frac{\left(\sum_{h=1}^{H} N_h s_h\right)^2}{N^2 \left(\frac{B^2}{4}\right) + \sum_{h=1}^{H} N_h s_h^2}$$

- <u>Necessary Total Sample Size for Estimating the <u>Population Total</u></u>:

$$n = \frac{\left(\sum_{h=1}^{H} N_h s_h\right)^2}{\frac{B^2}{4} + \sum_{h=1}^{H} N_h s_h^2}$$

- <u>Allocating Total Sample Size When Estimating Population <u>Mean or Total</u></u>

$$n_h = n \left(\frac{N_h s_h}{\sum_{h=1}^{H} N_h s_h}\right)$$

- <u>Necessary Total Sample Size for Estimating the</u> <u>Population Proportion</u>:

$$n = \frac{\left(\sum_{h=1}^{H} N_h \sqrt{\bar{p}_h(1-\bar{p}_h)}\right)^2}{N^2\left(\dfrac{B^2}{4}\right) + \sum_{h=1}^{H} N_h \bar{p}_h(1-\bar{p}_h)}$$

- <u>Allocating Total Sample Size When Estimating Population</u> <u>Proportion</u>

$$n_h = n\left(\frac{N_h \sqrt{\bar{p}_h(1-\bar{p}_h)}}{\sum_{h=1}^{H} N_h \sqrt{\bar{p}_h(1-\bar{p}_h)}}\right)$$

Cluster Sampling
- The population is first divided into N separate groups of elements called <u>clusters</u>.
- We would define the frame as the list of N clusters.
- Ideally, each cluster is a representative small-scale version of the population (i.e. <u>heterogeneous group</u>).
- A simple random sample of n clusters is then taken.
- All elements within each sampled (chosen) cluster form the sample.
- <u>Advantage</u>: The close proximity of elements can be cost effective (I.e. many sample observations can be obtained in a short time).
- <u>Advantage</u>: Cluster sampling tends to provide better results than stratified sampling when the elements within the clusters are heterogeneous.
- <u>Disadvantage</u>: This method generally requires a larger total sample size than simple or stratified random sampling.
- <u>Example</u>: A primary application is area sampling, where clusters are city blocks or other well-defined areas.

Notation Used Below
N = number of clusters in the population
n = number of clusters selected in the sample
M_i = number of elements in cluster i
M = number of elements in the population
$\bar{M}$ = average number of elements in a cluster
x_i = total of all observations in cluster i
a_i = number of observations in cluster i with a certain characteristic

Population Mean
- <u>Point Estimator</u>:

$$\bar{x}_c = \frac{\sum_{i=1}^{n} x_i}{\sum_{i=1}^{n} M_i}$$

- Estimate of the Standard Error of the Mean:

$$s_{\bar{x}_c} = \sqrt{\left(\frac{N-n}{Nn\bar{M}^2}\right)\frac{\sum_{i=1}^{n}(x_i - \bar{x}_c M_i)^2}{n-1}}$$

- Interval Estimate:

$$\bar{x}_c \pm z_{\alpha/2}s_{\bar{x}_c}$$

- Approximate 95% Confidence Interval Estimate:

$$\bar{x}_c \pm 2s_{\bar{x}_c}$$

Population Total
- Point Estimator:

$$\hat{X} = M\bar{x}_c$$

- Estimate of the Standard Error of the Total:

$$s_{\hat{X}} = Ms_{\bar{x}_c}$$

- Interval Estimate:

$$M\bar{x}_c \pm z_{\alpha/2}s_{\hat{X}}$$

- Approximate 95% Confidence Interval Estimate:

$$M\bar{x}_c \pm 2s_{\hat{X}}$$

Population Proportion
- Point Estimator:

$$\bar{p}_c = \frac{\sum_{i=1}^{n}a_i}{\sum_{i=1}^{n}M_i}$$

- Estimate of the Standard Error of the Proportion:

$$s_{\bar{p}_c} = \sqrt{\left(\frac{N-n}{Nn\bar{M}^2}\right)\frac{\sum_{i=1}^{n}(a_i - \bar{p}_c M_i)^2}{n-1}}$$

- Interval Estimate:

$$\bar{p}_c \pm z_{\alpha/2}s_{\bar{p}_c}$$

- Approximate 95% Confidence Interval Estimate:

$$\bar{p}_c \pm 2s_{\bar{p}_c}$$

Systematic Sampling

- If a sample size of *n* is desired from a population containing *N* elements, we might sample one element for every n/N elements in the population.
- We randomly select one of the first n/N elements from the population list.
- We then select every n/Nth element that follows in the population list.
- This method has the properties of a simple random sample, especially if the list of the population elements is a random ordering.
- <u>Advantage</u>: The sample usually will be easier to identify than it would be if simple random sampling were used.
- <u>Example</u>: Select every 100<u>th</u> listing in a telephone book after the first randomly selected listing.

KEY CONCEPTS

<u>CONCEPT</u>	<u>EXAMPLES</u>	<u>EXERCISES</u>
Simple Random Sampling		
Estimates of Population Total	①	1
Determining the Sample Size	2	2
Estimates of Population Proportion	③	3
Stratified Simple Random Sampling		
Estimates of Population Mean	④	4
Estimates of Population Total	⑤	5
Estimates of Population Proportion	6	6
Cluster Sampling		
Estimates of Population Mean	⑦	4
Estimates of Population Total	8	5
Estimates of Population Proportion	9	6

◯ Excel Used

EXAMPLES

EXAMPLE 1

Simple Random Sampling: Population Total Estimates

Innis Winchell owns and operates Innis Investments with 200 clients. A sample of 40 clients has been taken to obtain various demographic data and information about the clients' investment objectives. The sampled clients' net worth (in $thousands) are shown below.

410	508	479	555	366	566	509	560
338	588	512	512	564	378	406	348
612	296	395	393	443	684	593	391
447	365	360	319	432	333	404	573
795	625	521	403	610	578	622	407

a) Estimate the total net worth for the population (all clients).

b) Estimate the standard error of the population total (and round it to the nearest thousand).

c) Develop an approximate 95% confidence interval for the total net worth.

SOLUTION 1

First, we will manually compute the estimates.

a) Point estimate of total net worth of clients:

$$\bar{x} = \frac{\sum_{i=1}^{n} x_i}{n} = 480$$

$$\hat{X} = N\bar{x} = 200(480) = 96,000 \text{ thousand} = \$96,000,000$$

b) Estimate of standard error of total net worth:

$$s_{\hat{x}} = N s_{\bar{x}} = N \sqrt{\frac{N-n}{N}} \left(\frac{s}{\sqrt{n}} \right) = 200 \sqrt{\frac{200-40}{200}} \left(\frac{115}{\sqrt{40}} \right) = 3,252.6912 \text{ thousands}$$

$$= \$3,252,691$$

c) Approximate 95% confidence interval for total net worth:

$$N\bar{x} \pm 2 s_{\hat{x}} = 96,000 \pm 2(3,252.691)$$
$$= 89,494.618 \text{ to } 102,505.382 \text{ thousands}$$
$$= \$89,494,618 \text{ to } \$102,505,382$$

Now, we will use Excel to compute our estimates.

Formula Worksheet:

	A	B	C	D
1	Client	Worth	Population Size	200
2	1	410,000	Sample Size	=COUNT(B2:B41)
3	2	338,000	Sample Mean	=AVERAGE(B2:B41)
4	3	612,000	Sample Std. Dev.	=STDEV(B2:B41)
5	4	447,000		
6	5	795,000	Std. Error of Mean	=(SQRT((D1-D2)/D1))*(D4/SQRT(D2))
7	6	510,000	Std. Error of Total	=D1*D6
8	7	588,000	Bound on Samp. Error	=2*D7
9	8	296,000		
10	9	365,000	Point Est. (Pop. Tot.)	=D1*D3
11	10	625,000	Lower Limit (Pop. Tot.)	=D10-D8
12	11	475,000	Upper Limit (Pop. Tot.)	=D10+D8

Note: Rows 13-41 are not shown.

The results in the value worksheet below are virtually the same as those we computed manually. Any difference is due to our rounding the sample standard deviation (114,998.1) to 115,000 in our manual calculations.

Value worksheet:

	A	B	C	D
1	Client	Worth	Population Size	200
2	1	410,000	Sample Size	40
3	2	338,000	Sample Mean	480,000.00
4	3	612,000	Sample Std. Dev.	114,998.10
5	4	447,000		
6	5	795,000	Std. Error of Mean	16,263.19
7	6	510,000	Std. Error of Total	3,252,637.45
8	7	588,000	Bound on Samp. Error	6,505,274.91
9	8	296,000		
10	9	365,000	Point Est. (Pop. Tot.)	96,000,000.00
11	10	625,000	Lower Limit (Pop. Tot.)	89,494,725.09
12	11	475,000	Upper Limit (Pop. Tot.)	102,505,274.91

Note: Rows 13-41 are not shown.

EXAMPLE 2

Simple Random Sampling: Determining the Sample Size

Refer again to the Innis Investments problem in Example 1. One year later Innis wants to again survey his clients. He now has 325 clients and wants to set a bound of $5 million on the error of the estimate of their total net worth. What is the appropriate sample size?

SOLUTION 2

We are solving for the sample size necessary for estimating a population total with a bound of $5 million on the sampling error of estimate.

Recall from Solution 1 that $s = 115$ (rounded to the nearest thousand).

Necessary sample size:

$$n = \frac{Ns^2}{\left(\frac{B^2}{4N}\right) + s^2} = \frac{325(115)^2}{\left(\frac{5,000^2}{4(325)}\right) + 115^2} = 132.43$$

He will need a sample size of 133. This is more than three times the size of the original sample of 40, due to a larger population ($N = 325$ rather than the original 200) and a smaller error bound ($B = \$5.0$ million rather than the original $6.5 million).

EXAMPLE 3

Simple Random Sampling: Population Proportion Estimates

Refer again to the Innis Investments problem in Example 1. The sample of 40 clients (from a total of 200 clients) were asked if they favor fixed income investments. Twelve of the 40 clients replied "yes."

a) Estimate the population proportion favoring fixed income investments.

b) Estimate the standard error of the proportion.

c) Estimate an approximate 95% confidence interval for the population proportion.

SOLUTION 3

First, we will manually compute the estimates.

a) Point estimate of the population proportion favoring fixed-income investments:

$$\bar{p} = \frac{12}{40} = .30$$

b) Estimate of the standard error of the proportion:

$$s_{\bar{p}} = \sqrt{\left(\frac{N-n}{N}\right)\left(\frac{\bar{p}(1-\bar{p})}{n-1}\right)} = \sqrt{\left(\frac{200-40}{200}\right)\left(\frac{.3(1-.3)}{200-1}\right)} = .029$$

c) Approximate 95% confidence interval:

$$\bar{p} \pm 2s_{\bar{p}} = .300 \pm 2(.029) = .242 \text{ to } .358$$

Now, we will use Excel to compute our estimates.

Formula Worksheet:

	A	B	C	D
1	Client	Favor?	Population Size	200
2	1	No	Sample Size	=COUNTA(B2:B41)
3	2	No	Response of Interest	Yes
4	3	No	Count for Response	=COUNTIF(B2:B41,D3)
5	4	Yes	Sample Proportion	=D4/D2
6	5	Yes		
7	6	No	Std. Error of Propor.	=SQRT(((D1-D2)/D1)*(D5*(1-D5))/(D1-1))
8	7	No	Bound on Samp. Error	=2*D7
9	8	Yes		
10	9	No	Point Est. (Pop. Pro.)	=D5
11	10	Yes	Lower Limit (Pop. Pro.)	=D10-D8
12	11	No	Upper Limit (Pop. Pro.)	=D10+D8

Note: Rows 13-41 are not shown.

Value Worksheet:

	A	B	C	D
1	Client	Favor?	Population Size	200
2	1	No	Sample Size	40
3	2	No	Response of Interest	Yes
4	3	No	Count for Response	12
5	4	Yes	Sample Proportion	0.3
6	5	Yes		
7	6	No	Std. Error of Propor.	0.0291
8	7	No	Bound on Samp. Error	0.0581
9	8	Yes		
10	9	No	Point Est. (Pop. Pro.)	0.3
11	10	Yes	Lower Limit (Pop. Pro.)	0.2419
12	11	No	Upper Limit (Pop. Pro.)	0.3581

Note: Rows 13-41 are not shown.

EXAMPLE 4

Stratified Simple Random Sampling: Population Mean Estimates

Mill Creek Co. has used stratified simple random sampling to obtain demographic information and preferences regarding health care coverage for its employees and their families.

The population of employees has been divided into 3 strata on the basis of age: under 30, 30-49, and 50 or over. The sample data are shown below.

Stratum	N_h	n_h	Annual Family Dental Expense Mean	Std.Dev.	Proportion Married
Under 30	100	30	$250	$75	.60
30-49	250	45	400	100	.70
50 or Over	125	30	425	130	.68
	475	105			

a) Estimate the mean annual dental expense for a family.

b) Estimate the standard error of the mean.

c) Develop an approximate 95% confidence interval for the mean annual dental expense.

SOLUTION 4

First, we will manually compute the estimates.

a) Point estimate of the mean annual dental expense:

$$\bar{X}_{st} = \sum_{h=1}^{3}\left(\frac{N_h}{N}\right)\bar{X}_h = \left(\frac{100}{475}\right)250 + \left(\frac{250}{475}\right)400 + \left(\frac{125}{475}\right)425$$

$$= \$375$$

b) Estimate of the standard error of the mean:

$$S_{\bar{X}_{st}} = \sqrt{\left(\frac{1}{N^2}\right)\sum_{h=1}^{3}N_h(N_h - n_h)\frac{s_h^2}{n_h}} = \sqrt{\left(\frac{1}{475^2}\right)19,390,972}$$

$$= 9.27$$

c) Approximate 95% confidence interval for the mean annual dental expense:

$$\bar{X}_{st} \pm 2s_{\bar{X}_{st}} = 375 \pm 2(9.27) = 356.46 \text{ to } 393.54$$

An approximate 95% confidence interval for the mean annual family dental expense is $356.46 to $393.54.

Now, we will use Excel to compute our estimates.

Formula Worksheet:

	A	B	C	D	E	F	G
1	Stra-tum	Mean	Std. Dev.	Popul. Size	Strat. Size	Partial Calculations for Std. Dev.	Mean
2	< 30	250	75	100	30	=(D2/$D$5)*B2	=D2*(D2-E2)*(C2^2/E2)
3	30-49	400	100	250	45	=(D3/$D$5)*B3	=D3*(D3-E3)*(C3^2/E3)
4	> 50	425	130	125	30	=(D4/$D$5)*B4	=D4*(D4-E4)*(C4^2/E4)
5			Total			=SUM(F2:F4)	=SUM(G2:G4)
6							
7			Standard Error of Mean			=SQRT(1/D5^2*G5)	
8			Bound on Sampling Error			=2*F7	
9			Pt. Estimate (Pop.Mean)			=F5	
10			Lower Limit (Pop.Mean)			=F9-F8	
11			Upper Limit (Pop.Mean)			=F9+F8	

Value Worksheet:

	A	B	C	D	E	F	G
1	Stra-tum	Mean	Std. Dev.	Popul. Size	Strat. Size	Partial Calculations for Std. Dev.	Mean
2	< 30	250	75	100	30	52.6316	1,312,500.00
3	30-49	400	100	250	45	210.5263	11,388,888.89
4	> 50	425	130	125	30	111.8421	6,689,583.33
5			Total	475	105	375	19,390,972.22
6							
7			Standard Error of Mean			9.2706	
8			Bound on Sampling Error			18.5411	
9			Pt. Estimate (Pop.Mean)			375	
10			Lower Limit (Pop.Mean)			356.4589	
11			Upper Limit (Pop.Mean)			393.5411	

EXAMPLE 5

Stratified Simple Random Sampling: Population Total Estimates

Refer again to the Mill Creek Co. data in Example 4.

a) Estimate the total family dental expense (for all the employees).

b) Develop an approximate 95% confidence interval for the total family dental expense.

SOLUTION 5

First, we will manually compute the estimates.

a) Point estimate of the total family expense for all employees:
$$\hat{X} = N\bar{x}_{st} = 475(375) = 178,125 = \$178,125$$

b) Approximate 95% confidence interval for the total family expense for all employees:
$$\hat{X} \pm 2Ns_{\bar{x}_{st}} = 178,125 \pm 2(475)(9.27) = 178,125 \pm 8,807$$
$$= \$169,318 \text{ to } \$186,932$$

Now, we ill use Excel to compute the estimates.

Formula Worksheet:

	A	B	C	D	E	F	G
1	Stra-tum	Mean	Std. Dev.	Popul. Size	Strat. Size	Partial Calculations for Std. Dev.	Mean
2	< 30	250	75	100	30	=(D2/$D$5)*B2	=D2*(D2-E2)*(C2^2/E2)
3	30-49	400	100	250	45	=(D3/$D$5)*B3	=D3*(D3-E3)*(C3^2/E3)
4	> 50	425	130	125	30	=(D4/$D$5)*B4	=D4*(D4-E4)*(C4^2/E4)
5			Total	=SUM(D2:D4)	=SUM(E2:E4)	=SUM(F2:F4)	=SUM(G2:G4)
6							
7					Standard Error of Total	=D5*SQRT(1/D5^2*G5)	
8					Bound on Sampling Error	=2*F7	
9					Pt. Estimate (Pop.Total)	=D5*F5	
10					Lower Limit (Pop.Total)	=F9-F8	
11					Upper Limit (Pop.Total)	=F9+F8	

Value Worksheet:

	A	B	C	D	E	F	G
1	Stra-tum	Mean	Std. Dev.	Popul. Size	Strat. Size	Partial Calculations for Std. Dev.	Mean
2	< 30	250	75	100	30	52.6316	1,312,500.00
3	30-49	400	100	250	45	210.5263	11,388,888.89
4	> 50	425	130	125	30	111.8421	6,689,583.33
5			Total	475	105	375	19,390,972.22
6							
7					Standard Error of Total	4,403.52	
8					Bound on Sampling Error	8,807.04	
9					Pt. Estimate (Pop.Total)	178,125.00	
10					Lower Limit (Pop.Total)	169,317.96	
11					Upper Limit (Pop.Total)	186,932.04	

EXAMPLE 6

Stratified Simple Random Sampling: Population Proportion Estimates

Refer again to the Mill Creek Co. data in Example 4.

a) Estimate the population proportion that are married.

b) Estimate the standard error of the proportion married.

c) Estimate an approximate 95% confidence interval for the population proportion married.

SOLUTION 6

a) Point estimate of the proportion married:

$$\bar{p}_{st} = \sum_{h=1}^{3}\left(\frac{N_h}{N}\right)\bar{p}_h = \left(\frac{100}{475}\right).6 + \left(\frac{250}{475}\right).7 + \left(\frac{125}{475}\right).68 = .6737$$

b) Estimate of the standard error of the proportion:

$$s_{\bar{p}_{st}} = \sqrt{\left(\frac{1}{N^2}\right)\sum_{h=1}^{3}N_h(N_h - n_h)\frac{\bar{p}_h(1-\bar{p}_h)}{n_h - 1}} = \sqrt{\left(\frac{1}{475^2}\right)391.637}$$

$$= .0417$$

c) Approximate 95% confidence interval for the proportion:

$$\bar{p}_{st} \pm 2s_{\bar{p}_{st}} = .6737 \pm 2(.0417) = .5903 \text{ to } .7571$$

EXAMPLE 7

Cluster Sampling: Population Mean Estimates

There are 40 high schools in Cooper County. School officials are interested in the effect of participation in athletics on academic preparation for college.

A cluster sample of 5 schools has been taken and a questionnaire administered to all the seniors on the football team at those schools. There are a total of 1200 high school seniors in the county playing football. Below are data obtained from the questionnaire.

School	Number of Players	Average SAT Score	Number Planning to Attend College
1	45	840	15
2	20	980	16
3	30	905	12
4	38	880	18
5	40	970	23
Total	173		84

a) Estimate the population mean SAT score.

b) Estimate the standard error of the mean SAT score.

c) Develop an approximate 95% confidence interval for the mean SAT score.

SOLUTION 7

First, we will manually compute the estimates.

a) Point estimate of the population mean SAT score:

$$\bar{X}_c = \frac{\sum\limits_{i=1}^{5} x_i}{\sum\limits_{i=1}^{5} M_i} = \frac{45(840) + 20(980) + \dots + 40(970)}{45 + 20 + 30 + 38 + 40} = 906$$

b) Estimate of standard error of the population mean:

$$s_{\bar{x}_c} = \sqrt{\left(\frac{N-n}{Nn\bar{M}^2}\right)\frac{\sum\limits_{i=1}^{5}(x_i - \bar{x}_c M_i)^2}{n-1}}$$

$$= \sqrt{\left(\frac{1200 - 173}{1200(173)(30)^2}\right)\frac{18{,}541{,}944}{5 - 1}} = 5.0478$$

c) Approximate 95% confidence interval estimate of the population mean SAT score:

$$\bar{X}_c \pm 2s_{\bar{x}_c} = 906 \pm 2(5.0478) = 896 \text{ to } 916$$

Now, we will use Excel to compute the estimates.

Formula Worksheet:

	A	B	C	D	E	F
1	School (i)	Players (M$_i$)	Avg. Score	Tot. Score (x$_i$)	(x$_i$-x$_c$(M$_i$))^2	
2	1	45	840	=B2*C2	=(D2-$D$8*B2)^2	
3	2	20	980	=B3*C3	=(D3-$D$8*B3)^2	
4	3	30	905	=B4*C4	=(D4-$D$8*B4)^2	
5	4	38	880	=B5*C5	=(D5-$D$8*B5)^2	
6	5	40	970	=B6*C6	=(D6-$D$8*B6)^2	
7	Total	=SUM(B2:B6)		=SUM(D2:D6)	=SUM(E2:E6)	
8			Avg.	=D7/B7		
9	Number of Elements in Popul.				1200	
10	Number of Clusters in Population				40	
11	Average Number of Elements in Cluster				=F9/F10	
12	Number of Clusters in Sample				5	
13	Standard Error of Total				=SQRT((((F9-B7)/(F9*B7*F11^2))*(E7/(F12-1)))	
14	Bound on Sampling Error				=2*F13	
15	Point Estimate (Pop.Mean)				=D7/B7	
16	Lower Limit (Pop.Mean)				=F15-F14	
17	Upper Limit (Pop.Mean)				=F15+F14	

Value Worksheet:

	A	B	C	D	E	F
1	School (i)	Players (M$_i$)	Avg. Score	Tot. Score (x$_i$)	(x$_i$-x$_c$(M$_i$))^2	
2	1	45	840	37800	8,901,427	
3	2	20	980	19600	2,172,642	
4	3	30	905	27150	1,522	
5	4	38	880	33440	998,844	
6	5	40	970	38800	6,492,186	
7	Total	173		156790	18,566,622	
8			Avg.	906.3006		
9	Number of Elements in Popul.				1200	
10	Number of Clusters in Population				40	
11	Average Number of Elements in Cluster				30	
12	Number of Clusters in Sample				5	
13	Standard Error of Total				5.05111	
14	Bound on Sampling Error				10.1022	
15	Point Estimate (Pop.Mean)				906.30	
16	Lower Limit (Pop.Mean)				896.20	
17	Upper Limit (Pop.Mean)				916.40	

EXAMPLE 8

Cluster Sampling: Population Total Estimates

Refer again to the Cooper County school data in Example 7.

a) Estimate the population total SAT score (for all 1200 students).

b) Estimate the standard error of the population total SAT score.

c) Develop an approximate 95% confidence interval for the population total SAT score.

SOLUTION 8

a) Point estimate of the population total SAT score:
$$\hat{X} = M\bar{x}_c = 1200(906) = 1,087,200$$

b) Estimate of the standard error of the point estimate of population total:
$$s_{\hat{X}} = Ms_{\bar{x}_c} = 1200(5.0478) = 6,057.36$$

c) Approximate 95% confidence interval estimate of the population total SAT score:
$$M\bar{x}_c \pm 2s_{\hat{X}} = 1200(906) \pm 2(6,057.36)$$
$$= 1,087,720 \pm 12,114.72$$
$$= 1,075,605.28 \text{ to } 1,099,834.72$$

EXAMPLE 9

Cluster Sampling: Population Proportion Estimates

Refer again to the Cooper County school data in Example 7.

a) Estimate the population proportion that are planning to attend college.

b) Estimate the standard error of the estimate of the proportion planning to attend college.

c) Estimate an approximate 95% confidence interval for the population proportion planning to attend college.

SOLUTION 9

a) Point estimate of population proportion planning to attend college:
$$\bar{p}_c = \frac{\sum_{i=1}^{5} a_i}{\sum_{i=1}^{5} M_i} = \frac{84}{173} = .49$$

b) Estimate of standard error of the point estimate of the population proportion:

$$s_{\bar{p}_c} = \sqrt{\left(\frac{N-n}{Nn\overline{M}^2}\right) \frac{\sum_{i=1}^{n}(a_i - \bar{p}_c M_i)^2}{n-1}}$$

$$s_{\bar{p}_c} = \sqrt{\left(\frac{1200-173}{1200(173)(30)^2}\right) \frac{(15 - .49(45))^2 + ... + (23 - .49(40))^2}{5-1}}$$

$$s_{\bar{p}_c} = .0141368$$

c) Approximate 95% confidence interval estimate of the population proportion planning college:

$$\bar{p}_c \pm 2s_{\bar{p}_c} = .49 \pm 2(.0141368) = .49 \pm .0282736$$
$$= .4617264 \text{ to } .5182736$$

EXERCISES

EXERCISE 1

Simple Random Sampling: Population Total Estimates

Currently, the residents of Vista West, a 650-unit apartment complex, are individually billed by the utility company for their gas and electricity usage. The owner of Vista West is considering eliminating the individual gas and electric meters and providing the utilities for "free" (after he increases everyone's rent by an across-the-board amount).

A random sample of 50 apartments was selected and the average monthly utility (gas and electric) expense for each apartment is shown below.

91	78	93	57	75	52	99	80	73	62
71	69	72	89	66	75	79	75	72	76
104	74	62	68	97	105	77	65	80	109
85	97	88	68	83	68	71	69	67	74
62	82	98	101	79	105	79	69	62	73

a) Estimate the total utility expense for the population (all residents).

b) Estimate the standard error of the population total.

c) Develop an approximate 95% confidence interval for the total utility expense.

EXERCISE 2

Simple Random Sampling: Population Proportion Estimates

Refer again to the Vista West apartment problem in Exercise 1, specifically part (c). For the sample of size 50, the bound on the error of the estimate of the total utility expense was $2,432.46. What is the appropriate sample size for a bound of $2,000.00 on the error of the estimate of the total utility expense?

EXERCISE 3

Simple Random Sampling: Determining the Sample Size

Refer again to the Vista West apartment problem in Exercise 1. The sample of 50 residents (from a total of 650 residents) were asked if they were in favor of paying $75.00 more per month for rent and having the landlord pay their gas and electric bill. Thirty seven of the 50 residents replied "yes."

c) Estimate the population proportion favoring the utility proposal.

d) Estimate the standard error of the proportion.

c) Estimate an approximate 95% confidence interval for the population proportion favoring the utility proposal.

EXERCISE 4

Stratified Simple Random Sampling: Population Mean Estimates

Solectrix, a contract assembler of electronic components, has used stratified simple random sampling to obtain demographic and retirement fund contribution information pertaining to its employees.

The population of employees has been divided into 3 strata on the basis of job classification: manager, assembler, and clerk. The sample data are shown below.

| | | | Monthly Retirement Fund Contribution | | Proportion |
Stratum	N_h	n_h	Mean	Std.Dev.	Married
Managers	50	10	$350	$75	.70
Assemblers	625	70	100	30	.40
Clerks	125	20	150	45	.35
	800	100			

a) Estimate the mean monthly retirement fund contribution of an employee.

b) Estimate the standard error of the mean.

c) Develop an approximate 95% confidence interval for the mean monthly retirement fund contribution.

EXERCISE 5

Stratified Simple Random Sampling: Population Total Estimates

Refer again to the Solectrix data in Exercise 4.

a) Estimate the total workforce retirement fund contribution.

b) Develop an approximate 95% confidence interval for the total workforce retirement fund contribution.

EXERCISE 6

Stratified Simple Random Sampling: Population Proportion Estimates

Refer again to the Solectrix data in Exercise 4.

a) Estimate the population proportion that are married.

b) Estimate the standard error of the proportion married.

c) Estimate an approximate 95% confidence interval for the population proportion married.

EXERCISE 7

Cluster Sampling: Population Mean Estimates

There are 35 student chapters of the American Society of System Analysts (ASSA) at universities throughout the U.S. Officials at ASSA headquarters are interested in learning more about the profile of its student membership.

A cluster sample of 4 student chapters has been taken and a questionnaire administered to all the members at those schools. There are a total of 1300 student chapters nationwide. Below are data obtained from the questionnaire.

Student Chapter	Number of Members	Avg. Number of Credit Hours	Number Planning to Attend Grad. Sch.
1	55	90	9
2	20	104	3
3	40	96	9
4	35	102	6
Total	150		27

a) Estimate the population mean number of credit hours.

b) Estimate the standard error of the mean number of credit hours.

c) Develop an approximate 95% confidence interval for the mean number of credit hours.

EXERCISE 8

Cluster Sampling: Population Total Estimates

Refer again to the ASSA student chapters data in Exercise 7.

a) Estimate the population total number of credit hoursl (for the 1300 ASSA students).

b) Estimate the standard error of the population total number of credit hours.

c) Develop an approximate 95% confidence interval for the population total number of credit hours.

EXERCISE 9

Cluster Sampling: Population Proportion Estimates

Refer again to the ASSA student chapters data in Exercise 7.

a) Estimate the population proportion that are planning to attend graduate school.

b) Estimate the standard error of the estimate of the proportion planning to attend graduate school.

c) Estimate an approximate 95% confidence interval for the population proportion planning to attend graduate school.

SELF-TEST

TRUE/FALSE

___ 1. The development of the frame precedes sampling.

___ 2. An advantage of cluster sampling is that it generally requires a smaller total sample size than simple random sampling.

___ 3. Systematic sampling is a nonprobabilistic method of sampling.

___ 4. Interviewer error is an example of sampling error.

___ 5. A sampling unit may include several elements.

FILL-IN-THE-BLANK

1. If inferences from a sample are to be valid, the sampled population must be representative of the _____ population.

2. _____ error can be minimized by proper interviewer training, good questionnaire design, and careful coding and transferring of the data.

3. The best choice of a sample size usually involves a trade-off between cost and _____.

4. In cluster sampling, the primary issue in choosing a sample size is selecting the number of _____.

5. If it is necessary to provide statements about the precision of estimates made, a _____ sampling method must be used.

MULTIPLE CHOICE

___ 1. A probability sampling method in which we randomly select one of the first k elements and then select every k th element thereafter is
   a) stratified random sampling
   b) cluster sampling
   c) systematic sampling
   d) convenience sampling

___ 2. The standard deviation of a point estimator is the
   a) standard error
   b) sample statistic
   c) point estimate
   d) sampling error

____ 3. Which one of the following sampling methods is classified as a nonprobability sampling method?
   a) stratified random sampling
   b) cluster sampling
   c) systematic sampling
   d) convenience sampling

____ 4. Sampling error can be minimized by
   a) training the interviewers
   b) properly choosing a sample design
   c) pretesting the questionnaire
   d) aligning the sample population with the target population

____ 5. A bound on the sampling error equal to two times the standard error of the point estimator will provide an interval estimate with what approximate level of confidence?
   a) 90%
   b) 95%
   c) 97.5%
   d) 99%

ANSWERS

EXERCISES

1) a) $\hat{X} = \$51,025$
   b) $s_{\hat{x}} = \$1,216.23$
   c) $\$48,592.54$ to $\$53,457.46$

2) $n = 71.33 = 72$

3) a) $\bar{p} = 37 / 50 = .74$
   b) $s_{\bar{p}} = .060204$
   c) $.61959$ to $.86041$

4) a) $\bar{X}_{st} = 123.4375$
   b) $s_{\bar{X}_{st}} = 3.2867$
   c) $\$116.84$ to $\$130.01$

5) a) $\hat{X} = \$98,750.00$
   b) $\$93,491.28$ to $\$104,008.72$

6) a) $\bar{p}_{st} = .2408$

   b) $s_{\bar{p}_{st}} = .046954$

   c) .1469 to .3347

7) a) $\bar{x}_c = 96.27$

   b) $s_{\bar{x}_c} = .51078$

   c) 95.25 to 97.29 credit hours

8) a) $\hat{X} = 125,151$

   b) $s_{\hat{X}} = 664.014$

   c) 123,822.97 to 126,479.03

9) a) $\bar{p}_c = .180$

   b) $s_{\bar{p}_c} = .01537$

   c) .14926 to .21074 (or about 15% to 21%)

TRUE/FALSE

1) True
2) False
3) False
4) False
5) True

FILL-IN-THE-BLANK

1) targeted
2) nonsampling
3) precision
4) clusters
5) probabilistic

MULTIPLE CHOICE

1) c
2) a
3) d
4) b
5) b

CHAPTER 19

Statistical Methods
for Quality Control

Statistical Process Control

Acceptance Sampling

LEARNING OBJECTIVES

1. Learn about the importance of quality control and how statistical methods can assist in the quality control process.

2. Learn about acceptance sampling procedures.

3. Know the difference between consumer's risk and producer's risk.

4. Be able to use the binomial probability distribution to develop acceptance sampling plans.

5. Know what is meant by multiple sampling plans.

6. Be able to construct quality control charts and understand how they are used for statistical process control.

7. Know the definitions of the following terms:

producer's risk	assignable causes
consumer's risk	common causes
acceptance sampling	control charts
acceptable criterion	upper control limit
operating characteristic curve	lower control limit

REVIEW

Quality Terminology
- Quality is "the totality of features and characteristics of a product or service that bears on its ability to satisfy given needs."
- Quality assurance refers to the entire system of policies, procedures, and guidelines established by an organization to achieve and maintain quality.
- The objective of quality engineering is to include quality in the design of products and processes and to identify potential quality problems prior to production.
- Quality control consists of making a series of inspections and measurements to determine whether quality standards are being met.

Statistical Process Control (SPC)
- The goal of SPC is to determine whether the process can be continued or whether it should be adjusted to achieve a desired quality level.
- If the variation in the quality of the production output is due to assignable causes (operator error, worn-out tooling, bad raw material, . . .) the process should be adjusted or corrected as soon as possible.
- If the variation in output is due to common causes (variation in materials, humidity, temperature, . . .) which the manager cannot control, the process does not need to be adjusted.

SPC Hypotheses
- SPC procedures are based on hypothesis-testing methodology.
- The <u>null hypothesis</u> H_0 is formulated in terms of the production process being in control.
- The <u>alternative hypothesis</u> H_a is formulated in terms of the process being out of control.
- As with other hypothesis-testing procedures, both a <u>Type I error</u> (adjusting an in-control process) and a <u>Type II error</u> (allowing an out-of-control process to continue) are possible.

Control Charts
- SPC uses graphical displays known as <u>control charts</u> to monitor a production process.
- Control charts provide a basis for deciding whether the variation in the output is due to common causes (in control) or assignable causes (out of control).
- Two important lines on a control chart are the <u>upper control limit</u> (UCL) and <u>lower control limit</u> (LCL).
- These lines are chosen so that when the process is <u>in</u> control, there will be a high probability that the sample finding will be between the two lines.
- Values outside of the control limits provide strong evidence that the process is <u>out</u> of control.
- Patterns of data within the control limits can also indicate potential quality control problems and suggest that corrective action may be warranted.
- Over time, more and more data points will be added to the control chart.
- Every time a point is plotted on the control chart, we are carrying out a hypothesis test.
- The most important use of a control chart is in <u>improving the process</u>.

Types of Control Charts
- An $\bar{x}$ chart is used to monitor the mean of the measurements in a sample.
- An <u>R chart</u> is used to monitor the range of the measurements in the sample.
- A <u>p chart</u> is used to monitor the proportion defective in the sample.
- An <u>np chart</u> is used to monitor the number of defective items in the sample.
- The major difference among the four above charts is what the vertical axis measures.

$\bar{x}$ Chart
- An $\bar{x}$ <u>chart</u> is used if the quality of the output is measured in terms of a <u>variable</u> such as length, weight, temperature, and so on.
- The decision to continue or to adjust the production process is based on the mean value, $\bar{x}$, found in a sample of the output.

Control Limits for an $\bar{x}$ Chart: Process μ and σ Known
- The general practice is to define as reasonable any value of $\bar{x}$ that is within 3 standard deviations above or below the mean value.
- The upper control limit (UCL) and lower control limit (LCL) are:
$$UCL = \mu + 3\sigma_{\bar{x}}$$
$$LCL = \mu - 3\sigma_{\bar{x}}$$
- If a value of $\bar{x}$ is within the LCL-to-UCL interval, we will assume that the process is in control.

Control Limits for an $\bar{x}$ Chart: Process μ and σ Unknown
- Usually, the process mean and standard deviation must be estimated by using samples that are selected from the process when it is assumed to be operating in control.
- The upper control limit (UCL) and lower control limit (LCL) are:

$$UCL = \bar{\bar{x}} + A_2\bar{R}$$
$$LCL = \bar{\bar{x}} - A_2\bar{R}$$

where: $\bar{x}$ = overall sample mean
   $\bar{R}$ = average range
   A_2 = a constant that depends on n; taken from <u>Factors for Control Charts</u> table

- We can think of A_2 as a multiplier (coefficient) for $\bar{R}$ to make it approximately equal to $3\sigma_{\bar{x}}$.

Using Excel to Construct an $\bar{x}$ Chart
Assuming the sample data for each of the k samples and the control chart factor A_2 have already been entered in the worksheet, the general steps in constructing an $\bar{x}$ chart are as follows:
- The <u>mean of each sample</u>, $\bar{x}_j$, is computed using the <u>AVERAGE</u> function.
- The <u>overall sample mean</u>, $\bar{\bar{x}}$, is computed using the <u>AVERAGE</u> function.
- The <u>range of each sample</u> is computed using the <u>MAX</u> and <u>MIN</u> functions.
- The <u>average range</u>, $\bar{R}$, is computed using the <u>AVERAGE</u> function.
- The <u>lower control limit</u>, LCL, is computed by formula using $\bar{\bar{x}}$, A_2, and $\bar{R}$.
- The <u>upper control limit</u>, UCL, is computed by formula using using $\bar{\bar{x}}$, A_2, and $\bar{R}$.
- The <u>control chart</u> is produced by using the <u>Chart Wizard</u> tool and selecting <u>XY Scatter Chart with Data Points Connected by Lines</u>.
- Four lines, each consisting of k plotted points, are drawn on the chart:
  - The <u>UCL</u> is a straight, horizontal line.
  - The <u>center line</u> is a straight, horizontal line representing $\bar{\bar{x}}$.
  - The <u>LCL</u> is a straight, horizontal line.
  - The <u>sample means</u>, $\bar{x}_j$, are represented by an upward/downward bending line.
- The resulting chart will need to be edited in terms of size, scales, fonts, and labels to satisfy your own preferences.

R Chart
- An *R* chart is used to monitor and control the <u>variability</u> of a process.
- It is more common to monitor the variability of the process by using the <u>range</u> instead of the standard deviation because the <u>range is easier to compute</u>.
- If the sample size is greater than 10, a standard deviation chart (<u>s chart</u>) is generally preferred.
- If the *R* chart indicates that the process is out of control, the $\bar{x}$ Chart should not be interpreted until the *R* chart indicates the process variability is in control.

Control Limits for an *R* Chart
- The upper control limit (UCL) and lower control limit (LCL) are:

$$UCL = \bar{R}D_4$$

$$LCL = \bar{R}D_3$$

where: D_3 and D_4 are constants that depend on *n*; taken from <u>Factors for Control Charts</u> table

Using Excel to Construct an *R* Chart
Assuming the sample data for each of the *k* samples and the control chart factors D_3 and D_4 have already been entered in the worksheet, the general steps in constructing an *R* chart are as follows:
- The <u>range of each sample</u> is compute using the <u>MAX</u> and <u>MIN</u> functions.
- The <u>average range</u>, $\bar{R}$, is computed using the <u>AVERAGE</u> function.
- The <u>lower control limit</u>, LCL, is computed by formula using $\bar{R}$ and D_3.
- The <u>upper control limit</u>, UCL, is computed by formula using $\bar{R}$ and D_4.
- The <u>control chart</u> is produced by using the <u>Chart Wizard</u> tool and selecting <u>XY Scatter Chart with Data Points Connected by Lines</u>.
- Four lines, each consisting of *k* plotted points, are drawn on the chart:
  - The <u>UCL</u> is a straight, horizontal line.
  - The <u>center line</u> is a straight, horizontal line representing $\bar{R}$.
  - The <u>LCL</u> is a straight, horizontal line.
  - The <u>sample ranges</u>, R_j, are represented by an upward/downward bending line.
- The resulting chart will need to be edited in terms of size, scales, fonts, and labels to satisfy your own preferences.

p Chart
- Control charts that are based on data indicating the presence of a defect or the number of defects are <u>attribute control charts</u>.
- A *p* chart is an attribute control chart. It is used to monitor the proportion of defective items.
- The decision to continue or to adjust the production process will be based on $\bar{p}$, the proportion of defective items found in a sample of the output.

Control Limits for a *p* Chart
- The sampling distribution of $\bar{p}$ can be used to determine the variation that can be expected in $\bar{p}$ values for a process that is in control.
- The standard deviation of $\bar{p}$ is called the <u>standard error of the proportion</u> and is denoted as $\sigma_{\bar{p}}$.
- <u>If *p* is known</u>, the formula for $\sigma_{\bar{p}}$ is:

$$\sigma_{\bar{p}} = \sqrt{\frac{p(1-p)}{n}}$$

- If p is unknown, we treat all the data as one large sample and compute the overall sample proportion, denoted here as $\bar{\bar{p}}$. In this case, the formula for $\sigma_{\bar{p}}$ is:

$$\sigma_{\bar{p}} = \sqrt{\frac{\bar{\bar{p}}(1-\bar{\bar{p}})}{n}}$$

- The sampling distribution of $\bar{p}$ can be approximated by a normal distribution if the following conditions are met: $np \geq 5$ and $n(1-p) \geq 5$.
- The upper control limit (UCL) and lower control limit (LCL) are:
- If p is known: UCL $= p + 3\sigma_{\bar{p}}$ and LCL $= p - 3\sigma_{\bar{p}}$
- If p is unknown: UCL $= \bar{\bar{p}} + 3\sigma_{\bar{p}}$ and LCL $= \bar{\bar{p}} - 3\sigma_{\bar{p}}$

Using Excel to Construct a *p* Chart

Assuming the number of defective items found in each of the k samples and the sample size n have already been entered in the worksheet, the general steps in constructing a p chart are as follows:

- The <u>proportion defective for each sample</u>, $\bar{p}_j$, is computed by formula using n.

- If p is unknown, the <u>overall proportion defective</u>, $\bar{\bar{p}}$, is computed using the <u>AVERAGE</u> function.

- The <u>standard error of the proportion</u>, $\sigma_{\bar{p}}$, is computed by formula using p (if it is known) or $\bar{\bar{p}}$ (if p is unknown) and n.

- The <u>lower control limit</u>, LCL, and <u>upper control limit</u>, UCL, are computed by formulas using p (if it is known) or $\bar{\bar{p}}$ (if p is unknown), $\sigma_{\bar{p}}$, and the constant 3.

- The <u>control chart</u> is produced by using the <u>Chart Wizard</u> tool and selecting <u>XY Scatter Chart with Data Points Connected by Lines</u>.

- Four lines, each consisting of k plotted points, are drawn on the chart:
  - The <u>UCL</u> is a straight, horizontal line.
  - The <u>center line</u> is a straight, horizontal line representing p (if known) or $\bar{\bar{p}}$ (if p is unknown).
  - The <u>LCL</u> is a straight, horizontal line.
  - The <u>sample proportions</u>, $\bar{p}_j$, are represented by an upward/downward bending line.

- The resulting chart will need to be edited in terms of size, scales, fonts, and labels to satisfy your own preferences.

np Chart

- An *np* Chart is an <u>attribute chart</u> developed for the number of defective items observed in a sample.
- The information provided by an *np* chart is equivalent to the information provided by a *p* chart.
- If a particular process is judged to be out of control on the basis of a *p* chart, the same conclusion about the process would result based on an *np* chart.

Control Limits for an *np* Chart

- Whenever the sample size is large ($np \geq 5$ and $n(1-p) \geq 5$), the distribution of the number of defective items observed in a sample size *n* can be approximated by a normal distruibution with mean *np* and standard deviation $\sqrt{np(1-p)}$.
- The upper control limit (UCL) and lower control limit (LCL) are:

$$UCL = np + 3\sqrt{np(1-p)}$$
$$UCL = np - 3\sqrt{np(1-p)}$$

Note: If computed LCL is negative, set LCL = 0

Using Excel to Construct an *np* Chart

Assuming the number of defective items found in each of the *k* samples, the sample size *n*, and the probability, *p*, of observing a defective item when the process is in control have already been entered in the worksheet, the general steps in constructing an *np* chart are as follows:

- The standard deviation of the number of defective items observed in a sample is computed by formula using *n* and *p*.
- The lower control limit, LCL, and upper control limit, UCL, are computed by formulas using *n*, *p*, and the constant 3.
- The control chart is produced by using the Chart Wizard tool and selecting XY Scatter Chart with Data Points Connected by Lines.
- Four lines, each consisting of *k* plotted points, are drawn on the chart:
  - The UCL is a straight, horizontal line.
  - The center line is a straight, horizontal line representing *np*.
  - The LCL is a straight, horizontal line.
  - The number of defective items found in each of the *k* samples are represented by an upward and downward bending line.
- The resulting chart will need to be edited in terms of size, scales, fonts, and labels to satisfy your own preferences.

Interpretation of Control Charts

- The location and pattern of points in a control chart enable us to determine, with a small probability of error, whether a process is in statistical control.
- A primary indication that a process may be out of control is a data point outside the control limits.
- Certain patterns of points within the control limits can be warning signals of quality problems. These patterns include: a large number of points on one side of center line, or six or seven points in a row that indicate either an increasing or decreasing trend.

Acceptance Sampling

- Acceptance sampling is a statistical method that enables us to base the accept-reject decision on the inspection of a sample of items from the lot.
- A lot might be an incoming shipment of raw material or purchased parts for example.
- Acceptance sampling has advantages over 100% inspection including: less expensive, less product damage, fewer inspectors involved, . . . and more.

- The general steps of acceptance sampling are:
    - After a lot is received, a sample is selected for inspection.
    - The inspection results are compared to quality specifications.
    - If the quality is satisfactory, the lot is accepted.
    - If the quality is not satisfactory, the lot is rejected and managers must decide the disposition of the lot.
- Acceptance sampling is based on hypothesis-testing methodology.
- The hypothesis are: H_0: Good-quality   and H_a: Poor-quality lot
- As with other hypothesis-testing procedures, both a <u>Type I error</u> (rejecting a good-quality lot) and a <u>Type II error</u> (accepting a poor-quality lot) are possible.
- Because the probability of a Type I error creates a risk for the producer of the lot, it is known as the <u>producer's risk</u>.
- Because the probability of a Type II error creates a risk for the consumer of the lot, it is known as the <u>consumer's risk</u>.

Probability of Accepting a Lot
- The number of defective items in a sample of n from a large lot has a binomial probability distribution.
- The probability of x defectives in the sample is:

$$f(x) = \frac{n!}{x!(n-x)!} p^x (1-p)^{(n-x)}$$

where: p = proportion of defective items in lot
- A graph of the probability of accepting the lot versus the percent defective in the lot, for a given n value and given c value, is called the <u>operating characteristic (OC) curve</u>.

Selecting an Acceptance Sampling Plan
- In formulating a plan, managers specify two values for the fraction defective in the lot.
    - α = the probability that a lot with p_0 defectives will be rejected.
    - β = the probability that a lot with p_1 defectives will be accepted.
- Then the values of n and c are selected that result in an acceptance sampling plan that comes closest to meeting both the α and β requirements specified.

Multiple Sampling Plans
- A <u>multiple sampling plan</u> uses two or more stages of sampling.
- At each stage the <u>decision possibilities</u> are: a) stop sampling and accept the lot, b) stop sampling and reject the lot, or c) continue sampling.
- The specifics of the plan are as follows:
    - Initially a sample of n_1 items is selected.
    - If the number of defective items x_1 is less than or equal to c_1, accept the lot.
    - If x_1 is greater or equal to c_2, reject the lot.
    - If x_1 is between c_1 and c_2, select a second sample of n_2 items.
    - Determine the total number of defectives from the first sample (x_1) and the second sample (x_2).
    - If $x_1 + x_2 \leq c_3$, accept the lot; otherwise reject the lot.
- Multiple sampling plans often result in a <u>smaller total sample size</u> than single-sample plans with the same Type I error and Type II error probabilities.

CONCEPT	EXAMPLES	EXERCISES
Control Charts		
$\bar{x}$ Chart: μ and σ Known	1	1
R Chart	②	2
$\bar{x}$ Chart	③	2
p Chart	④	3
np Chart	⑤	3
Acceptance Sampling		
Probability of Accepting a Lot	6	4
Selecting an Acceptance Sampling Plan	7	4
Constructing an OC Curve	⑧	5
Producer's Risk and Consumer's Risk	6,7,8	4,5

◯ Excel Used

EXAMPLES

EXAMPLE 1

$\bar{x}$ Chart: μ and σ Known

The weight of bags of cement filled by Granite Rock Company's packaging process is normally distributed with a mean of 50 pounds and a standard deviation of 1.5 pounds when the process is in control. What should the control limits be for a sample mean, $\bar{x}$, chart if 9 bags are sampled at a time?

SOLUTION 1

The sampling distribution (mean and standard deviation) of $\bar{x}$ is used to determine what values of $\bar{x}$ are reasonable if the process is in control. Because the filling weights (x) are normally distributed, the sampling distribution of $\bar{x}$ is normal for any sample size. Thus, the sampling distribution of $\bar{x}$ is a normal probability distribution with mean μ and standard deviation $\sigma_{\bar{x}}$

The standard error of the mean, $\sigma_{\bar{x}}$, is a function of the population standard deviation, σ, and the sample size, n. The standard error of the mean is computed as follows:

$$\sigma_{\bar{x}} = \sigma / \sqrt{n} = 1.5 / \sqrt{9} = 0.5$$

The general practice in quality control is to define as reasonable any value of $\bar{x}$ that is within 3 standard deviations above or below the mean value of $\bar{x}$. Thus, the upper and lower control limits for the $\bar{x}$ chart for Granite Rock Co. are computed as follows:

$$UCL = \mu + 3\sigma_{\bar{x}} = 50 + 3(.5) = \underline{51.5}$$
$$LCL = \mu - 3\sigma_{\bar{x}} = 50 - 3(.5) = \underline{48.5}$$

EXAMPLE 2

R Chart

Granite Rock Company produces masonry cement and packages it in bags that have the label "50 pounds." Granite does not know the true mean and standard deviation for the weights of the output from the bag-filling process. Nevertheless, It wants to develop control charts for monitoring the variation in the weight. Granite has taken twenty 5-bag samples while the process was believed to be in control. The weights of the five bags in each of the twenty samples have been entered into a worksheet as shown below. Construct an appropriate R chart for the bag-filling process..

Data Worksheet:

	A	B	C	D	E	F
1	**Sample**	**Observ. 1**	**Observ. 2**	**Observ. 3**	**Observ. 4**	**Observ. 5**
2	1	50.22	49.91	50.05	50.12	49.79
3	2	50.13	50.09	50.17	50.23	50.04
4	3	50.30	50.11	49.91	49.89	50.09
5	4	49.91	50.20	50.16	50.05	50.24
6	5	50.11	49.89	49.94	50.17	49.88
7	6	49.78	50.07	49.78	49.79	50.04
8	7	49.84	49.92	50.11	50.04	49.81
9	8	50.08	49.88	49.90	49.97	49.78
10	9	49.89	50.10	50.14	49.99	49.90
11	10	50.11	50.16	50.20	50.06	50.06
12	11	49.86	49.79	50.06	50.11	49.97
13	12	49.99	50.03	49.92	50.17	50.19
14	13	50.20	49.81	49.89	49.88	50.11
15	14	49.84	49.97	50.08	50.22	49.82
16	15	50.30	49.83	50.04	49.78	50.23
17	16	50.04	50.19	49.92	50.17	50.01
18	17	49.90	50.16	49.86	49.98	49.83
19	18	49.95	50.02	50.13	49.91	49.89
20	19	50.07	49.85	49.89	50.27	49.78
21	20	50.03	49.94	50.00	49.79	50.07

SOLUTION 2

Using Excel's Chart Wizard

Enter Data: The data for the bag weights for the 20 samples selected by Granite Rock are entered into a worksheet we will call <u>Data</u>. We will refer to the Data worksheet in the process of constructing a second worksheet for developing our R chart. The discussion that follows pertains to the second worksheet.

Enter Functions and Formulas: Column A contains the sample numbers 1-20. Column B contains the formulas needed to compute the range for each sample from the data in cells B2:F21 of the Data worksheet. In these formulas we use the MAX and MIN functions and we refer to cell addresses in the Data worksheet. (Note that the worksheet name followed by an exclamation point, Data!, must precede a cell reference when the cells referred to are in another worksheet.) The AVERAGE function is used in cell B22 to compute the average of the ranges for the 20 samples.

In order to compute the LCL and UCL, we must know D_3 and D_4. These values are obtained from the table below (in the $n = 5$ row) and entered into cells D23 and D24, respectively. The formulas in cells C2:C21 are identical; they compute the LCL by multiplying D_3 (cell D23) times the average range (cell B22). The formulas in cells D2:D21 are also identical; they provide the average range. Finally, the formulas in cell E2:E21 (also identical) are used to compute the UCL by multiplying D_4 (cell D24) times the average range (cell B22).

Factors for x bar and R Control Charts					
n	d_2	A_2	d_3	D_3	D_4
2	1.128	1.880	0.850	0	3.267
3	1.693	1.023	0.888	0	2.574
4	2.059	0.729	0.880	0	2.282
5	2.326	0.577	0.864	0	2.114
6	2.534	0.483	0.848	0	2.004
7	2.704	0.419	0.833	0.076	1.924
8	2.847	0.373	0.820	0.136	1.864
9	2.970	0.337	0.808	0.184	1.816
⋮	⋮	⋮	⋮	⋮	⋮

Formula Worksheet:

	A	B	C	D	E
1	Samp.	*R*	LCL	Mean	UCL
2	1	=MAX(Data!B2:F2)-MIN(Data!B2:F2)	=$D$23*$B$22	=$B$22	=$D$24*$B$22
3	2	=MAX(Data!B3:F3)-MIN(Data!B3:F3)	=$D$23*$B$22	=$B$22	=$D$24*$B$22
4	3	=MAX(Data!B4:F4)-MIN(Data!B4:F4)	=$D$23*$B$22	=$B$22	=$D$24*$B$22
5	4	=MAX(Data!B5:F5)-MIN(Data!B5:F5)	=$D$23*$B$22	=$B$22	=$D$24*$B$22
6	5	=MAX(Data!B6:F6)-MIN(Data!B6:F6)	=$D$23*$B$22	=$B$22	=$D$24*$B$22
20	19	=MAX(Data!B20:F20)-MIN(Data!B20:F20)	=$D$23*$B$22	=$B$22	=$D$24*$B$22
21	20	=MAX(Data!B21:F21)-MIN(Data!B21:F21)	=$D$23*$B$22	=$B$22	=$D$24*$B$22
22	*R*bar	=AVERAGE($B$2:$B$21)			
23			D_3	0	
24			D_4	2.114	

Note: Rows 7-19 are hidden.

Value Worksheet:

	A	B	C	D	E
1	Samp.	*R*	LCL	Mean	UCL
2	1	0.43	0	0.32	0.6807
3	2	0.19	0	0.32	0.6807
4	3	0.41	0	0.32	0.6807
5	4	0.33	0	0.32	0.6807
6	5	0.29	0	0.32	0.6807
20	19	0.49	0	0.32	0.6807
21	20	0.28	0	0.32	0.6807
22	*R*bar	0.322			
23			D_3	0	
24			D_4	2.114	

We see in the resulting worksheet above the values for the upper limit, lower limit, and center line in our *R* chart. Now we are ready to draw the *R* chart.

Apply Tools: We will use Excel's Chart Wizard to construct the *R* chart from the data in cells A2:E21 of our worksheet.

Constructing an *R* Chart

Step 1 Select cells A2:E21
Step 2 Select the **Chart Wizard** button on main toolbar
Step 3 When the Chart Wizard-Step 1 0f 4-**Chart Type** dialog box appears:
Choose **XY (Scatter)** in the **Chart Type** list
Choose **Scatter with data points connected by lines** from the Chart Subtype display
Select **Next >**

Step 4 When the Chart Wizard-Step 2 of 4- **Chart Source Data** dialog box appears:
Select **Next >**

Step 5 When the **Chart Wizard-Step 3 of 4-Chart Options** dialog box appears:
Select the **Titles** tab and then
Type **R Chart for Granite Rock Co.** in the **Chart title** box
Type **Sample Number** in the **Value (X)** axis box
Type **Sample Range R** in the **Value (Y)** axis box
Select the **Legend** tab and then
Remove the check in the **Show Legend** box
Select the **Gridlines** tab and then
Remove the check in the **Major Gridlines** box
Select **Next >**

Step 6 When the **Chart Wizard- Step 4 of 4 – Chart Location** dialog box appears:
Specify a location for the chart
Select **Finish**

With practice and patience, you can alter the chart initially produced by Excel to look like the one below or to suit your personal preferences. A right-click on almost any item in the chart will bring up a menu of alteration options.

R Chart:

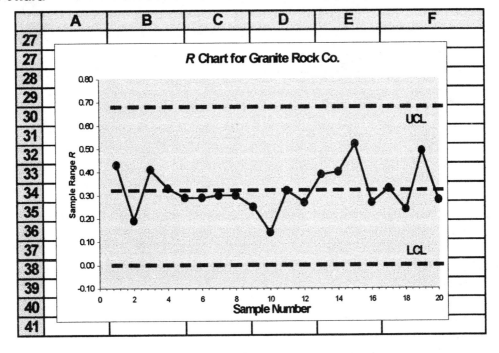

EXAMPLE 3

$\bar{x}$ Chart

Refer again to the background information and data for the Granite Rock Co. in Example 2. Construct an appropriate $\bar{x}$ chart for the bag-filling process.

SOLUTION 3

Using Excel's Chart Wizard

Enter Data: The data for the bag weights for the 20 samples selected by Granite Rock are entered into a worksheet we will call <u>Data</u>. We will refer to the Data worksheet in the process of constructing a second worksheet for developing our $\bar{x}$ chart. The discussion that follows pertains to the second worksheet. Our second worksheet is a continuation of the worksheet we developed for Example 2; for this reason we start here with row 28.

Enter Functions and Formulas: Column A contains the sample numbers 1-20. Column B contains the formulas needed to compute the mean for each sample from the data in cells B2:F21 of the Data worksheet. In these formulas we use the AVERAGE function and we refer to cell addresses in the Data worksheet. (Note that the worksheet name followed by an exclamation point, Data!, must precede a cell reference when the cells referred to are in another worksheet.) The AVERAGE function is used in cell B49 to compute the average of the 20 sample means.

In order to compute the LCL and UCL, we must know A_2. This value (0.577) is obtained from the Control Chart Factors table (shown in Solution 2) and entered into cell D50. The formulas in cells C29:C48 are identical; they compute the LCL by multiplying A_2 (cell D50) times the overall sample mean (cell B49). The formulas in cells D29:D48 are also identical; they provide the overall sample mean. Finally, the formulas in cell E29:E48 (also identical) are used to compute the UCL by multiplying A_2 (cell D50) times the overall sample mean (cell B49).

Formula Worksheet:

	A	B	C	D	E
28	Sample	*x* bar	LCL	Mean	UCL
29	1	=AVERAGE(Data!B2:F2)	=$B$49-$D$50*$B$22	=$D$50	=$B$49+$D$50*$B$22
30	2	=AVERAGE(Data!B3:F3)	=$B$49-$D$50*$B$22	=$D$50	=$B$49+$D$50*$B$22
31	3	=AVERAGE(Data!B4:F4)	=$B$49-$D$50*$B$22	=$D$50	=$B$49+$D$50*$B$22
32	4	=AVERAGE(Data!B5:F5)	=$B$49-$D$50*$B$22	=$D$50	=$B$49+$D$50*$B$22
33	5	=AVERAGE(Data!B6:F6)	=$B$49-$D$50*$B$22	=$D$50	=$B$49+$D$50*$B$22
47	19	=AVERAGE(Data!B20:F20)	=$B$49-$D$50*$B$22	=$D$50	=$B$49+$D$50*$B$22
48	20	=AVERAGE(Data!B21:F21)	=$B$49-$D$50*$B$22	=$D$50	=$B$49+$D$50*$B$22
49	Mean	=AVERAGE(B29:B48)			
50				A_2 0.577	

Note: Rows 34-46 are hidden.

Value Worksheet:

	A	B	C	D	E
28	Sample	x bar	LCL	Mean	UCL
29	1	50.018	49.824	50.01	50.195
30	2	50.132	49.824	50.01	50.195
31	3	50.060	49.824	50.01	50.195
32	4	50.112	49.824	50.01	50.195
33	5	49.998	49.824	50.01	50.195
47	19	49.972	49.824	50.01	50.195
48	20	49.966	49.824	50.01	50.195
49	Mean	50.010			
50					
51				A_2 0.577	

We see in the resulting worksheet above the values for the upper limit, lower limit, and center line for our $\bar{x}$ chart. Now we are ready to draw the $\bar{x}$ chart.

Apply Tools: We will use Excel's Chart Wizard to construct the $\bar{x}$ chart from the data in cells A29:E48 of our worksheet. The steps to follow are nearly identical to those we outlined in Solution 2 where we were constructing an R chart. Refer to Solution 2 for details. You can alter the chart initially produced by Excel to look like the one below or to suit your personal preferences. A right-click on almost any item in the chart will bring up a menu of alteration options.

$\bar{x}$ Chart:

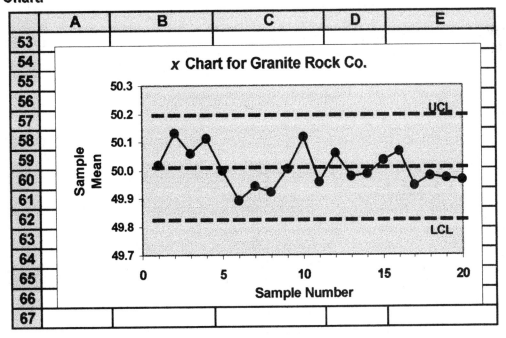

EXAMPLE 4

p Chart

Every check cashed or deposited at Norwest Bank must be encoded with the amount of the check before it can begin the Federal Reserve clearing process. The accuracy of the check encoding process is of upmost importance. If there is any discrepancy between the amount a check is made out for and the encoded amount, the check is defective.

Twenty samples, each consisting of 250 checks, were selected and examined when the encoding process was known to be operating correctly. The number of defective checks found in the twenty samples are listed below.

4	1	5	3	2	7	4	5	2	3
2	8	5	3	6	4	2	5	3	6

Construct a p chart for the check encoding process, assuming each sample has 250 checks.

SOLUTION 4

Using Excel's Chart Wizard

Enter Data: The identifying sample number and the number of defective checks for the 20 samples selected by Norwest Bank are entered into the worksheet in columns A and B.

Enter Functions and Formulas: We compute the proportion of checks that are defective in each sample by entering the formula =B2/250 into cell C2 and then copying it to cells C3:C21. The overall proportion of defective checks for the 20 samples, the estimate of p, is computed by entering the formula =AVERAGE(C2:C21) into cell C22. The estimated standard error of the proportion, $\sigma_{\bar{p}}$, is computed by entering the following formula into cell C23:

$$=SQRT(C22*(1-C22)/250)$$

The formulas in cells D2:D21 are identical; they compute the lower control limit. The LCL generally equals the estimated p <u>minus</u> three times the standard error of the proportion ($C$22-3*$C$23). However, if this calculation results in a negative value, the LCL is set equal to zero. For this reason we use the MAX function to select the greater of the two values: 0 and ($C$22-3*$C$23).

The formulas in cells E2:E21 are also identical; they provide the overall proportion of defective checks. Finally, the formulas in cell F2:F21 (also identical) are used to compute the UCL which equals the estimated p <u>plus</u> three times the standard error of the proportion ($C$22-3*$C$23).

Formula Worksheet:

	A	B	C	D	E	F
1	Sample	Number Defect.	Proportion Defective	LCL	CL	UCL
2	1	4	=B2/250	=MAX(0,$C$22-3*$C$23)	=$C$22	=$C$22+3*$C$23
3	2	1	=B3/250	=MAX(0,$C$22-3*$C$23)	=$C$22	=$C$22+3*$C$23
4	3	5	=B4/250	=MAX(0,$C$22-3*$C$23)	=$C$22	=$C$22+3*$C$23
5	4	3	=B5/250	=MAX(0,$C$22-3*$C$23)	=$C$22	=$C$22+3*$C$23
20	19	3	=B20/250	=MAX(0,$C$22-3*$C$23)	=$C$22	=$C$22+3*$C$23
21	20	6	=B21/250	=MAX(0,$C$22-3*$C$23)	=$C$22	=$C$22+3*$C$23
22	**Estimated *p***		=AVERAGE(C2:C21)			
23	**Estim. Std. Error**		=SQRT(C22*(1-C22)/250)			

Note: Rows 6-19 are hidden.

Value Worksheet:

	A	B	C	D	E	F
1	Sample	Number Defect.	Proportion Defective	LCL	CL	UCL
2	1	4	0.016	0	0.0160	0.0398
3	2	1	0.004	0	0.0160	0.0398
4	3	5	0.020	0	0.0160	0.0398
5	4	3	0.012	0	0.0160	0.0398
20	19	3	0.012	0	0.0160	0.0398
21	20	6	0.024	0	0.0160	0.0398
22	**Estimated *p***		0.016			
23	**Estim. Std. Error**		0.00794			

We see in the resulting worksheet above the values for the upper limit, lower limit, and center line for our *p* chart. Now we are ready to draw the *p* chart.

Apply Tools: We will use Excel's Chart Wizard to construct the *p* chart from the data in cells A2:A21 and C2:C21 of our worksheet. (We will not be graphing the number of defectives data in column B.) The steps to follow are outlined below.

Constructing an *p* Chart

    Step 1 Select cells A2:A21 and D2:F21
    Step 2 Select the **Chart Wizard** button on main toolbar
    Step 3 When the Chart Wizard-Step 1 0f 4-**Chart Type** dialog box appears:
            Choose **XY (Scatter)** in the **Chart Type** list
            Choose **Scatter with data points connected by lines** from the Chart subtype display
            Select **Next >**
    Step 4 When the Chart Wizard-Step 2 of 4- **Chart Source Data** dialog box appears:
            Select **Next >**

Step 5 When the **Chart Wizard-Step 3 of 4-Chart Options** dialog box appears:
        Select the **Titles** tab and then
            Type *p* **Chart for Norwest Bank** in the **Chart title** box
            Type **Sample Number** in the **Value (X)** axis box
            Type **Sample Proportion *p*** in the **Value (Y)** axis box
        Select the **Legend** tab and then
            Remove the check in the **Show Legend** box
        Select the **Gridlines** tab and then
            Remove the check in the **Major Gridlines** box
        Select **Next >**
Step 6 When the **Chart Wizard- Step 4 of 4 – Chart Location** dialog box appears:
        Specify a location for the chart
        Select **Finish**

    With practice and patience, you can alter the chart initially produced by Excel to look like the one below or to suit your personal preferences. A right-click on almost any item in the chart will bring up a menu of alteration options.

p **Chart:**

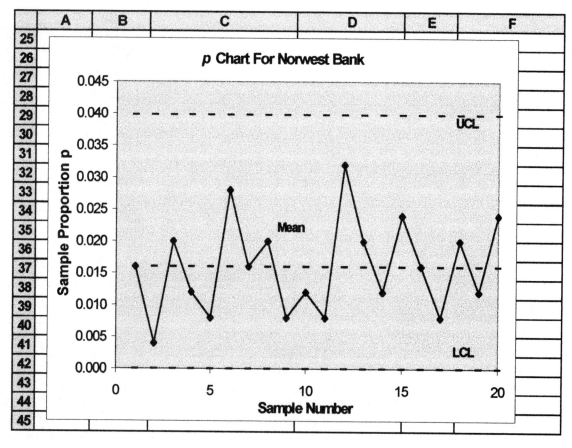

EXAMPLE 5

np Chart

Refer again to the background information and data for Norwest Bank in Example 4. Construct an appropriate *np* chart for the check encoding process..

SOLUTION 5

Using Excel's Chart Wizard

With just a few modifications to the worksheet developed in Solution 4, we can construct an *np* chart for Norwest Bank.

Enter Data: The data is already entered. See Solution 4 for details.

Enter Functions and Formulas: The proportion of checks that are defective in each sample, as well as the overall proportion of defective checks, are already computed. The estimated standard error is computed by entering the following formula into cell C23:

$$=SQRT(250*C22*(1-C22))$$

The one new item in this worksheet is the estimated average number of defective checks per sample of 250, denoted *np*. We compute the estimated *np* by entering the formula =250*C22 into cell C24.

The formulas in cells D2:D21 are identical; they compute the lower control limit. The LCL generally equals the estimated *np* <u>minus</u> three times the standard error ($C$24-3*$C$23). However, if this calculation results in a negative value, the LCL is set equal to zero. For this reason we use the MAX function to select the greater of the two values: 0 and ($C$24-3*$C$23).

The formulas in cells E2:E21 are also identical; they provide the expected number of defective checks. Finally, the formulas in cell F2:F21 (also identical) are used to compute the UCL which equals the estimated *p* <u>plus</u> three times the standard error ($C$24-3*$C$23).

Formula Worksheet (Note: Rows 6-19 are hidden):

	A	B	C	D	E	F
1	Sample	Number Defect.	Proportion Defective	LCL	CL	UCL
2	1	4	=B2/250	=MAX(0,$C$24-3*$C$23)	=$C$24	=$C$24+3*$C$23
3	2	1	=B3/250	=MAX(0,$C$24-3*$C$23)	=$C$24	=$C$24+3*$C$23
4	3	5	=B4/250	=MAX(0,$C$24-3*$C$23)	=$C$24	=$C$24+3*$C$23
5	4	3	=B5/250	=MAX(0,$C$24-3*$C$23)	=$C$24	=$C$24+3*$C$23
20	19	3	=B20/250	=MAX(0,$C$24-3*$C$23)	=$C$24	=$C$24+3*$C$23
21	20	6	=B21/250	=MAX(0,$C$24-3*$C$23)	=$C$24	=$C$24+3*$C$23
22	**Estimated *p***		=AVERAGE(C2:C21)			
23	**Estim. Std. Error**		=SQRT(250*C22*(1-C22))			
24	**Estimated *np***		=250*C22			

We see in the resulting worksheet below the values for the upper limit, lower limit, and center line in our *np* chart. Now we are ready to graph the *np* chart.

Apply Tools: We will use Excel's Chart Wizard to construct the *n* chart from the data in cells A2:B21 and D2:F21of our worksheet. (We will not be graphing the proportion defective data in column C.) . The steps to follow are nearly identical to those we outlined in Solution 4 where we were constructing a *p* chart. Refer to Solution 4 for details. You can alter the chart initially produced by Excel to look like the one below or to suit your personal preferences. A right-click on almost any item in the chart will bring up a menu of alteration options.

Value Worksheet:

	A	B	C	D	E	F
1	Sample	Number Defect.	Proportion Defective	LCL	CL	UCL
2	1	4	0.016	0	4.00	9.952
3	2	1	0.004	0	4.00	9.952
4	3	5	0.020	0	4.00	9.952
5	4	3	0.012	0	4.00	9.952
20	19	3	0.012	0	4.00	9.952
21	20	6	0.024	0	4.00	9.952
22	Estimated *p*		0.0160			
23	Estim. Std. Error		1.9839			
24	Estimated *np*		4.0000			

Note: Rows 6-19 are hidden.

np Chart:

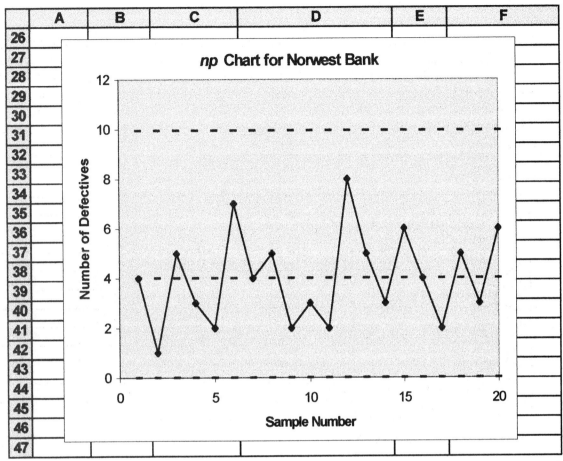

EXAMPLE 6

Probability of Accepting a Lot

Ledd Electronics has received a large shipment of power supply units for the desktop computers being assembled. The units are coming from a new supplier and Ledd is not sure what the actual defect rate will be for this component. Ledd is considering an acceptance sampling plan with $n = 30$ and $c = 1$.

a) Find the probability of accepting a lot when the defect rate is 2%, 4%, and 6%.

b) What happens to the producer's risk as the defect rate increases?

c) What happens to the consumer's risk as the defect rate increases?

SOLUTION 6

a) The maximum number of defective units that can be found in a sample of 30 units and still deem the shipment as being acceptable is 1. Therefore, the probability of accepting the lot equals the probability of 0 or 1 defectives. The probability of rejecting the lot equals the probability of there being 2 or more defectives in the sample.

The probability of x defectives in the sample is:

$$f(x) = \frac{n!}{x!(n-x)!} p^x (1-p)^{(n-x)}$$

where: p = the proportion of defectives in the lot
n = the sample size

For example, the probability of 0 defectives when $n = 30$ and $p = .02$ is computed as:

$$f(0) = \frac{30!}{0!(30!)} .02^0 (.92)^{30} = .54548$$

Continuing in this manner, the calculations can be summarized as follows:

Defect Rate p	$P(x = 0)$	$P(x = 1)$	Probab. of Accepting (Consumer's Risk, β) $P(x \leq 1)$	Probab. of Rejecting (Producer's Risk, α) $P(x \geq 2)$
.02	.54548	.33397	.87945	.12055
.04	.29386	.36732	.66118	.33882
.06	.15626	.29921	.45547	.54453

b) Refer to the table above where the acceptance criterion, c, has been held constant at 1. The chance that a lot will contain 2 or more defectives will increase as the expected number of defectives in the lot increases.

c) We see that the consumer's risk decreases as the defective rate increases.

EXAMPLE 7

Selecting an Acceptance Sampling Plan

An acceptance sampling plan with $n = 20$ and $c = 1$ has been designed with a producer's risk of .12.

a) Was the value of p_0 equal to .02, .03, .04, or .05?

b) What is the consumer's risk associated with this plan if p_1 is .08?

c) Assume the consumer's risk found in (b) is unacceptably high. Which modification of the sampling plan will result in the greater reduction of the consumer's risk, increasing n to 30 or decreasing c to 0?

SOLUTION 7

a)

Defect Rate p	$P(x = 0)$	$P(x = 1)$	Probab. of Accepting (Consumer's Risk, β) $P(x \leq 1)$	Probab. of Rejecting (Producer's Risk, α) $P(x > 1)$
.02	.66761	.27249	.94010	.05990
.03	.54379	.33637	.88016	.11984
.04	.44200	.36834	.81034	.18966
.05	.35848	.37735	.73583	.26417

b) $n = 20, c = 1, p_1 = .08$ $\quad$ $P(x = 0) = .188693$
$\qquad\qquad\qquad\qquad\qquad\quad$ $P(x = 1) = \underline{.328162}$
$\qquad\qquad\qquad\qquad\qquad\quad$ $P(x \leq 1) = .516855$ = Consumer's Risk

c) $n = 30, c = 1$ $\quad$ $P(x \leq 1) = .081966 + .213825 = .295791$
$\quad$ $n = 20, c = 0$ $\quad$ $P(x = 0) = .188693$
$\quad$ Decreasing c to 0 results in the lowest consumer's risk.

EXAMPLE 8

Constructing an Operating Characteristic Curve

Dock 4 Exports receives a particular style of candle holder in large lots from a wholesaler. When Dock 4 receives a shipment, a random sample of 20 candle holders are inspected to determine if they meet the product quality specifications. If any defectives are detected in the sample, the lot is rejected and returned to the wholesaler.

Graph the operating characteristic curve for this acceptance sampling plan. Using the graph, determine the approximate probability (producer's risk) that the plan will reject a lot that has a .03 defective rate.

SOLUTION 8

Using Excel's BINOMDIST Function and Chart Wizard

Enter Data: The integer values 0, 1, 2, ..., 29, 30 are entered into cells A4:A34. These represent the percentage of defectives in a lot, ranging from 0% to 30%. (Generally, it is not necessary to graph the OC curve beyond a 30% defective rate because the curve is essentially flat at that point.) Next, the value of n, which is 20, is entered into cell D1 and the value of c, which is 1, is entered into cell D2. Finally, identifying labels should be entered into cells A1:A3, C1, and C2.

Enter Functions and Formulas: We will compute the cumulative probability of accepting a lot with each of the defective rates listed in cells A5:A34 by using the BINOMDIST function in cells B5:B34. (We simply enter the value 0 into cell B4 because the BINOMDIST function returns an error message when we try to enter a value of 0 for p.)

The BINOMDIST function's first argument is the value of *x* for which we are computing a cumulative probability. Dock 4 Exports will accept a lot if the number of defectives, *x*, is less than or equal to *c*, the acceptance criterion. For this reason, we use the value of *c*, in cell D2, as the first argument in the function. The second argument is the value of *n* which is in cell D1. The third argument is the lot defect rate whose value is in cell A5 (we must convert it from a percentage to a proportion by dividing by 100). We will input TRUE as the last argument because we want a cumulative probability returned by the function. To summarize, the following formula is entered into cell B5 and then copied to cells B6:B34.

$$=\text{BINOMDIST}(\$D\$2,\$D\$1,A5/100,TRUE)$$

Formula Worksheet:

	A	B	C	D
1	Percent	Probability	*n* =	20
2	Defective	of Accepting	*c* =	1
3	in the Lot	the Lot		
4	0	1.00000		
5	1	=BINOMDIST($D$2,$D$1,A5/100,TRUE)		
6	2	=BINOMDIST($D$2,$D$1,A6/100,TRUE)		
7	3	=BINOMDIST($D$2,$D$1,A7/100,TRUE)		
8	4	=BINOMDIST($D$2,$D$1,A8/100,TRUE)		
9	5	=BINOMDIST($D$2,$D$1,A9/100,TRUE)		
30	26	=BINOMDIST($D$2,$D$1,A30/100,TRUE)		
31	27	=BINOMDIST($D$2,$D$1,A31/100,TRUE)		
32	28	=BINOMDIST($D$2,$D$1,A32/100,TRUE)		
33	29	=BINOMDIST($D$2,$D$1,A33/100,TRUE)		
34	30	=BINOMDIST($D$2,$D$1,A34/100,TRUE)		

Note: Rows 10-29 are hidden.

Value Worksheet:

	A	B	C	D
1	Percent	Probability	*n* =	20
2	Defective	of Accepting	*c* =	1
3	in the Lot	the Lot		
4	0	1.00000		
5	1	0.98314		
6	2	0.94010		
7	3	0.88016		
8	4	0.81034		
9	5	0.73584		
30	26	0.01946		
31	27	0.01551		
32	28	0.01230		
33	29	0.00972		
34	30	0.00764		

We now have the data needed to plot an OC curve for an aceeptance sampling plan with $n = 20$ and $c = 1$.

Apply Tools: The following steps describe how to use the Chart Wizard to graph an OC curve from the data in our worksheet.

Step 1 Select cells A4:

Step 2 Select the **Chart Wizard** button

Step 3 When the **Chart Wizard-Step 1 of 4-Chart Type** dialog box appears:
> Choose **XY (Scatter)** in the **Chart type** list
> Choose **Scatter with data points connected by lines** from the
>> **Chart sub-type** display
>
> Select **Next >**

Step 4 When the **Chart Wizard-Step 2 of 4-Chart Source Data** dialog box appears
> Select **Next >**

Step 5 When the **Chart Wizard-Step 3 of 4-Chart Options** dialog box appears:
> Select the **Titles** tab and then
>> Type **Operating Characteristic Curve** in the **Chart title** box
>> Enter **Percent Defective in the Lot** in the **Value (X)** axis box
>> Enter **Probability of Accepting the Lot** in the **Value (Y)** axis box
>
> Select the **Legend** tab and then
>> Remove the check in the **Show Legend** box
>> Select **Next >**

Step 6 When the **Chart Wizard-Step 4 of 4-Chart Location** dialog box appears:
> Specify the location for the new chart
> Select **Finish** to display the ogive

Using the OC curve below, we see that the probability of rejecting a lot with .03 defective is approximately .06.

Operating Characteristic (OC) Curve:

	B	C	D	E	F	G	H	I
1	Probability	$n =$ 20						
2	of Accepting	$c =$ 1						
3	the Lot							
4	1.00000							
5	0.98314							
6	0.94010							
7	0.88016							
8	0.81034							
9	0.73584							
10	0.66045							
11	0.58686							
12	0.51686							
13	0.45160							
14	0.39175							
15	0.33757							
16	0.28910							
17	0.24615							
18	0.20843							
19	0.17556							
20	0.14713							
21	0.12269							
22	0.10183							

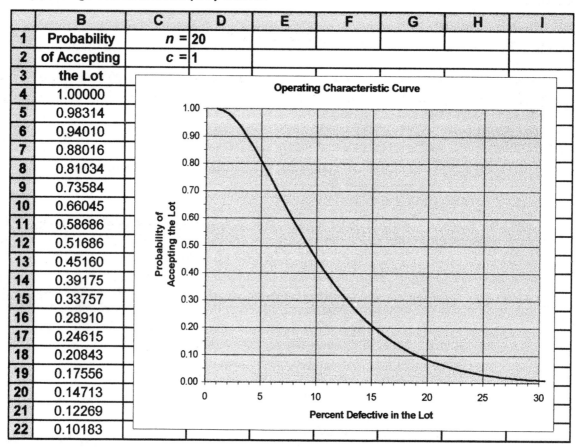

You can alter the chart initially produced by Excel to look like the one above or to suit your personal preferences. A right-click on almost any item in the chart will bring up a menu of alteration options.

EXERCISES

EXERCISE 1

$\bar{x}$ Chart: μ and σ Known

A process that is in control has a mean of $\mu = 56.5$ and a standard deviation of $\sigma = 3.4$. What should the control limits be for a sample mean chart if samples of size 8 are taken?

EXERCISE 2

$\bar{x}$ and R Charts

A process sampled 30 times with a sample of size nine resulted in $\bar{\bar{x}}$ = 12.7 and $\bar{R}$ = 0.8. Compute the upper and lower control limits for the $\bar{x}$ and $\bar{R}$ charts for this process.

EXERCISE 3

p and np Charts

Snipper, Inc. manufactures lawnmowers that require minor, final assembly by the customer. A sealed plastic bag containing the hardware (nuts, bolts, washers, and so on) needed for final assembly is included with each lawnmower shipped.

During a week of normal, in-control operation, twenty samples of 200 bags of hardware were examined for content (hardware type and count) accuracy. A total of 104 bags of the 4000 examined failed to have the correct contents.

a) Compute the upper limit, center line, and lower limit for a p chart.

b) Compute the upper limit, center line, and lower limit for an np chart.

EXERCISE 4

Selecting an Acceptance Sampling Plan

To inspect incoming shipments of components, a manufacturer is considering samples of sizes 12, 15, and 18. Use binomial probabilities to select a sampling plan that provides a producer's risk of α = .12 when p_0 is .04 and a consumer's risk of β = .08 when p_1 is .25.

EXERCISE 5

Constructing an OC Curve

A U.S. manufacturer of video cassette recorders purchases a circuit board from a Taiwanese firm. The circuit boards are shipped in lots of 2000. The acceptance sampling procedure uses 12 randomly selected circuit boards. The acceptance number is 1.

a) Construct an operating characteristic curve for this acceptance sampling plan.

b) If p_0 is .03 and p_1 is .20, what are the producer's and consumer's risks for this plan?

SELF-TEST

TRUE/FALSE

___ 1. No corrective action is necessary when output variations are due to common causes.

___ 2. The consumer's risk is the probability of rejecting good-quality lot.

___ 3. If the R chart indicates that the process is out of control, the $\bar{x}$ chart should not be interpreted until the R chart indicates the process variability is in control.

___ 4. If we were to conclude that a particular process is out of control on the basis of a p chart, we might not come to the same conclusion on the basis of an np chart.

___ 5. If all data points plotted on a control chart lie inside the control limits, the process is in statistical control.

FILL-IN-THE-BLANK

1. _____ refers to the entire system of policies, procedures, and guidelines established by an organization to achieve and maintain quality.

2. Operator error and incorrect machine settings are examples of _____ causes.

3. An operating characteristic curve is based on a _____ probability distribution.

4. A control chart that is based on data indicating the presence of a defect or the number of defects is called a(n) _____ control chart.

5. In the context of statistical process control, the _____ hypothesis is formulated in terms of the process being out of control.

MULTIPLE CHOICE

___ 1. If the value of c in a single-stage acceptance sampling plan is increased, with n remaining constant, the probability of accepting the lot
    a) increases
    b) decreases
    c) remains the same
    d) might increase or decrease, depending on the percent defective in the lot

____ 2. The general practice in quality control is to set the control chart's upper and lower control limit values equal to the variable's mean value +/-
   a)   1 standard deviation
   b)   2 standard deviations
   c)   2.5 standard deviations
   d)   3 standard deviations

____ 3. The sample result plotted on an *np* control chart is
   a) *n*
   b) *p*
   c) *np*
   d) the number of defectives in the sample

____ 4. The second stage of a two-stage acceptance sampling plan is executed (additional items are sampled) when the first-stage result is
   a) $x_1 > c_1$
   b) $c_1 < x_1 < c_2$
   c) $x_1 \geq c_2$
   d) $x_1 \geq c_1 + c_2$

____ 5. The producer's risk is the probability of
   a)   a Type I error
   b)   a Type II error
   c)   accepting a poor quality lot
   d)   not rejecting a null hypothesis that is false

ANSWERS

EXERCISES

1) UCL = 60.11, CL = 56.5, LCL = 52.89

2) $\bar{x}$ chart: UCL = 12.97, LCL = 12.43; $\bar{R}$ chart: UCL = 1.453, LCL = 0.147

3) a) UCL = .0598, CL = .0260, LCL = 0
    b) UCL = 11.952, CL = 5.200, LCL = 0

4) *n* = 15, *c* = 1

5) b) $\alpha = .05$, $\beta = .275$

TRUE/FALSE

1) True
2) False
3) True
4) False
5) False

FILL-IN-THE-BLANK

1) Quality assurance
2) assignable
3) binomial
4) attributes
5) alternative

MULTIPLE CHOICE

1) a
2) d
3) d
4) b
5) a

Appendix

TABLE 1   Areas for the Standard Normal Distribution

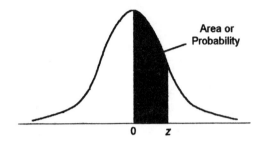

Area or Probability

0   z

Entries in the table give the area under the curve between the mean and z standard deviations above the mean. For example, for z = 1.25 the area under the curve between the mean and z is .3944.

z	.00	.01	.02	.03	.04	.05	.06	.07	.08	.09
.0	.0000	.0040	.0080	.0120	.0160	.0199	.0239	.0279	.0319	.0359
.1	.0398	.0438	.0478	.0517	.0557	.0596	.0636	.0675	.0714	.0753
.2	.0793	.0832	.0871	.0910	.0948	.0987	.1026	.1064	.1103	.1141
.3	.1179	.1217	.1255	.1293	.1331	.1368	.1406	.1443	.1480	.1517
.4	.1554	.1591	.1628	.1664	.1700	.1736	.1772	.1808	.1844	.1879
.5	.1915	.1950	.1985	.2019	.2054	.2088	.2123	.2157	.2190	.2224
.6	.2257	.2291	.2324	.2357	.2389	.2422	.2454	.2486	.2518	.2549
.7	.2580	.2612	.2642	.2673	.2704	.2734	.2764	.2794	.2823	.2852
.8	.2881	.2910	.2939	.2967	.2995	.3023	.3051	.3078	.3106	.3133
.9	.3159	.3186	.3212	.3238	.3264	.3289	.3315	.3340	.3365	.3389
1.0	.3413	.3438	.3461	.3485	.3508	.3531	.3554	.3577	.3599	.3621
1.1	.3643	.3665	.3686	.3708	.3729	.3749	.3770	.3790	.3810	.3830
1.2	.3849	.3869	.3888	.3907	.3925	.3944	.3962	.3980	.3997	.4015
1.3	.4032	.4049	.4066	.4082	.4099	.4115	.4131	.4147	.4162	.4177
1.4	.4192	.4207	.4222	.4236	.4251	.4265	.4279	.4292	.4306	.4319
1.5	.4332	.4345	.4357	.4370	.4382	.4394	.4406	.4418	.4429	.4441
1.6	.4452	.4463	.4474	.4484	.4495	.4505	.4515	.4525	.4535	.4545
1.7	.4554	.4564	.4573	.4582	.4591	.4599	.4608	.4616	.4625	.4633
1.8	.4641	.4649	.4656	.4664	.4671	.4678	.4686	.4693	.4699	.4706
1.9	.4713	.4719	.4726	.4732	.4738	.4744	.4750	.4756	.4761	.4767
2.0	.4772	.4778	.4783	.4788	.4793	.4798	.4803	.4808	.4812	.4817
2.1	.4821	.4826	.4830	.4834	.4838	.4842	.4846	.4850	.4854	.4857
2.2	.4861	.4864	.4868	.4871	.4875	.4878	.4881	.4884	.4887	.4890
2.3	.4893	.4896	.4898	.4901	.4904	.4906	.4909	.4911	.4913	.4916
2.4	.4918	.4920	.4922	.4925	.4927	.4929	.4931	.4932	.4934	.4936
2.5	.4938	.4940	.4941	.4943	.4945	.4946	.4948	.4949	.4951	.4952
2.6	.4953	.4955	.4956	.4957	.4959	.4960	.4961	.4962	.4963	.4964
2.7	.4965	.4966	.4967	.4968	.4969	.4970	.4971	.4972	.4973	.4974
2.8	.4974	.4975	.4976	.4977	.4977	.4978	.4979	.4979	.4980	.4981
2.9	.4981	.4982	.4982	.4983	.4984	.4984	.4985	.4985	.4986	.4986
3.0	.4986	.4987	.4987	.4988	.4988	.4989	.4989	.4989	.4990	.4990

TABLE 2   *t* Distribution

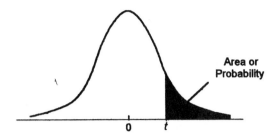

Area or Probability

Entries in the table give *t* values for an area or probability in the upper tail of the *t* distribution. For example, with 10 degrees of freedom and a .05 area in the upper tail, $t_{.05} = 1.812$.

Degrees of Freedom	Area in Upper Tail				
	.10	.05	.025	.01	.005
1	3.078	6.314	12.706	31.821	63.657
2	1.886	2.920	4.303	6.965	9.925
3	1.638	2.353	3.182	4.541	5.841
4	1.533	2.132	2.776	3.747	4.604
5	1.476	2.015	2.571	3.365	4.032
6	1.440	1.943	2.447	3.143	3.707
7	1.415	1.895	2.365	2.998	3.499
8	1.397	1.860	2.306	2.896	3.355
9	1.383	1.833	2.262	2.821	3.250
10	1.372	1.812	2.228	2.764	3.169
11	1.363	1.796	2.201	2.718	3.106
12	1.356	1.782	2.179	2.681	3.055
13	1.350	1.771	2.160	2.650	3.012
14	1.345	1.761	2.145	2.624	2.977
15	1.341	1.753	2.131	2.602	2.947
16	1.337	1.746	2.120	2.583	2.921
17	1.333	1.740	2.110	2.567	2.898
18	1.330	1.734	2.101	2.552	2.878
19	1.328	1.729	2.093	2.539	2.861
20	1.325	1.725	2.086	2.528	2.845
21	1.323	1.721	2.080	2.518	2.831
22	1.321	1.717	2.074	2.508	2.819
23	1.319	1.714	2.069	2.500	2.807
24	1.318	1.711	2.064	2.492	2.797
25	1.316	1.708	2.060	2.485	2.787
26	1.315	1.706	2.056	2.479	2.779
27	1.314	1.703	2.052	2.473	2.771
28	1.313	1.701	2.048	2.467	2.763
29	1.311	1.699	2.045	2.462	2.756
30	1.310	1.697	2.042	2.457	2.750
40	1.303	1.684	2.021	2.423	2.704
60	1.296	1.671	2.000	2.390	2.660
120	1.289	1.658	1.980	2.358	2.617
∞	1.282	1.645	1.960	2.326	2.576